Outsiders and Others

OUTSIDERS AND OTHERS

Queer Friendships in Novels by Hermann Hesse

OSCAR VON SETH

Södertörns högskola

Comparative Literature
Critical and Cultural Theory
School of Culture and Education
& Baltic and East European Graduate School

(CC BY 3.0)

Södertörns högskola
(Södertörn University)
Library
SE-141 89 Huddinge

www.sh.se/publications

Parts of chapters four and five have been published previously as Oscar von Seth,
"Tracing the Wolf in Hermann Hesse's *Der Steppenwolf*," in *Squirrelling: Human–
Animal Studies in the Northern-European Region*, ed. Amelie Björck, Claudia Lindén,
and Ann-Sofie Lönngren (Huddinge: Södertörns högskola, 2022), 119–140.

Cover image: Fabien Chesseboeuf, 2022
Graphic form: Per Lindblom & Jonathan Robson

Stockholm 2022

Södertörn Doctoral Dissertations 202
ISSN 1652–7399

ISBN 978-91-89504-00-4 (print)
ISBN 978-91-89504-01-1 (digital)

Your friend is your needs answered.
He is your field which you sow with love and reap with thanksgiving.
And he is your board and your fireside.
For you come to him with your hunger, and you seek him for peace.

– Khalil Gibran, *The Prophet*

Friendship … is a virtue, or involves virtue; and also it is one of the most indispensable requirements of life.

– Aristotle, *Nicomachean Ethics*

Well, it seems to me that the best relationships, the ones that last, are frequently the ones that are rooted in friendship. You know, one day, you look at the person and you see something more than you did the night before. Like a switch has been flicked somewhere. And the person who was just a friend is suddenly the only person you can ever imagine yourself with.

– Special Agent Dana Scully, *The X-Files*
(season 6, episode 8, "The Rain King")

Abstract

This dissertation explores how characters who embody outsiderness and/or otherness intersect with and connote queerness—such as, for instance, homoeroticism and nonconformism—in the novels *Peter Camenzind* (1904) and *Der Steppenwolf* (1927) by German-language author Hermann Hesse (1877–1962).

In most of Hesse's novels, the narrative revolves around a male protagonist who is characterized as an outsider. This outsider comes to know himself through friendship with another man. The friend is desired by the outsider and tends to embody some form of otherness; he is almost always portrayed as different—rebellious, beautiful, enigmatic, and inspiring—and he comes to play a key role in the protagonist's personal development and journey through life. The hypothesis in this study is that the friendships formed by these characters are queer friendships, that is, that they challenge heteronormative conceptions of relationality, sexuality, and desire.

The study's main theoretical apparatus encompasses a selection of queer theories and concepts, including (among others) José Esteban Muñoz's conceptualization of the horizon as a signifier for "queer utopia" as well as Heather Love's thoughts on "backwardness." Eve Kosofsky Sedgwick's early queer-theoretical work on male homosocial desire and Jack Halberstam's recent theorizing about sexuality and wildness are also drawn on.

The study begins with an overview chapter on Hesse's authorship that provides historical context followed by two parts (one on *Peter Camenzind* and one on *Der Steppenwolf*) with three analytical chapters each. The overview chapter revolves around certain norm-challenging aspects of Hesse's time and reception. Hesse was active alongside the German homosexual emancipation movement and emerging field of sexology in the early 1900s, and his work was embraced by contemporary countercultures such as the German *Wandervogel* groups and by later anti-conformist movements like beatniks and hippies. Despite these connections, however, Hesse's novels have rarely been interpreted with an ambition to emphasize queerness.

The common thread in the study's six analytical chapters is depictions of queer friendship. In each chapter, one character is in primary focus. This character's portrayal as an outsider or Other (or both) is examined. In some instances, the protagonist is the key person of interest; at other times, the protagonist's friend is in focus.

Chapter one, "Romantic Friendship in a *Bildungsroman*," centers on Peter, the outsider-protagonist in *Peter Camenzind*, and his homosocial bond with the character Richard. The chapter examines how defining traits of the

Bildungsroman (novel of formation) and the concept of romantic friendship intersect in the novel. Chapter two, "Without Leaving Children Behind," explores heterosexual ambivalence, which Peter conveys in his interactions with women, which is interpreted as a manifestation of queerness. While the chapter concerns a number of female characters, Peter's friend Elisabeth is the key character. Chapter three, "Facing the Other," focuses on Peter's friend Boppi. The otherness ascribed to Boppi through his disability is examined, as well as the ways that disability works as a catalyst for expressions of "queer/crip kinship" in the text.

Chapter four, "Tracing the Wolf," examines a key expression of otherness in *Der Steppenwolf*, namely, the animality of its protagonist, the wolf-man (and outsider) Harry Haller. This chapter is different from the others in that it does not revolve around queer friendship per se. Rather, it emphasizes the antithesis of friendship, that is, a bond built on animosity, a major characteristic in the relationship between the human part and the wolf part of the protagonist. Chapter five, "The Function of Hermine," explores the fluid gender expressions and queer characteristics of Harry's friend Hermine. Hermine is a character whose otherness mirrors the protagonist's dual nature. Chapter six, "Queer Sounds, Times, and Places," puts the spotlight on Pablo, another of Harry's friends, and examines how the novel's portrayal of sounds (such as jazz music), times (the conflict between the old and the new), and places (like the dance floor) connote queerness in various ways.

Ultimately, this dissertation demonstrates that Hermann Hesse's stories include queerness both in the shape of nonconformity in the characters, and in norm-challenging sexuality and the prevalence of homoeroticism. In addition, *Peter Camenzind* and *Der Steppenwolf* convey that queerness is essential to their protagonists' longings to become whole and in the ways that the novels portray completeness.

Keywords: Hermann Hesse; *Peter Camenzind*; *Der Steppenwolf*; outsiderness; otherness; queer friendship; homoeroticism; nonconformism; homosexuality; bisexuality; Bildungsroman; romantic friendship; heterosexual ambivalence; disability; animality; gender

Sammanfattning (Summary in Swedish)

Den här avhandlingen undersöker hur karaktärer som skildras genom utanförskap och/eller annanhet samspelar med och konnoterar queerhet – som till exempel homoerotik och icke-konformism – i romanerna *Peter Camenzind* (1904) och *Der Steppenwolf* (1927) av den tyskspråkige författaren Hermann Hesse (1877–1962).

I de flesta av Hesses romaner kretsar berättelsen kring en manlig huvudperson som skrivs fram som en outsider. Denna outsider lär känna sig själv genom vänskap med en annan man. Vännen åtrås av huvudpersonen och förkroppsligar vanligtvis någon form av annanhet; han framställs nästan alltid som annorlunda – rebellisk, vacker, gåtfull och inspirerande – och får en nyckelroll i huvudpersonens utveckling och resa genom livet. Den här studiens hypotes är att de vänskaper som dessa karaktärer bildar är queera vänskaper, det vill säga relationer som utmanar heteronormativa föreställningar om relationalitet, sexualitet och begär.

Studiens huvudsakliga teoretiska ramverk utgörs av ett antal queerteorier och queerbegrepp, bland annat José Esteban Muñozs konceptualisering av horisonten som en symbol för en "queer utopi", liksom Heather Loves reflektioner om queera figurer i litteraturhistorien. Dessutom tillämpas Eve Kosofsky Sedgwicks queera teorier om manligt homosocialt begär, samt Jack Halberstams teoretiserande kring sexualitet och vildhet.

Studien inleds med ett översiktskapitel om Hesses författarskap som ger en historisk kontext. Översiktskapitlet följs av två delar (en om *Peter Camenzind* och en om *Der Steppenwolf*) med tre analyskapitel per del. I översiktskapitlet fokuseras det på vissa normbrytande aspekter av den tidsepok Hesse var verksam i, samt mottagandet av hans romaner. Hesse var aktiv parallellt med den homosexuella emancipationsrörelsen och sexologiforskningen i Tyskland i början av 1900-talet. Hans texter hyllades dessutom av dåtidens motkulturrörelser som de tyska *Wandervogel*-grupperna och senare av antikonformister som beatniks och hippies. Trots dessa kopplingar har Hesses romaner sällan tolkats med en ambition att uppmärksamma queerhet.

Det genomgående temat i studiens sex analyskapitel är queer vänskap. Varje kapitel fokuserar på en karaktär som skildras genom utanförskap eller annanhet (eller både och). I vissa fall är det huvudpersonen som är i fokus; i andra fall är det huvudpersonens vän.

Kapitel ett handlar om titelfiguren i *Peter Camenzind* (en outsider) och hans homosociala relation med karaktären Richard. Kapitlet undersöker hur bildningsromanens konventioner och romantisk vänskap samverkar i texten. I kapitel två tolkas heterosexuell ambivalens, som präglar Peters relationer med kvinnor, som uttryck för queerhet. Kapitlet berör flera kvinnliga karaktärer men Peters vän Elisabeth är nyckelpersonen. Kapitel tre fokuserar på Peters vän Boppi. Kapitlet undersöker den annanhet som tillskrivs Boppi på grund av hans funktionsvariation, samt förbindelsen mellan queerhet och annanhet i männens relation.

I kapitel fyra undersöks ett centralt uttryck för annanhet i *Der Steppenwolf*, nämligen den djuriskhet som karaktäriserar romanens varg/människa-protagonist (och outsider) Harry Haller. Detta kapitel är annorlunda jämfört med de övriga då det inte uttryckligen kretsar kring queer vänskap. Snarare betonar kapitlet en motsats till vänskap, det vill säga en relation byggd på fientlighet, vilket präglar förhållandet mellan vargen och människan inuti huvudpersonen. Kapitel fem utforskar flytande genusuttryck och queera egenskaper hos Harrys vän Hermine. Hermine är en karaktär vars annanhet speglar huvudpersonens dubbelnatur. Och slutligen, med fokus på karak-tären Pablo, ytterligare en av Harrys vänner, undersöker kapitel sex hur romanens skildringar av ljud (som jazzmusik), tid (konflikten mellan gam-malt och nytt), och platser (som dansgolv) konnoterar queerhet på olika sätt.

Sammantaget visar avhandlingen att Hermann Hesses berättelser inklud-erar queerhet både i form av icke-konformism i karaktärerna, och genom normbrytande sexualitet och homoerotik. Utöver detta förmedlar *Peter Camenzind* och *Der Steppenwolf* att queerhet spelar en avgörande roll vad gäller huvudpersonernas längtan efter att bli hela, samt för de sätt på vilka romanerna skildrar fullkomlighet.

Contents

Preface

In *Wanderung* (*Wandering*, 1920), which is a collection of autobiographical texts by Hermann Hesse (1877–1962), the prose and poems express the author's profound wanderlust and affection for the grand mountain land-scapes around his home village in Montagnola, Switzerland. Throughout Hesse's life he yearned to be free from the constraints of modernity. He believed that nature has the potential to rekindle one's spirit.

Now I believe that as well.

Hesse's affection for nature occupied my mind when my boyfriend Robert and I began wandering the King's Trail in northern Sweden in the summer of 2021. There was, at the time, less than a year to go before the public defense of this dissertation.

As we came out of the lush, deep, bewitching woods there was an open landscape in front of us. In the distance we saw the mountains through which we would hike for six days to come. The setting was romantic—birds were singing, there were clouds in the sky—and although there was an imminent chance of rain it did not dampen our mood. These enchanting natural surroundings had a soothing effect on us both. While we wandered through them, I came to the realization that Hesse's writings have provided me with a similar sort of comfort since I began my doctoral studies in the fall of 2017.

Contrary to many of Hesse's readers (oftentimes they are adolescents), I was already thirty-five when I experienced my first Hesse novel. However, when I finally did become acquainted with him and as his characters, something within me simply fell into place. The way Hesse's pure prose spoke to me ignited something that I cannot quite put into words, something that has now made me devote half a decade to studying his work. The result is this book, which will provide an account of themes in Hesse's writing that entice my curiosity, such as friendship, sexuality, gender transgression, male homo-social desire, outsiderness, and otherness.

Hermann Hesse is one of the most widely read German-language authors of the twentieth century. He was awarded the Nobel Prize for Literature in 1946. In most of his novels, the narrative revolves around a male protagonist who is characterized as an outsider. This outsider comes to know himself through friendship with another man. The friend is desired by the outsider and tends to embody some form of otherness; he is almost always portrayed as different—rebellious, beautiful, enigmatic, and inspiring—and comes to play a key role in the protagonist's personal development and journey through life. The hypothesis in this study is that the friendships formed by these characters are queer friendships, that is, that they challenge heteronormative conceptions of relationality, sexuality, and desire.

Apart from Hermann Hesse himself, the main characters in the two novels that are of primary focus in the following have, at this point, become equivalent to old friends of mine. The eponymous protagonist in *Peter Camenzind* (1904) as well as the wolf-man Harry Haller in *Der Steppenwolf* (1927) are, like me, travelers. While Peter is a wanderer, Harry is a runner, and the paces of these characters (as well as the prose that gives them life) mirror the way this study materialized. When I began my PhD endeavor, I delved deep into *Peter Camenzind* and experienced its lyrical passages slowly. When I read *Der Steppenwolf* two years later and started to grasp the scope of my project (which incidentally also began to stress me out), I found myself devouring the text with a pace befitting a running wolf. Both novels make me feel like I am right there beside the protagonists. For the last five years, I have, in a sense, had the privilege of being Peter's and Harry's co-traveler.

My experience of reading Hesse's novels—I feel that he speaks directly to me—is not an uncommon testament. Hesse has an almost uncanny ability to make his readers feel seen, heard, and accepted. Although I have occupied myself intensely with his work for a long time now, it keeps inspiring me, which contradicts what most people have told me about completing a PhD: "As you're approaching the public defense, you'll have grown tired of your object of study," they said.

Not me.

Enjoying the wonders of the natural world is one of the many things that I have learned from the writings of Hermann Hesse. I want to continue experiencing his stories and travel alongside his characters. This is as true today as it was during Robert's and my hike along the King's Trail last summer.

As we wandered, I gazed toward the horizon. With a flutter of excitement, I imagined the many adventures ahead. Being able to finally share this work with you is the beginning of one of those journeys.

Stockholm, March 2022

Introduction: "Be Yourself"

Outsiders and Others in Hesse's Fiction

In Colin Wilson's *The Outsider* (1956), the outsider figure in Western literature is defined as someone who is at odds with society. Wilson defines the Outsider as a man, a misanthropic, nihilistic individual who despises ordinary people and their social conventions.[1] At the same time, the Outsider is characterized by a yearning to cease being an outsider, which, however, does not involve conforming to the ideals of the society he disgusts. "Above all," Wilson writes, "[the Outsider] would like to know how to express himself, because that is the means by which he can get to know himself and his unknown possibilities."[2]

Wilson continuously discusses the Outsider in singular, thereby emphasizing its strong individuality. The Outsider is also someone who first and foremost is devoted to his own self-exploration. Wilson proposes that this lone, nonconforming, truth-seeking character is a recurring figure in the novels of Hermann Hesse.

As underscored by Wilson and many other scholars, Hesse's novels have always been beacons to readers in the margins. Ingo Cornils reminds us that "Hesse advocated in his writings a sense of responsibility to one's own potential that resonates with readers who feel encouraged to know that someone is on their side when they are 'the odd one out.'"[3] From the nonconformity in *Unterm Rad* (*Beneath the Wheel*, 1906) and theme of independence in *Knulp* (1915), to the spiritual ideals in *Siddhartha* (1922) and the theme of insight in *Narziß und Goldmund* (*Narcissus and Goldmund*, 1930), Hesse's texts provide opportunities to absorb oneself in the lives of outsiders and Others.

Throughout this study, concepts of "otherness" will be recurring focus points. Otherness can be described as a characteristic in "the Other," a figure

---

[1] Colin Wilson's definition of the Outsider as an exclusively *male* literary figure is a narrow one. Since Wilson's book excludes women completely—both female writers and female characters—and argues that outsiders (men) are the ones who know "the truth" about the human condition, *The Outsider* reinforces, in no subtle manner, the old-fashioned idea that female subjectivity holds no truth-claim and cannot be considered universal.

[2] Colin Wilson, *The Outsider* (London: Pan, 1963), 220.

[3] Ingo Cornils, "Introduction: From Outsider to Global Player — Hermann Hesse in the Twenty-First Century," in *A Companion to the Works of Hermann Hesse*, ed. Ingo Cornils (Rochester, NY: Camden House, 2009), 12.

that occurs within various frameworks.[4] The notions of otherness that will be drawn on herein will be explained throughout. Suffice it to say, for now, that overall, in Hesse's fiction, otherness tends to appear in portrayals of difference that challenge conceptions of what is considered normal. As we shall see, Hesse's outsiders and Others challenge heteronormativity in equal measure—however, not always in identical fashion. While both figures are characterized as *different*, the outsider is always the novel's protagonist, whereas the Other is the friend he makes—an individual who is desired and idealized.

Hesse's outsider-protagonists (and sometimes the Others) possess a quality referred to as *Eigensinn* (self-will). According to Hesse, an individual who possesses Eigensinn adheres to a single sacred law: "dem Gesetz in sich selbst, dem 'Sinn' des 'Eigenen'."[5] (the law in itself, one's "sense" of "self."[6]) Hesse is convinced that Eigensinn is the most important of virtues, but unlike the worldly things that exist in accordance with their own self-will—such as stones, grass, animals, and flowers—most humans follow other laws, he argues, mainly a sort of law of the majority. This law of the majority mirrors the modern definition of what a "norm" is, namely a way of behaving or thinking that most people adhere to and/or agree with, but which is also challenged by those who cannot, or choose not to, conform to the norm.

Conforming to society's norms, in Hesse's view, prohibits us from truly being ourselves. Eigensinn, therefore, is a concept that can be found in all of his novels. It is a defining characteristic in Hesse's outsider-protagonists, who

[4] In phenomenology, for example, the Other is identified as being an integral element in the self-image of an individual. In short, the Other's difference makes the characteristics of the Self evident. Another commonly invoked definition of otherness can be found in the writing of Edward W. Said, whose *Orientalism* (1978)—a groundbreaking text in the field of postcolonial studies—describes how Western societies' notions about (and conceptualizations of) "the East" are inextricably linked with imperialist beliefs. Said's book emphasizes how Western culture subjects the East to "othering," that is, portraying it as radically different and inferior. This practice can include both exotification and viewing the Other as primitive and frightening. As such, Said's conceptualization of otherness has been proven useful in research on race and ethnicity. While Said's theorizing could be an interesting starting point when examining Hesse's work, this study will make use of frameworks of otherness that are better suited for interpretations of *Peter Camenzind* and *Der Steppenwolf*.

[5] Hermann Hesse, "Eigensinn," in *Eigensinn macht Spaß: Individuation und Anpassung*, ed. Volker Michels (Frankfurt am Main: Insel, 2002), 84.

[6] The present study features both German and English quotes from Hesse's texts. All translations into English were made by the author of this book and appear in parenthesis immediately following the original German. Under the heading "About the Translations," an extended explanation is given of the reasons for not using prior translations.

can be said to march to the beat of their own drums.[7] However, as this study will acknowledge, outsiders in Hesse's fiction also seek affinity with other people (oftentimes desperately), which the texts' iterations of queer friendships make evident.

The Eigensinn of Hesse's outsiders—for instance, the eponymous characters of *Demian* (1919) and *Peter Camenzind*, and of course Harry Haller, the protagonist in *Der Steppenwolf*—animates the self-development of the readers themselves. The theme of individuation—which, in Hesse's novels, often takes the shape of rebelliousness against normative processes of socialization, in which distinctive personal traits and exceptional characteristics are subdued—makes his writing especially attractive to young readers. David G. Richards argues that Hesse's novels "have consistently appealed to youth in chaotic times and when traditional authority is questioned and resisted, and certain of his novels and stories have appealed especially to young people who are attempting to find and define themselves as individuals in rigid and authoritarian societies."[8]

Richard's arguments stem from the injunction *Sei Du Selbst* (Be yourself) which can be found throughout Hesse's oeuvre. In plain language, Hesse maintains:

> "Sei Du Selbst" ist das ideale Gesetz, zu mindest für den jungen Menschen, es gibt keinen andern Weg zur Wahrheit und zur Entwicklung.[9]

> ("Be yourself" is the ideal law, at least for the young, there is no other way to truth and development.)

Furthermore, in *Zarathustras Wiederkehr* (*Zarathustra's Return*, 1919)—which is a spiritual sequel to *Also sprach Zarathustra* (*Thus Spoke Zarathustra*, 1883–1885) by Friedrich Nietzsche (1844–1900)—Hesse suggests

---

[7] Hesse suggests that only two things on earth are *not* blessed with a natural inclination toward Eigensinn: "Einzig der Mensch und das von ihm gezähmte Haustier sind dazu verurteilt, nicht der Stimme des Lebens und Wachstums zu folgen, sondern irgendwelchen Gesetzen, die von Menschen aufgestellt sind und die immer von Zeit zu Zeit wieder von Menschen gebrochen und geändert werden." (Hesse, "Eigensinn," 85–86.) (Only humans and their domestic animals are condemned not to follow the voice of life and growth [Eigensinn/self-will], but to follow other laws established by humans, laws that are inevitably broken and changed by humans from time to time.)

[8] David G. Richards, *Exploring the Divided Self: Hermann Hesse's* Steppenwolf *and its Critics* (Columbia: Camden House, 1996), 1.

[9] Hermann Hesse, "Eigensinn macht Spaß," in *Eigensinn macht Spaß: Individuation und Anpassung*, ed. Volker Michels (Frankfurt am Main: Insel, 2002), 9.

that being oneself is not a mere expression of individuality but a means to make the whole world a better place:

> Sei du selbst, so ist die Welt reich und schön! Sei *nicht* du selbst, sei Lügner und Feigling, so ist die Welt arm und scheint dir der Verbesserung bedürftig.[10]

> (Be yourself, then the world is rich and beautiful. If you are not yourself, if you are a liar and a coward, then the world will be poor and in need of improvement.)

As the quote above shows, Hesse addresses his readership directly. He did so throughout his life, not just figuratively but literally, by personally answering tens of thousands of letters from young people who sought his counsel.[11] Hesse's writings—and the author himself—have always roused in readers a sense of being recognized and respected for who they truly are.

Hesse's Appeal to Countercultures

Hesse's popularity among the young can be traced to the publication of his debut novel *Peter Camenzind* in 1904.[12] The German youth movement groups called *Wandervogel* (Ramblers, or Migratory birds)—who rebelled against industrialization by hiking in the countryside and advocated an existence in harmony with nature—embraced the novel because they identified parallels to their own ideals within it.[13] Theodore Saul Jackson cites three major similarities between Hesse and the Wandervogel groups: first, they "shared an affinity for nature as well as movement within nature. A second commonality is the desire to guide and advise young persons. Finally, they were both critical of the German school system and the customs and rigidity of the bourgeois lifestyle which accompanied it."[14]

---

[10] Hermann Hesse, *Zarathustras Wiederkehr: Ein Wort an die deutsche Jugend* (Bern: Stämpfli & Cie, 1919), 29.

[11] See Hermann Hesse, *Die Antwort bist du selbst: Briefe an junge Menschen*, ed. Volker Michels (Frankfurt am Main: Insel, 2000).

[12] Before being published as a full-length novel in 1904, *Peter Camenzind* was serialized in the journal *Die Neue Rundschau* the previous year. (Ralph Freedman, *Hermann Hesse: Pilgrim of Crisis. A Biography* [New York: Pantheon, 1978], 111.)

[13] Despite similarities between the ideals of the Wandervogel movement and Hesse, the author himself was never convinced of the link between the two. Ralph Freedman writes: "If [Hesse] disapproved of the Youth Movement, he did so mostly because he disliked any organized form of living that might threaten the integrity of the individual life. He did not, however, disapprove of the return to nature or the quest for ideals or the romance of the simple life." (Ibid., 110.)

[14] Theodore Saul Jackson, "Hermann Hesse as Ambivalent Modernist" (PhD diss., Washington University, 2010), 105–106, doi: https://doi.org/10.7936/K71R6NKW (accessed January 14, 2022).

Hesse's avid affection for nature permeates much of his work and, as we shall see in chapter one, *Peter Camenzind* is a particularly colorful expression of his affection. The novel's call for a Rousseauesque "return to nature" made Hesse, overnight, "a figurehead of a counterculture—one of the first of the twentieth century," Gunnar Decker writes, and continues: "Before long the Wandervogel and reformist movements of all kinds would heed and take as their own the call that he issued in *Peter Camenzind*—just as, sixty years later, a global counterculture youth movement would adopt *Steppenwolf*."[15]

In the decades following Hesse's death, he gained an almost prophet-like status in North America.[16] During the 1960s and 70s, most of Hesse's novels were in print in the United States and *Siddhartha* and *Der Steppenwolf* gained leagues of devoted fans. *Siddhartha*, with its themes of spiritual seeking and interconnectedness, was immensely attractive to hippies and other free-thinkers. Scott MacFarlane writes that the book "articulated an underlying Eastern philosophy predicated on the oneness of everything, a notion heartily embraced by most adherents of the counterculture."[17] And *Der Steppenwolf*, with its animality theme, mystical elements, and passages of hedonistic excesses turned out to be equally embraced. As Gary Lachman puts it, the book "brought Hesse to a generation of angry young men and beatniks who saw in his exploration of strange mental states and anti-conformism a precursor to themselves."[18]

Due to the popularity of these novels, they were made into Hollywood films. *Siddhartha* (Conrad Rooks, 1972) was made with an all-Indian cast of actors to great critical acclaim, and two years later *Steppenwolf* (Fred Haines, 1974) was released. Joseph Mileck calls this period a "Hesse boom" that not only brought Hesse millions of new readers (students, beatniks, hippies) and a wave of literary scholarship, but also gave rise to coffee shops, restaurants, bookshops, and theaters bearing names from his stories, as well as a rock band named Steppenwolf.[19] Hesse became a pop-cultural phenomenon as well as "a veritable rallying point for protest and change," Mileck asserts, "a

---

[15] Gunnar Decker, *The Wanderer and His Shadow*, trans. Peter Lewis (Cambridge, MA: Harvard University Press, 2018), 220.

[16] See Theodore Ziolkowski, "Saint Hesse among the Hippies," *American-German Review* 35, no. 2 (1969): 19–23.

[17] Scott MacFarlane, *The Hippie Narrative: A Literary Perspective on the Counterculture* (Jefferson, NC: McFarland & Co, 2007), 88.

[18] Gary Lachman, *Turn Off Your Mind: The Mystic Sixties and the Dark Side of the Age of Aquarius* (New York: Disinformation, 2001), 120.

[19] Joseph Mileck, "Trends in Literary Reception: The Hesse Boom," *The German Quarterly* 51, no. 3 (1978): 348–350.

kindred soul, support, and inspiration for an enthusiastic following of dissidents, seekers, and estranged loners drawn from both the establishment and the subculture."[20] Also, as David G. Richards suggests, "the primary factor in [Hesse's] popular success may be his uncompromising commitment to the discovery and development of the self."[21] This is especially evident among counterculture readers who respond not only to the themes in the texts but also to the author's presence within them.

The theme of self-development is a recurring motif in Hesse's writings. It is frequently depicted through contemplative inner journeys of the protagonists, of which *Die Morgenlandfahrt* (*Journey to the East*, 1932)—in which a religious sect of fictional characters (some from Hesse's previous texts) make an eastward pilgrimage—and Hesse's magnum opus, *Das Glasperlenspiel* (*The Glass Bead Game*, 1943), are prime examples. Hesse's narratives are often characterized by the search for contentment and truth, and they are almost always influenced by the author's own life. Beginning with Hugo Ball's biography *Hermann Hesse: Sein Leben und sein Werk* (1927), scholarship has frequently emphasized correlations between the author's life and his work.[22] When addressing the fact that Hesse labeled his writings *Seelenbiographien* (biographies of the soul), Ingo Cornils states that "Hesse explored his innermost thoughts and feelings as a starting point for constructing characters that serve as case studies both for the narrator and for the reader, who might or might not sense an affinity with them."[23] Similarly, Ralph Freedman writes: "One of the trademarks of Hermann Hesse's work, which in part accounts for his various waves of great popularity, is the reciprocal relationship between his personal life and his art. More

[20] Mileck, "Trends in Literary Reception," 350.

[21] Richards, *Exploring the Divided Self*, 7.

[22] Eugene Stelzig's study from 1988 examines "what it means to be an 'autobiographical writer' by considering Hesse's fictions of the self as exemplary instances of the relationship between life and art, biography and autobiography, in the subjective tradition of modern literature." (Eugene Stelzig, *Hermann Hesse's Fictions of the Self: Autobiography and the Confessional Imagination* [Princeton: Princeton University Press, 1988], ix–x.) Stelzig's study follows Joseph Mileck's Hesse-biography from 1978 in which it is suggested that Hesse was a writer who documented his life in confessional form for therapeutic purposes. "Hesse's protagonists are self-projections," Mileck writes, "not only in their concerns, thoughts, and feelings, but even in their persons and experiences and, with rare exception, in the worlds in which they live and the circles in which they move." (Joseph Mileck, *Hermann Hesse: Life and Art* [Berkeley: University of California Press, 1978], xii.) Also, Lewis W. Tusken argues that "[t]he biographical approach to understanding Hesse is especially helpful, not only because it details the circumstances under which his works were written but also because it helps to determine his *Erzählhaltung*—his stance toward his subject matter—and, thus, to reveal his message in relation to his own ability to 'live it' at a given time." (Lewis W. Tusken, *Understanding Hermann Hesse: The Man, His Myth, His Metaphor* [Columbia: University of South Carolina Press, 1998], 2.)

[23] Cornils, "Introduction," 8.

directly than most writers, he used his work as a means of managing his psychological crises and used the crises as the subject and form of the work in order to overcome them."[24]

Attention to the bond between Hesse's life and work is persistent. In a biography from 2012, Gunnar Decker states that in Hesse's writing "the constant interplay between the internal and the external brings together auto-biographical accounts with reflection and a sense of enchantment through new myth making."[25] Biographical approaches such as the ones referred to hitherto are rewarding. But a key reason as to why queer aspects in Hesse's writing are seldom emphasized might in fact be that scholars want to avoid insinuating that Hesse himself was a closeted homosexual (of which neither proof nor indications can be found). While it is certainly interesting to speculate on Hesse's *intentions* with certain recurring aspects in his texts, it bears underscoring that those intentions are not necessarily connected with the author's own experiences.

Approaching Hesse's Writing from a Queer Angle

Overall, this study concerns Hesse's texts rather than his personal life. However, some biographical aspects will be mentioned in the following, since these provide context to the significance of Eigensinn and the "Be yourself" ideal in the author's characters.

As shown in Decker's biography, during Hesse's adolescent years he faced predicaments that came to shape his authorship.[26] His parents decided early that he was to study theology and become a teacher or a priest. Until he was allowed to pursue his own dream—that of becoming a writer—he was unable to find his place in the world. Hesse's formative years were therefore difficult. He had mental breakdowns, attempted suicide, and ran away from his boarding school.[27] The young Hermann Hesse, Decker explains, "found himself caught up in the workings of a system that was geared to either clipping the wings of anything that contradicted the prevailing norm or excluding the disruptive and irritating element. This process now brought it home to him that it did not take much to become an outsider, or even a heretic."[28] In order to manage Hesse's insurgent behavior he was treated by a

---

[24] Freedman, *Pilgrim of Crisis*, 289–290.
[25] Decker, *The Wanderer and His Shadow*, 3–4.
[26] Ibid., 64–87.
[27] Later on, Hesse drew on this episode for inspiration to the events in *Unterm Rad*, wherein one of the primary characters also flees from a repressive boarding school.
[28] Decker, *The Wanderer and His Shadow*, 69–70.

"faith healer and 'devil exorcist'," and when that failed, his parents sent their "problem child" to an insane asylum.[29]

In the semi-autobiographical *Kurzgefaßter Lebenslauf* (*Brief Curriculum Vitae*, 1924), the Eigensinn of Hesse himself is clearly conveyed. The text paints a picture of the young aspiring author as being just as rebellious as many of his future literary outsiders:

> Gebote aber haben leider stets eine fatale Wirkung auf mich gehabt, mochten sie noch so richtig und noch so gut gemeint sein ... Ich brauchte nur das "Du sollst" zu hören, so wendete sich alles in mir um, und ich wurde verstockt.[30]

> (Sadly, orders have always had a fatal impact on me, no matter how true or well-intentioned they are. I only had to hear the "You shall" for a shift to occur in me and make me disobedient.)

Following the nonconformity of Hesse's youth, his lifestyle can be said to have remained somewhat alternative throughout his life, as he was frequently torn between bachelorhood and married life. "Hesse's biography," Theodore Saul Jackson writes, "reveals great tensions between these two poles—tensions that jeopardized his first two marriages inasmuch as he required extended amounts of time spent away from his families."[31]

Another, even more prominent, aspect of Hesse's alternative lifestyle can be seen in the documentary *Freak Out!* (Carl Javiér, 2014) and in *Die Literatur der Lebensreform* (2016). Both Javiér's documentary and Kathrin Geist's chapter in the anthology mention Hesse's stay in the early 1900s at Monte Verità, a colony in the Swiss Alps where the community cornerstones were the anti-establishment ideals of the *Lebensreformbewegung* (the social movement for life reform). Geist describes the colony's ideals in the following way: "Here one longs from liberation from established norms, and for a healthy, natural, and vegetarian way of life (which at this time is a political issue) in an ever more technological and industrialized world."[32] Being part

---

[29] Decker, *The Wanderer and His Shadow*, 74.

[30] Hermann Hesse, *Kursgefaßter Lebenslauf*, in *Sämtliche Werke. Band 12: Autobiographische Schriften II. Selbstzeugnisse. Erinnerungen. Gedenkblätter und Rundbriefe*, ed. Volker Michaels (Frankfurt am Main: Suhrkamp, 2003), 46.

[31] Jackson, "Ambivalent Modernist," 167.

[32] Kathrin Geist, "Der Nacktkletterer vom Monte Verità: Hermann Hesses *In den Felsen* als kritische Auseinandersetzung mit der Lebensreform," in *Die Literatur der Lebensreform: Kulturkritik und Aufbruchstimmung um 1900*, ed. Thorsten Carstensen and Marcel Schmid (Bielefeld: transcript, 2016), 195. ("Man sehnt sich nach Befreiung von etablierten Normen, nach gesunder, naturnaher, vegetarischer

of this social movement—with its vegetarianism, nudism, and "free love ideals"—makes Hesse a fitting role model for the future hippie movement.[33]

Following the thematic aspects of Hesse's writing that have been referred to above—such as the frequency of protagonists personifying Eigensinn, their search for self-knowledge, their devotion to nonconformism, and their status as outsiders in society—rebellious and norm-challenging qualities in the authorship emerge. These rebellious and norm-challenging qualities will be emphasized throughout this study to cast light on other queer characteristics in *Peter Camenzind* and *Der Steppenwolf*, such as the texts' homoerotic content.

Before we continue, a word on the selection of the primary study material. The reason for focusing on *Peter Camenzind* and *Der Steppenwolf* is twofold. First, these novels differ greatly in style and can be said to represent two very different stages of Hesse's career, which will hopefully provide an overview of the evolution of certain tropes and themes that he was fond of.[34] And second, as Gunnar Decker has stated, both novels were heavily embraced by countercultures, which makes them interesting when one's ambition is to emphasize queerness. The enthusiasm for these texts by Wandervogel and hippie movements establishes them as not only anti-traditional but also—in the sense that they challenge conceptions of what it means to be normal in society—as queer. Overall, the call embedded in Hesse's authorship to "Be yourself" can be seen as a queer stance since it relies on a refusal to conform

Lebensweise [was zu dieser Zeit durchaus ein Politikum ist] in einer sich technisierenden und industrialisierenden Welt.") The translation into English is made by the author of this book.

[33] For further reading on Hesse's stay at Monte Verità, see Martin Radermacher, "Hermann Hesse – Monte Verità: Wahrheitssuche abseits des Mainstreams zu Beginn des 20. Jahrhunderts," *Zeitschrift für junge Religionswissenschaft* 6 (2011), doi: https://doi.org/10.4000/zjr.710 (accessed January 14, 2022).

[34] "Dividing Hesse's works into an early and a mature period has become a commonplace among critics," David G. Richards writes, "and is sanctioned by the author's own evaluation." (Richards, *Exploring the Divided Self*, 2.) Richards clarifies that the bisection of these periods occurs in 1916–1917 and is attributed to Hesse's personal experiences with psychoanalysis. After authoring *Demian* in 1917, Hesse began to express a tendency to distance himself from his previous work (of which *Peter Camenzind* is part), work that was often characterized as entertainment or escapism. Novels from this period, however, "are not cheaply escapist; they offer," Theodore Saul Jackson argues, "as all of Hesse's novels do, examples of psychological *rejuvenation* from the stresses of modern life." (Jackson, "Ambivalent Modernist," 4.) In Hesse's mature period (in which *Der Steppenwolf* is a key text), the author was, according to Richards, "no longer willing to cater to the tastes and desires of the public." (Richards, *Exploring the Divided Self*, 3.) He began instead to write primarily for *himself*. As argued by Joseph Mileck, however, regardless how one divides Hesse's authorship into periods or phases, "the center about which his creative activity revolves [the individual versus society] and about which his vivid imagination and his unusual mastery of language weave their varied tapestry remains constant." (Joseph Mileck, "The Prose of Hermann Hesse: Life, Substance and Form," *The German Quarterly* 27, no. 3 [1954]: 171.)

to the norms of majority culture both in terms of identity and sexuality, as we shall see.

Given Hesse's themes and fans, it is curious that, with a limited number of exceptions (examples will be given under the heading "Research Background"), his novels have not been labeled especially queer. The lack of queer readings of Hesse's texts is even more confusing considering that the author himself suggested their queer potentiality, specifically in the shape of homoerotic desire between men. In a letter in 1931 regarding the possible homoeroticism between male characters in his novels *Roßhalde* (1914), *Knulp*, and *Narziß und Goldmund*, Hesse confirmed the following: "Daß diese Freundschaften, weil zwischen Männern bestehend, völlig frei von Erotik seien, ist ein Irrtum."[35] (It is a mistake to assume that these friendships, because they exist between men, are completely free of eroticism.) While the following readings will not consider eroticism and sex as equivalent (the former, for instance, can characterize a text without including any actual sexual activity), Hesse's statement indicates that he was aware of the existence of homosexuality and that he is inviting readers to interpret his work queerly.

Thus, in accordance with Hesse's authorial invitation, the general aim of this study is to examine how characters who embody outsiderness and/or otherness in *Peter Camenzind* and *Der Steppenwolf* intersect with and connote queerness, such as, for instance, homoeroticism and nonconformism. The study will attempt to answer how queerness is manifested in the novels, as well as (in particular) what role friendship plays in their portrayals of queerness. Further distinctions in this general aim will be explained and developed in the subsequent analytical chapters.

Queer Theories

Since the inception of "queer" as a theoretical term, many have argued that it raises questions rather than provides answers. Having arisen out of the research field Gay and Lesbian Studies during a series of North American conferences in the early 1990s—initially intended as a light-minded provocation that combined queer activism and the more "respectable" concept of theory—queer theory quickly became a radical analytic tool that gained traction within the humanities.

Over time, queer theory has evolved into a powerful means of critiquing inequalities based on sexual identity (among other things). "When signalling an unapologetic, anti-assimilationist stance," Noreen Giffney explains, "[the

---

[35] Hermann Hesse, *Briefe* (Frankfurt am Main: Suhrkamp, 1964), 49.

term] queer champions those who refuse to be defined in the terms of, and by the (moral) codes of behavior and identification set down by, the dominant society."[36] Queer theory's refusal to be pinned down and defined in any easy terms—attempting instead to be self-reflexive and in constant flux—makes it a difficult concept to summarize. Complicating matters further, there is no one, all-encompassing, or "original" queer theory in the singular. As Donald E. Hall proposes, there are "only many different voices and sometimes overlapping, sometimes divergent perspectives that can loosely be called 'queer theories.'"[37]

The signifying trait of most queer theories is critique of norms such as those relating to sexuality, gender, relationality, and desire, most often heteronormativity, which is the system of norms that determines how we understand gender and sexuality. "Queer theory," Rachel Carroll writes, "approaches heterosexuality as a normative category of sexed, gendered and sexual identity which serves both to support the binary logic by which 'hetero-' and 'homosexual' identities are produced and to perpetuate the construction of homosexual identities as deviant and abnormal."[38] Heteronormativity stipulates that all human beings are supposed to be heterosexual. This means that women and men (which are often the only two fathomable genders in heteronormative contexts) should embody what Judith Butler calls "stable gender identities" that match their biological sexes (also known as cisgender).[39]

Butler's pioneering queer-theoretical work challenges the heteronormative idea that natural sexuality concerns women and men who desire each other for the sole purpose of reproduction. Individuals who refuse to conform to such a way of life—like many who identify within the LGBTQIA+ spectrum (that is, lesbians, gays, bisexuals, trans people, queers/questioning people, intersex individuals, those who are asexual, as well as allies and others)—risk losing not only social, economic, and political privileges, but

---

[36] Noreen Giffney, "Introduction: The 'q' Word," in *The Ashgate Research Companion to Queer Theory*, ed. Noreen Giffney and Michael O'Rourke (Farnham: Ashgate, 2009), 3.

[37] Donald E. Hall, *Queer Theories* (Basingstoke: Palgrave Macmillan, 2003), 5.

[38] Rachel Carroll, "Introduction: feminism, queer theory and heterosexuality," in *Rereading Heterosexuality: Feminism, Queer Theory and Contemporary Fiction*, ed. Rachel Carroll (Edinburgh: Edinburgh University Press, 2012), 2.

[39] In Judith Butler's early work within queer theory, she developed the idea of "gender performativity" which, in broad strokes, consists of the notion that one cannot "be a gender" without "doing gendered acts." Gender, Butler suggests, is a performative social construct—an idea that challenges the heteronormative conception of gender as "natural." For further reading on Butler's concept of gender performativity, see her groundbreaking work *Gender Trouble: Feminism and the Subversion of Identity* (New York: Routledge, 1990), as well as *Undoing Gender* (New York: Routledge, 2004).

also becoming systematically marginalized and met with prejudice, hate, and often various forms of violence.

Considering that queer as a theoretical term can hold a variety of meanings—it is an adjective (something *is* queer), a verb (one can *queer* something; that is, bring queerness to it or elevate its inherent queer potential), and an adverb (for instance reading *queerly*)—its applicability as a critical tool can be vast. As a contemporary identity category, queer also implies taking control over how one is defined. It mirrors, in this regard, how Hesse's protagonists define themselves as outsiders in society.

Although there were no queer theories in Hesse's time, what most certainly did exist, albeit with a different terminology, in the late nineteenth and early twentieth centuries, were queer people. While one should be mindful when using terms like homosexual, queer, or gay in descriptions of individuals from that time, as underscored by Robert Deam Tobin, "it seems self-evident that, for those sexually interested in members of their own sex, the sense of identity must have changed significantly in the late nineteenth-century as new vocabularies of 'urning,' 'invert,' and 'homosexual' arose, backed up with scientific, medical and cultural—rather than religious—evidence."[40]

The sexology discourse in the German-speaking world at the turn of the twentieth century (to which Tobin refers) will be discussed at length later. For the moment it suffices to say that throughout this study, terms like homosexual and queer will be used when discussing themes, tropes, contexts, and characters in Hesse's texts, although not always interchangeably. The label homosexuality will mostly be used when discussing homoeroticism and same-sex romance, whereas the term queer figures as a signifier of how certain aspects of Hesse's texts (such as homoeroticism and nonconformism) challenge heteronormative perceptions about sexuality, identity, relationality, and desire.

A Couple of Queer-Theoretical Concepts

Under this heading, some queer-theoretical concepts that are of significance in the upcoming readings of *Peter Camenzind* and *Der Steppenwolf* will be explained. These concepts have been formulated within a field of queer studies called "queer temporality," within which the concept of "queer time" is broadly described as temporal contexts in which heteronormative life

---

[40] Robert Deam Tobin, *Peripheral Desires: The German Discovery of Sex* (Philadelphia: University of Pennsylvania Press, 2015), xiv.

patterns do not have hegemonic status. In Jack Halberstam's *In a Queer Time and Place* (2005), queer time is said to be "about the potentiality of a life unscripted by the conventions of family, inheritance, and child rearing."[41]

Queer time, however, is not unaffected by heteronormativity.[42] A central point of interest in the field has been the perpetual adolescence that queers are reduced to within majority culture, especially in those instances when they do not marry or become parents. Although some temporal aspects in *Peter Camenzind* and *Der Steppenwolf* will be examined in this study, queer temporality will not be used as an overarching theoretical framework. Rather, the study will make use of a couple of concepts that have been formulated within that field.

One of these concepts is Heather Love's "backwardness," which she devised in *Feeling Backward: Loss and the Politics of Queer History* (2007). Love writes that "[t]he history of Western representation is littered with the corpses of gender and sexual deviants. Those who are directly identified with same-sex desire most often end up dead; if they manage to survive, it is on such compromised terms that it makes death seem attractive."[43] This treatment of characters that defy norms of gender and sexuality forces readers of older literature to witness unsettling iterations of queer subjectivity. As typical aspects in portrayals of queerness, Love mentions, for instance, loneliness, loss, self-hatred, shame, and failure.

Love's work shows that when one reads about queers in historic texts, one must have thick skin and be prepared to wallow in all sorts of suffering, darkness, and (of course) death. The reader must be ready to accept what she describes as "the historical 'impossibility' of same-sex desire."[44] While such iterations connote hopelessness and might be depressing, readers should not, however, refrain from "feeling backward" and attempt to embrace them:

---

[41] Jack Halberstam, *In a Queer Time and Place: Transgender Bodies, Subcultural Lives* (New York: New York University Press, 2005), 2.

[42] For further reading on the concept of queer temporality, see, e.g., Lee Edelman, *No Future: Queer Theory and the Death Drive* (Durham: Duke University Press, 2004). In this polemical work against "reproductive futurism," Edelman argues that in normative culture the figure of the Child is pinned against the queer subject, which is labeled "narcissistic," "antisocial," and "future negating." Edelman suggests that we, as queers, refuse this social and political order by boldly embracing negativity. The field of queer temporality also includes work by scholars such as Elizabeth Freeman, Carla Freccero, and several others.

[43] Heather Love, *Feeling Backward: Loss and the Politics of Queer History* (Cambridge, MA: Harvard University Press, 2007), 1.

[44] Ibid., 4.

> Although many queer critics take exception to the idea of a linear, triumphal-
> ist view of history, we are in practice deeply committed to the notion of
> progress; despite our reservations, we just cannot stop dreaming of a better
> life for queer people. … Such utopian desires are at the heart of the collective
> project of queer studies and integral to the history of gay and lesbian identity.
> Still, the critical compulsion to fix—at least imaginatively—the problems of
> queer life has made it difficult to fully engage with such difficulties. Critics
> find themselves in an odd position: we are not sure if we should explore the
> link between homosexuality and loss, or set about proving that it does not
> exist.[45]

One might certainly ask what we stand to gain by embracing the sadness of
the past. Love argues that since contemporary queer identities are shaped by
the damage done to us throughout history, "[p]aying attention to what was
difficult in the past may tell us how far we have come, but that is not all it will
tell us; it also makes visible the damage that we live with in the present."[46]

Love's idea of backwardness is useful within queer-focused scholarship
because it forces us not to become blinded by progress, instead remaining
realistic about the conditions under which queer people *have lived* and *still
live*. Backwardness, in Love's definition, is a concept with a double implication. On the one hand, it is "a queer historical structure of feeling" and on
the other hand, it can be used "as a model for queer historiography."[47] As
such, it is both an emotional condition that can be identified in queer
historical subjects (such as characters in a literary text) and a means for
scholars to approach queer (literary) history.

Studying literature that concerns or is affected by the dark history of queer
subjectivity need not to be an entirely depressing affair, however. Like stars
in the night sky or a lighthouse beacon on a stormy sea, specks of light such
as expressions of queer companionship, affection, desire, and romance, truly
stand out in the dark. In the following readings of Hesse's novels, such
expressions, which this study calls "queer specks of light," will be traced and
emphasized.

At times in this study, it will be argued that some of the queerness in
Hesse's texts is alluded to, not only metaphorically as a narrative technique,
but also by the characters that populate his stories. Since queer voices have
been systematically silenced by history, it is hardly surprising that in the early

---

[45] Love, *Feeling Backward*, 3.
[46] Ibid., 29.
[47] Ibid., 146.

twentieth-century, queer literary characters sometimes seem to hide their desires. Such "hidden queerness" in older texts makes Christopher Nealon's writing relevant here: "The many ways contemporary queer readers and critics have invested pre-Stonewall writing and images with romance or nostalgia or distaste all point to the funny communicability of shadow-relations and secret emotions across time, as if they acquire heft only in the long term, where the difficulty of the problems they want to solve (like historical isolation and suffering) can emerge in their full intractability."[48] Nealon argues that because of the systematic silencing of queer subjectivity in history, queerness can sometimes only find ways to materialize over time. Therefore, current queer-theoretical approaches become fruitful methodologies in readings of older literature.

In addition to Heather Love's idea of backwardness, another concept from the field of queer temporality that will be referenced later is what José Esteban Muñoz calls "queer utopia." In *Cruising Utopia: The Then and There of Queer Futurity* (2009), Muñoz draws on Ernst Bloch's reflections on hope and utopia and argues that "[q]ueerness is a longing that propels us onward, beyond romances of the negative and toiling in the present. Queerness is that thing that lets us feel that this world is not enough, that indeed something is missing."[49] In Muñoz's work the concept of utopia is regarded as a fervent insistence on something new, something better, and something dawning.[50] "Utopian queerness," in Muñoz's view, is a *potentiality*: "Queerness," he writes, "is essentially about the rejection of a here and now and an insistence on potentiality or concrete possibility for another world."[51] Muñoz's suggestion is to recognize queerness as *not yet here*. Queerness can still be felt, however, "as the warm illumination of a horizon imbued with potentiality."[52] The horizon is a signifier for utopian queerness in Muñoz's work, and often, he states, "we can glimpse the worlds proposed and promised by queerness

---

[48] Christopher S. Nealon, *Foundlings: Lesbian and Gay Historical Emotion Before Stonewall* (Durham: Duke University Press, 2001), 178.

[49] José Esteban Muñoz, *Cruising Utopia: The Then and There of Queer Futurity* (New York: New York University Press, 2009), 1.

[50] This description of utopia does not differ in any major way from most other definitions of the concept. Ruth Levitas explains that "the ultimate importance of utopia lies in its connection with progress and thus in its social role." (Ruth Levitas, *The Concept of Utopia* [Syracuse, NY: Syracuse University Press, 1990], 13.) In Levitas's book she examines how utopia is used, for instance, by Marx, Engels, Herbert Marcuse, and Ernst Bloch. What sets Muñoz apart from these thinkers (and the principal reason as to why their writings do not constitute primary theoretical sources in this study) is how Muñoz connects utopia with various examples of queerness.

[51] Muñoz, *Cruising Utopia*, 1.

[52] Ibid.

in the realm of the aesthetic. The aesthetic, especially the queer aesthetic, frequently contains blueprints and schemata of a forward-dawning futurity."[53]

Hypothesizing that one can read certain characters in Hesse's novels as queer (queer in the sense that, for instance, they challenge heteronormative conceptions of sexuality by cultivating homoeroticism), the conditions under which these fictional subjects exist on the page—at times having to hide their desires from the rest of society—will likely make longing for a queer utopia highly relevant to them. These characters' longings for something new, something better, or something dawning will be identified in this study and examined in conjunction with what Heather Love calls the historical impossibility of same-sex desire.

Other queer-theoretical concepts will be drawn on and explained throughout. These concepts, as well as those described above, will be referenced to varying extents, and are not drawn on in every analytical chapter. Moreover, the theoretical concepts of interest here do not constitute a complete description of the conceptual apparatus of queer theories.

"Reading the Queer"

Under this heading, the "method" that will be utilized in this study will be described. Placing the word method within quotation marks refers to the fact that within literature studies, modes of interpreting are constantly critiqued, re-assessed, and developed. Toril Moi even argues that literary scholars do not rely on methods at all:

> The way we (literary critics) talk about what we do (often under headings such as "method" or "approach" and the like) is at odds with what we actually do. We mistake political and existential investments for methods, specific practices of reading. … What we—literary critics—call different "methods of reading" are really different interests, and different views of what is important in literature (and life).[54]

In broad terms, the way with which Hermann Hesse's writing will be approached in this study falls into the category of "queer readings," a reading tradition that began with the development of queer theory in the 1990s. Eve Kosofsky Sedgwick, whose *Between Men: English Literature and Male Homosocial Desire* (1985) and *Epistemology of the Closet* (1990) are early

---

[53] Muñoz, *Cruising Utopia*, 1.
[54] Toril Moi, *Revolution of the Ordinary: Literary Studies after Wittgenstein, Austin, and Cavell* (Chicago: The University of Chicago Press, 2017), 179.

examples of queer readings, equates this reading style with that of a child who "is reading for important news about herself, without knowing what form that news will take; with only the patchiest familiarity with its codes; without, even, more than hungrily hypothesizing to what questions this news may proffer an answer."[55] In other words, reading queerly is, in Sedgwick's view, a subjective, adventurous, and pleasurable act in which curiosity, surprise, and the ability to venture into a text *with an open mind* is essential.[56]

Moreover, reading queerly aims at highlighting and activating the queer potential of texts. Equal to the queer-theoretical imperative to critique various kinds of norms (in this study, heteronormativity especially), the purpose of many of the early queer readings (such as Sedgwick's books) was to question and destabilize the hegemony of heterosexuality in literature. Reading queerly turned into a practice in which the reader placed emphasis on a text's silences, tensions, and inconsistencies (what might be charac-terized as "reading between the lines"), thereby divulging a text's dormant and/or ignored queerness.[57]

As queer readings were adopted within literary and cultural studies, they drew heavily on the "symptomatic readings" that had originated in the early 1980s with the writings of Fredric Jameson among others.[58] Sedgwick's early work, for instance, can be said to follow Jamesonian thought in that it sometimes seeks the unspoken meanings behind the surfaces of texts. This style of interpretation—to assume that surfaces are deceptive and that the real meaning can be exposed by the reader—went on to become an immensely

---

[55] Eve Kosofsky Sedgwick, "Paranoid Reading and Reparative Reading; or, You're So Paranoid, You Probably Think This Introduction Is About You," in *Novel Gazing: Queer Readings in Fiction*, ed. Eve Kosofsky Sedgwick (Durham: Duke University Press, 1997), 2–3.

[56] Sedgwick's idea that reading queerly demands "childlike imagination" correlates with views on reading that Hermann Hesse himself perpetuated. In the essay "Vom Bücherlesen" ("On Reading Books," 1920), Hesse suggests that there are three types of readers and that any person can belong to any type (or all three at the same time) at any time. The first type is a naïve reader who reads objectively. The second type reads with openness to a myriad of textual meanings. The third type is a playful reader, in every way comparable to a child, who places as much significance on *association* as on what is actually printed on the page. (Hermann Hesse, "Vom Bücherlesen," in *Die Welt der Bücher: Betrachtungen und Aufsätze zur Literatur*, ed. Volker Michels [Frankfurt am Main: Suhrkamp, 1977], 188–193.)

[57] Katri Kivilaakso, Ann-Sofie Lönngren, and Rita Paqvalén, "Förord," in *Queera läsningar*, ed. Katri Kivilaakso, Ann-Sofie Lönngren, and Rita Paqvalén (Hägersten: Rosenlarv, 2012), 10.

[58] Fredric Jameson argues that texts are never "just texts," they require interpretation, something he describes as an "allegorical practice" wherein the interpreter actually "rewrites" the object that is studied. (Fredric Jameson, *The Political Unconscious: Narrative as a Socially Symbolic Act* [London: Methuen, 1981], ix–x.) The rewriting process of which Jameson speaks concerns not only the text in itself but the previous scholarly reception of that text. Eve Kosofsky Sedgwick's early books, for example, are critical of previous interpretations that have failed to acknowledge queer meanings in the work she analyzes, like that of Shakespeare and Henry James.

influential interpretative practice within literary studies for almost three decades.

Over the course of the last fifteen years, however, the symptomatic reading style has been questioned by several scholars, not least by Sedgwick herself. Already in 1997, in her influential essay on "reparative reading," Sedgwick voiced her concerns, arguing that within queer theory and other progressive critical paradigms, Paul Ricoeur's "hermeneutics of suspicion," a practice of deciphering that he developed in his writing on Freud, Marx, and Nietzsche—is a *paranoid* interpretive practice that has become "widely understood as a mandatory injunction rather that a possibility among other possibilities."[59]

Although Sedgwick acknowledges that Ricoeur's contribution has merit, she advocates a more diverse style of interpretive inquiry, since suspicious hermeneutics, she writes, "may have had an unintentionally stultifying side-effect: they may have made it less rather than more possible to unpack the local, contingent relations between any given piece of knowledge and its narrative/epistemological entailments for the seeker, knower, or teller."[60] In other words, reading suspiciously can make it challenging to identify conditions that are inherent to the object of study. Instead of aiding in clarifying what a text says, the suspicious interpreter, Sedgwick warns us, might inadvertently construe something it does not say.[61]

As an alternative, Sedgwick suggests reading reparatively, a style that in contrast to the traditional queer reading does not primarily aim at exposing the ways with which literary texts reproduce political inequities, but rather at repairing damage: "to read from a reparative position," Sedgwick writes, "is to surrender the knowing, anxious paranoid determination that no horror, however apparently unthinkable, shall ever come to the reader *as new*: to a reparatively positioned reader, it can seem realistic and necessary to experience surprise. Because there can be terrible surprises, however, there can also be good ones."[62]

---

[59] Sedgwick, "Paranoid Reading," 5.

[60] Ibid., 4.

[61] It is worth noting that all forms of hermeneutics are not inherently suspicious. For the literary hermeneutic, Peter Szondi explains, one goal is to overcome the historical distance to texts: "The hermeneuticist is a translator," he writes, "a mediator, who uses his linguistic knowledge to make intelligible what is not understood, what is *no longer* understood. He does this by replacing the no longer intelligible word with another one belonging to the current state of the language." (Peter Szondi, *Introduction to Literary Hermeneutics* [Cambridge: Cambridge University Press, 1995], 6.) This un-suspicious mode of interpretive inquiry can be seen as a sort of transference of meaning from one temporal context to another.

[62] Sedgwick, "Paranoid Reading," 24.

The queer specks of light that will be given attention in this study—that is, positive or hopeful representations of queerness—are comparable to the "good surprises" that Sedgwick refers to. Tracing such specks in Hesse's texts thus draws on the reparative reading tradition. Instead of paranoia (which in Sedgwick's opinion means adopting the stance that texts are always already guilty of sexism, or homophobia, transphobia, funk-phobia, and/or racism that the reader can expose through critical interpretation), reading reparatively is not about disclosing the horrors of queer subjectivity as it is represented in literature history, but about opening oneself up to something other than *identifying* these issues. Heather Love's endeavor in *Feeling Backward*, for example, is clearly indebted to the reparative reading style in that she, as a reader and a scholar, attempts to embrace the sadness of the past. When Love addresses what to do with "sad old queens and long-suffering dykes who haunt the historical record," she suggests the following: "By including queer figures from the past in a positive genealogy of gay identity, we make good on their suffering, transforming their shame into pride after the fact."[63] In addition, when reading reparatively, a queer reader's own, possibly ambivalent, feelings about belonging to a historically stigmatized group are counteracted. Sedgwick's concept therefore goes beyond being just a method. Essentially, the point of reading reparatively becomes less about repairing texts and more about repairing their readers.

Others who have voiced criticism of the symptomatic reading style are Stephen Best and Sharon Marcus, who, in a special issue of the multidisciplinary journal *Representations* (2009), made us familiar with "surface reading" as an alternative to symptomatic reading's distrust of textual surfaces. Best and Marcus explain that surface reading means to focus on "what is evident, perceptible, apprehensible in texts; what is neither hidden nor hiding; what, in the geometrical sense, has length and breadth but no thickness, and therefore covers no depth."[64] Being attentive to what appears on the surface inspires a more straightforward style of reading, they argue, in which texts are taken at face value and are described accurately, on their own terms.

In *Between Women: Friendship, Desire, and Marriage in Victorian England* (2007), Sharon Marcus remarks that surface readings are never completely devoid of critical or interpretative efforts, but that their goal (rather than plunging the depths of texts) is to draw attention to surface meanings that previous research has failed to notice. Although Marcus

---

[63] Love, *Feeling Backward*, 32.
[64] Stephen Best and Sharon Marcus, "Surface Reading: An Introduction," *Representations* 108, no. 1 (2009): 9.

employs a rather dogmatic surface reading method in her book—a style she playfully (or ironically) labels "just reading"—she writes: "just reading recognizes that interpretation is inevitable: even when attending to the givens of a text, we are always only—or just—constructing a reading."[65] Her argument shows that surface reading *affects* and *is affected* by symptomatic reading. These reading styles depend on each other because, Marcus writes, "only by attending to what other critics have been unable to explain can subsequent critics build a more capacious interpretive framework."[66]

Toril Moi, Stephen Best, and Sharon Marcus all mirror the current trend within the humanities to attempt other reading styles than the symptomatic one. So does Rita Felski in *The Limits of Critique* (2015), in which she argues that Ricoeur's suspicious hermeneutics—which she treats as synonymous with reading *critically*—ought not to be considered the definitive mode of literary inquiry. "Because we are convinced that things are not as they seem," she writes, "we are driven to decode and decipher, to push beyond the obvious, to draw out what is unseen or unsaid."[67] There is a danger in this sort of critical examination, Felski suggests, because "[t]o suspect something … is not to know it for a fact: it is to speculate and second-guess rather than to be sure. A mistrust of someone's motives is compounded by the nagging fear that our own mistrust may not be justified and that we could be jumping to unwarranted and unjust conclusions."[68]

On the one hand, reading suspiciously may result in interpretations that will take us to places where we have not yet been. On the other hand, a suspicious-minded reader also runs the risk of having their interpretations being labeled speculative. An easy way of dismissing the validity of queer readings, for instance, is to propose that one "reads too much into things." Although the focus of the early style of queer readings was often the unspoken or concealed meaning of texts, Alexander Doty disputed this accusation already in 1993: "Queer readings," he argued, "aren't 'alternative' readings, wishful or willful misreadings, or 'reading too much into things' readings."[69] Doty underlines that rather than queering a seemingly heterosexual narrative—which might be seen as ascribing queer meaning to a text—queer readings emphasize *what is already there*. Jenny Björklund explains this prac-

---

[65] Sharon Marcus, *Between Women: Friendship, Desire, and Marriage in Victorian England* (Princeton: Princeton University Press, 2007), 75.

[66] Ibid., 76.

[67] Rita Felski, *The Limits of Critique* (Chicago: The University of Chicago Press, 2015), 38.

[68] Ibid.

[69] Alexander Doty, *Making Things Perfectly Queer: Interpreting Mass Culture* (Minneapolis: University of Minnesota Press, 1993), 16.

tice as "reading the queerness" of a text, which is a form of surface reading.[70] This way of reading will constitute this study's methodological basis.

According to Björklund, when reading a text's queerness, one operates from the notion that norm-challenging qualities in the work is found on the text's surface rather than hidden between the lines. Björklund together with Ann-Sofie Lönngren subsequently state that reading practices that are critical toward symptomatic reading "focus on understanding what is present in the text and what it tries to communicate, rather than reading it against the grain, with suspicion and an aim to reveal its hidden ideological content."[71] Besides, Björklund suggests, queer readings are not only suitable for heteronormative texts but can involve texts that are explicitly queer. In fact, she writes that "to point out manifest queer themes in a text can be just as subversive, especially since such themes are often ignored by straight audiences."[72]

That queer themes are systematically ignored (or, as the defense of such ignorance can be labeled, "accidentally overlooked") solidifies the usefulness of "acknowledgment" to this study, a concept that Toril Moi has developed from ideas of Stanley Cavell. Moi explains:

> The concept of acknowledgment helps us to understand why even the most stunning reading of a text doesn't block the way for new ones. Different brilliant readings aren't competing to reveal the same (absolutely certain) knowledge of the text, as if the text only offered us one truth. ... Rather, different readings reveal different readers' different ways of acknowledging the text. To acknowledge the text in the right way, each reader needs to work out his or her own position in relation to it.[73]

Following Moi, acknowledging specific aspects in a literary work—like queerness—has nothing to do with attempting to formulate an all-encompassing truth about that work. Any interpretation of any text depends on who is reading it.

Donna Haraway's concept of "situated knowledge"—that is, feminist objectivity based on embodiment and experience—therefore becomes relevant.[74] Situated knowledges are especially useful within feminist, post-

---

[70] Jenny Björklund, "Queer Readings/Reading the Queer," *Lambda Nordica* 23, no. 1–2 (2018): 7–15.

[71] Jenny Björklund and Ann-Sofie Lönngren, "Now You See It, Now You Don't: Queer Reading Strategies, Swedish Literature, and Historical (In)visibility," *Scandinavian Studies* 92, no. 2 (2020): 197.

[72] Björklund, "Queer Readings/Reading the Queer," 8.

[73] Moi, *Revolution of the Ordinary*, 209.

[74] For further reading on the concept of "situated knowledge," see chapter nine in Donna Haraway, *Simians, Cyborgs, and Women: The Reinvention of Nature* (New York: Routledge, 1991), 183–201.

colonial, and queer paradigms since they support the claim that embodied experiences of marginalization, discrimination, and alienation are essential to knowledge production. They also suggest that one's personal experiences dictate one's interests and affect how one reads. While the concept of acknowledgment, in this respect, may seem entwined with a reader's subjectivity, Moi also states that acknowledgment "can serve as an antidote to the idea that to read a text is to impose our own pre-existing theories on it. It can also free us from the idea that all readings must begin in suspicion."[75]

Alongside this broad applicability of the concept of acknowledgment, any interpretation of any text also depends on *when* the text is read. Different temporal contexts will likely result in varied acknowledgments, which illuminates the importance of re-reading older texts and expanding their interpretive possibilities. Readings that acknowledge expressions of queer subjectivity in Hesse's novels, for example, might be especially rewarding at this point in time.

As the discussion above has shown, the various modes of interpreting employed by literary scholars are, rather than methods, best described as styles of reading that are shaped by political and existential attachments to works that tickle our interests.[76] This study will read the queerness in Hesse's *Peter Camenzind* and *Der Steppenwolf,* which means that the novels' surface signs of queerness will be emphasized and interpreted. As such, the present study can, in short, be designated a "queer surface reading."

Queer aspects in Hesse's texts will be traced and examined in chapters one through six. Male homosociality and homoeroticism (themes that will be explained in detail and discussed under the next heading) are examples of such aspects, as well as the presence of sexual ambivalence in the characters. Additionally, queer specks of light in the novels—that is, representations of queer companionship, affection, desire, and romance—will be emphasized, embraced, and celebrated. This way of approaching Hesse's texts should neither be regarded as "reading between the lines" nor as "reading too much into things," but as allowing their surface signs of profound meaning to be taken seriously.

---

[75] Moi, *Revolution of the Ordinary,* 205.

[76] Cf. Rita Felski, *Hooked: Art and Attachment* (Chicago: The University of Chicago Press, 2020.) In this work, Felski argues that "being hooked" is as central when it comes to appreciating high art as when experiencing pop-cultural entertainment.

Male Friendship and Homoeroticism

In *Queer Friendship: Male Intimacy in the English Literary Tradition* (2018), George E. Haggerty explains that friendship, in the classical world, "was celebrated as among the highest human achievements. Nothing was more likely to lead to the divine than looking for it in the eyes of a friend."[77] Throughout Haggerty's study it is shown that male friendship in literature often become "tantamount to a marriage between men," which makes the concept of friendship multifaceted, he argues.[78]

Haggerty's study aims at "exploring the complexities of male–male relations beyond the simple labels of sexuality."[79] It shows that male relationships in literature can be eroticized for many reasons, such as "obsession, or competition or rivalry, in ways that animate the text and give it emotional power."[80] In Haggerty's view, what makes a friendship between men categorizable as queer depends on an intertwinement of male relationality and homoeroticism, but also on characteristics that do not exclusively revolve around sexuality. As such, Haggerty's conception correlates with this study's position that queer friendships challenge heteronormative conceptions of not only sexuality and desire, but also various forms of relationality.

Since most of Hesse's novels treat friendship between men as integral to their characters' journeys through life, the concept of male friendship and its connection with homoeroticism will be discussed under this and the following heading. This connection—or intertwinement—has roots in ancient Greek and Roman culture (which will be accounted for shortly), and to queer scholars like Eve Kosofsky Sedgwick the connection has proven rewarding when interpretating literature. In *Between Men*, for instance, Sedgwick argues that heteromasculine male bonding is an unstable concept, characterized as much by homophobia as homoeroticism, and it is therefore sexually ambiguous.[81]

Sedgwick states that the word homo*social*—which describes social relationships between individuals of the same sex—clearly is formed in correlation with the word homo*sexual*. She illustrates this with the concept of the "erotic triangle." Drawing on René Girard's early work about rivalry in

---

[77] George E. Haggerty, *Queer Friendship: Male Intimacy in the English Literary Tradition* (Cambridge: Cambridge University Press, 2018), 1.

[78] Ibid., 3.

[79] Ibid., 12.

[80] Ibid., 64.

[81] See Eve Kosofsky Sedgwick, *Between Men: English Literature and Male Homosocial Desire* (New York: Columbia University Press, 1985), 1–5.

romance novels, Sedgwick postulates that English-language literature beginning with Shakespeare, has been modelled according to this thesis:

> [I]n any erotic rivalry, the bond that links the two rivals is as intense and potent as the bond that links either of the rivals to the beloved … Girard seems to see the bond between rivals in an erotic triangle as being even stronger, more heavily determinant of actions and choices, than anything in the bond between either of the lovers and the beloved. And within the male-centered novelistic tradition of European high culture, the triangles Girard traces are most often those in which two males are rivals for a female; it is the bond between males that he most assiduously uncovers.[82]

With a variety of Western texts as examples, Sedgwick builds on Girard's argument and shows that since literature is characterized by a form of male bonding that is endorsed by patriarchal culture, it is inherently homosocial. Sedgwick's work shows that in homosocial texts women are frequently devoid of agency and function as commodities to be exchanged between men.[83] Her study thus illuminates that in erotic triangles between two men and a woman, the woman comes to signify something unreachable. She often figures in the peripheries of the narrative, and when she does gain a central position, she is likely placed on a symbolic pedestal where she is ascribed a certain "value" (mostly due to virginal purity) that confirms her function as merchandise.

There are common denominators between Sedgwick's notions of male homosocial desire and the intertwinement of male friendship and homoeroticism in Classical antiquity. For instance, Plato's *Symposium* (385–370 BC), a series of speeches given in praise of Eros, the god of love and desire, is a notable example of the homoerotic implications of male homosocial bonds in that era. The text's celebratory speeches are given by a group of men attending a banquet, among them the philosopher Socrates and the Athenian statesman Alcibiades. Their speeches acknowledge Eros both as erotic love and as inspiration to develop qualities such as courage, honor, and faithfulness among men. Plato's *Symposium* refers to the practice of "pederasty"— a physically intimate same-sex relationship between an adult man (*erastes*, the lover) and a younger man (*eromenos*, the beloved, commonly a teenager, sometimes labeled "the favorite")—which in Classical antiquity was a socially recognized bond.

[82] Sedgwick, *Between Men*, 21.
[83] Ibid., 25–26.

The purpose of this type of relationship was to perpetuate the younger man's philosophical education and its homoerotic content has been widely studied and interpreted.[84] Though homosexual activities between the lover and beloved did occur, feelings that went beyond physical pleasures—like romantic feelings—generally befell the younger man and was reserved for when he was young: "For in truth there is no sort of valor more respected by the gods than this which comes of love," Plato writes, "yet they are even more admiring and delighted and beneficent when the beloved is fond of his lover than when the lover is fond of his favorite."[85] Alcibiades's concluding speech in *Symposium*, however, which is directed not at Eros but at Alcibiades's old lover Socrates, is an example of male–male romantic attachment that has persisted into adulthood.

Usually, however, what was regarded most noble within pederasty was the life-long love for the other's good character; essentially, the enduring and idealized friendship between the men. The over-arching sociopolitical potential embedded in such a bond is evident in the following: "if we could somewise contrive to have a city or an army composed of lovers and their favorites," Plato writes, "they could not be better citizens of their country than by thus refraining from all that is base in a mutual rivalry for honor; and such men as these, when fighting side by side, one might almost consider able to make even a little band victorious over all the world."[86] As the quote indicates, Plato's idealization of love between men aimed at convincing soldiers to defend their land against enemies. In essence, the soldiers' intimate relations would motivate them to fight with strength, courage, and conviction.

While actual homosexual activity and love for one's friend's noble character were not always equally prevalent within pederast relationships, they paved the way for a lingering intertwinement of male friendship and homoeroticism in Western history. Quoted by Lillian Faderman, Michel de Montaigne (1533–1592), for example, wrote passionately about male friendship, suggesting "that love between two men could cause them to 'mix

---

[84] See, e.g., Kenneth James Dover, *Greek Homosexuality* (London: Duckworth, 1978); *Homosexuality in Greece and Rome: A Sourcebook of Basic Documents*, ed. Thomas K. Hubbard (Berkeley: University of California Press, 2003); and David Konstan, *Friendship in the Classical World* (Cambridge: Cambridge University Press, 1997).

[85] Plato, *The Symposium of Plato*, trans. R. G. Bury (Cambridge: Heffner and sons, 1909), 180a–b.

[86] Ibid., 178e–179a.

and blend in each other with so complete a mixing that they efface and never again find the seam that joined them.'"[87]

Montaigne's view on friendship clearly derives from the male same-sex bonds of Classical antiquity, Faderman emphasizes. However, "Montaigne distinguishes this love from homosexuality as practiced by the Greeks by pointing out that in the latter, there was generally a great disparity in age and vocation between the lovers, and that the relationship was often founded on the corporeal beauty of the youth alone."[88] As we can see, in Montaigne's view, the homoerotic implications of male friendship had evolved from the pederasty model and could, in the early modern period, signify a *mutually romantic bond.*

Such a bond is generally labeled a "romantic friendship," an intimate and affectionate relationship between two people of the same sex (a sort of predecessor to queer friendship). Romantic friendship has been predominantly used to describe same-sex friendships before the middle of the 1800s. After the emergence of homosexuality as a category in the mid-nineteenth century, the physical intimacy of romantic friendships—which up until then had been considered perfectly natural—was met with suspicion and anxiety. Even so, friendship ideals with roots in Classical antiquity were not forgotten or concealed in Europe. In Germany, for instance at the time when Hermann Hesse received his education, and when he began his literary endeavors, the homoerotic signifiers of Greek classicism were neither obscure nor overlooked. Clayton J. Whisnant states that since a classical education had a continuing importance in the nineteenth and early twentieth centuries, the homoeroticism of ancient Greece was not only well-known but also became "a fundamental feature of Germany's educated elite."[89] Although Hesse never completed his education, as a bookseller's apprentice at the turn of the century he certainly became familiar with literature from Classical antiquity.[90]

---

[87] Lillian Faderman, *Surpassing the Love of Men: Romantic Friendship and Love Between Women from the Renaissance to the Present* (London: Women's Press, 1985), 65.

[88] Ibid.

[89] Clayton J. Whisnant, *Queer Identities and Politics in Germany: A History 1880–1945* (New York: Harrington Park Press, 2016), 135.

[90] Hesse's knowledge of Classical antiquity extended beyond his work as a bookseller's apprentice. First, the injunction "Be yourself" that permeates his authorship derives from the ancient Greek aphorism "Know thyself" inscribed above the entrance of the Temple of Apollo in Delphi. Second, Hesse was familiar with the works of Homer and Vergil (see Ernst Rose, *Faith from the Abyss: Hermann Hesse's Way from Romanticism to Modernity* [New York: New York University Press, 1965], 12, 15.), as well as the work of Ovid (see Salvatore Campisi, "Hermann Hesse and the Dialectics of Time," [PhD diss.,

The Field of German Sexology and the Homosexual Emancipation Movement

In addition to being a novelist, poet, and painter, Hermann Hesse was a politically astute and socially conscious thinker who wrote extensively about aesthetics, war, intellectual history, and politics.[91] In fact, Kocku von Stuckrad maintains that Hesse "belongs to the leading intellectuals who explicitly reflected on the societal, political, and cultural transformations that shook Europe during the first half of the twentieth century."[92]

Hesse rarely took an active part in public debates, although he could hardly be considered uninformed, and since he acknowledged homoeroticism in some of his novels, it is not implausible that he was also conscious of the field of sexology (the scientific study of human sexuality) and the homosexual emancipation movement in the German-speaking world around the turn of the twentieth century.[93] These historical contexts are closely entangled and will be accounted for in the following, because they form an important backdrop for tracing queerness in *Peter Camenzind* and *Der Steppenwolf*.

When studying the history of queer identities, Germany is of chief significance. Clayton J. Whisnant writes: "The first homosexual activists were German; the first writer to coin the term *homosexual* was a German-speaking Hungarian who moved from one German city to another for much of his adult life. Berlin's gay life became internationally renowned (or infamous, depending on your point of view) by the 1920s."[94] Because the historic contexts in focus here were heavily characterized by what was discussed

University of Salford, 2010], 125, doi: https://www.yumpu.com/en/document/view/7240583/hermann-hesse-and-the-dialectics-of-time-salvatore-c-p- [accessed January 14, 2022].) And third, Hesse's final novel *Das Glasperlenspiel* is greatly influenced by Plato's *Republic* (circa 375 BC). For an extended examination of the complex similarities between these works, see Charles Senn Taylor, "The Platonism of Hesse's 'Das Glasperlenspiel'," *Monatshefte* 74, no. 2 (1982): 156–166.

[91] Further reading on Hermann Hesse's views on politics, war, intellectual history, and aesthetics include Hermann Hesse, *My Belief: Essays on Life and Art*, ed. Theodore Ziolkowski, trans. Denver Lindley, with two essays trans. Ralph Manheim (St. Albans: Triad/Panther Books, 1978); and Hermann Hesse, *Krieg und Frieden: Betrachtungen zu Krieg und Politik seit dem Jahr 1914* (Zürich: Fretz & Wasmuth, 1946).

[92] Kocku von Stuckrad, "Utopian Landscapes and Ecstatic Journeys: Friedrich Nietzsche, Hermann Hesse, and Mircea Eliade on the Terror of Modernity," *Numen* 57, no. 1 (2010): 88.

[93] In Walter Sorell's biography of Hesse, Hesse's awareness of the political climate of his time is addressed. Sorell explains that while Hesse seldom actively took part in the political occurrences of his time, he was not unaware of what was happening. However, Sorell argues, "we cannot expect this nonconformist, who admittedly was happiest working in his garden or cell, to rush to the barricades … His faith in himself was as a writer, and his task, as he saw it, was to reach his readers with his ideas and counsel." (Walter Sorell, *Hermann Hesse: The Man Who Sought and Found Himself* [London: Oswald Wolff, 1974], 60.)

[94] Whisnant, *Queer Identities*, 4.

under the previous heading—namely an intense intertwinement of male friendship and homoeroticism—they are of interest to this study.

The world's first homosexual magazine, *Der Eigene* (*The Self-Owner*), which started issuing in 1896, makes the intertwinement visible. Created by Adolf Brand (1874–1945), *Der Eigene* contained love poems, images, and essays on social, political, and aesthetic aspects of male same-sex love, which, Harry Oosterhuis underlines, was "repeatedly associated with friendship."[95] At this point in time, the common term for friendship was sexually ambiguous, and in male homosexual contexts it functioned as a sort of code word for same-sex activity. Moreover, we see it in the label *Freundschaftsbund* (Friendship League), which was used to describe the many homosexual organizations in Germany in the early decades of the twentieth century.

According to James D. Steakley's study *The Homosexual Emancipation Movement in Germany* (1975), there were at least twenty-five such organizations in 1923: "For example: in Berlin, the *Bund der Freunde und Freundinnen* (League of Friends) held conferences on scientific, literary, and artistic subjects and also organized social events."[96] In their name, *League of Friends*, the friendship/homosexuality correlation is evident. While referring predominantly to the Weimar era (1919–1933), Whisnant also underscores the correlation and claims that the most common alternative to "homosexual" was "friend," which had a specific purpose: "Instead of bringing the sexual aspect of relationships to the foreground as *homosexual* did, *friend* and *friendship* put the emphasis on the emotional and personal content of relationships."[97] Whisnant concludes that using the term friendship as a synonym for homosexuality served to validate (and naturalize) same-sex bonds. Moreover, the ambiguity that still today characterizes the German word *Freund* is interesting to note, as the word not only means "friend" but also "boyfriend." This ambivalence continues to bring its connotation within the sexology discourse and the German homosexual emancipation movement to mind.

In addition to the above-mentioned correlations, the titles of two homosexual magazines from the 1920s, publications that followed the trend established in *Der Eigene*, namely *Freundschaft und Freiheit* (*Friendship and*

---

[95] Harry Oosterhuis, "Homosexual Emancipation in Germany Before 1933: Two Traditions," in *Homosexuality and Male Bonding in Pre-Nazi Germany: The Youth Movement, the Gay Movement and Male Bonding before Hitler's Rise: Original Transcripts from Der Eigene, the First Gay Journal in the World,* ed. Harry Oosterhuis and Hubert Kennedy (New York: Haworth Press, 1991), *16*.

[96] James D. Steakley, *The Homosexual Emancipation Movement in Germany* (Salem, NH: Ayer, 1982), 82.

[97] Whisnant, *Queer Identities*, 153.

Freedom) and *Die Freundschaft* (*The Friendship*), clearly equates homo-eroticism with same-sex friendship. The same comparison is visible in the *Gemeinschaft der Eigenen* (Community of Self-Owners) which was founded by Adolf Brand in 1903 with the slogan "Bund für Freundschaft und Freiheit" (Society for Friendship and Freedom).[98] Oosterhuis explains that contrary to Magnus Hirschfeld (1868–1935) and the *Wissenschaftliches-humanitäres Komitee* (Scientific-Humanitarian Committee), whose aim was proving that homosexuality was a biological phenomenon, the masculinists in the Community of Self-Owners stressed a cultural significance of male homo-eroticism that was rooted in the romantic friendship tradition.[99] Additionally, as Max Kramer has shown, many *Männerbunde* (associations of men) in Germany in the early twentieth century were characterized by an ethos that verged on the homoerotic.[100] Robert Deam Tobin underscores that these Männerbunde "harbored antiliberal, antibourgeois, [and] antimodernist tendencies."[101] The masculinist culture within them mirrored Plato's esti-mation in *Symposium* that the reason why men seek the company of other men—for love, intimacy, and eroticism—"is due not to shamelessness but to daring, manliness, and virility."[102] Among other things, the upcoming readings of *Peter Camenzind* and *Der Steppenwolf* will show that Hesse's writing tends to align itself with ideals of the Männerbunde, such as male

---

[98] While Adolf Brand's importance for the early gay liberation movement is undeniable (at least for homosexual *men*), he adhered to ideals such as misogyny and *völkisch* nationalism (racist-nationalist sentiments). Oosterhuis writes: "Brand's frequent use of abusive language in his writings showed his militant and somewhat quick-tempered character: he did not mince words. Many times he got mixed up in public quarrels, scandals, and trials." (Oosterhuis, "Homosexual Emancipation," 3.) When moralists accused *Der Eigene* of lewdness, Brand sometimes defended its homoerotic depictions of men by arguing that "showing male nudity was in the interest of 'racial health and purity.'" (Ibid., 4.) Also, the Community of Self-Owners had a misogynistic foundation: "the Community enthused for an anarchistic utopia which would put women firmly in their place as child-bearers and domestic servants and usher in a new era of male comradeship." (Steakley, *Homosexual Emancipation Movement*, 61.) Although Brand had no overt affiliations with the Nazi Party, being a fervent masculinist who perpetuated misogynistic, nationalistic, and racist ideals, he was never arrested when Hitler rose to power in the 1930s. At one point Nazi storm troopers raided his home and confiscated journals, photographs, and books, but because Brand was a married man, his life was never threatened by the Nazis, as hypothesized by Oosterhuis. (Oosterhuis, "Homosexual Emancipation," 7.) Brand and his wife died in an American bombing raid in 1945.

[99] Ibid., 8.

[100] See Max Kramer, "From Georg Simmel to Stefan George: Sexology, Male Bonding, and Homo-sexuality," *German Studies Review* 41, no. 2 (2018): 275–279. For further reading, see, e.g., Ulrike Brunotte, *Zwischen Eros und Krieg: Männerbund und Ritual in der Moderne* (Berlin: Wagenbach, 2004); and Claudia Bruns, *Politik des Eros. Der Männerbund in Wissenschaft, Politik und Jugendkultur (1880–1934)* (Köln: Böhlau, 2008).

[101] Tobin, *Peripheral Desires*, 53.

[102] Plato, *The Symposium of Plato*, 192a.

bonding, homoeroticism, and *völkisch* nationalism, which were integral elements in these groups' ideological foundation.[103]

In the early 1900s when *Peter Camenzind* was published, ambiguities surrounding male friendship and homosexual male relationships was a heated topic in Germany. In the decades leading up to the First World War, conservative forces dreaded that "if Germans, particularly men, could not master their sexual desires and could not obey religious authority on sexual matters, their mastery over the rest of their human selves would falter."[104] It was believed that if male homosexuality was not strictly policed, Germany would succumb to chaos. Susanne zur Nieden explains that during this time homosexual men were labeled "enemies of the state."[105] This notion was enhanced by some high-profile public cases in the era, such as a couple of "homosexual scandals" within Kaiser Wilhelm II's government.[106] A consequence of these scandals was the political instrumentalization of homophobia, in all political camps, which zur Nieden asserts lasted for decades after the end of the Second World War.

At the same time, sexual conservatism had been challenged in German-speaking Europe for a long time and voices within the field of sexology continuously drew attention to homosexuality as an issue worthy of serious scrutiny. Oosterhuis writes: "Already in the forties and fifties of the 19th century some German physicians who acted as expert witnesses for law courts, where they were required to prove acts of sodomy [a term that most

---

[103] For an in-depth look at the intertwinement of masculinity, homosexuality, and fascism in the German context, see Klaus Theweleit, *Männerphantasien* (Frankfurt am Main: Roter Stern, 1977–1978). In these two volumes, Theweleit examines the desires of men in the German *Freikorps* (proto-fascist paramilitary groups) who came to play a fundamental role in the rise of Nazism. See also chapter 11, "Leadership, *Bund*, and Eros," in George L. Mosse, *The Crisis of German Ideology: Intellectual Origins of the Third Reich* (New York: Grosset & Dunlap, 1964).

[104] Laurie Marhoefer, *Sex and the Weimar Republic: German Homosexual Emancipation and the Rise of the Nazis* (Toronto: University of Toronto Press, 2015), 25.

[105] Susanne zur Nieden, "Einleitung," in *Homosexualität und Staatsräson: Männlichkeit, Homophobie und Politik in Deutschland 1900–1945*, ed. Susanne zur Nieden (Frankfurt: Campus, 2005), 7–10.

[106] One of the "homosexual scandals" concerned Friedrich Alfred Krupp, a steel manufacturer who in the early years of the twentieth century used the influence of government allies, including Kaiser Wilhelm II, to defend himself against allegations of homosexuality. It is believed that Krupp committed suicide in 1902 because of the allegations. The Eulenburg affair, yet another scandal involving the Kaiser, took place in 1907–1909. In this scandal several prominent members of the government were accused of homosexual conduct. This controversy received a lot of publicity and, just like the Oscar Wilde trials in England, it created a heated public debate about homosexuality. For further reading, see Robert Aldrich, *The Seduction of the Mediterranean: Writing, Art and Homosexual Fantasy* (London: Routledge, 1993); and James D. Steakley, "Iconography of a Scandal: Political Cartoons and the Eulenburg affair," in *Hidden from History: Reclaiming the Gay and Lesbian Past*, ed. Martin Duberman, Martha Vicinus, and George Chauncey, Jr. (New York: NAL, 1989).

commonly referred to anal intercourse], devoted studies to the character and the emotional lives of sodomites."[107]

The interest in male–male sexual behavior—as well as public defense of individuals engaging in homosexual acts—was spearheaded by the lawyer and activist Karl Heinrich Ulrichs (1826–1895) who in the 1860s began to publicly defend *Urninge* (Uranians), a term derived from the Greek god Uranus describing men who are sexually attracted to other men. Before Ulrichs, most nineteenth-century theories of sexuality had relied on Christianity's conception of morality and therefore labeled homosexuality as unnatural. Ulrichs instead acknowledged the naturalness of homosexuality and argued that the gender of homosexual men was neither male nor female; rather, the homosexual man had a male physique but "the soul of a woman." Ulrichs wrote the following in 1864: "We Urnings constitute a special class of human gender. We are our own gender, a third sex, equivalent to the species of men and women. … The Urning is not a man but a type of feminine being who is female not only in the realm of sexual feelings. His entire spiritual organism, his entire spiritual temperament and character is feminine."[108] According to Oosterhuis, Ulrichs's claim underscored that "male-male love was not unnatural because the urning loved in accordance with his immutable inborn nature."[109]

Among the sexologists who shared Ulrichs's views and/or expressed ideas that correlated with them were the German-Hungarian writer Karl-Maria Kertbeny (1824–1882), who in addition to being vocal about legal rights for homosexuals is known for having coined the term "homosexuality" in 1869.[110] Another sexologist influenced by Ulrichs was Carl Friedrich Otto Westphal (1833–1890), whose article "Die Konträre Sexualempfindung" ("The Contrary Sexual Tendency," 1869) explained (in Oosterhuis's words): "the 'contrary sexual tendency' as an inborn instinct that corresponded to a certain effeminacy in a male. Since the tendency was pathological, according to Westphal, he preferred medical treatment to legal prosecution."[111]

---

[107] Oosterhuis, "Homosexual Emancipation," 12.

[108] Karl Heinrich Ulrichs, *Vindex: Social-juristische Studien über mannmännliche Geschlechtsliebe* [1864], in *Forschungen über das Rätsel der mannmännlichen Liebe (Leipzig: Max Spohr, 1898), quote lifted from* Ralph M. Leck, *Vita Sexualis: Karl Ulrichs and the Origins of Sexual Science* (Urbana: University of Illinois Press, 2016), 40.

[109] Oosterhuis, "Homosexual Emancipation," 13.

[110] See, e.g., Judith Takács, "The Double Life of Kertbeny," in *Past and Present of Radical Sexual Politics: Working Papers: Fifth Meeting of the Seminar "Socialism and sexuality", Amsterdam, October 3–4, 2003,* ed. Gert Hekma (Amsterdam: Mosse Foundation, 2004), 51–62.

[111] Oosterhuis, "Homosexual Emancipation," 13.

In *Psychopathia Sexualis* (1886), psychiatrist Richard von Krafft-Ebing also drew on Ulrichs's ideas and wrote that "if the homosexual feels perverse, it is not his fault, but the fault of an abnormal condition natural to him. His sexual instinct may be aesthetically very repugnant, but, from his morbid stand-point, it is natural."[112] Since von Krafft-Ebing saw homosexuality as a natural phenomenon (like Westphal and Ulrichs before him), he called for compassion for homosexuals rather than punishment.

Apart from the hitherto mentioned sexologists, another important name in the field is Sigmund Freud (1856–1939), whose ideas about homosexuality, at times, correlated with work by German sexologists like Hirschfeld, Krafft-Ebing, and Ulrichs.[113] Another Austrian sexologist is Otto Weininger (1880–1903) whose *Geschlecht und Charakter* (*Sex and Character*, 1903) became widely read after his suicide.[114] And a final name worth mentioning is German psychiatrist Albert Moll (1862–1939) who in 1891 wrote the first scientific study that solely concerned homosexuality. While Moll's work is greatly indebted to other sexologists, his contribution is unique because it provided "the first documented, ethnographic description of Berlin's homosexual subculture."[115]

Among all these sexologists, however, it is Ulrichs that remains truly revolutionary, Ralph M. Leck argues, "because he linked his pioneering sexual science to a radical demand for sexual revolution."[116] Ulrichs's trailblazing and radical thinking paved the way for the German homosexual emancipation movement (the first of its kind in the world), which, however, came to include deeply opposing perspectives.

---

[112] Richard von Krafft-Ebing, *Psychopathia Sexualis: With Especial Reference to the Antipathetic Sexual Instinct*, trans. Franklin S. Klaf (London: Mayflower-Dell, 1965), 382.

[113] For a short overview on Freud's thoughts regarding homosexuality vis-à-vis some of the German sexologists, see Tobin, *Peripheral Desires*, 70–71.

[114] Apart from being influential within the field of sexology, Otto Weininger was a misogynist who perpetuated antisemitic and homophobic conceptions. At the same time, he was himself a closeted homosexual of Jewish descent. Some aspects of his work correlated with and were used within the racist-nationalist ideology of the Nazis. For further reading, see Daniel Steuer's introduction in Otto Weininger, *Sex and Character: An Investigation of Fundamental Principles*, ed. Daniel Steuer with Laura Marcus, trans. Ladislaus Löb (Bloomington: Indiana University Press, 2005). Steuer points out that apart from remembering Weininger as associated with misogynism, homophobia, and antisemitism, there are "those that see him as a critic of alienation in the modern age, and an agent of human emancipation." (xi.)

[115] Robert Beachy, "To Police *and* Protect: The Surveillance of Homosexuality in Imperial Berlin," in *After* The History of Sexuality: *German Genealogies With and Beyond Foucault*, ed. Scott Spector, Helmut Puff, and Dagmar Herzog (New York: Berghahn Books, 2012), 112.

[116] Leck, *Vita Sexualis*, 1–2.

On one side of the movement were Magnus Hirschfeld and the Scientific-Humanitarian Committee (which was founded in 1897).[117] Hirschfeld held the belief that homosexuality was biological and followed Ulrichs's conception of Uranians as a third sex. The aim of his committee was public education about homosexuality and advocacy for individuals who had fallen victim to blackmail, but first and foremost it was dedicated to the repeal of Paragraph 175, which was the provision of the German Criminal Code that made homosexual acts illegal. On the opposing side of the movement—adhering to a contrasting ideal—were *Der Eigene*, Adolf Brand, and the masculinists in the Community of Self-Owners, who believed in a cultural significance of homoeroticism and male friendship.[118]

Between the early 1900s when *Peter Camenzind* was published and 1927 when *Der Steppenwolf* came out, the field of German sexology as well as the conditions for homosexuals underwent significant changes. As we have seen, at the time of *Peter Camenzind*'s publication, conversations about homosexuality were largely influenced by the homosexual scandals within the government, which established homosexual men as enemies of the state. While homosexuality was still illegal when *Der Steppenwolf* was published two decades later, certain conditions for same-sex desiring individuals had, in practice, improved.

In-between the two World Wars, extensive queer subcultures developed in many of the larger German cities. There were bars, same-sex balls, clubs, and queer cabarets, and Robert Beachy has shown that Berlin police officials were remarkably tolerant of these venues as early as the 1890s.[119] This tolerance (while not completely unconditional) paved the way for what is often referred to as the "Golden Twenties," an era of German homosexual history that has been famously depicted in, for instance, the writings of Christopher Isherwood (1904–1986) like *Mr Norris Changes Trains* (1935) and *Goodbye to Berlin* (1939), and in the subsequent film adaptation of Isherwood's stories, the renowned Academy Award-winning musical *Cabaret* (Bob Fosse, 1972).

---

[117] Hirschfeld also headed the world's first institute for the scientific study of sexuality, Institut für Sexualwissenschaft, between 1919–1933.

[118] For further reading on Hirschfeld, Brand, and their polarized perspectives during the homosexual emancipation movement in Germany, see Marita Keilson-Lauritz, "Tanten, Kerle und Skandale: Die Geburt des 'modernen Homosexuellen' aus den Flügelkämpfen der Emanzipation," in *Homosexualität und Staatsräson: Männlichkeit, Homophobie und Politik in Deutschland 1900–1945*, ed. Susanne zur Nieden (Frankfurt: Campus, 2005), 81–99.

[119] See Beachy, "To Police *and* Protect," 109–115.

In 1922, in Berlin, there were around eighty homosexual venues where queer individuals could meet.[120] These improved social conditions for queers, however, ended abruptly when the Nazis came to power in 1933, and disappeared completely during the horrors of the Second World War.[121]

While the Golden Twenties provided a subculture that embraced a range of queer identities—from lesbians to cross-dressers to gay men—the gender ideals for homosexual men were constricted in-between the World Wars, as a sort of "militarized masculinity" became the prevailing norm. Jason Crouthamel has shown that the First World War was a turning point for the homosexual emancipation movement in Germany because the war made *comradeship* central to the definition of homosexual identity.[122] "In the Weimar Republic," he writes, "competing strands of the homosexual emancipation movement shared a new image of a homosexual 'warrior' activist for whom 'friendship', the widely used euphemism for homosexual love, and 'comradeship' were conflated."[123] Since majority culture tended to perceive homosexual men as effeminate traitors (enemies of the state), gay activists used their military service and experiences in the trenches as proof of their manliness. This militarized masculinity ideal became widely celebrated across the spectrum of competing homosexual rights organizations. Even Hirschfeld's Committee, Crouthamel states, "employed the militarised language of the trenches, and the new image of a gay warrior-activist, to justify the abolition of Paragraph 175. 'Comradeship' cultivated in the war proved that gay men were normal, integrated members of society who deserved equal rights."[124] As Crouthamel's discussion about comradeship

---

[120] For a closer look at queer subcultures in Berlin in the Golden Twenties, see Wolfgang Theis and Andreas Sternweiler, "Alltag im Kaiserreich und in der Weimarer Republik," in *Eldorado: Homosexuelle Frauen und Männer in Berlin 1850–1950; Geschichte, Alltag und Kultur* ed. Michael Bollé (Berlin: Frölich & Kaufmann, 1984), 48–73.

[121] For a conclusive overview of queer history during the Nazi regime, see Richard Plant, *The Pink Triangle: The Nazi War Against Homosexuals* (New York: H. Holt, 1986); and Whisnant, *Queer Identities*, 204–241.

[122] For a detailed description of the homosocial intimacy (bordering on homoeroticism) that characterized the relationships between German soldiers in the First World War, see Jason Crouthamel, "Love in the Trenches: German Soldiers' Conceptions of Sexual Deviance and Hegemonic Masculinity in the First World War," in *Gender and the First World War*, ed. Christa Hämmerle, Osvald Überegger, and Birgitta Bader Zaar (London: Palgrave Macmillan, 2014), 52–71. Crouthamel discloses that during the First World War, "heterosexual men felt safe experimenting with homosocial bonds to alleviate the stress of life at the front" and that "[t]he front enabled homosexual men to find other homosexual men in an environment more tolerant of same-sex relations than pre-war culture." (Ibid., 60–61.)

[123] Jason Crouthamel, "'Comradeship' and 'Friendship': Masculinity and Militarisation in Germany's Homosexual Emancipation Movement after the First World War," *Gender & History* 23, no. 1 (2011): 111.

[124] Ibid., 119.

demonstrates, male friendship continued to be intimately intertwined with homoeroticism and homosexuality in-between the World Wars, if not more so than before.

At this point, two details about the intertwinement of male friendship and homoeroticism in the historic contexts that have been described here should be discussed further. First, there is the conceptual link between the title of Adolf Brand's *Der Eigene* and the *Eigen*sinn in Hesse's writing, which is interesting to note as the name of the publication and Hesse's term signify more or less the same thing. As previously discussed, Eigensinn, in Hesse's view, means to be nonconforming, knowing one's self-worth and "being oneself." *Der Eigene* and its English title *The Self-Owner* refer to the same qualities. While the magazine's title has been translated in other ways, such as *The Exceptional* and *The Special One*,[125] Brand's understanding and application of the term correlates with Hesse's. Though Brand certainly viewed exceptionality and being special as integral elements in homosexual men—and that those qualities are also implied in the magazine's title—he explained that "*Der Eigene* represents the right of personal freedom and the sovereignty of the individual to the farthest consequence."[126] In Brand's statement, the emphasis on freedom and individuality can be said to mirror Hesse's profound belief in individualism.

Second, it should be pointed out that, although there are no indications that Hesse was familiar with Brand's publication, *it was familiar with him*. Because of the prevalence of male friendship in Hesse's writings he is mentioned in an issue from 1925. The article that refers to him is about the significance of homoeroticism between men in the German Youth Movement such as the Wandervogel groups (we will return to the homoeroticism/Wandervogel connection in chapter one, "Romantic Friendship in a *Bildungsroman*"). The article labels Hesse a model for the movement's rejection of the stagnated institutions of the past.[127] In so doing, it contextually links Hesse's work with the homoeroticism of the male friendships that were the primary focus of *Der Eigene*, and therefore underlines why a

---

[125] Robert Deam Tobin uses the title *The Exceptional*, while Clayton J. Whisnant employs the name *The Special One*. See Robert Deam Tobin, *Warm Brothers: Queer Theory and the Age of Goethe* (Philadelphia: University of Pennsylvania Press, 2000), 199; and Whisnant, *Queer Identities*, 137.

[126] Oosterhuis, "Homosexual Emancipation," 22. Oosterhuis quotes Adolf Brand in *Der Eigene* 1920, no. 10.

[127] St. Ch. Waldecke, "Eros in the German Youth Movement," in *Homosexuality and Male Bonding in Pre-Nazi Germany: The Youth Movement, the Gay Movement and Male Bonding before Hitler's Rise: Original Transcripts from Der Eigene, the First Gay Journal in the World*, ed. Harry Oosterhuis and Hubert Kennedy (New York: Haworth Press, 1991), 205.

queer reading of Hesse's texts—in which attention to friendship is given—is worthwhile.

Research Background

Research with a primary emphasis on friendship in Hesse's writing is scarce, as are readings that directly address homoeroticism or queerness. Themes that have been of greater interest include religious aspects in Hesse's writing,[128] Hesse and music,[129] the influence of Jungian thought on Hesse's authorship,[130]

plinks between Hesse and Nietzsche,[131] and the interrelation of Hesse's life and art (that is, the previously mentioned biographical research). In Jürgen Below's *Hermann Hesse Bibliographie: Sekundärliteratur 1899–2007*, some 25,000 titles of German and international secondary literature are listed, out of which more than 1,200 are monographs. Therefore, attempting to provide a conclusive account of the research on Hesse's work is close to impossible, at least within the scope of this study.

[128] Research emphasizing religious aspects in Hesse's writing include, e.g., Oskar Seidlin, "Hermann Hesse: The Exorcism of the Demon," in *Hermann Hesse: A Collection of Criticism*, ed. Judith Liebmann (New York: McGraw-Hill, 1977), 7–28; and Adrian Hsia, "Siddhartha," in *A Companion to the Works of Hermann Hesse*, ed. Ingo Cornils (Rochester, NY: Camden House, 2009), 149–170.

[129] The research field on Hesse and music is large and some of that research will be drawn on in chapter six. For further reading on musical elements in Hesse's writing, see Theodore Ziolkowski, *The Novels of Hermann Hesse: A Study in Theme and Structure* (Princeton: Princeton University Press, 1967), 178–228; Julia Moriz, "Die musikalische Dimension der Sprachkunst: Hermann Hesse, neu gelesen," (PhD diss., Hamburg University, 2007), doi: https://ediss.sub.uni-hamburg.de/bitstream/ediss/1206/1/Dissertation.pdf (accessed January 14, 2022); Mark Christian Thompson, *Anti-Music: Jazz and Racial Blackness in German Thought Between the Wars* (Albany: State University of New York Press, 2018), 57–87; C. Immo Schneider, "Hermann Hesse and Music," in *A Companion to the Works of Hermann Hesse*, ed. Ingo Cornils (Rochester, NY: Camden House, 2009), 373–394; Maddalena Fumagalli, "Pablo contra Mozart? Das 'magische Teater' der Musik," in *Hermann-Hesse-Jahrbuch. Band 1*, ed. Mauro Ponzi (Tübingen: Max Niemeyer, 2004), 111–120; as well as several texts in the anthology *"Magischer Einklang": Dialog der Künste im Werk Hermann Hesses*, ed. Henriette Herwig and Sikander Singh (Göttingen: Wallstein, 2011).

[130] A common move in research on *Der Steppenwolf* is to examine its relation to the theories of Carl Jung. The fact that Hesse sought therapy from J. B. Lang (a student of Jung's), and had conversations with Jung himself, has prompted plenty of scholarly work that highlights the influence of Jungian thought on Hesse's authorship. For an overview of these inquires, see Richards, *Exploring the Divided Self*, 111–141; Emmanuel Maier, "The Psychology of C.G. Jung in the Works of Hermann Hesse [An Abridgment]," (PhD diss., New York University, 1953), doi: http://hesse.projects.gss.ucsb.edu/papers/maier.pdf (accessed January 14, 2022); and for further reading on Hesse's personal relationship with Jung, see Miguel Serrano, *C.G Jung and Hermann Hesse: A Record of Two Friendships*, trans. Frank MacShane (London: Routledge and Kegan Paul, 1971).

[131] For further reading on the link between Hesse and Nietzsche, see Herbert W. Reichert, *The Impact of Nietzsche on Hermann Hesse* (Mt. Pleasant, MI: Enigma Press, 1972); and von Stuckrad, "Utopian Landscapes," 78–102.

One theme that appears regularly in the research on Hesse's work that is of interest here is the *dualisms* that characterize his writing, polarities he attempts to synthesize. Wilbur B. Franklin argues that "[t]hroughout Hesse's work there is the longing to find a reconciliation of opposites, to discover an absolute behind the polarity in man's nature."[132] Franklin underscores that the main dualism emerges in Hesse's protagonists, who are torn between their *Geist* (mind or spirit) and their *Natur* (natural instincts). This dualism creates ambiguity in the authorship, Franklin proclaims, then he adds: "Whenever one looks at the polarities in Hesse, one discovers that Geist and Natur have a masculine and a feminine interpretation. … Conflict exists between the creative sensuality (feminine) and the controlling intellectuality (masculine)."[133]

This masculine/feminine polarity signals that gender and sexuality are themes of relevance in Hesse's texts. Lewis W. Tusken argues that "the interplay of masculine–feminine metaphors … reveal that most other duality motifs are but variations on this theme,"[134] at least from *Demian* and onward. However, Tusken sees the masculine and feminine themes as primarily manifested in representations of the "father-world" and "mother-world," which in Hesse's earlier novels have more clear boundaries than in the later ones. While it is binary, this thematic masculine/feminine interaction suggests that gender and sexuality are negotiated in Hesse's fiction, and because they are negotiated, they may have transgressive potential.

In addition to Wilbur B. Franklin, others who have emphasized dualisms in Hesse's work are, for instance, Theodore Saul Jackson, who argues that "Hesse transcends typical one-sided views of modernity by suggesting and implementing syntheses of the polar opposites (past/future, purity/diversity, nature/culture) between which the modern individual is drawn."[135] To these antitheses Salvatore Campisi adds themes such as "light and darkness, mind and matter, separation and unity, life and death,"[136] between which Hesse's artistry oscillates, he argues. Campisi also writes: "The gap or distance

---

[132] Wilbur B. Franklin, "The Concept of 'the Human' in the Work of Hermann Hesse and Paul Tillich," (PhD diss., University of St Andrews, 1977), 60, doi: https://core.ac.uk/download/pdf/96709396.pdf (accessed January 14, 2022).
[133] Ibid., 61. Emphasis in original.
[134] Lewis W. Tusken, "A Mixing of Metaphors: Masculine-Feminine Interplay in the Novels of Hermann Hesse," *The Modern Language Review* 87, no. 3 (1992): 626.
[135] Jackson, "Ambivalent Modernist," 12.
[136] Campisi, "Dialectics of Time," 9.

between opposites is a source of knowledge and insight for Hesse,"[137] which is likely a reference to the author's own life-long pursuit of balance.

Walter Sorell, one of Hesse's biographers, adds:

> For Hesse … life consisted of a constant fluctuation between two poles, of a relentless oscillation between the two cornerstones of existence. He never tired of pointing to the duality of life since he never completely escaped from being pulled from one extreme to the other. On the other hand, he never ceased to recognise the connecting threads in the fabric of life between these often frightening contrasts and to show us the oneness behind the puzzle of diversity.[138]

Drawing on Sorell's quote—especially its concluding reference to a "puzzle of diversity" being the basis for "oneness" in Hesse's work—the hypothesis that Hesse's authorship, alongside polarities such as past/future, nature/culture, life/death, and femininity/masculinity, also would include the dualism *homosexuality/heterosexuality* is far from unlikely.

There are, however, those who outright oppose the possibility of homosexual content in Hesse's works. Lewis W. Tusken, for instance, claims that interpretations that suggest homosexual connotations are "confused" since they fail to grasp the metaphorical purpose of character relationships in Hesse's fiction, which he argues is a primarily "stylistic device."[139] For this study, it is interesting to note that there are those who believe that when a synthesis is achieved in Hesse's texts it does so within the confounds of a male friendship. Walter Naumann, for example, states that throughout Hesse's work "we find two characters who complete each other because they embody … opposite tendencies. These antagonists are always two men, two friends."[140] Their relationship, he continues, resembles a "marriage" in which "an individual is educated in the highest sense through a person who is destined for him and inescapably linked to him."[141] Sorell arrives at a similar conclusion. He underscores that for Hesse to compose unity in his texts, "[h]is device was the representation of two human beings who, in reality, symbolise the two extreme poles in man. We only have to think of *Demian*

---

[137] Campisi, "Dialectics of Time," 19.

[138] Sorell, *The Man Who Sought*, 115.

[139] Tusken, *Understanding Hermann Hesse*, 49–50, 53. Curiously, Tusken's informative chapter on *Peter Camenzind* gives no clear examples of what metaphors in the shape of friendships might actually signify.

[140] Walter Naumann, "The Individual and Society in the Work of Hermann Hesse," *Monatshefte* 41, no. 1 (1949): 37.

[141] Ibid.

and *Sinclair, Narcissus* and *Goldmund, Siddhartha* and *Govinda*. Essentially, they all personify the two basic opposites: contemplation and action, introversion and extroversion."[142] Bearing in mind that the concept of male friendship, ever since Classical antiquity, has been intertwined with homoeroticxism, syntheses constituted by male friendship in Hesse's work have queer potential.

As previously stated, the lack of research emphasizing queerness or homoeroticism in Hesse's writing is curious. One might very well ponder: Are these themes possibly viewed as so obvious that they need not to be mentioned? Or might this gap in the vast research field relate to Jenny Björklund's previously mentioned argument that queer themes in texts are often overlooked or ignored by readers?

To some extent, readers with queer sensibilities have embraced Hesse's writing and acknowledged its queer content. While Hesse's lifelong friend Thomas Mann (whose homosexuality is well-known) was not a queer reader in the scholarly sense, he is said to have responded enthusiastically to the "homoerotic metaphysics" in *Demian*, a novel that spoke of "something that hit a nerve" in him.[143] Another of Hesse's contemporaries, Robert Musil, wrote critically about *Peter Camenzind* in 1910, frustratedly pondering if he was the only one who could detect its homoeroticism.[144] Yet another example can be found in Edmund White's coming-of-age tale *A Boy's Own Story* (1982), which is one of the most recognized North American examples of gay-themed literature. White's novel suggests that reading the works of Hesse is a sort of initiation rite for homosexual men.[145]

---

[142] Sorell, *The Man Who Sought*, 117.

[143] Anthony Heilbut, *Thomas Mann: Eros and Literature* (New York: Knopf, 1996), 335, 470. Apart from responding enthusiastically to the latent homoeroticism in *Demian*, Mann wrote an introduction to the 1948 English translation of the novel. While Hesse and Mann had different literary styles, their mutual respect for each other's writing and political convictions made them life-long friends and public defenders of one another. Hesse's admiration for Mann made him base the character Thomas von der Trave—Magister Ludi in *Das Glasperlenspiel*—on him. And Mann referred to Hesse as the "closest and dearest friend of my literary generation." For further reading on the friendship between Hesse and Mann, see, e.g., *Der Briefwechsel Hermann Hesse–Thomas Mann*, ed. Anni Carlsson (Frankfurt am Main: Suhrkamp, 1968).

[144] Robert Musil, "Über echte deutsche Dichter [Um 1910]," in *Gesammelte Werke. 2, Prosa und Stücke. Kleine Prosa, Aphorismen. Autobiographisches. Essays und Reden. Kritik*, ed. Adolf Frisé (Reinbek bei Hamburg: Rowohlt, 1978), 1303–1304.

[145] When the protagonist in *A Boy's Own Story* is acquainted with two colorful characters who become his queer community, these characters quickly establish a link between Hermann Hesse's writings and the queerness they themselves embody: "Soon after I first met Fred and Marilyn they decided I must learn German in order to read the novels of Hermann Hesse, at that time [the 1950s] still largely untranslated. Hesse's mix of suicide, mysticism and sexual ambiguity had launched them into a thrilling void." (Edmund White, *A Boy's Own Story* [London: Picador, 2016], 99.)

Among the scholarly examples in which homoerotic aspects of Hesse's work are addressed, Kamakshi P. Murti's "'Ob die Weiber Menschen seyn?' Hesse, Women, and Homoeroticism" (2009), Craig Bernard Palmer's "The Significance of Homosexual Desire in Modern German Literature" (1997), a chapter in Steven Bruhm's *Reflecting Narcissus: A Queer Aesthetic* (2000), and Anjeana Kaur Hans's "Defining Desires: Homosexual Identity and German Discourse 1900–1933" (2005) are noteworthy. In his reading of *Der Steppenwolf*, Palmer highlights the novel's many fluid expressions of gender and sexuality, and suggests that "[t]he intersection of heterosexual and homosocial desires in this novel is homosexual."[146] Additionally, Palmer is critical of research in which it is claimed that male friends in Hesse's novels are "double self-projections" of the author himself.[147] Not only do such analyses trivialize the homoerotic significance of male homosociality, he argues, but they also convert the homoerotic aspects of the texts into expressions of the author's narcissism. In studies that label both protagonist (outsider) and friend (Other) as two sides of one character's personality, "the desire of one for the other is not homoerotic," Palmer writes, "because they do not exist as autonomous individuals, but rather it is narcissistic and self-reflexive."[148]

Murti's essay argues that the unexplored homoerotic dimension in Hesse's fiction could help explain why his female characters are reduced to objects, muses, or allegories. Murti shows that the question in her title, "Ob die Weiber Menschen seyn?" ("Whether Women are Human Beings"), is "central to an understanding of Hesse in a homoerotic frame,"[149] and that the absence of women with clear subject positions turns male bonding in various Hesse-novels into "an escape from heterosexual responsibility."[150] Her thoughts on *Narziß und Goldmund* in particular—a story about lifelong friendship between two monks in the Middle Ages—illuminate the signi-

[146] Craig Bernard Palmer, "The Significance of Homosexual Desire in Modern German Literature," (PhD diss., Washington University, 1997), 2, doi: http://hesse.projects.gss.ucsb.edu/papers/palmer-chap5.pdf (accessed January 14, 2022).

[147] Palmer's critique is mainly directed at Joseph Mileck, who, regarding the "double self-projections" in Hesse's work, has written the following: "the protagonist is almost always what Hesse thought himself to be, and the close friend is almost always what Hesse would have liked to be, or had to become to fulfill himself." (Mileck, *Life and Art*, 36.) The same idea is identifiable in Oskar Seidlin's interpretation of "doubles" in Hesse's writing. Seidlin writes: "each of Hesse's major books has a double focus, has two heroes which are 'two' in the sense in which a schizophrenic is 'two'." (Seidlin, "The Exorcism of the Demon," 12.)

[148] Palmer, "The Significance of Homosexual Desire," 10.

[149] Kamakshi P. Murti, "'Ob die Weiber Menschen seyn?' Hesse, Women, and Homoeroticism," in *A Companion to the Works of Hermann Hesse*, ed. Ingo Cornils (Rochester, NY: Camden House, 2009), 265.

[150] Ibid., 270.

ficance of homoeroticism in Hesse's writing. Narziß's erotic desire for Goldmund is openly referred to in the novel, which is underscored in Bruhm's study as well. *Narziß und Goldmund*, Bruhm writes, is "a novel whose queer longings it would take a heart of stone to read without noticing."[151] The many women with whom the character Goldmund engages sexually never come close to being as important to him as his friend Narziß. Murti writes that "[t]he women Goldmund encounters within the parameters of accepted social and sexual behavior have no individuality. His vagabond life takes him from village to village, from woman to woman."[152] But it is the bond between the men that endures and their profound affection for each other remains the key manifestation of love in the text. Here it is worth emphasizing that in the recent film adaptation *Narziss und Goldmund* (Stefan Ruzowitzky, 2020) the homoerotic aspects of the story are openly acknowledged, which shows that queer meanings in Hesse's work are finally starting to be more generally recognized.

In Anjeana Kaur Hans's study, it is stated that *Der Steppenwolf* "situates non-heterosexual desire as the primary indicator not of an individual's sexual identity, but rather as the constitutive element in an ideal of identity that is explicitly opposed to the bourgeois ideal."[153] This study also criticizes Hesse's treatment of non-heterosexual desire as a representation of "something else than what it is." It is underlined by Hans that elevating characters who embody queer forms of desire (such as Hermine and Pablo in *Der Steppenwolf*) "to the status of pure soul, 'eternal ones,' enacts a definitional process that essentially denies them physical reality … By constructing desire as something divorced from physicality," she remarks, "[Hesse] undermines the notion of homosexual desire as 'real.'"[154]

---

[151] Steven Bruhm, *Reflecting Narcissus: A Queer Aesthetic* (Minneapolis: University of Minnesota Press, 2000), 99. While Bruhm's queer approach to Hesse's work makes it a thrilling read, his reflections seldom correlate with the interpretations made in this study. Drawing on psychoanalytic theories, Bruhm focuses on Hesse's *Demian* and *Narziß und Goldmund* and argues that the two novels' complex relationships between mothers, sons, and creativity renders creative expression a sublimation of homoerotic desire. "For Hesse," Bruhm argues, "homosexuality is as crucial to the development of the artist's whole personality as is the disembodied abstractness of ideas and the heteronormative search for the mother." (Ibid., 98.)

[152] Murti, "'Ob die Weiber Menschen seyn?'," 289.

[153] Anjeana Kaur Hans, "Defining Desires: Homosexual Identity and German Discourse 1900–1933," (PhD diss., Harvard University, 2005), 114.

[154] Ibid., 139.

Apart from Murti, Palmer, Bruhm, and Hans, a limited number of scholars have examined homoeroticism in Hesse's writings,[155] and most often they only briefly refer to the homoerotic aspects in the texts. An example can be seen in Colin Wilson's writing, in which he does acknowledge "strong homosexual overtones" in the male friendships in *Peter Camenzind, Unterm Rad, Narziß und Goldmund,* and *Das Glasperlenspiel,* but brushes these overtones off as primarily belonging to the "sacred friendships" of the romantic tradition.[156] Other than Murti's essay and Palmer's study, Harley Ustus Taylor's "Homoerotic Elements in the Novels of Hermann Hesse" (1967) is the only other analysis that *primarily* explores homoeroticism. Taylor suggests that to Hesse's characters, "the need for a rewarding friendship with a member of the same sex and the need for sexual fulfillment are closely akin."[157]

While Craig Bernard Palmer's reading of *Der Steppenwolf* emphasizes queerness, *Peter Camenzind* has not yet been extensively interpreted from a queer-theoretical angle. Another significant difference between these novels is that the former is extremely well-represented in the research field on Hesse's work, whereas the latter has not received as much scholarly attention. In the many Hesse-biographies, *Peter Camenzind* is usually only mentioned briefly,[158] and in a fairly recent companion to Hesse's work, *A Companion to the Works of Hermann Hesse* (2009), it is the only major novel beside *Die Morgenlandfahrt* that is not granted a chapter of its own.

Since Theodore Saul Jackson's previously quoted study emphasizes the theme of wandering in Hesse's writing—a theme that is especially prevalent in *Peter Camenzind*—it will be returned to in chapter one of this study. Other recent research that remarks upon *Peter Camenzind* and will be drawn on includes essays by Colin Riordan and Angelika Rauch-Rapaport in *Hermann Hesse Today = Hermann Hesse Heute* (2005). Riordan's text concerns the idyllic aspects of nature in *Peter Camenzind,* and Rauch-Rapaport's text argues that the inability of Hesse's male protagonists to have meaningful and lasting relationships with women originates in their insecure attachments to their mothers. Rauch-Rapaport points out that most female characters in

---

[155] See Freedman, *Pilgrim of Crisis,* 115–117; Franklin, "The Concept of 'the Human'," 44–45 and 80–83; and (albeit more focused on the masculine/feminine dualism than homoerotic content and implications) Tusken, "A Mixing of Metaphors," 626–635.

[156] Colin Wilson, *Hermann Hesse* (London: Village Press, 1974), 11, 17, 38.

[157] Harley Ustus Taylor, "Homoerotic Elements in the Novels of Hermann Hesse," *West Virginia University Philological Papers* 16, (1967): 66.

[158] See, e.g., Hugo Ball, *Hermann Hesse: Sein Leben und sein Werk* (Berlin: S. Fischer, 1927), 96–117; and Mileck, *Life and Art,* 32–34.

Hesse's work are elevated as unattainable, ideal beings and hence, in the case of *Peter Camenzind*, "heterosexual happiness … is merely observed and dreamed about."[159] Curiously, Rauch-Rapaport alludes to the fact that romantic love between men is a potential element in the novel, but does not, however, elaborate on this idea.

We will shortly delve into this study's queer readings, but first, it bears repeating that since research with a primary emphasis on friendship in Hesse's writing is scarce—and that the readings that do address homo-eroticism or queerness are not perfectly aligned with the aim of this study—research by other scholars than the ones mentioned above will be referred to and drawn on throughout. The findings of these scholars seldom include references to the themes of interest here, but they will, nevertheless, help make what is queer in Hesse's work clear.

About the Translations

This study will feature both German and English quotes from Hesse's texts. The translations into English are made by the author of this book and they appear in parentheses immediately following the original German.

There are two reasons for choosing not to use any of the existing English translations of Hesse's work. The first derives from Walter Benjamin's thoughts on translation as a sort of balancing act between transferring form, content, and meaning, where the latter is more important than linguistic exactness. "The task of the translator," Benjamin writes, "consists in finding that intended effect [*Intention*] upon the language into which he is translating which produces in it the echo of the original."[160] In fact, Benjamin argues, "all great texts contain their potential translation between the lines."[161] The translations made herein aim to be sensitive to queer potential in Hesse's writing and acknowledge said potential *in the very translation process*. Drawing on Benjamin's ideas, however, does not mean to imply that queerness can *only* exist "between the lines." Overall, drawing on Benjamin, the subsequent translations do not aim at providing linguistically elegant renditions of Hesse's prose. Rather, they aim to be sensitive to the texts' literal meanings.

---

[159] Angelika Rauch-Rapaport, "The Melancholic Structure of the Mind: The Absence of Object Relations in the Work of Hermann Hesse," in *Hermann Hesse Today = Hermann Hesse Heute*, ed. Ingo Cornils and Osman Durrani (Amsterdam: Rodopi, 2005), 85.

[160] Walter Benjamin, "The Task of the Translator," trans. Harry Zohn, in *The Translation Studies Reader*, ed. Lawrence Venuti (London: Routledge, 2000), 19–20.

[161] Ibid., 23.

The second reason for not studying existing English translations of Hesse's writing follows a point made by Theodore Ziolkowski: "There is no standard translation of Hesse's works [and] the available ones are sometimes misleading at crucial points."[162] Furthermore, translations of Hesse's texts are often different in tone, form, and pace, which for a study such as this complicates the choice of one over the other, which is a problem especially relevant regarding *Der Steppenwolf*. The primary reason for not using one of *Der Steppenwolf*'s existing English translations is that at least four have been published after Basil Creighton's first version in 1929, and all of them criticize or outright reject their predecessors. In 1963, for example, the opening note on the revised translation of Creighton's original stated that the translators, Joseph Mileck and Horst Frenz, "were intent upon a more exact and more readily understood rendition" which would correct the earlier "misleading translations."[163] Demonstrating the enormous contemporary international interest in Hesse, that same year also saw another translation of *Der Steppenwolf* by Walter Sorell.

More recently, in 2010, Thomas Wayne provided a version that discarded Mileck and Frenz's "improvements" on Creighton's translation. In Wayne's version, the ambition was to adhere more faithfully to Hesse's original. Finally, there is David Horrocks's translation from 2012 in which he rejects Sorell's 1963 version. One of Horrocks's goals is to provide a less masculine-gendered version of Hesse's novel. For instance, he translates the word *Mensch* into "human being" instead of "man." Moreover, he translates the novel's catchphrase, "Nur für verrückte," which is commonly translated into "For Madmen Only," into "For Mad *People* Only." These choices are timely and add depth to the novel. However, Horrocks also chooses to alter the name of Hermine (a central character) to the English-sounding "Hermione," which somewhat obfuscates the similarity between the German-sounding "Hermine" (female) and "Hermann" (male), who is another character in the novel. In Hesse's original text, the similarity between these names actually emphasizes gender transgression as one of the story's major themes. (Gender transgression in *Der Steppenwolf* will be examined in detail in chapter five, "The Function of Hermine.")

All things considered, comparing the various translations of Hesse's work with the interpretations made here is beyond the scope of this study.

---

[162] Ziolkowski, *The Novels of Hermann Hesse*, 11.

[163] See Hermann Hesse, *Steppenwolf*, trans. Basil Creighton, updated by Joseph Mileck and Horst Frenz (New York: Bantam Books, 1963).

Outline

This overview chapter will be followed by two parts with three analytical chapters each. Their common thread is portrayals of queer friendship in Hesse's novels. In each chapter, one character will be in primary focus, with an emphasis on these characters' portrayals as outsiders or Others (or both). In some instances, the protagonist is the key person of interest; at other times, the protagonist's friend is in focus.

The study's first part is entitled "The Wanderer: Peter Camenzind" and contains three chapters on Hesse's debut novel. Chapter one, "Romantic Friendship in a *Bildungsroman*," centers on Peter, the outsider-protagonist in *Peter Camenzind*, and his homosocial bond with the character Richard. The chapter examines how defining traits of the *Bildungsroman* (novel of formation) and the concept of romantic friendship intersect in the novel. Chapter two, "Without Leaving Children Behind," explores heterosexual ambivalence, which Peter conveys in his interactions with women, which is interpreted as a manifestation of queerness. While the chapter concerns a number of female characters, Peter's friend Elisabeth is the key character. Chapter three, "Facing the Other," focuses on Peter's friend Boppi. The otherness ascribed to Boppi through his disability is examined, as well as the ways that disability works as a catalyst for expressions of "queer/crip kinship" in the text.

The second part of the study, "The Runner: Steppenwolf," devotes three chapters to *Der Steppenwolf*. Chapter four, "Tracing the Wolf," examines a key expression of otherness in *Der Steppenwolf*, namely, the animality of its protagonist, the wolf-man (and outsider) Harry Haller. This chapter is different from the others in that it does not revolve around queer friendship per se. Rather, it emphasizes the antithesis of friendship, that is, a bond built on *animosity*, a major characteristic in the relationship between the human part and the wolf part of the protagonist. Chapter five, "The Function of Hermine," explores the fluid gender expressions and queer characteristics of Harry's friend Hermine. Hermine is a character whose otherness mirrors the protagonist's dual nature. Chapter six, "Queer Sounds, Times, and Places," puts the spotlight on Pablo, another of Harry's friends, and examines how the novel's portrayal of sounds (such as jazz music), times (the conflict between the old and the new), and places (like the dance floor) connote queerness in various ways.

PART 1
The Wanderer: Peter Camenzind

Romantic Friendship in a *Bildungsroman*

"The Most Noble of Youth's Pleasures"

In the overview chapter, we touched upon how the German Wandervogel groups embraced *Peter Camenzind* wholeheartedly, as they identified their own ideals (the Rousseauesque "return to nature") within it. But even more so, the young men's interest in Hesse's novel suggests that it can be interpreted as homoerotic. As James D. Steakley has shown, drawing on Hans Blüher's best-selling book *Die deutsche Wandervogelbewegung als erotisches Phänomen* (*The German Wandervogel Movement as an Erotic Phenomenon*, 1912), within the Wandervogel movement, "neither comradeship nor even friendship but outright homoeroticism was the binding force [and] the founders and original leaders of the early movement had all been homosexual."[164] The fact that these groups embraced *Peter Camenzind* can thus be said to indicate that the novel includes themes that mirror homoerotic sentiments and sensibilities. Because of this, it is curious that when emphasizing expressions of queerness in Hesse's work, none of the recent queer-focused research (like the interpretations by Kamakshi P. Murti and Craig Bernard Palmer) mention *Peter Camenzind*. Murti even claims that it was *Demian* (published thirteen years after Hesse's debut novel) that "offered a first clear glimpse of Hesse's recognition of alternative sexualities."[165]

To highlight how queerness manifests itself in *Peter Camenzind*, this chapter will examine how defining traits of the Bildungsroman and the concept of romantic friendship intersect in the novel. As mentioned earlier, romantic friendship can be seen as a predecessor to what is herein regarded a queer friendship, that is, a bond that challenges heteronormative conceptions of relationality, sexuality, and desire. *Peter Camenzind* is a novel in which such bonds are shown to be of great, if not primary, importance. Its protagonist, Peter, describes friendships between men as "das edelste

---

[164] Steakley, *Homosexual Emancipation Movement*, 56. For further reading on the homoerotic foundation of the German Wandervogel groups, see pages 52–56 in Steakley's book, as well as John Alexander Williams, "Ecstasies of the Young: Sexuality, the Youth Movement, and Moral Panic in Germany on the Eve of the First World War," *Central European History* 34, no. 2 (2001): 163–189; and Max Fassnacht, "On the Ground of Nature: Sexuality and Respectability in *Die Freundschaft*'s *Wandervogel* Stories," *Journal of Homosexuality* 68, no. 3 (2021): 434–460.

[165] Murti, "'Ob die Weiber Menschen seyn?'," 290.

Jugendglück"[166] (the most noble of youth's pleasures), and: "Edler und beglückender aber als der Ruhm und der Wein und die Liebe und die Weisheit war meine Freundschaft." (60) (My friendship was nobler and brought more happiness than glory and wine and love and wisdom.) As a keyword in Peter's assessment of male friendship, the term *edel* (noble) brings Plato's *Symposium* to mind, since the homoerotically charged friendships between men in that text are defined with the same term.[167]

Summary of Key Events in *Peter Camenzind*

The story in *Peter Camenzind* goes like this: The eponymous character is born in a quiet village in the Swiss Alps. In his adolescence he leaves the village to go to university and to experience the world. Peter is an outsider but over the course of his school years he undergoes an intense intellectual and spiritual journey, while at the same time enjoying a close friendship with Richard, a charming young musician.

After the experiences at the university, Peter begins to wander the landscapes of Germany, Italy, France, and Switzerland, enamored with the wonders, beauty, and simplicity of nature. He is faced with diverse hardships and heartbreak throughout the novel, and he eventually develops an unhealthy alcohol habit that he does not overcome until the end of the story.

Alongside the friendship with Richard, Peter forms an intimate bond with Boppi, a disabled man with whom he lives for a while. He also makes the acquaintance of Elisabeth, a woman he considers proposing to. Elisabeth, however, is engaged to another man so she and Peter become friends instead. Both Boppi and Elisabeth influence Peter in ways that further his personal growth.

After learning all he needs to know about life—having experienced intimate companionship, love, and loss—Peter finally returns home, now a grown man.

The Bildungsroman Genre

As we shall see in this chapter, Peter Camenzind's life experiences are constantly linked to *Bildung* (education, or learning) and the novel thereby places itself within the category of the Bildungsroman, also known as the

---

[166] Hermann Hesse, *Peter Camenzind*, in *Sämtliche Werke. Band 2: Die Romane. Peter Camenzind, Unterm Rad, Gertrud*, ed. Volker Michaels (Berlin: Suhrkamp, 2001), 36. Further references will be given by page number in parenthesis.
[167] See, for example, Plato, *The Symposium of Plato*, 183d.

"novel of formation." In the German context this genre is characterized by "novels that depict a young protagonist's development towards personal maturity and social integration."[168] Or, in Colin Wilson's words: "The Bildungsroman is a sort of laboratory in which the hero conducts an experiment in living. For this reason, it is a particularly useful medium for writers whose main concern is a philosophical answer to the practical question: What shall we do with our lives?"[169]

Evidently, Bildung should not be understood as exclusively connected with education in schools but as learning about life in a broader sense. Hesse's novels are apt examples of this broader meaning, which has been pointed out by various scholars. Ingo Cornils, for instance, writes that "Hesse's heroes experience a similar development as do those of the traditional Bildungs-roman, with the vital difference that instead of going through a number of stages that educate them and allow them to find their places in society, they go on an 'interior journey' that brings them face to face with their 'true' selves."[170] The broad implication of Bildung in Hesse's work is also evident in the author's own attitude toward school, "not as a propagator of truth, but of lies,"[171] as Theodore Saul Jackson writes. Jackson's study links the theme of walking in Hesse's texts with Bildung: "Walking is rebellious for Hesse," he states, "not because it is forbidden by authority, but because it serves as an alternative to the established school system. It moves the protagonist both literally and figuratively away from the static authority of school."[172]

The term Bildungsroman was popularized in the early twentieth century by Wilhelm Dilthey (1833–1941) and it was regarded, Tobias Boes writes, as "the poetic expression of the Enlightenment concept of Bildung [which] might be described as a process of teleological and organic growth, in the manner of a seed that develops into a mature plant according to inherent genetic principles."[173] This growth—a natural evolution from one stage to another—is mimicked in the narrative trajectory of the Bildungsroman, which, according to Karl Morgenstern (1770–1852), portrays "the Bildung of

---

[168] Todd Kontje, "The German Tradition of the Bildungsroman," in *A History of the Bildungsroman*, ed. Sarah Graham (Cambridge: Cambridge University Press, 2019), 10.

[169] Wilson, *The Outsider*, 54. Emphasis in original.

[170] Cornils, "Introduction," 8. Emphasis in original.

[171] Jackson, "Ambivalent Modernist," 96.

[172] Ibid., 115.

[173] Tobias Boes, "Modernist Studies and the Bildungsroman: A Historical Survey of Critical Trends," *Literature Compass* 3, no. 2 (2006): 232. Emphasis in original.

the hero in its beginnings and growth to a certain stage of completeness."[174] Completeness, in Morgenstern's definition, usually takes the shape of a happy ending in which the protagonist triumphs in heterosexual romance. The concluding marriages in two key examples of Bildungsromane, Johann Wolfgang von Goethe's *Wilhelm Meisters Lehrjahre* (1795–96) and Jane Austen's *Pride and Prejudice* (1813), are examples of such endings.

The goal of the Bildungsroman, Jill Ehnenn explains, "is development for societal assimilation and to that end, often the reader observes the hero reaching the happy ending by ultimately settling in love and/or vocation."[175] The genre thus promotes a heteronormative sort of logic that Martin Swales also underscores. Swales argues that even though the Bildungsroman primarily concerns itself with the self-realization and inner life of an individual hero, it relies heavily on the protagonist's ultimate recognition of "practical reality," that is, career, family and marriage, which are rendered essential to the hero's development.[176] Similarly, Franco Moretti has stressed that the Bildungsroman has a drive toward normality and "has accustomed us to looking at normality *from within* rather than from the stance of its exceptions; and it has produced a phenomenology that makes normality interesting and meaningful *as* normality."[177] Furthermore, Moretti confirms, normality in Bildungsromane is achieved through successful heterosexual marriages and its protagonist "either marries or, in one way or another, must leave social life."[178]

In recent decades, however, scholars have begun to challenge the heteronormative foundation of the genre. Meredith Miller, for instance, has shown that Bildungsromane that are set in all-male educational environments—such as E. M. Forster's *Maurice* (written in 1913–1914 but published in 1971)—express homoerotic tendencies and queer desires.[179] And Jill Ehnenn has established that by using disability and non-heterosexuality to contrast

---

[174] Morgenstern's quote is lifted from Lothar Köhn, *Entwicklungs- und Bildungsroman: Ein Forschungsbericht* (Stuttgart: Metzler, 1969), 5. Emphasis in original.

[175] Jill Ehnenn, "Reorienting the *Bildungsroman*: Progress Narratives, Queerness, and Disability in *The History of Sir Richard Calmady* and *Jude the Obscure*," *Journal of Literary & Cultural Disability Studies* 11, no. 2 (2017): 154.

[176] Martin Swales, *The German Bildungsroman from Wieland to Hesse* (Princeton: Princeton University Press, 1978), 28–29.

[177] Franco Moretti, *The Way of the World: The Bildungsroman in European Culture* (London: Verso, 1987), 11.

[178] Ibid., 23.

[179] Meredith Miller, "Lesbian, Gay and Trans Bildungsromane," in *A History of the Bildungsroman*, ed. Sarah Graham (Cambridge: Cambridge University Press, 2019), 246–248.

normative ideals "the Bildungsroman trains readers to recognize differ-ence."[180]

A similar approach is utilized by Courtney J. Andree who criticizes the Bildungsroman's narrow focus on normative development and challenges the genre's heteronormativity by contrasting it with queer alternatives: "By embracing forms of negativity, non-reproduction, and failure," Andree writes, "[the Bildungsroman's] queer/crip subjects … are empowered to live life on alternative terms."[181] As the works of these scholars suggest, if one looks closely, the Bildungsroman has plenty of queer potential.

Desiring Male Friendship

In Hesse's novels, outsiders like Peter Camenzind tend to pay a high price for their freedom and self-determination. They are often lonely and isolated, and Thomas E. Colby writes: "often they seem engaged in a desperate search for a new community, one that can be reconciled with their personal, and in the conventional sense, anti-social code."[182]

The "desperate search for a new community" to which Colby refers is clearly identifiable in *Peter Camenzind*, in which Peter's desire for friendship is awoken in his early school years, long before he goes to university and meets Richard: "Noch stärker und lebendiger war eine andere Sehnsucht in mir. Ich wollte gern einen Freund haben." (22) (Even stronger and more vivid was another longing within me. I wanted to have a friend.)

Peter yearns for male companionship with an intensity that leads him to follow an older boy called Kaspar Hauri around, hoping to be noticed by him and engaged with socially. Kaspar embodies traits perceived by Peter as masculine: "Er hatte eine sichere und stille Art zu gehen und dazusein, trug den Kopf männlich fest und ernst." (22) (He had a confident and carefree way of walking and being present, he wore his head high in a masculine and serious manner.)

It is certainly possible to interpret Peter's interest in Kaspar as a younger boy's adoration for an older one. Kaspar would, in such an interpretation, be a manifestation of that to which Peter aspires, a masculine model into which Peter himself will grow in time. Peter's jealousy and disdain for those blessed by Kaspar's company indicate something beyond idolization, however: "Ich

---

[180] Ehnenn, "Reorienting the *Bildungsroman*," 155. Emphasis in original.
[181] Courtney J. Andree, "*Bildung* Sideways: Queer/Crip Development and E. M. Forster's 'Fortunate Failure'," *Journal of Literary & Cultural Disability Studies* 12, no. 1 (2018): 27.
[182] Thomas E. Colby, "The Impenitent Prodigal: Hermann Hesse's Hero," *The German Quarterly* 40, no. 1 (1967): 19.

war auf jeden Spießbürger eifersüchtig, den er grüßte." (22) (I was jealous of every philistine he greeted.) Hesse's use of *eifersüchtig* (jealous) to describe Peter's feelings, instead of the less romantically coded term *neidisch* (envious), points to Peter's emotions having little (if anything) to do with envy of Kaspar's more evolved masculinity. Peter's experience of jealousy connotes a queer sort of desire.

To Peter's disappointment, he never gets to form a friendship with Kaspar Hauri. Instead, he gets to know a boy his own age and a friendship with an unequal premise begins: "Ich gewann seine Freundschaft nicht ohne Mühe, und der flotte kleine Altersgenosse benahm sich stets ein klein wenig gönnerhaft gegen mich." (22) (I did not win his friendship without effort and the carefree little fellow always patronized me a little bit.) The relationship ends sourly when Peter discovers that the boy is impersonating him in a derogatory manner to other boys in school: "Es sah sich sehr komisch an und war so witzig und lieblos als möglich gemacht." (23) (It looked very silly and was done as ridiculously and callously as possible.)

It is noticeable that Peter describes the act as *lieblos* (callous, cruel, heartless, loveless) since it indicates what he hopes to receive from a male friend. Peter desires the opposite of a callous relationship, that is, an affectionate and loving bond. Hand in hand with the queer connotations surrounding Peter's desire for Kaspar, his idea of friendship is confirmed to be deeper than common camaraderie. Wilbur B. Franklin corroborates this idea: "Friendship is important in Hesse's understanding of love. He seems to grasp the significance of this relationship, whereas the depth of the male/female sexual relationship is not to be found in his work."[183] If we recall the ambiguities around friendship and homosexuality in the era when *Peter Camenzind* was written, Peter's understanding of friendship—that he equates it with an intimate and affectionate bond between men—can be interpreted as homoerotic.

After the incident with the demeaning boy, Peter experiences the remainder of his pre-university school years without friends. In late adolescence, when he goes off to Zürich to study at the university, he finally meets Richard:

> Die Jugend trat mich an in der Gestalt eines schönen, jungen Menschen, der in derselben Stadt studierte und im ersten Stockwerk meines Hauses zwei hübsche Zimmer gemietet hatte. Jeden Tag hörte ich ihn unten Klavier spielen … Dann sah ich den hübschen Jungen das Haus verlassen, ein Buch oder

---

[183] Franklin, "The Concept of the 'Human'," 80.

> Notenheft in der Linken, in der Rechten die Zigarette, deren Rauch hinter seinem biegsam schlanken Gang verwirbelte. (37)

> (Youth approached me in the form of a beautiful young man who studied in the same city and rented two fine-looking rooms on the first floor of my house. Every day I heard him playing the piano downstairs. I watched the handsome young man leave the house with a book or sheet music in his left hand, a cigarette in his right, the smoke swirling behind him as he gracefully strolled.)

Richard is introduced with an emphasis on his appearance. He is described both as *schön* (beautiful) and *hübsch* (handsome), which indicates desire in Peter's gaze. Also, smoke "swirls" behind Richard "as he gracefully strolls," a description indicating that Peter perceives this man as both sophisticated and exciting.

What is most striking in Richard's introductory passage is the sentence: "Mich zog eine scheue Liebe zu ihm hin" (37) (A shy love drove me toward him), which can be seen as indicating romantic intentions on Peter's part. In Harley Ustus Taylor's examination of homoerotic elements in Hesse's novels, he writes: "When friendships develop, almost always because the protagonist has been chosen by a stronger complementing nature, there is sometimes a tendency for the passive friend to confuse feelings of friendship with the stirrings of his awakening sexual desire."[184] Taylor's observation suits *Peter Camenzind*.

When visiting Richard's apartment, observing him playing the piano, Peter's desire is conspicuous. Not only does he watch Richard "mit heimlicher Lust" (38) (with secret desire), but he is also overwhelmed with feelings of "Zärtlichkeit und Achtung." (39) (tenderness and admiration.) Both these quotes establish that Peter experiences romantic and sexual desire for the man. Although Sigmund Freud, who was no stranger to unconscious desires, admired *Peter Camenzind* and called it "one of his favorite readings,"[185] the queerness in Peter's feelings for Richard is not unconscious in a Freudian sense, but identifiable on the text's surface.

As we shall see, when the bond between Peter and Richard is formed, it is reminiscent of a romantic friendship. Harry Oosterhuis explains that between 1750 and 1850 in Germany, romantic friendships could be both loving and erotic:

---

[184] Taylor, "Homoerotic Elements," 64.
[185] Freedman, *Pilgrim of Crisis*, 117.

> The typically German expression *Freundesliebe* (love between friends)
> originates from the *Sturm und Drang* [Storm and Stress] period, when in
> many university towns literary "Societies of Friends" were founded in which
> men wrote each other passionate letters, dedicated real love poems to one
> another, embraced and kissed each other warmly and shed many tears when
> they had to take leave of one another or met again after a long absence.[186]

The German literary "Storm and Stress movement" to which Oosterhuis
refers emphasized themes such as nature, emotion, and individualism. As
such, Hesse's fiction (*Peter Camenzind* in particular) fits perfectly within this
category, although the author's artistic endeavors commenced long after the
heyday of the movement.

Regarding Hesse's writing and the romantic friendship ideal, Craig
Bernard Palmer argues: "whether Hesse identified with the homosocial or the
homosexual aspects of the romantic friendship cult, it was clearly a concept
that he refused to discard on account of its untimeliness."[187] While romantic
friendship may have been an intentional model for male bonds in Hesse's
fiction, one must remember that the introduction of homosexuality as a
category in the mid-nineteenth century affected how romantic friendship
was regarded. Since such liaisons were now met with suspicion and anxiety,
Hesse's fervent application of male friendships in his novels suggest either
that they are *not* to be regarded as romantic in the classic tradition, or that
Hesse *did not mind* that they could be understood as homoerotic (or even
homosexual). As we saw in the overview chapter (in Hesse's letter confirming
homoeroticism in his novels), the latter is a likely option.

Now we will examine the homoeroticized language in *Peter Camenzind*
and show that it is an expression of the sort of sexual ambiguity that Eve
Kosofsky Sedgwick claims characterizes heteromasculine male bonding.
Several expressions in Hesse's text concern Peter's portrayal of Richard as a
handsome man. Richard "sah prachtvoll aus" (38) (looked gorgeous), he is
described as having a "[hübscher] Kopf" (38) (pretty head) and is called "Der
schöne Student." (38) (the beautiful student.) And Richard is fascinated by
Peter's muscular body: "Vor andern renommierte er damit und war stolz,
einen Freund zu haben, der ihn einhändig hätte erdrücken können." (62) (He
bragged to others and was proud to have a friend who, with one hand, could
hug him to death.) Additionally, when Peter is observing Richard play pool,

---

[186] Oosterhuis, "Homosexual Emancipation," 9.
[187] Palmer, "The Significance of Homosexual Desire," 3–4.

he confesses that he takes immense pleasure in watching him: "es war eine Lust, ihn dabei zu betrachten." (62) (it was a pleasure to watch him do it.)

The homoeroticized language used when describing Peter and Richard's feelings for one another mirrors English Renaissance literature's "romantic language," which was commonly used to describe same-sex friendship. Lillian Faderman writes: "The language that English writers used to describe friendship was barely distinguishable from the language of erotic love."[188] Why is it then reasonable to argue that Hesse's application of such language is interpretable as queer? Well, if the present analysis were to be exclusively dedicated to examining linguistic aspects of Hesse's writing, one might be able to argue that the homoeroticized language in *Peter Camenzind* is *not* queer—in essence, that it does not break with the wide-ranging literary convention to which Faderman refers. In this study, however, more than mere linguistic aspects of Hesse's novel are examined, such as themes, tropes, and characters, as well as its historical context. Besides, as Faderman has shown elsewhere, female same-sex relationships can be categorized as queer regardless of their inclusion of actual sexual practices.[189] The same could very well be true of a male same-sex bond.

As argued by Harley Ustus Taylor, "Hesse's concern with the homoerotic element in male friendships is evidenced, in its simplest form, by the use of situations involving descriptions of the beauty of the male body,"[190] which has been exemplified above. What makes Richard's frequently declared beauty queer is that it challenges the heteronormative conception that men should only desire women. Peter describes him:

> [Richard] war schön und heiter an Leib und Seele, und das Leben schien für ihn keine Schatten zu haben. … Sein Gang und seine Sprache und sein ganzes Wesen war geschmeidig, wohllaut und liebenswert. Oh, wie er lachen konnte! (60)

> (Richard was beautiful and cheerful in both body and soul, there seemed to be no shadows in his life. His manner, how he talked, everything about him was supple, sweet-sounding, and lovable. Oh, how he could laugh!)

Richard's happy manner adds a certain flair to him. His character is described as bright, free, and flourishing, and his affinity for laughter makes him quite

---

[188] Faderman, *Surpassing the Love of Men*, 66.
[189] See Lillian Faderman, *Odd Girls and Twilight Lovers: A History of Lesbian Life in Twentieth-Century America* (London: Penguin, 1992).
[190] Taylor, "Homoerotic Elements," 64.

the gay individual in the multifaceted meaning of the word. Before the 1960s, the term "gay" mainly referred to being jolly or joyful, and in *The Random House Dictionary of the English Language* it is explained that "[gay] suggests a lightness of heart or liveliness of mood that is openly manifested."[191] Over time, however, the term has become synonymous with homosexual men who are characterized by carefree, cheerful, and bright personalities (among other things). While the idea that homosexual men by default are lighthearted, cheerful, and happy is no longer commonplace,[192] the potential to read Richard as a gay man (in the double meaning of the word) is enhanced when Peter depicts his likeability and happiness like this:

> [W]as wir an ihm liebten und bewunderten, war nicht Witz und Geist, sondern die unbezwingliche Heiterkeit seines lichten, kindlichen Wesens, welche jeden Augenblick hervorbrach und ihn mit einer leichten, fröhlichen Atmosphäre umgab. (41)

> (What we loved and admired about him was not his wit and spirit, rather the determined serenity of his bright, childlike nature, which burst forth at every moment and surrounded him with an easy, happy aura.)

Needless to say, being a happy man does not automatically make one homosexual. In the interpretive context of this novel, however (with its homoeroticized language), Richard's gay character affects how his sexuality can be understood.

In addition, Richard's childlike nature suggests that he is not yet fully formed, which mirrors the notion that before boys grow into normative heterosexuality—that is, in their formative years, most often in educational contexts—they go through a phase in which homosexual desire is as viable (potentially even more so) as heterosexual desire. Here, yet another link to the homoerotic aspects of *Symposium* becomes visible. Plato's text conveys that while homosexual activities between the lover (the older man) and the beloved (the younger one) did occur, feelings that transcended physical pleasures—like romantic feelings—were usually reserved for the younger

---

[191] *The Random House Dictionary of the English Language* [The Unabridged Ed.], ed. Jess Stein (New York: Random House, 1969), 587.

[192] David M. Halperin explains that the term gay has a history of an all-too "cheery insistence on how happy we [are] all supposed to be." (David M. Halperin, *How to be Gay* [Cambridge, MA: The Belknap Press of Harvard University Press, 2012], 75.) This "happy" implication of gayness "merely [invokes] the specter it [is] all too obviously struggling to exorcize, the specter of a sad and pathetic homosexuality." (Ibid.)

man. Hesse's focus on two *young* men in *Peter Camenzind,* whose attitudes toward each other express ambiguousness regarding their sexualities, thus correlates with the romantic aspect of Classical antiquity's male same-sex bonds. It transcends the conventional dynamic within a pederasty relationship, however, and makes same-sex romance possible. Moreover, since the purpose of a pederasty relationship was to provide the younger man with philosophical education, the link between *Symposium* and *Peter Camenzind*—a novel about Bildung—is hard to question.

Turning to Nature

As previously mentioned, nature is a theme that stands out in *Peter Camenzind,* and, as we soon shall see, is oftentimes interwoven with the themes of Bildung and romantic friendship.

Colin Wilson argues that when Hesse chose Switzerland as the setting for his debut novel, it was a result of his love for Gottfried Keller's *Der grüne Heinrich* (*Green Henry,* 1855) "and because he wanted to place his hero in an idyllic landscape of mountains and lakes."[193] Like *Peter Camenzind, Der grüne Heinrich* is a Bildungsroman that portrays the effects of the shift from romanticism to realism in life and art. Keller's novel is greatly influenced by Rousseau's "return to nature ideal," which, as we shall see shortly, also characterizes *Peter Camenzind.*

From the very first sentences and throughout Hesse's novel, nature is cherished and elevated as an element vital to the protagonist's wellbeing. The key activity that underscores nature's importance is *wandering,* as Theodore Saul Jackson's study shows. "The act of walking," Jackson writes, "becomes a cipher for the metaphysical journeys [Hesse's] characters undertake. Hesse transforms walking into a leitmotif that seems to propel the characters through their spiritual journeys, giving them comfort on the way, past and present, and allowing them to develop metaphysical syntheses between the extremes of modernity."[194] A link between nature, wandering, and outsiderness emerges in *Peter Camenzind,* since the protagonist reminds us of a vagabond. According to Wilbur B. Franklin, the vagabond is a common character in Hesse's fiction: "he is usually the kind of person who gives in to 'nature,' i.e., he lives an unrestrained life, without consideration for social

---

[193] Wilson, *Hermann Hesse,* 8.
[194] Jackson, "Ambivalent Modernist," 80.

concerns. He experiences loneliness but also a radical freedom."[195] These qualities are all embodied by Peter.

Alongside his debut novel, Hesse's reverence for nature can be seen in his autobiographical *Wanderung*, in which time spent in nature signifies rebirth.[196] Hesse elevates nature as ideal, something to love, cherish, and even desire, which bestows it with queer connotations. Essentially, in Hesse's work, one's love for nature is a form of affection that exists beyond conventional understandings of love. Hesse's own words strengthen this claim when he says the following about wanderers:

> Unser Wandertreib und Vagabundentum ist zu einem großen Teil Liebe, Erotik. ... Wir Wanderer sind darin geübt, Liebeswünsche gerade um ihrer Unerfüllbarkeit willen zu hegen, und jene Liebe, welche eigentlich dem Weib gehörte, spielend zu verteilen an Dorf und Berg, See und Schlucht.[197]

> (To a large extent, our wanderlust and vagabonding lives are love itself, eroticism. We wanderers have been trained to cherish love as something that cannot be reached, and, with ease, to give our affection—which actually belongs to women—to land and mountain, lake and valley.)

The themes of wandering and affection for nature in *Peter Camenzind* place the novel firmly within the framework of Rousseau's thoughts on nature. Rousseau compared the state of nature with a time and place before the rise of civilization, when human beings were uncorrupted by society. In this natural state, individuals wander the world freely with only sporadic interaction with other wanderers.[198] As we can see, Hesse's outsider ideal also corresponds to Rousseau's notion of nature.

Beyond its correlation to Rousseauesque ideals, *Peter Camenzind* corresponds to other frameworks. First, Peter's affection for nature makes the novel an example of the neo-Romantic literary tradition, of which Colin Riordan writes: "After an early aversion to Romanticism, Hesse in the late 1890s

---

[195] Franklin, "The Concept of the Human'," 62.

[196] Hermann Hesse, *Wanderung. Aufzeichnungen* [1920], in *Sämtliche Werke. Band 11: Autobiographische Schriften 1*, ed. Volker Michaels (Berlin: Suhrkamp, 2003), 10. The quote goes as follows: "Die Welt ist schöner geworden. Ich bin allein, und leide nicht unter dem Alleinsein. Ich wünsche nichts anders ... Ich bin begierig, reif zu werden. Ich bin bereit zu sterben, bereit wiedergeboren zu werden." (The world has become more beautiful. I am alone but do not suffer from being so. I do not wish for anything else. I am eager to become ripe, ready to die, ready to be reborn.)

[197] Ibid., 12.

[198] For a conclusive explanation of Rousseau's thoughts on the state of nature, see Jean-Jacques Rousseau, *The Social Contract* and *The First and Second Discourses* [1762, 1750, 1755], ed. Susan Dunn (New Haven: Yale University Press, 2002).

becomes a great enthusiast both for German Romanticism and the 'Neuro-mantik' which is often interpreted as a reaction to the swift pace of industrialisation, urbanisation and social change which characterises this period in Germany."[199] Riordan states: "in [*Peter Camenzind*] industry and technology are very much in the background while nature is foregrounded as an idyllic refuge still available if you know how to appreciate it."[200] His quote emphasizes the novel's anti-modernist core.

Second, according to Ernst Rose, Hesse's early work can be said to belong within *Heimatkunst* (Regional Art), a literary movement that was embraced by the Wandervogel groups:

> They [the Wandervogel groups] read the regional writers who from 1900 on had drawn together in a Heimatkunst movement in defiance of so-called hothouse and asphalt literature. The Heimatkunst poets perpetuated the village and country tales of an earlier period—the literature of the Swiss masters Jeremias Gotthelf and Gottfried Keller ... Young Hesse seemed to belong among these regional writers [which] stamped him as a romantic escapist. Until 1914 there was little evidence in his writing to refute that image.[201]

Third, as mentioned in the overview chapter, the ideals of the Lebensreform movement also parallel *Peter Camenzind*'s idealization of nature (and Hesse's writing in general). The thematic and ideological range of the Lebensreform movement in the early twentieth century included food reform, natural medicine, *Freikörperkultur* (nudism), and *Gartenstadtbewegung* (Garden City movement, in which the aim was to build communities with small houses surrounded by undeveloped green areas). In general, the Lebens-reform movement stressed that urban life was harmful because it detached humans from nature.[202]

These three frameworks can all be associated with *Peter Camenzind*, wherein nature bestows the protagonist with happiness and comfort. Much of the first chapter revolves around lyrical descriptions of the beautiful Alps close to Peter's home village:

---

[199] Colin Riordan, "Hermann Hesse and the Ecological Imagination," in *Hermann Hesse Today = Hermann Hesse Heute*, ed. Ingo Cornils and Osman Durrani (Amsterdam: Rodopi, 2005), 98.

[200] Ibid., 101.

[201] Rose, *Faith from the Abyss*, 16. Emphasis in original.

[202] See Thorsten Carstensen and Marcel Schmid, "Die Literatur der Lebensreform. Kontexte, Orte und Autoren," in *Die Literatur der Lebensreform: Kulturkritik und Aufbruchstimmung um 1900*, ed. Thorsten Carstensen and Marcel Schmid (Bielefeld: transcript, 2016), 9–26.

> Berge, See, Sturm und Sonne waren meine Freunde, erzählten mir und erzogen mich und waren mir lange Zeit lieber und bekannter als irgend Menschen und Menschenschicksale. Meine Lieblinge aber, die ich dem glänzenden See und den traurigen Föhren und sonnigen Felsen vorzog, waren die Wolken. (15)

> (The mountains, lakes, the storm, and sun were my friends, they talked to me and educated me, and for a long time they were dearer and more familiar to me than people and their destinies. But my favorites, the ones I preferred to the glistening lake and the gloomy pines and the sunny cliffs, were the clouds.)

Clouds are especially important to the novel's protagonist. They signify, on the one hand, a desire to explore that comes natural to him, and on the other hand, they are symbols for journeying itself.[203] "The young Camenzind," Lewis W. Tusken writes, "equates the clouds with man's dreams; they are symbols of wanderings, the souls of humankind hovering between time and eternity."[204] Peter describes them as "das ewige Sinnbild alles Wanderns, alles Suchens, Verlangens und Heimbegehrens." (16) (the eternal symbol of all that wanders, seeks, desires, and longs for home.)

Peter has always hiked in the Alps, even as a child, which corresponds to a description of wanderers that Hesse makes in *Wanderung*. Hesse explains that wanderers treat borders as irrelevant; he labels wanderers "guides to the future."[205] Therefore, Peter's childhood hikes can be seen as signifiers of what the future has in store for him; that is, that he is destined to leave the village and receive an education, have new experiences, and wander the world in search of happiness.

While playfully following clouds as a ten-year-old boy, Peter comes to climb his first mountain. This is an event that opens his eyes to the vastness of the world: "Zugleich aber zitterte etwas in mir gleich dem Zeiger des Kompasses mit unbewußtem Streben mächtig jener großen Ferne entgegen." (17) (At the same time, there was something inside me that trembled, like the pointer of a compass that drew me toward the great beyond with a subcons-

---

[203] Cf. Peter Baer Gontrum, "Natur- und Dingsymbolik als Ausdruck der inneren Welt Hermann Hesses" (PhD diss., Munich, 1958), 27.

[204] Tusken, *Understanding Hermann Hesse*, 49.

[205] Hesse writes: "Der Wanderer ist in vielen Hinsichten ein primitiver Mensch, so wie der Nomade primitiver ist als der Bauer. Die Überwindung der Seßhaftigkeit aber und die Verachtung der Grenzen machen Leute meines Schlages [Wanderer] trotzdem zu Wegweisern in die Zukunft." (Hesse, *Wanderung*, 7.) (The wanderer is in many ways a simple person, just as the nomad is simpler than the farmer. Even so, in overcoming laziness and disregarding borders, people like me [wanderers] become guides to the future.)

cious and powerful longing.) Standing on the mountaintop, a profound yearning is awoken in Peter, a desire for knowledge (Bildung) that brings him to Zürich and Richard (the romantic friendship), as well as a similar scene in a natural setting. Peter and Richard's romantic friendship can be said to fully begin when they climb a mountain together, a scene that mirrors Peter's climb as a ten-year-old boy:

> Während dieses gemeinsamen Stehens und Lauschens überrann mich mit köstlichem Schauer die Empfindung, zum erstenmal neben einem Freunde zu stehen und so zu zweien in schöne, rosig verwölkte Lebensweiten zu blicken. (39)

> (While standing together and listening, I sensed for the first time with a sweet shiver that I was standing next to a friend and glancing toward a future draped in beautiful rosy clouds.)

This description is an almost perfect example of José Esteban Muñoz's conceptualization of the horizon as signifying queer utopia. Recalling Muñoz's argument that queer aesthetics often contain blueprints of a queer future—a future that is utopian and "in the making"—makes Peter's hopefulness interesting. If we posit that *Peter Camenzind* belongs within a queer aesthetics framework, would we not be able to identify yearning in its characters, especially yearning for a future in which the limitations of the present have dissolved? Interpreted with a basis in Muñoz's statement, the scene between Peter and Richard on the mountaintop becomes imbued with queer potentiality, as the future of their relationship, quite literally, is *on the horizon*.

Muñoz's conception of utopian queerness has a noteworthy relation to Andreas Kiryakakis research on Hesse, in which the ideal of *Heimat* (home, or homeland) is investigated. Kiryakakis differentiates between three types of Heimat in Hesse's writing: "the geographic or parental, the ideal or spiritual, and the metaphysical."[206] The first two are present in *Peter Camenzind*, whereas the third—the metaphysical Heimat—can be found primarily in *Der Steppenwolf* (more on that in the second part of this book).

Peter Camenzind's first type of Heimat, the geographic or parental, is Peter's home-village Nimikon in the Swiss Alps. The second type of Heimat—the ideal or spiritual—shares traits with the utopian queerness that

---

[206] Andreas Kiryakakis, *The Ideal of Heimat in the Works of Hermann Hesse* (New York: Peter Lang, 1988), 5.

the novel's horizon points toward. The queer horizon (the ideal Heimat) and clouds symbolizing "all that wanders, seeks, desires, and longs for home" become signifiers for the queer utopia that the romantic friendship promises (which is comparable with a spiritual Heimat).[207]

In Hesse's longer quote above, the juxtaposition of the romantic friendship, the queer potentiality represented by the horizon, and the Romantic natural setting is important since in German-speaking Europe in the early twentieth century, neo-Romantic themes that suffused art and literature were frequently mentioned in homosexual magazines (such as *Der Eigene* and *Die Freundschaft*).[208] In this era, Clayton J. Whisnant explains, a correlation existed between homosexuality and the kind of story in which one has affection for nature:

> [M]any authors saw the countryside as a space for refuge, relaxation, and sexual discovery. A large number of the stories in the lesbian press used natural settings such as the mountains or the seashore. One can easily interpret these stories as a firm rejection of the identification between homosexuality and modernity made by so many moralizing figures at the time. Most commonly, the characters are presented as fleeing the city ... Escape from the routine and social conventions of civilization allows new pleasures to be discovered, new forms of self to be explored, and new kinds of relationships to be established.[209]

Drawing on Whisnant's account, the fact that Peter's romantic friendship with Richard is established in nature becomes important for this reading. "At least implicit in much Romantic art and literature," Whisnant suggests, "was a critique of the controlling and stifling tendencies of society."[210] In light of this idea, Peter and Richard's turn to nature becomes an escape from society's heteronormative constraints, which underlines a nature/culture dualism in

---

[207] Alongside *Peter Camenzind*, the concept of queer utopia occurs rather regularly in Hesse's writing. The concept's manifestation in *Der Steppenwolf* will be examined later. Additionally, queer utopias are present in both *Narziß und Goldmund* and *Das Glasperlenspiel*. Both novels contain queerness similar to that which is queer in *Peter Camenzind* and *Der Steppenwolf*, that is, male homosocial relationships that are characterized by homoeroticism. But even more so, the settings of *Narziß und Goldmund* and *Das Glasperlenspiel* are utopian in that they are "imaginary societies," as Walter Naumann calls them (Naumann, "The Individual and Society," 38). *Das Glasperlenspiel* in particular, which is Hesse's final novel, portrays a vision for the future as a male homosocial realm (it takes place in 2025). As such, one could argue that when Hesse imagines the future he expresses a sort of queer-utopian potential.

[208] See Whisnant, *Queer Identities*, 132.

[209] Ibid.

[210] Ibid., 133.

the text. Instead of remaining in the city with its social conventions, the men travel to a mountain where a "new kind of relationship" can commence.

Moreover, *Peter Camenzind*'s employment of nature as a space where queer desires can be cultivated shares traits with a strategy used by homosexual individuals in Germany at the time. As pointed out by Max Fassnacht: "Weimar Germany's homosexual emancipation movement sought to associate itself with nature as means of portraying homosexuality in a positive light."[211] In essence, to associate oneself with the beauty of German nature (in a national-romantic way) aimed at normalizing one's outsiderness as a queer person and take part in national identity. Fassnacht arrives at this conclusion by examining "Wandervogel stories" about male bonding and nature that were published in one of the homosexual magazines of the era. He suggests that "publishing stories with themes of homoeroticism and nature [likely was] a way of presenting a model of homosexual respectability."[212] The juxtaposition of homoeroticism and nature in Hesse's novel is certainly perceivable as serving such a purpose.

At the same time, Peter and Richard turning to nature *together* contradicts a common trope in Hesse's writing, namely that nature is the setting in which one's *independence* is cultivated.[213] Jackson writes that "nature seems to provide in [the] early works of Hesse an arena outside the civilized and cultural world in which the individual is free to wrangle with societal and spiritual forces without threatening the imposed politeness which reigns indoors."[214] The outsider-protagonists in *Knulp* and *Unterm Rad*, for instance, wander alone. Not only does Peter and Richard's joint hike up the mountain underline the link between *Peter Camenzind* and the homoerotically connoted Wandervogel groups (young men that hiked *together*), but it also breaks with Hesse's overall idea of cultivating one's independence in nature.

From the moment on the mountaintop and onward, Peter is not alone anymore but glances toward a colorful future with a companion next to him, which beside his desire for knowledge is what he has yearned for. The scene on the mountain is a queer speck of light in the text, and the dreamy setting

---

[211] Fassnacht, "On the Ground of Nature," 435.

[212] Ibid., 441.

[213] Hesse exemplifies his conception of independence with the symbol of *trees*. He honors, especially, trees that stand firmly by themselves. Their sole purpose, he writes, is: "ihr eigenes, in ihnen wohnendes Gesetz zu erfüllen, ihre eigene Gestalt auszubauen, sich selbst darzustellen." (Hesse, *Wanderung*, 20.) (to fulfill the law that resides within them, to grow and build up their individual shape, to become themselves.)

[214] Jackson, "Ambivalent Modernist," 91.

and Peter's "sweet shiver" differ greatly from the previously mentioned portrayals of male friendship in the novel. This romantic friendship being established in a natural setting—a space where Peter feels comfortable, happy, and hopeful about the future—thus accentuates Richard's importance in Peter's life. It suggests that from now on these men are in their right element. Whatever follows in their relationship is thereby conceivable as just as natural as the movements of the free-flowing clouds.

Transcending the Romantic Friendship

After a short while, Peter's feelings of jealousy show up again, much like in the experience with Kaspar Hauri. Once again, we see that Peter's jealousy has nothing to do with envy but is rooted in feelings of rejection:

> Freundschaften schloß ich keine mehr, da ich Richard ausschließlich und mit Eifersucht liebte. Auch den Frauen, mit denen er viel und vertraut umging, suchte ich ihn zu entziehen. (42)

> (I did not make any more friends since I jealously loved only Richard. I tried to keep him from women, with whom he frequently and familiarly spent time.)

The probability of heterosexual romance triggers jealousy and fear of rejection in Peter, which suggests that he regards the relationship with Richard as more than friendship. Peter and Richard's bond is, in fact, reminiscent of a regular romance. They behave like lovers, squabble about little things and make up after arguing in a romantic fashion. Peter narrates:

> [Richard] faßte mich um den Kopf, rieb nach orientalischem Liebesbrauch seine Nasenspitze an der meinen und liebkoste mich, bis ich ärgerlich lachend mich ihm entzog; die Freundschaft aber war wieder heil. (42)

> (Richard placed his hands on both sides of my head and with the tip of his nose against mine—the Oriental custom of love—he cuddled me until I withdrew with an annoyed giggle and our friendship was mended.)

This intimacy is indicative of the special status of the men's bond. Ralph Freedman also emphasizes this bond and writes that no encounters "involving real touch and feeling ... exist in the episodes with the women."[215]

---

[215] Freedman, *Pilgrim of Crisis*, 116.

Physical intimacy does not occur in Peter's and Richard's other social relations, but as the nose-rubbing description shows (as well as the previously-
quoted passage about having a friend who "could hug one to death"),
physicality does take place in their relationship.

Even though both Peter and Richard occasionally engage in heterosexual
practices, such as flirtation with women, their relationship stands out as
paramount. They prioritize each other and privilege their bond in place of
relationships with women, which challenges heteronormative conceptions of
how romantic and sexual liaisons are supposed to be organized.

One of the most playful expressions of how the men's bond provides a
context in which they are allowed to experience intimacy free from heteronormative constraints is a scene in which Peter and Richard are skinny
dipping in a mountain lake. There they pretend to be the siren-like water
spirit Lorelei and a seaman charmed by her beauty. In this scene, the men's
nakedness accentuates a potent connection with one of the pillars of the
Lebensreform movement, namely nudism. While Kathrin Geist's analysis of
Hesse's relationship to the Lebensreform ideals primarily concerns his short
story *In den Felsen* (*Among the Rocks*, 1907), *Peter Camenzind* projects similar ideas regarding nature. Both texts also concern renunciation of modern
life. In Geist's assessment, Hesse's writing perpetuates the idea that nakedness is a means of becoming part of nature and something that reminds us of
the primordial human condition before civilization.[216] Her idea is evident in
Peter Camenzind. The text conveys that being naked in nature is therapeutic
and that the therapeutic benefits of being naked are entangled with male
friendship and homoeroticism. As nakedness is portrayed as natural,
homoeroticism between men comes to connote naturalness as well.

As they are playing naked in the lake a group of tourists pass by, and Peter
and Richard hide before they are spotted. From their hiding place Richard
scares the tourists and compares his actions to the painting *Pan frightening a
shepherd* by Symbolist painter Arnold Böcklin (1827–1921), curiously
adding: "'Es waren aber leider Frauenzimmer dabei.'" (61) ("Sadly, there were
also women in the group.")

Böcklin was a painter who, in Ernst Rose's description, "stood for a
romantic aestheticism which populated nature with mythological figures."[217]
He was also a native of Basel, the town where Hesse worked in a bookstore at
the turn of the twentieth century. Hesse was influenced by Böcklin's "lively

---

[216] Geist, "Der Nacktkletterer," 198–199.
[217] Rose, *Faith from the Abyss*, 16.

colors" and nature images, and it was through the eyes of this painter that Hesse viewed the Swiss Alps, Rose explains.[218] In Böcklin's painting *Pan frightening a shepherd*, the Greek goat-god Pan frightens a male shepherd by emerging naked from some rocks. Richard mentions this particular painting while expressing discontent with the presence of women, establishing male homosociality as his preferred method of socializing.[219] Pan's homoerotic connotations (in Greek mythology he desired beautiful young men and was often depicted with a large, erect penis) give the young men's nakedness in the Lorelei/seaman game an amplified queer meaning.

Additionally, Peter and Richard hiding from the tourists corresponds to an idea mentioned in the overview chapter regarding queer voices having been systematically silenced by history. It was suggested that because of this treatment, queer literary characters in the early twentieth century sometimes purposefully hide their desires. Peter and Richard's reason for hiding comes across as having little (if anything) to do with conventions about male nakedness in the presence of women. It appears that they hide, on the one hand, because they are interrupted in an erotic game that mimics a heterosexual encounter, and, on the other hand, to avoid the heteronormative judgment that arises with a female presence. As we can see, the homoeroticism that characterizes this scene is both hidden (from the other characters) and in plain sight (on the surface of the text for the reader to acknowledge).

The above-mentioned expression of queerness—that is, the homoeroticized language and practices that challenge heteronormative conceptions of relationality—contrast with the novel's references to heterosexuality. While the text provides several indications of male homoeroticism, the presence of heterosexuality and women is constantly characterized by ambivalence. These observations will be examined in detail in the next chapter, but for now, suffice it to say that Peter prefers to view women from afar. He puts them on pedestals and idealizes them, which, in a sense, makes them unreachable. Even when women are in his immediate surroundings, the text conveys a palpable distance. For example, during an uncomfortable date with a woman with whom Peter at one point has a relationship, the couple is on a night tour in a boat. At the time, Peter compares heterosexual dating with a theatrical performance:

---

[218] Rose, *Faith from the Abyss*, 16–17.

[219] For a reference to the queer connotations of Pan, see, e.g., Louis Crompton, *Homosexuality and Civilization* (Cambridge, MA: The Belknap Press of Harvard University Press, 2003), 2.

> Das Schöne und Poetische der ganzen abendlichen Szenerie, das Sitzen im
> Kahn, die Sterne, der laue, ruhige See und alles das beängstigte mich, denn es
> kam mir vor wie eine schöne Theaterdekoration, in deren Mitte ich eine
> sentimentale Szene agieren müsse. (53)

> (The beauty and poetry of the evening scenery, to sit in the boat, under the
> stars, on the calm sea, made me anxious, because it seemed like a beautiful
> theater décor, in which I, in the center, had to act a sentimental scene.)

In addition to accentuating a contrast between homosociality and heterosociality (a bond between individuals of different sexes), queerness is visible
in Peter's use of the verb *agieren* (act), since it settles that there are at least
two sides to him: one authentic and one acted, and that acting is necessary to
perform heterosexuality. As the pressure of performing heterosexuality arises
here, Peter, evidently, becomes anxious and does not want to partake.

When the scene above is juxtaposed with the following example, the contrast between homosociality and heterosociality become strikingly apparent:

> Noch viel erstaunter und glücklicher war ich aber, als [Richard] acht Tage
> später in einem vielbesuchten Biergarten Brüderschaft mit mir schloß, vor
> allen Leuten aufsprang, mich küßte und umfaßte und mit mir wie verrückt
> um den Tisch herum tanzte. (40)

> (I was even more astonished and happy when Richard, eight days later in a
> crowded Biergarten, announced our companionship by kissing and
> embracing me in front of everyone, and then led me in a wild dance around
> the table.)

Peter's response to Richard kissing him—"'Was werden die Leute denken?'
warnte ich ihn schüchtern." (40) (Nervously I warned him: "What will people
think?")—is interesting on two accounts. First, Peter's question demonstrates
that homoerotic desire occurs in the novel. Second, his apprehension shows
that such desire must be kept secret, as the previous example of swimming
naked also showed. In addition, the example in which Peter observes Richard
"with *secret* desire" indicate that the men's feelings for each other include
concealed same-sex yearnings. Evidently, both homoeroticism and what
appears to be homosexuality exist in this novel's fictional world and both
Peter and Richard know what those things are.

Another noteworthy aspect of Peter's reaction to Richard's kiss is that
Richard confirms their bond as romantic. Richard's response to Peter's
nervousness about what people might think of them is this: "'Sie werden

denken: die zwei sind außerordentlich glücklich oder ganz außerordentlich besoffen; die meisten werden gar nichts denken.'" (40) ("They will think that those two are enormously happy or enormously drunk; but most of them will not think anything at all.") Richard does not deny that what transpires is romantic, rather, a same-sex romance is recognized. Richard shows that he understands his own sexuality and reassures Peter that they have nothing to worry about. In so doing, their relationship transcends the romantic friendship. From this point on, Peter and Richard's relationship has crossed a line and it cannot really be considered a romantic friendship any longer. Rather, it can be interpreted as a romance between two homosexual men. This mirrors a statement in Ralph Freedman's research on Hesse, namely that Richard is "the novel's central love."[220]

Shortly after the kissing and dancing in the Biergarten, the men start socializing with Richard's friends, who are described in a colorful manner. Peter explains:

> [Ich] nahm an den Zusammenkünften [Richards] Freunde teil, verkehrte mit Franzosen, Deutschen, Russen, hörte sonderbare moderne Bücher vorlesen, trat da und dort in die Ateliers der Maler oder wohnte Abendgesellschaften bei, in denen eine Menge aufgeregter und unklarer junger Geister erschienen und mich wie ein phantastischer Karneval umgaben. (43)

> (I participated in the social gatherings of Richard's friends where I met Frenchmen, Germans, Russians, and heard peculiar modern books being read aloud. I found myself in painters' workshops and attended dinner parties at which a young crowd of eager, undecided, and spirited people appeared, who welcomed me into their amazing carnival.)

In the modernist culture described here—which echoes the conditions for queer people in the Golden Twenties and Weimar Berlin's intellectual bohemia—the men's romance runs little risk of coming across as deviant. Rather, it is presented as a progressive ideal which is associated with queer, colorful practices of celebration. Although this *phantastischer Karneval* (amazing carnival) contrasts with the men's previous escape to nature when establishing their relationship, this new context shows that Peter and Richard have found a group of like-minded individuals who make them feel comfortable about who they are. Choosing to surround themselves with creative and free-spirited individuals—elsewhere labeled "interessanten,

---

[220] Freedman, *Pilgrim of Crisis*, 115.

kunstliebenden und aparten Personen" (41) (interesting, art-loving, and unusual people)—seems ideal for a same-sex couple. As we can see, Peter and Richard choose a group of friends wherein their romance is significantly less likely to be condemned.

While the modernist culture referred to in the quote contrasts with the idealization of nature in *Peter Camenzind*, the nature/culture dualism can be seen as aiming toward a synthesis. Though Max Fassnacht's earlier argument is relevant (that in order to convey a respectable homosexuality, queer people in early twentieth-century Germany associated themselves with nature), urban life in the 1900s provided another sort of freedom. Many homosexuals, Clayton J. Whisnant asserts, "saw the city not as depraved at all but instead as a space that offered freedoms. For them the city was a place to get away from the closed-minded countryside."[221] Hesse's novel includes both contexts and Peter and Richard are part of both. While Peter prefers nature, he and Richard move freely between these contexts and are equally queer in both. As such, their romance becomes interpretable as an iteration of a synthesis incarnate.

"Southern Flight"

As Peter and Richard's time at the university reaches its end, when it is almost time for Richard to return to his home, the men make a journey together. To prolong their "[bitterer] Abschied" (63) (bitter farewell) they travel to Florence, Italy.

Peter has long yearned to visit Florence. "Die Stadt lag da, wie ich sie aus hundert Bildern und tausend Träumen kannte" (65) (The city lay before me as I knew it from a hundred pictures and a thousand dreams), he narrates, then adding: "Das beweglich freudige, harmlose toskanische Leben ging mir wie ein Wunder auf, und ich war bald heimischer, als ich je zu Hause gewesen war." (65) (The exuberant, uncomplicated Tuscan life seemed to me a miracle and soon I felt more at home there than I had ever been.)

Peter feeling at home in Florence is interesting since this city, from the mid-fifteenth century, is said to have had a widespread homosexual culture. Michael Rocke has described Florence as "a city where male same-sex relations were indeed extraordinarily common, so much so as to have earned the city an infamous reputation across Europe."[222] Elsewhere, Rocke has shown

---

[221] Whisnant, *Queer Identities*, 149.
[222] Michael Rocke, "The Ambivalence of Policing Sexual Margins," in *At the Margins: Minority Groups in Premodern Italy*, ed. Stephen J. Milner (Minneapolis: University of Minnesota Press, 2005), 55.

that the city's homosexual connotation is enhanced through the term *Florenzer* (Florentine) which, in fifteenth century Germany, could be used to refer to a sodomite.[223]

The thematic link between Florence's queerly connoted history and the fact that Peter and Richard choose this particular place as their travel destination indicates that their relationship can be understood as a same-sex romance. Florence Tamagne makes a similar assertion about the writings of E. M. Forster, in which Italy is described as a sunny, open-minded "homosexual paradise" that contrasts Puritanical England.[224] The portrayal of Italy in Forster's novels shares many traits with the country's description in *Peter Camenzind*. When one sees Peter and Richard's relationship as a same-sex romance, the fact that homosexuality became legal in Italy in 1889, whereas it was not fully legalized in Germany until 1994, underlines the significance of choosing this country as their travel destination. In James D. Steakley's study of the German homosexual emancipation movement, it is mentioned that Karl Ulrichs himself travelled to Italy to escape heteronormativity.[225] While conversations about homosexuality were possible in Germany at the time (as the field of sexology demonstrates), and while queer subcultures existed in major German cities, one must remember that Germany was far from a queer utopia. As the "homosexual scandals" make evident, threats of blackmail, social stigmatization, and legal prosecution were common. Steakley thus labels Ulrichs's journey to Italy a "southern flight," which was a usual move among homosexuals at the time and is depicted, for instance, in Thomas Mann's *Der Tod in Venedig* (*Death in Venice*, 1912).

So, by journeying to Florence, Peter and Richard escape the stifling heteronormative atmosphere in their home country, and while there is a considerable gap between the peak of the commonness of same-sex relationships in fifteenth century Florence and the era in which *Peter Camenzind* was written, Peter discloses: "in Florenz genoß ich die beständige Vorstellung

---

[223] Michael Rocke, *Forbidden Friendships: Homosexuality and Male Culture in Renaissance Florence* (New York: Oxford University Press, 1996), 3.

[224] Florence Tamagne, *A History of Homosexuality in Europe: Volume 1 & 2: Berlin, London, Paris 1919–1939* (New York: Algora, 2006), 142. Moreover, the queer connotations of Italy (Florence in particular) can be found in the work of another homosexual writer (beside E. M. Forster), namely Oscar Wilde. While never completed, Wilde wrote a play called *A Florentine Tragedy* which has an example of an erotic triangle with homosocial desire at the center. Another queer connotation can be seen in Hesse's own biography of Giovanni Boccaccio (1313–1375) whose *The Decameron* (probably composed between 1349–1353) takes place in Florence and includes homoerotic content. For further reading on the homoeroticism in *The Decameron*, see Carla Freccero, *Queer/Early/Modern* (Durham: Duke University Press, 2006), 43–47.

[225] Steakley, *Homosexual Emancipation Movement*, 22.

vom Leben des Quattrocento." (66) (in Florence I enjoyed the stable presence of fifteenth century life.) While Hesse's text does not give a conclusive answer as to whether Peter is aware of Florence's queer connotations, his and Richard's southern flight constitutes a queer speck of light, since during the trip they reach the pinnacle of their happiness:

> [W]ir hatten beide das kräftige Gefühl, unseres Glückes würdig, einem reichen, neuen Leben entgegenzugehen. … [W]ir wußten fester als je, daß wir einer dem andern notwendig und einer des andern fürs Leben sicher waren. (66)

> (Both of us had the strong feeling of being worthy of our happiness, to encounter a rich, new life. We knew more firmly than ever that we needed each other and were sure of each other for life.)

These proclamations mirror the scene on the mountain when Peter and Richard gaze toward the horizon and a future together. They feel worthy of their current happiness and share a desire not to go their separate ways. But what does the "rich new life" that awaits them entail? Might it be possible that the next step for Peter and Richard is one which leads to their romance being out in the open?

José Esteban Muñoz's conception of the future as queerness's domain supports such a hypothesis: "to access queer visuality," Muñoz writes, "we may need to squint, to strain our vision and force it to see otherwise, beyond the limited vista of the here and now."[226] Possibly, Peter and Richard imagine what lies beyond their "here and now" by mimicking heterosexual marriage and that social institution's belief in "until death do us part." In the men's promise to one another, we see an iteration of George Haggerty's point about literary male friendships as "marriages between men." Also, Walter Naumann's previously quoted conception becomes relevant, that is, that Hesse's work makes male friendships resemble marriages between individuals of opposite tendencies who educate each other "in the highest sense."

What the men are expressing when they say that they are sure of each other "for life" is herein understood as a visualization of a queer utopia that challenges the heteronormativity of their time. Taking the text's surface seriously, *fürs Leben* (for life) indicates a lifelong homosocial bond that does not include future wives. However, such a lifelong bond is abruptly made

---

[226] Muñoz, *Cruising Utopia*, 22.

impossible. The scene when the men part ways after the trip is characterized by melancholy, because Peter and Richard find it truly hard to separate:

> In Zürich nahm Richard Abschied. Zweimal stieg er wieder aus dem Eisenbahnwagen, um mich zu küssen, und nickte mir noch, so lange es ging, vom Fenster aus zärtlich zu. (67)

> (Richard said goodbye in Zürich. He got out of the railroad car twice to kiss me and then nodded tenderly to me through the window for as long as he possibly could.)

The scene depicts intimacy, tenderness, and affection. But this is the last time Peter and Richard get to see each other. Only two weeks later Richard drowns in a river.

Having suddenly lost Richard leaves Peter in a state of profound sorrow: "ich war im Kern der Seele krank und hatte ein Grauen vor allem Lebendigen." (67) (I was sick in the core of my soul and dreaded everything living.) Grief-stricken, Peter travels to Paris where he drifts around without purpose. He writes for a magazine while simultaneously engaging in a decadent lifestyle: "Ich bekenne, daß ich einen Irrweg um den andern ging, allerlei Schmutz gesehen habe und darin gesteckt bin." (68) (I confess that I chose several sinful paths, saw all kinds of filth, and allowed myself to get stuck in it.) After the time in Paris, Peter develops an unhealthy alcohol habit that intensifies during the middle section of the novel, and it will be a while before he experiences anything resembling happiness again.

At the end of the novel, Peter returns home to the mountain village to care for his elderly father and to write about "das schöne Geheimnis der Liebe." (98) (the beautiful secret of love.) Hesse's text implies that the beautiful secret is love of nature itself. Colin Riordan proposes that "[t]he key to Hesse's understanding of nature at this time is that the important relationship is not that between the individual and society, but between the individual and the cosmos."[227] In general, Peter's bond with nature is treated as more important than his relationships with people, which challenges normative conceptions of relationality. And when Peter imagines writing about beautiful nature environments, he even finds it difficult to insert humans in the fictional settings, because, he explains:

---

[227] Riordan, "Ecological Imagination," 101.

Mit Erstaunen nahm ich wahr, daß der Mensch von der übrigen Natur sich vor allem durch eine schlüpfrige Gallert von Lüge unterscheidet, die ihn umgibt und schützt. (99–100)

(I realized with astonishment that human beings differ from the rest of nature, above all because of a slippery jelly of lies which surrounds and protects them.)

The quote clarifies that Peter cherishes nature—which he (for the most part) appreciates in solitude—in a way that he does not cherish people. The Alps surrounding Peter's home village are a refuge bestowing him with comfort and privacy. There is one person, however, with whom he shared his beloved nature. The relationship with Richard was established in a natural setting that despite the presence of two humans did not come across as unnatural. Therefore, it is significant that the previous quote occurs after Richard's death. When Richard is no longer around, Peter regards people as surrounded by "a slippery jelly of lies," which implies that while the men's romance was kept secret from others, their relationship was never a lie. Rather, it seems to have been the truest and most noble part of Peter's youth.

In presenting the romantic relationship between Peter and Richard as natural—and enhancing its naturalness with an actual natural setting— Hesse's text can be said to criticize the belief that homosexuality should be regarded as *un*natural, a notion that was being heavily contested by all branches of the homosexual emancipation movement in the early 1900s.

"It Is Merely the Friendship of My Student Years That I Miss"

In a reading of *Wilhelm Meisters Lehrjahre* (commonly regarded as the Bildungsroman-genre's blueprint), Claudia Lindén suggests that the Bildungsroman is perceivable as inherently queer. For the protagonist to complete his Bildung, however, all queerness must disappear from the story at the end, she argues.[228] As indicated by Franco Moretti, the end of the Bildung must entail the ending of male homosocial bonds. Richard's death in *Peter Camenzind* is certainly perceivable as an example of such heteronormative enforcement.

---

[228] Claudia Lindén, "It Takes a Real Man to Show True Femininity. Gender-transgression in Goethe's and Humboldt's concept of Bildung," in *The Humboldtian Tradition: Origins and Legacies*, ed. Peter Josephson, Thomas Karlsohn, and Johan Östling (Leiden: Brill Publisher, 2014), 69.

At the end of the story, the elimination of all characters (except for the protagonist) embodying queerness—here, Richard and later on also Peter's disabled friend Boppi—pushes Peter toward a lifestyle where homosociality is to be replaced with heterosexual relationality and marriage, and in this regard, *Peter Camenzind* resembles a classic Bildungsroman. Here we might recall Martin Swales's argument that the Bildungsroman rests on its protagonist's final recognition of "practical reality," which he defines as career, family, and marriage.

Even though Hesse's novel can be regarded a classic Bildungsroman, it does challenge these genre conventions since as an adult, Peter still praises the noble friendship of his youth:

> Ich weiß auch heute in der Welt nichts Köstlicheres als eine ehrliche und tüchtige Freundschaft zwischen Männern, und wenn mich einmal an nachdenklichen Tagen etwas wie ein Jugendheimweh befällt, so ist es allein um meine Studentenfreundschaft. (60)

> (Still today I know nothing more delightful in this world than a sincere and strenuous friendship between men, and on melancholic days when I long for my youth, it is merely the friendship of my student years that I miss.)

The quote shows that memories of Richard linger in Peter's mind throughout his life. Queerness as such has not disappeared completely from the story when it ends.

After Richard's death he lives on in Peter's memory. Therefore, Peter comes to give voice to Heather Love's conception of backwardness as "a queer historical structure of feeling"—an emotional condition in a queer literary character, characterized, for example, by loneliness and loss. Additionally, Peter's journey of formation does not end in "practical reality" (in Swales's definition). Career-wise, Peter returns to a simple, non-intellectual existence in the mountains where he lives near nature, far from the urban spaces where he got his education. He does not form a family in a heteronormative sense, a type of life that he, quite remarkably, since the very beginning of the story, has opted out of: "ich [werde] auch vermutlich einmal sterben … ohne Kinder dazulassen." (9) (I will probably also die one day without leaving children behind.) Peter's conviction shows that he has always known he will not conform to heteronormativity. In essence, he rejects heteronormative life patterns.

Throughout Peter's life he discounts what José Esteban Muñoz calls "straight time"—a temporality that lets queers know "that there is no future but the here and now of our everyday life. ... The only futurity promised [by straight time]," Muñoz writes, "is that of reproductive majoritarian heterosexuality."[229] Straight time, essentially, is an understanding of time that elevates heterosexual/reproductive relationships as correct and natural. As we have seen, Peter's idea of the future is *not* characterized by heteronormative family life but instead represented by the horizon, toward which he gazes with Richard, imagining a brighter future with him.

---

[229] Muñoz, *Cruising Utopia*, 22.

CHAPTER 2

"Without Leaving Children Behind"

The Queerness of Peter's Heterosexual Ambivalence

Whereas male homosociality is portrayed as natural in *Peter Camenzind*, most of the text's references to heterosexuality—which are primarily visible when women are included in Peter's social life—are accompanied by ambivalence in the novel's protagonist. Peter's bond with Elisabeth, however, differs from other relationships between people of different sexes in the text. If we are to clarify how and why the bond between these two can be understood as a queer friendship, we need first to observe Peter's overall attitude toward women.

Drawing on the work of Lee Edelman, José Esteban Muñoz writes that queers, "especially those who do not choose to be biologically reproductive, a people without children, are, within the dominant culture, people without a future. They are cast as people who are developmentally stalled, forsaken, who do not have the complete life promised by heterosexual temporality."[230] Peter embodies this type of "futurelessness" in two ways that accentuate queerness. First, Richard's sudden death denies him a queer-utopian future. And second, he does not participate in reproductive practices.

At the end of the previous chapter, it was mentioned that Peter never forms a family of his own. When his story begins, he confesses that he will likely die someday "without leaving children behind." This statement turns out to be an early allusion to heterosexual ambivalence in the protagonist— an ambivalence that can be understood as queer, as we shall see.

How does he, as a young boy, know that he will probably not have children when he becomes an adult? Which are the surrounding factors that contribute to this very specific idea? When attempting to answer these questions, Peter's view of his parents and the other men and women in the village becomes significant, since he perceives their lives to be tedious and scripted:

> [J]eder spielt solang er kann seine Rolle mit, tritt dann zögernd in den Kreis der Unbrauchbaren und taucht schließlich ins Dunkel unter, ohne daß viel Aufsehens davon gemacht würde. (9)

---

[230] Muñoz, *Cruising Utopia*, 98.

(Everyone plays their role for as long as they can, then slowly enters the circle of the useless and finally plunges into darkness without any fuss being made about it.)

The quote shows that Peter views the circular and heteronormative lifestyle of the men and women in the village as gloomy and hopeless. Furthermore, as he is clearly doubting whether engaging in traditional heterosexual practices such as procreating is the right path for him—he longs for another type of life—the novel's queerness becomes even more pronounced.

If we recall Peter's nightly boat tour with a woman with whom he has a relationship at one point (the painter Erminia Aglietti), we know that he compares heterosexual practices to acting. Men and women "play their roles," Peter claims, which implies that they follow staked-out paths through life. Peter's own life, however, does not evolve in such a fashion. He gets to go to school in a large city, travel, and meet lots of people, and his comment at the beginning of the novel about not having children underscores that all his experiences ought to be observed with this statement in mind. As a young boy, Peter suspects that he is somehow different from the other villagers. All in all, his idea about not conforming to the heterosexual practice of parenting conveys an inherent uncertainty about heterosexuality in him, which comes to affect how his relationships with women can be interpreted.

The First Love: Rösi Girtanner

It has been pointed out by Micaela Mecocci that while women in Hesse's fiction play all sorts of roles—friend, sister, lover, or mother—they are almost always characterized as Others.[231] That is, women are portrayed as passive, without agency, and devoid of spirituality.[232] Under the following headings

---

[231] Micaela Mecocci, "Die Bedeutung der weiblichen Gestalten in Hermann Hesses Prosa," in *Hermann-Hesse-Jahrbuch. Band 1*, ed. Mauro Ponzi (Tübingen: Max Niemeyer, 2004), 73–76.

[232] The conception of woman as Other has its foundation in Simone de Beauvoir's *La Deuxième Sexe* (*The Second Sex*, 1949) in which de Beauvoir argues that men are considered the norm, whereas women are Other. As opposed to young boys, young girls, de Beauvoir explains, are fostered into *passiveness*. In cultures where men are encouraged to trust their strength and sovereignty, women are allotted a strictly corporeal existence which makes them stuck in a structure that denies them power and personal agency. For further reading, see Simone de Beauvoir, *The Second Sex*, trans. H. M. Parshley (London: Jonathan Cape, 1953).

we will demonstrate that female characters and heterosexual ambivalence come to affect the ways with which queerness occurs in *Peter Camenzind*.[233]

There are four women with whom Peter is socially involved. These relations, in various ways, create expectations of heterosexuality in and around him. Overall, we shall see that when women are concerned, Peter is either openly suspicious of them—"[ich hatte] immer noch ein leises Mißtrauen gegen die Frauen" (95) (I was still slightly mistrustful of women)—or keeps them at a distance, as this quote shows:

> Um von der Liebe zu reden – darin bin ich zeitlebens ein Knabe geblieben. Für mich ist die Liebe zu Frauen immer ein reinigendes Anbeten gewesen, eine steile Flamme meiner Trübe entlodert, Beterhände zu blauen Himmeln emporgestreckt. ... [D]ie Frauenliebe [hat] mir so viel Bitteres als Süßes eingebracht; zwar blieben die Frauen auf dem hohen Sockel stehen, mir aber verwandelte sich die feierliche Rolle des anbetenden Priesters allzuleicht in die peinlich-komische des genarrten Narren. (25–26)

> (Where love is concerned, I have remained a boy my entire life. For me, the love of women was always a cleansing form of worship, a sharp flame that pierced through my somber being, hands in prayer raised toward the blue skies. The love of women has brought me as much bitter as sweet; even though women remained on their high pedestals, I all too easily had to change the solemn role of an adoring priest for the embarrassing role of a swindled fool.)

As the quote affirms, when it comes to love, Peter has "remained a boy his entire life." This might refer to him having never reached adulthood in a heteronormative sense—that is, not becoming a parent—as well as never having lost his virginity with a woman, thus never becoming what hetero-masculine culture would designate a "real man."

Furthermore, the quote shows that the love of women (which implies that there are also other kinds of love, such as *love of men*) is an ambivalent affair to Peter. It is a "form of worship," he says, which does not signify a corporeal relationship. First, terms like "worship" and "pedestal" contrast with the closeness in his relationship with Richard. And second, while praying can be

---

[233] Among other things, this study emphasizes various forms of otherness in Hesse's *fiction*. However, it bears mentioning that after Hesse's escape from his boarding school as an adolescent, he came to regard himself as an Other (*ein Anderer*), someone who was different from everyone around him. Otherness, in other words, was a concept to which Hesse had a personal connection. For further reading, see York-Gothart Mix, "'Ja, ich bin ein Anderer' – Hermann Hesses Konzept des Eigensinns Genese und kulturkritischer Impetus," in *Der Grenzgänger Hermann Hesse: Neue Perspektiven der Forschung*, ed. Henriette Herwig and Florian Trabert (Freiburg i. Br.: Rombach, 2013), 359–369.

seen as an activity that brings an individual closer to one's deity in a spiritual way, the act signifies distance rather than being physically close to another being.

One might ask whether this distance, which is enhanced through the placement of women on pedestals, renders women unreachable (for worshipping purposes) or—as a means of escaping the normative pressures of heterosexuality—keeps them comfortably at bay? There is, in any case, ambivalence at work here, which is also noticeable at the end of the passage, where Peter once more associates his feelings for women with role-playing.

Evidently, there is quite a gap between Peter and women. This gap is most visible in Peter's relation to his first love, Rösi Girtanner, who he desires from afar. Peter is seventeen years old when he falls for her: "Sie war schön, und ich bin stolz darauf, daß ich mein Leben lang immer nur in sehr schöne Frauenbilder verliebt war." (23) (She was beautiful, and I am proud that I, throughout my life, have always loved beautiful women.)

Peter really falls for this girl. It is indisputable that Hesse's text gives voice to an intense sort of love. Ambivalence, however, is also present. Peter's proclamation therefore becomes an expression of what Kalle Berggren has termed "straight inoculation," that is, a "rhetorical means of sustaining a contested heterosexual identity."[234] In essence, straight inoculation implies that after announcing one's love for a woman, one can express palpably homoerotic tendencies and still pass for a heterosexual. To Peter, falling for Rösi seems to serve this purpose.

Interestingly, the term Peter uses about women, *Frauenbilder*, means (in a literal sense) "images of women" rather than "women." Peter falling in love with *images* of women corresponds to the previously cited worship which is herein understood as a nonsexual form of desire. The women to whom Peter refers are always objects to gaze *at* rather than subjects to engage *with*, which corresponds Kamakshi P. Murti's argument (see the overview chapter) regarding women in Hesse's fiction, who are mostly reduced to objects without clear subject positions.[235] "In a male-defined and male-structured image of the self," she writes, "women either slowly relinquish their femaleness, disappearing into the male persona, or they remain ... on an idealized or allegorical plane of being."[236] For example, none of Hesse's main characters

---

[234] Kalle Berggren, "Reading Rap: Feminist Interventions in Men and Masculinity Research" (PhD diss., Uppsala University, 2014), 38.
[235] Cf. Claudia Karstedt, *Die Entwicklung des Frauenbildes bei Hermann Hesse* (Frankfurt am Main: Peter Lang, 1983).
[236] Murti, "'Ob die Weiber Menschen seyn?'," 271.

are women. And in his final novel, *Das Glasperlenspiel*, female characters have been made obsolete; in the province Castalia where the novel takes place *every single character is male.*[237]

With a basis in Murti's arguments, the term Frauenbilder can be read as a blend of the expressions *Frauenzimmer* and *Weibsbild*, which were and still are pejorative German expressions used about women. The fact that Peter uses an amalgamation of two misogynistic terms while simultaneously emphasizing Rösi's beauty signals the following: his feelings are not only ambivalent, but also ambiguous and open to interpretation.

The language of the protagonist when he is talking about women often conveys misogynistic semantics and ideas. In this chapter, differences between how Peter talks about women and how he talks about men will become clear, albeit this is not done with the intent of normalizing his anti-feminine remarks. The purpose of emphasizing Peter's misogynistic comments is to underline how relationships between men are privileged in this novel, which, as we shall see, affects its readability as a narrative about queerness (such as queer friendship).

While misogyny should not be understood as a prerequisite for male homosexuality, in a heteronormative context in which one's opportunity to express a non-heterosexual identity is diminished—and wherein non-normative forms of sexualities are pathologized or in other ways punished—a homosexual man (if we agree to interpret Peter as a homosexual man) may have accumulated a lot of bitterness that comes to be expressed via misogynistic language. The point here is that since heteronormativity limits Peter's possibilities of desiring men and creates pressure to desire women, feelings of resentment arise that are directed toward the latter. Rather than regarding this resentment as an embedded part of male homosexuality, the misogynistic language in the novel ought instead to be seen as an effect of heteronormativity.

Peter wants to look at Rösi from afar, but he does not want her to look back at him: "Dennoch verlangte mich nicht danach, von ihr bemerkt zu werden." (27) (Still, I did not want to be noticed by her.) What does Peter fear that Rösi would see if she saw him? The answer is indicated in this passage:

---

[237] Walter Sorell points out that even in Hesse's *Gertrud*, "the central figure is not Gertrud but the crippled musician Kuhn." (Sorell, *The Man Who Sought*, 124.)

> Und dann dachte ich auch oft an Rösi und hatte wieder das böse, rechthaberische Gefühl meines bauernhaften Unvermögens, je in der "Welt" einen sicheren und beweglichen Mann abzugeben. (30)

> (And then I often thought of Rösi and once more experienced the malicious, self-possessed feeling of being an inadequate peasant, one who would never be able to become a confident, flexible man of the "world.")

Having left the tedious but familiar village-life for an urban, modern space where Peter must find his place clearly affects him negatively. He sees himself as a country-boy lost in a big city which is not the self-image he wishes to project to Rösi, whose higher-class status is commented on several occasions. She is described as *adlig* (aristocratic) and belongs to "[einen] alten, vornehmen und gesegneten Haus." (26) (an old, distinguished, and fortunate house.)

As we can see, because of their differences in class, Peter prefers not to be seen by Rösi at all. Rösi embodies a higher class ideal and throughout the novel it is this aspect of her character (rather than being a woman) that is paramount in the way she is depicted. Peter's fixation on Rösi's higher class determines what sort of desire he is experiencing. In this first love of his, the text communicates that when it comes to choosing a woman to love, Peter considers class to be of greater importance than sexual desire. In effect, Rösi becomes a mere signifier for urban life and the expectations on Peter to succeed. Peter's unwillingness to be noticed by her is a manifestation of his performance anxiety. He has been given a chance to distinguish himself through an education in the city (which few if any of the people from his village have ever gotten). The opportunity creates pressure, and a consequence is that Peter's first experience of heterosexual relationality is characterized by an intense anxiety to conform.

Rösi's presence in Peter's life deepens his anxiety which he must manage somehow. When it gets overwhelming Peter returns to nature, a familiar setting where he feels safe:

> Ich entzog mich, lief ins Freie und staunte mit wunderlicher Träumerei in die Welt. Nun sah ich plötzlich, wie schön und farbig alles war, wie Licht und Atem durch alle Dinge floß, wie klargrün der Fluß und wie rot die Dächer und wie blau die Berge waren. (26)

> (I withdrew, went out into the open and marveled at the world with curiosity. Suddenly, I saw how beautiful and colorful everything was, how the light and

life flowed through everything, how clear-green the river was, how red the roofs, and how blue the mountains were.)

It is noteworthy that in Peter's reverence for nature the term *world* is not framed by quotation marks whereas earlier, when speaking of urban life (which is represented by Rösi), Peter admitted that he would never become a man of that "world."

The tension between nature's naturalness and the city's unnaturalness affects how Peter's heterosexual ambivalence is depicted. We see this in a scene in which he travels from the city to the countryside to pick flowers for Rösi. On the train ride leaving the city he is not at all anxious. On the train ride back, however, with a small bouquet of white flowers in his hand, Peter's anxiety about returning is unmistakable:

> Nun waren alle heimischen Berge versunken, und eine breite, niedere, hellgrüne Landschaft drängte sich hervor. Das hatte mich bei meiner ersten Reise gar nicht berührt. Diesmal aber ergriff mich Unruhe, Angst und Trauer, als wäre ich verurteilt, weiter in immer flachere Länder hinein zu fahren und die Berge und das Bürgerrecht der Heimat unwiederbringlich zu verlieren. Zugleich sah ich immer das schöne, schmale Gesicht der Rösi vor mir stehen, so fein und fremd und kühl und meiner unbekümmert, daß mir Erbitterung und Schmerz den Atem verhielt. (28)

> (Now all the mountains that I knew from my home had sunk, and a broad, low, bright green landscape spread around me. This view had not bothered me on my first trip. This time, however, I was seized by anxiety, fear, and grief as if I was condemned to continue travelling into ever flatter landscapes and irretrievably lose the mountains and the belonging to my homeland. At the same time, I saw the beautiful, slim face of Rösi before me, so elegant, distant, and dismissive, as well as unconcerned by the fact that my bitterness and pain made it difficult to breathe.)

When Peter returns to the city, he feels like he does not belong there: "Ich fühlte, daß ich nicht mehr heimisch war." (28) (I felt that I was not at home.) Nevertheless, he gives Rösi the flowers, but never meets her in person—instead he leaves them on her doorstep without a note: "Niemand sah mich, und ich erfuhr nie, ob Rösi meinen Gruß zu sehen bekommen habe." (29) (No one saw me, and I never learned whether Rösi saw my greeting or not.)

What is interesting about Peter's endeavor is that after having performed the romantic gesture of picking flowers for a girl, he is content with leaving them (anonymously) on her doorstep. He seems, in fact, rather relieved that he does not have to meet her in person. Peter's flower-picking effort is heterosexually tentative, but what he calls "love" for Rösi does not make him readable as a heterosexual man. On the contrary, when it comes to expressions of intimacy, desire, and affection, the relationship with Richard far exceeds the shallow experiment described above.

Finally, Peter confesses:

> Diese meine erste Liebe fand nie einen Abschluß, sondern verklang fragend und unerlöst in meine Jugendjahre und lief neben meinen späteren Verliebtheiten wie eine stille ältere Schwester mit. (29)

> (This first love of mine never came to an end but faded unanswered and unresolved throughout my teenage years and accompanied my later infatuations like a quiet older sister.)

It is a nonsexual description of a first love for sure, especially because of its "quiet older sister" simile. Shortly afterwards, when Peter is acquainted with Richard, he describes big-city women like Rösi like this:

> Die modisch eleganten, hoffärtigen Weiber der Reichen kamen mir wie Pfauen im Hühnerhofe vor, hübsch, stolz und ein wenig lächerlich. (37)

> (The fashionably elegant, superior, and rich women seemed like peacocks in the hen house to me, pretty, proud, and somewhat ridiculous.)

Compared to the bond with Richard—in which Richard's beauty and lovability is continuously underscored—the difference between Peter's desire for women (as it is expressed in his love for Rösi) and his desire for men is strikingly evident.

A Masculine Countertype

Peter's attitude toward his first female love interest clearly indicates that when it comes to heterosexual relationality, he is experiencing ambivalence. Interestingly, heterosexual ambivalence turns out to be closely entwined with expressions of masculinity in the novel.[238]

---

[238] Although there are plenty of theories within gender studies on the topic of masculinity (and some of them would surely be rewarding when examining masculinity in Hesse's work), this study makes exclusive use of George Mosse's "countertype" and "stereotype" concepts, since they neatly align with portrayals of outsiderness in *Peter Camenzind*.

In *The Image of Man: The Creation of Modern Masculinity* (1996), George Mosse shows that throughout the modern era (including the time when Hesse was writing *Peter Camenzind*), the construction of masculinity was founded on a *stereotype* whose self-controlling ability, proper appearance, stability, and morals reflected the normative patterns of modern society:

> [The masculine stereotype] needed an image against which it could define itself. Those who stood outside or were marginalized by society provided a countertype that reflected, as in a convex mirror, the reverse of the social norm. Such outsiders were either those whose origins, religion, or language were different from the rest of the population or those who were perceived as asocial because they failed to conform to the social norms.[239]

Examples of the countertype included men who contrasted with the active hard-working stereotype ideal, namely unsettled individuals such as vagrants or vagabonds (travelers that were characterized by not having families in a conventional sense, that is, the type of figures that frequent Hesse's fiction), as well as those who were without roots or territories of their own—criminals, homosexuals, the insane, men of color—basically anyone who did not fit into the narrow norm of the white bourgeois man, whose body and soul were believed to be in sync in a way that the countertype's were not.[240]

The link between body and soul in the masculine stereotype was emphasized through medicine, Mosse writes, which "made its contribution to the construction of modern masculinity through its assertion that a healthy mind and a healthy body are inseparable."[241] It was believed that the normative and desired form of masculinity was conditioned on a healthy body and mind. Undesired forms of masculinity thus became associated with various forms of sickness, such as physical or mental illness, non-normative sexuality, or disability. Undesired masculinity, or *unmanliness* (which characterized the countertype) was frequently accompanied by nervousness.

Mosse states that nervousness in men was usually associated with an improper or ragged outward appearance. Essentially, the countertype was recognizable because of his ugliness, abnormal physical proportions, and fidgety mannerisms. Therefore, robustness, Mosse writes, became a form of armor protecting the modern man from illnesses, frail nerves, and other

---

[239] George L. Mosse, *The Image of Man: The Creation of Modern Masculinity* (New York: Oxford University Press, 1996), 56.
[240] Ibid., 56–60.
[241] Ibid., 60.

forms of abnormality: "Sick and diseased men had ruined their nerves, which not only threatened to make them effeminate … but, through the state of their bodies and mind, documented their lack of manliness."[242]

Mosse's study discloses that unmanliness was a key characteristic of the countertype and that feminine men triggered an enormous anxiety in normative society. A "true man" was expected to defeat any possible female features of his nature, whereas homosexuals were either unable to overcome their unmanly qualities, or, in some especially frightening cases, managed to disguise their femininity and pass as heterosexual. Stereotypical masculine men were expected to be in control of their passions; thus, being *out of control* or unable to master one's desires came to be considered a female characteristic, whereby a lack of impulse control was undoubtedly viewed as an unmanly trait.[243]

When a literary character like Peter is compared with Mosse's countertype, it can make inherent queerness more visible, since by challenging normativity the masculine countertype is perceivable as a queer category. Mosse makes it clear that a homosexual man can be seen as an example of the countertype. However, the queer connotations of the figure are just as potent when one considers that the countertype explicitly challenges all kinds of norms. Recalling what was mentioned in the overview chapter about queer theories, challenging various forms of normativity is one of the—if not the most—significant feature of the modern definition of what queer is and does.

The principal theme that has permeated this chapter so far is ambivalence and, as we saw in the previous section about Peter's first love, his attitude toward Rösi is characterized by ambivalent feelings. It is therefore not surprising that when one takes a closer look at Peter with Mosse's reflections on the countertype in mind, ambivalence is near at hand. In addition, we will see another iteration of Hesse's frequent use of dualisms.

Peter is not only associated with the countertype; he is also associated with Mosse's masculine stereotype and thus embodies a dualism between manliness and unmanliness. There is a visible discrepancy in Peter that cor-

---

[242] Mosse, *The Image of Man*, 60.

[243] While the homoerotic idealization of masculinity, virility, and strength that was perpetuated within German Männerbunde, such as the Gemeinschaft der Eigenen, privileged a narrow form of masculinity, the homoerotically-centered masculine ethos of these groups can still (with an amount of goodwill) be regarded as a critique of heteromasculine culture—after all, the masculinists strove to destigmatize homosexual desire between men. However, in the early twentieth century, femininity in cis men (gay, straight, or bisexual) tended to be treated as undesirable. Being unmanly in dominant culture indicated sexual deviance, and in the eyes of the masculinists, being an unmanly homosexual man was also a violation of the norm.

responds to the ideas of the time, that the masculine ideal depended on a balance between a healthy body and a healthy mind. On the one hand, Peter's muscular body is vigorous and robust—he has "eine ungewöhnliche Körperkraft" (15) (an unusual physical strength), which makes him fit within the category of the masculine stereotype. Elsewhere, he also describes himself like this: "Mein Leben lang war ich stark und gesund gewesen, hatte nie eine ernste Krankheit gehabt" (109) (I have been strong and healthy all my life, I never had a serious illness), which accentuates his physio-stereotypical masculinity.

Peter's mind, on the other hand, is characterized by anxiety, nervousness, ambivalent feelings, and queerness, and he is thereby synonymous with the countertype. At the same time, Peter has no overtly feminine mannerisms and thereby passes for a heterosexual. We saw this ability to pass depicted in the previous chapter, in the example from the Biergarten when Peter and Richard dance together. So, because Peter does not look like a homosexual, instead embodying traits of the masculine stereotype, such as a proper, handsome appearance, he passes as a "true" heterosexual man even though he openly engages in a same-sex dance. Though when it comes to *alcohol*, one of the text's major themes and one with which Peter struggles deeply, he is not in control of his impulses. Lacking impulse control, as we know, was regarded an unmanly trait characteristic of the countertype. (Textual examples of Peter's alcoholism will be presented shortly under the heading "The girlfriend: Erminia Aglietti.")

Embodying traits from both the masculine stereotype and its countertype, Peter personifies a dualism of manliness and unmanliness that makes him readable as inherently ambivalent. Furthermore, because of the contingency between stereotypical masculinity and heterosexuality, the in-betweenness of Peter's masculine identity renders expressions of heterosexuality within him questionable.

Under the following heading, we shall see that the novel's expressions of heterosexual and masculine ambivalence are also interlinked with references to a specific vessel.

Boats as Bearers of Heterosexual and Masculine Meaning

It will soon become evident that expressions of heterosexuality and masculinity in *Peter Camenzind* tend to correlate with the presence of boats. As previously stated, Peter equates heterosexuality with a performative act. The passage in the text where that comparison is made depicts the date with

Erminia Aglietti, an encounter that takes place under a starry sky when the couple is sitting together in a boat. Because of this, the instability of heterosexuality in Hesse's text—that is, its performative basis—can be seen as connected with these vessels.

Primarily, however, boats in *Peter Camenzind* seem significant when male characters are to embody masculinity. Boats are thereby interpretable as bearers of masculine meaning. We see this in the portrayal of Peter's Uncle Konrad. Throughout the story Konrad is thematically associated with a boat and he is also characterized by being a fool, that is, one who does not conform to social norms.

In Peter's home village, fools are regarded like this:

> [Man war] froh an den paar Narren, welche zwar noch still und ernsthaft genug waren, aber doch einige Farbe und einige Gelegenheit zu Gelächter und Spott hereinbrachten. (10)

> (One was glad to have a few fools who were still mostly quiet and serious but brought some color to life and provided opportunities for laughter and ridicule.)

Narren (fools, or jesters) are needed to "bring color to life in the village," a life that for the men and women living there is a rather tedious, staked out, and heteronormatively scripted affair. Moreover, due to the oftentimes harsh weather conditions in the mountains, the villagers are prone to *Tiefsinn* (heavy-heartedness, or melancholy) which is said to be lessened by the presence of fools.

As we will see, by means of his foolishness, Uncle Konrad challenges village norms which makes it interesting that Hesse's text does not give a single indication about whether Konrad desires women. Neither is it mentioned whether he is married or has children. What we know is that Peter's own story ends with an equivalent outsider status—he neither marries, nor becomes a father—which creates a connection between him and his uncle.

Young Peter looks up to his uncle a lot, especially because Konrad tries to leave the village at one point. With the intent to broaden his limited horizons, Konrad's endeavor—which is portrayed as a flight attempt—is closely associated with him throughout the text. And, not surprisingly, Konrad's flight attempt involves a boat. In front of the entire village population, Konrad sets sail on the vessel. Initially his enterprise seems to be a success and to the amazement of the spectators Konrad sails away. Later that same night, however, having lost the boat's sail, he returns to the place where he started. This makes Konrad the laughingstock of the whole village and generates the mocking phrase "'Mußt Segel nehmen, Konrad!'" (12) ("You must raise the sail, Konrad!") among the villagers.

From a queer perspective it is significant that Konrad, who in the first chapter comes across as the most non-normative character in Hesse's novel, attempts to leave the heteronormative village but fails to do so. Because of his attempt to flee, leaving the village comes to signify opening oneself up to something other than tradition and the scripted lifestyle that village life allows. Perhaps then, because he himself has failed, Uncle Konrad paves the way for Peter to leave?

When Peter's father is contemplating the question of whether Peter should be allowed to leave to study, the father consults Konrad for help in the matter: "Natürlich war [Konrad] sofort dafür entflammt, daß ich lernen und später studieren und ein Gelehrter und Herr werden müsse." (19) (Of course, Konrad was instantly thrilled for my sake, that I would have an education and become a scholar and a gentleman.) Consulting Konrad conveys the patriarchal foundation of life in the village and, moreover, since Konrad can be associated with the Shakespearean fool—a figure of "wit and wisdom" whose purpose is not simply to provide "comic relief" but to speak the truth to other characters and the audience—the father is guaranteed an honest answer. As Konrad can be associated with the truth-telling fool in Shakespeare's plays and at the same time connotes queerness, we see that Hesse allows queerness a certain importance in *Peter Camenzind* that should not be understated.

Konrad's excitement convinces Peter's father and a decision is made that Peter is to leave for his studies, which bestows upon Peter a chance to develop as a young man without the narrowmindedness of the village population influencing his growth—an opportunity that Konrad himself, the perpetual village fool, never received. In Konrad's case, attempting to sail away and failing has tragic associations throughout the story. He tries to break out of the normative restrictions of his surroundings, but this attempt only confirms him as the village fool. Since foolishness is part of what makes Konrad readable as an iteration of Mosse's masculine countertype (a categorization that also diminishes his manliness), Konrad is coded as even more of a fool after his flight attempt. As he becomes more of a fool, he also loses any stereotypical masculinity he might have possessed to begin with. So, where Konrad is concerned, becoming "less of a man" is an effect of having been unable to master his sailboat, which makes that boat an object that conveys masculine meaning in the text.

It is interesting to note that the boat belongs to Peter's father, who, we learn, has an untroubled relationship to the vessel. His masculinity is never threatened by sailing failures since he keeps the boat safe on land, all year round. Once a year he tars the vessel, a process that is depicted with romantic language:

> [I]ch sah wieder den Vater in Hemdärmeln mit dem Pinsel hantieren, sah die bläulichen Wölkchen aus seiner Pfeife in die stillen Sommerlüfte steigen und die blitzgelben Falter ihre unsicheren, scheuen Flüge tun. An solchen Tagen zeigte mein Vater eine ungewöhnlich behagliche Laune. (14)

> (Once again, I saw my father in short shirtsleeves handling the brush; I saw the bluish clouds from his pipe rise in the calm summer atmosphere and the light-yellow butterflies fly shy and fleetingly. On such days my father was in an unusually relaxed mood.)

Since boats in *Peter Camenzind* are solely operated by male characters, it is relevant to observe that, throughout history (in the Western world), the domain of sailing has been dominated by men. As Suzanne J. Stark has shown, the notion that women do not belong at sea has a long and pervasive history: "They not only were weak," she writes, "hysterical, and feckless and distracted the men from their duties, but they also brought bad luck to the ships they travelled in; they called forth supernatural winds that sank the vessels and drowned the men."[244] The fact that boats themselves commonly have female names can be seen as a hint at attitudes toward heterosexuality in the men that handle them.

If we agree to view boats in Hesse's novel as meaningful when expressing heterosexuality, Konrad's heterosexuality turns out to be questionable, as he fails to master the masculine area of sailing. While Peter's father gives the boat its yearly care in a compassionate manner, conveying that his heterosexuality is stable, Konrad does not manage to master the boat and thus becomes less of a man. Nowhere in the novel is it indicated that Peter's father's relationship with Peter's mother is ambivalent. Up until her death, their marriage is portrayed as an uneventful but loving bond; for his part, Konrad has no heterosexual liaisons.

---

[244] Suzanne J. Stark, *Female Tars: Women Abord Ship in the Age of Sail* (London: Constable, 1996), 1.

One of the most significant mentions of boats that is linked to the protagonist occurs when Richard has drowned. Peter then experiences unbearable grief:

> Wie zwei rasche Nachen waren wir miteinander vorangestürmt, und Richards Nachen war der bunte, leichte, glückliche, geliebte, an dem mein Auge hing und dem ich vertraute, er würde mich zu schönen Zielen mitreißen. Nun war er mit kurzem Schrei versunken, und ich trieb steuerlos auf plötzlich verdunkelten Wassern umher. (67)

> (Like two quick small boats we had rushed forward, and Richard's boat was the colorful one, the light, happy and beloved one, the one upon whom my gaze had rested, the one who I believed would bring me to beautiful places. Now, with a brief cry, he had sunk, and I drifted around without any direction at all on the suddenly darkened waters.)

Not only does this passage convey Peter's grief in an emotional manner that contrasts his feelings for Rösi or Erminia (more on her shortly), but it also reactivates the nature/culture dualism that was discussed in the previous chapter.

Nature, as we saw, represents queer potential in *Peter Camenzind*, whereas culture (such as city life) mostly stands for heteronormativity and social conventions. Let us, therefore, when analyzing the aforementioned quote, view water (an expression of nature) as a signifier for queerness. This "queer water" comes to symbolize a sort of bottomless homosexual threat that men can keep at bay by remaining in their boats (or, like Peter's father, by keeping the boat safe on land). As opposed to the open water, one's boat comes to constitute a controlled existence, characterized by boundaries such as the railing. Men in *Peter Camenzind* must evidently stay within the edges of their boats to not get sucked into an "ocean of homosexuality" of sorts.

Being a failed sailor (as the example of Uncle Konrad shows) means being unable to master one's boat, that is, failing to express masculinity correctly. As *Peter Camenzind* shows, however, queer water does not provide complete release from heteronormativity. As proven by Richard's death, men who disregard heteronormativity to cultivate their same-sex desire are punished by drowning in their own indulgence.

The Girlfriend: Erminia Aglietti

Although this study underscores that heterosexuality in Peter is quite unlikely, he is, nevertheless, involved in an actual heterosexual relationship at one point in the story. At the height of his relationship with Richard, the Italian painter Erminia Aglietti is introduced and for a short while she becomes Peter's girlfriend.

According to Richard, who is acquainted with Erminia already, her skills as an artist are questionable but she herself is a beautiful woman. When he and Peter are looking at one of Erminia's paintings, he says: "es gibt keine schönere Malerin als die, die das gemacht hat." (43) (there is no painter more beautiful than she who has made this.) For looking at the developing Peter/Richard/Erminia triangle, Eve Kosofsky Sedgwick's conception of the erotic triangle is relevant. On the one hand, Richard's comment about Erminia's beauty indicates a potential rivalry between him and Peter, thereby accentuating homoerotic tension between the men. On the other hand, Erminia's entry into the mix makes her a rival for Richard's affection, reactivating Peter's jealousy.

Peter and Richard decide to visit Erminia at a party in her studio, a visit that heightens ambivalence in Peter:

> [W]ir gingen zusammen zur Aglietti, ich mit einigem inneren Widerstreben, denn der freie, etwas burschikose Verkehr Richards und seiner Kameraden mit Malweibern und Studentinnen hatte mir nie gefallen. (44)

> (Together we went to "the Aglietti," I with some inner reluctance, since I had never liked the slack and somewhat childish affairs that Richard and his comrades had with "women painters" and students.)

Yet again we see Peter's tendency to use pejorative terms when talking about women. His use of the term *Malweiber* ("woman painter") to describe Erminia is clearly demeaning. Peter expresses reluctance but he chooses to go with Richard to Erminia's party anyway, a choice that attests to his uncertainty. His ambivalence is detectable in his initial perception of Erminia. After being introduced to each other, Peter (in his typical fashion) glances at her from a distance:

> [D]as Gesicht erschien mir nicht schön. Der Schnitt war scharf und knapp, die Augen ein wenig streng, das Haar reich, schwarz und weich; was mich störte und fast abstieß, war die Farbe des Gesichts. Sie erinnerte mich

schlechterdings an Gorgonzola, und ich wäre nicht erstaunt gewesen, grüne Ritzen darin zu finden. (45)

(To me the face was not beautiful. The features were harsh and tense, the eyes a little strict, the hair rich, black, and soft; what bothered me and was off-putting was the color of the face. It reminded me of Gorgonzola, and it would not have surprised me to find green cracks in it.)

In Kathrine M. Rogers's *The Troublesome Helpmate* (1966), it is hypothesized that one of the reasons that misogyny plagues literary history is the fact that men have written about women more than the other way around. A consequence, Rogers argues, is that "some of the most prominent ideals in literature are of the mistress, the wife, the mother,"[245] figures that are denigrated by means of satiric "jokes." Rogers shows that oftentimes in literature, female characters interfere with the interests of male characters, which can be seen, for instance, in conventions such as "the bad wife/poor husband storyline." She adds that since women "have been described almost entirely from the male point of view, we have from all periods of literature a procession of selfish, exploitative, contentious, trying, bossy, unloving wives."[246] Although Erminia is not Peter's wife, her very presence as a love interest suggests a possibility of a future marriage.

However, thinking of Erminia as a love interest makes Peter's initial description of her even more curious. Equating her face to that of an Italian cheese is not only misogynistic but racist. It is thus rather remarkable when interpretations like Ralph Freedman's manage to heterosexualize the event and characterize Erminia as a woman "whose minutely described pale features resembled many Italian beauties Hesse had seen in life and on canvas."[247] Peter's perception expresses disgust, or at the very least extreme ambivalence.

Comparing the misogynistic portrayal of Erminia to Richard's introduction— in which he is associated with terms such as *schön* (beautiful), *hübsch* (handsome) and *Liebe* (love)—emphasizes quite a contrast. First, Peter clearly states that he does *not* find Erminia particularly beautiful, which might be interpreted as a jealous reaction to Richard finding her attractive. The fact that Peter shortly afterwards claims that he *loves* Erminia is therefore

---

[245] Kathrine M. Rogers, *The Troublesome Helpmate: A History of Misogyny in Literature* (Seattle: University of Washington Press, 1966), 266.

[246] Ibid.

[247] Freedman, *Pilgrim of Crisis*, 114.

paradoxical. Second, it highlights a discrepancy, because in the previous love experience with Rösi Girtanner, Peter noticeably narrated that he is proud to have always loved *beautiful* women.

In contrast to the story with Rösi, in this new heterosexual romance that takes shape, Peter is not the only one who gazes at his love interest from afar—Erminia also watches him back. This reciprocity is portrayed literally since Erminia uses Peter as a model for her paintings:

> In den nächsten Tagen saß ich ihr Stunde um Stunde. Es wurde dabei fast gar nichts gesprochen, ich saß oder stand ruhig und wie verzaubert da, hörte den weichen Strich der Zeichenkohle, sog den leichten Ölfarbegeruch ein und hatte keine andere Empfindung, als daß ich in der Nähe der von mir geliebten Frau war und ihren Blick beständig auf mir ruhen wußte. (51)

> (In the following days I modelled for her hour after hour. We rarely said a word to each other, I sat or stood quietly and with enchantment listened to the soft stroke of the charcoal, inhaled the fine smell of oil paint, and experienced no other sensation than that I was close to the woman I loved, knowing that her eyes constantly rested on me.)

It is interesting that Peter and Erminia hardly speak to each other. It is also telling that watching each other seems sufficient as a social form of interaction to them. While modern bourgeois ideals at the turn of the twentieth century made courtship between unmarried men and women less formalized than before, such expressions do not occur in *Peter Camenzind*. Note that in Peter and Erminia's relationship, no kissing, hand-holding or sexual activity takes place, ever. They look at each other but the context in which they do so is notably dispassionate.

Comparing this non-intimate sociality with Peter and Richard's relationship—especially the make-up gesture between the men, when they console each other after squabbling by rubbing their noses against each other—highlights the contrast. One could of course argue that no obvious hand-holding or sexual activity is portrayed in their relationship either. However, as we could see, *kissing, dancing, hugging, nose-rubbing, skinny dipping involving erotic playfulness*, and *queerness in the shape of homoerotic hints* do characterize their bond. Erotic hints like these are entirely absent in Hesse's depiction of Peter and Erminia's relationship.

Even though Peter's relationship with Erminia comes across as both nonsexual and nonerotic, heteronormativity triggers expectations of sexual engagement between them, which results in tremendous ambivalence in the protagonist. In Rogers's conception, one of the reasons that misogyny frequents literature has to do with "the belief that woman is less spiritual than man. She is supposed to be less capable than he of controlling lust, gluttony, anger, and greed, because these impulses are stronger in her and reason weaker."[248] Following this notion, Erminia's sexuality (which she as a woman is thought to be unable to control) constitutes a threat to the spiritual bond between Peter and Richard. As previously clarified, male same-sex relations make homoeroticism possible without forsaking spiritual ideals such as noble friendship.

All in all, as a portrayal of a romance, Peter and Erminia's relationship comes across as nonpassionate and unharmonious. One sees this lack of emotion in Peter's description of how he feels about her. In the same passage where he describes sitting for her sketches, he also describes his thoughts about the person one loves like this:

> Solche Gedankengänge sind wie gewisse Volks- und Soldatenlieder, worin tausenderlei Dinge vorkommen, der Refrain aber hartnäckig wiederkehrt, auch wo er durchaus nicht paßt. (51)

> (Such thoughts are like certain folk and soldier songs in which thousands of things occur and the refrain stubbornly returns, even where it does not fit at all.)

Evidently, rather than signaling completeness, this quote conveys dissonance. Heterosexuality is equated with a stubborn returning refrain which implies that Erminia's presence is creating pressure for Peter to perform heterosexuality.

Another effect of Erminia's presence in Peter's life is that his readability as a countertype is heightened. During their first encounter at the gathering in Erminia's studio, Peter accidentally makes a fool of himself by devouring the buffet's entire supply of ham. This makes him the laughingstock of the other guests:

> Da man nun leise lachte und ich eigene ironische Blicke einheimste, wurde ich wütend und verwünschte die Italienerin samt ihrem Schinken. (48)

---

[248] Rogers, *The Troublesome Helpmate*, 268.

> (As the others began to laugh, I could feel their ironic looks on me; this made
> me angry, and I cursed the Italian woman and her ham.)

Similar to the actions by which Uncle Konrad is labeled a fool, Peter's foolishness corresponds to George Mosse's idea of the countertype as unmanly.
Interpreted in this way, Peter devouring the entire supply of ham without any
impulse control has effects on his masculinity. In conjunction with the added
pressure of heterosexual performativity that Erminia generates, it is not
surprising that Peter then attempts a heterosexual relationship with her.
Essentially, Peter's romance with Erminia becomes an attempt to mend the
damage that was done to his manliness following the embarrassing incident
with the ham.

After the party, Peter's ambivalence and anxiety bring him to the top of a
hill where he has an emotional outburst:

> [I]ch … legte mich auf die Erde, sprang auf und stöhnte, stampfte den Boden,
> warf den Hut von mir, wühlte mit dem Gesicht im Gras, rüttelte an den
> Baumstämmen, weinte, lachte, schluchzte, tobte, schämte mich, war selig und
> todbeklommen. (50)

> (I lay down on the ground, jumped up and moaned, stamped the ground,
> threw my hat off, pressed my face to the grass, shook the tree trunks, cried,
> laughed, sobbed, raged, felt ashamed, was blessed, and deadly depressed.)

After the outburst he finds a tavern on a remote street: "[ich] trat willenlos
ein, trank zwei Liter Waadtländer und kam gegen Morgen schauderhaft
betrunken nach Hause." (50) (weak-willed I entered, drank two liters of wine
and in the morning, I came home terribly drunk.) As is evident, Peter is
experiencing ambivalence, and, even more so, a crisis of some sort.

The scene plants the seed to what is to become Peter's unhealthy alcohol
habit. In no unclear terms, Peter even discloses that it is his relationship with
Erminia that "erzog mich zum Zecher." (55) (turned me into a drinker.) He
goes on to describe alcohol as "ein Verführer und Bruder des Eros." (55–56)
(a seducer and a brother of Eros.) This is an interesting juxtaposition that
brings Plato's *Symposium* to mind yet again. While the guests in Plato's text
drink lots of wine throughout the evening, they never lose their heads (except
for Alcibiades who forgoes some of his self-restraint when he confesses his
love and admiration for Socrates). One of the main points of *Symposium* is
that self-control constitutes a major characteristic in an ideal man. Peter's

alcoholism signifies a *lack of control* as well as an escape from heterosexual responsibility.

Peter's growing addiction develops in parallel with an ever more prevalent anxiety in him, which is linked to Erminia's presence and heterosexuality. He narrates:

> [K]ein Tag ging ganz ohne Leid vorbei. Manchmal überfiel es mich nachts im Bett, daß ich stöhnte und mich bäumte und spät in Tränen entschlief. Oder es erwachte, wenn ich der Aglietti begegnet war. Meistens aber kam es am Spätnachmittag, wenn die schönen, lauen, müdemachenden Sommerabende begannen. Dann ging ich an den See, nahm ein Boot, ruderte mich heiß und müde und fand es dann unmöglich, nach Hause zu gehen. Also in einer Kneipe. (56–57)

> (Not a single day went by without suffering. Sometimes it came over me when I was in bed at night and I moaned, tossed, and turned, and fell asleep late in tears. Or it turned up after having met "the Aglietti." Mostly, however, it came over me in the late afternoon when the beautiful, mild, and slumberous summer evenings began. Then I went to the lake, took a boat, rowed myself hot and exhausted and found it impossible to return home. So, instead I went to a pub.)

It is obvious that Peter's emotional state is shaky. Performing heterosexuality is linked to terms such as *Leid* (suffering), "Liebeselend" (55) (love misery), and "Unglück." (60) (misfortune.) These terms provide a significant contrast between heterosexual and homosocial relationality in *Peter Camenzind*, and the longer quote above confirms one thing clearly: Peter's suffering arises specifically as a consequence of having met Erminia.

It is worth noting that in Peter's narration, Erminia is rarely addressed by her name. Instead, she is labeled in ways that are characterized either by formality or misogyny, such as *die Aglietti* ("the Aglietti"), *die Italienerin* (the Italian woman) or "[d]ie Malerin" (48) (the female painter), whereas Richard is constantly spoken of with his first name. This difference indicates that there is intimacy and affection in the men's bond which is not to be found in Peter's relationship with Erminia.

Note that the quote above includes a reference to a boat. To manage the anxiety that arises because of Erminia, Peter rows himself tired in a manner that projects an utmost desperation. Boats being bearers of masculine and heterosexual meaning in this novel makes his frantic rowing a symbol for the struggle to live up to heteronormativity. But the struggle ends in exhaustion and Peter turns to alcohol as an escape from his failures. From the perspective of Mosse, who states that lacking impulse control (of which alcoholism is an example) characterizes the countertype, Peter's alcohol abuse confirms an even deeper unmanliness. All in all, heterosexuality has grave effects on his health.

After Erminia's introduction, Peter's alcoholism escalates. His drinking makes him bitter, and he mocks the social practices of people in his surroundings; Peter is scornful of the heteronormative society to which he himself is unable conform:

> [N]un begann ich sie kritisch und ironisch zu betrachten. Mit Vorliebe erfand und erzählte ich kleine Geschichten, in welchen die Verhältnisse der Menschen untereinander lieblos und mit scheinbarer Sachlichkeit satirisch dargestellt und bitter verhöhnt wurden. (57–58)

> (From now on I began to view them [other people] critically and ironically. It amused me to invent and tell stories in which I, objectively, satirically, and bitterly, mocked their relationships and portrayed them as callous.)

It is evident that Peter longs for something else, something other than the heteronormativity of his surroundings. In his dreams there is "ein Ziel, ein Glück, eine Vollendung vor mir." (58) (a goal, a happiness, a completion that awaits me.) This longing, however, is difficult for him to define: "Ich wußte noch nicht," he narrates, "daß ich an einer Sehnsucht litt, welcher nicht Liebe noch Ruhm Grenze und Erfüllung sind." (58–59) (I did not yet know that I was suffering from a yearning that neither love nor glory could fulfill.) The completion Peter desires is herein interpreted as the utopian queerness he longs to cultivate with Richard. But their relationship is interrupted after Erminia's introduction, and the interruption corresponds to Rogers's previously discussed argument that misogynous perceptions in literature oftentimes derive from female characters interfering with the interests of male characters.

The interruption, however, only lasts a short while. The relationship with Erminia ends seemingly undramatically (the reader is not privy to a break-up scene), and Peter returns to Richard, who he has "ein wenig vernach-lässigt." (60) (neglected a little bit.) What follows in the story is the journey to Florence, after which the men part ways and Richard dies. This incident does not pave the way for Peter and Erminia's relationship to be resumed though. In fact, she subsequently disappears from the story without any fuss being made about it.

It was mentioned earlier that Peter spends some time in Paris after Richard's death. There he engages in a decadent lifestyle and his alcohol habits intensify. He becomes asocial, withdraws from others, and is completely consumed by his grief:

> Ich hatte das Gefühl einer schauerlichen Einsamkeit. Zwischen mir und den Menschen und dem Leben der Stadt, der Plätze, Häuser und Straßen war fortwährend eine breite Kluft. (70)

> (I felt terribly lonely. Between others and myself and the life of the city—the squares, houses, and streets—was a constant and wide gap.)

On top of his terrible loneliness, Peter wonders what "Hemmnis oder Dämon" (75) (obstacle or demon) possesses him. He narrates:

> Dabei hatte ich auch noch den sonderbaren Gedanken, mich für einen aparten, irgendwie zu kurz gekommenen Menschen zu halten, dessen Leiden niemand kenne, verstehe oder teile. (75)

> (At the same time, curiously, I also considered myself to be an unusual individual who had fallen short, and whose suffering nobody knew, could understand or share.)

As we can see, Peter describes his body and soul as being possessed by a demonic force. The imagery of having a demon inside signifies that there is something deviant within him. Peter's demonic possession—which utters itself via an unsympathetic, bitter, alienated, and grieving aura around him—makes him repellent to others. He is no longer hopeful that there is a brighter future ahead. Richard having suddenly died has erased the potential for a queer utopia.

Furthermore, Peter labels himself *apart* (special, or unusual), which from a queer-theoretical standpoint is noteworthy. Unusualness can be seen as a synonym for "weirdness," "oddness" or "strangeness" and is thus a signifier for queerness, which makes Peter's expressed isolation in the above-mentioned quote linked to Richard's sudden death. Before Richard passed away both men existed in a shared queerness that they considered normal, whereas Peter, at this point in the story, is completely alone in being queer (as far as he knows at least). The point here is this: The queerness that Peter considered normal when Richard was around is now deemed unusual because he is no longer alive.

The Friend: Elisabeth

It is now time to direct our attention toward this chapter's key character, Elisabeth, who is the third woman with whom Peter is socially involved. As previously mentioned, his bond with her is different from the other different-sex relationships in the text. When Peter meets Elisabeth his ambivalence toward heterosexuality is still prevalent, although it is not as profoundly and misogynistically articulated as during his relationship with Erminia.

Elisabeth is initially described as beautiful: "während des Betrachtens entdeckte ich allmählich mit naiver Finderfreude, daß sie sehr schön war." (79) (as I watched her, I began to discover with naïve joy that she was very beautiful.) In Peter's typical fashion he does, however, merely a moment later change his mind about her:

> Sie ging weg und wurde bald darauf genötigt, Klavier zu spielen. Sie spielte gut. Aber da ich hinzutrat, sah ich, daß sie nicht mehr so schön war. (79)

> (She walked away and shortly afterwards she was encouraged to play the piano. She played well but as I walked closer, I saw that she was not so beautiful anymore.)

Peter changing his mind about Elisabeth's beauty does not necessarily have to be interpreted as an expression of heterosexual ambivalence. His reaction likely arises because of her playing the piano: up until this point in the story, piano playing has been exclusively associated with Richard. When Richard was introduced, Peter narrated:

> Jeden Tag hörte ich ihn unten Klavier spielen und spürte dabei zum erstenmal etwas vom Zauber der Musik, der weiblichsten und süßesten Kunst. (37)

> (Every day I heard him playing the piano downstairs and for the first time I experienced the magic of music, the most feminine and sweetest of the arts.)

Elisabeth playing the piano seems to reawaken Peter's memories of Richard, which stirs up grief, makes him sad and bitter, and it accentuates his loneliness. Therefore, Peter's doubts regarding Elisabeth are likely not an expression of heterosexual ambivalence (as in the relationship with Erminia). While

Peter oscillates back and forth between finding Elisabeth beautiful and not finding her beautiful, she is portrayed with a radically different language than the other women. This is evident when Peter notices Elisabeth in an art museum and watches her:

> Sie stand in meiner Nähe vor einem großen Segantini und war ganz in das Bild versunken. Es stellte ein paar auf mageren Matten arbeitende Bauernmädchen dar, hinten die zackig jähen Berge, etwa an die Stockhorngruppe erinnernd, und darüber in einem kühlen, lichten Himmel eine unsäglich genial gemalte, elfenbeinfarbene Wolke. … Offenbar verstand Elisabeth diese Wolke, denn sie war ganz dem Anschauen hingegeben. … Die Schönheit und Wahrhaftigkeit eines großen Kunstwerkes zwang ihre Seele, selbst schön und wahrhaftig und unverhüllt sich darzustellen. Ich saß still daneben, betrachtete die schöne Segantiniwolke und das schöne von ihr entzückte Mädchen. Dann fürchtete ich, sie möchte sich umwenden, mich sehen und anreden und ihre Schönheit wieder verlieren, und ich verließ den Saal schnell und leise. (80)

> (She stood near me in front of a large Segantini painting and was completely immersed in the motif. A couple of peasant girls were pictured, working on a meagre meadow; behind them the steep, pointy hills, reminiscent of the Stockhorn mountain rose and above them, in a cool, clear sky, an indescribable and ingeniously painted ivory-colored cloud. Elisabeth clearly understood this cloud because she watched it with complete devotion. It was the beauty and truthfulness of this great work of art that made her soul present itself, equally beautiful, true, and sincere. I sat there quietly and watched the beautiful Segantini cloud and the beautiful girl that was enamored by it. Then I suddenly was frightened that she would turn around and see me, talk to me, and lose her beauty once more, so I left the museum hall quickly and quietly.)

First, let us linger on the cloud in the painting. Peter's narration emphasizes this cloud, which is not surprising given that his love for nature is conveyed with imagery involving these objects. As we have seen, clouds signify Peter's desire to explore and also his longing for nature when urban life becomes overwhelming. In essence, nature is a place where Peter feels safe. Therefore, in this context, Elisabeth sharing his affection for nature (which is expressed by her looking at a work by the Italian landscape painter Giovanni Segantini [1858–1899] who is particularly known for painting the Alps) signifies that she may be a safe person for Peter to be around.

Peter's evolving feelings for Elisabeth show that she neither evokes pressure to perform heterosexuality in the way that Erminia did, nor is it her higher-class status (which mirror Rösi's) that results in the ambivalent feelings in the museum. There is still uncertainty to be discerned, of course, and Peter leaves because he fears that Elisabeth would lose her beauty if she spoke, but this is likely due to Peter's wish to savor the beauty of the moment rather than to escape the pressures of heterosexuality.

One could argue that it is not Elisabeth's beauty as such that is acknowledged in the above-quoted passage but rather that she (like Peter) acknowledges *nature's* beauty, which is portrayed in Segantini's painting. In such an interpretation it is Elisabeth's fascination for the painting that leads to her own beauty being recognized by Peter. The splendor of the great work of art makes her attractiveness apparent. The fact that Elisabeth is a woman (women having previously been exclusively linked to heterosexuality) comes across as unthreatening when she is linked with nature in this way.

First and foremost, Elisabeth's presence seems to strengthen Peter's love of nature, whereas the potential for a heterosexual romance is downplayed in comparison. In Angelika Rauch-Rapaport's interpretation, Elisabeth is one of Hesse's "Madonna-like women" or "Earth Mothers," whose function in the text is to convey ideas or be an inspiration for the protagonist. "In general," Rauch-Rapaport writes, "Hesse's wanderers, though they do experience things, merely observe life, but are not entangled in it, a habit which gets them out of any commitment to another."[249] This lack of engagement certainly describes the heterosexual bonds in *Peter Camenzind*, but not the novel's homosocial relationships or the protagonist's affection for nature. Even Rauch-Rapaport herself states: "Community and mutual relations are side-stepped for an imagined harmony with elements of nature."[250] As we have seen already, nature is associated with the relationship between Peter and Richard. Nature's forests, mountains, and meadows are described in a similar manner as Richard is characterized; essentially, as *loveable*:

> Und so begann ich diese Dinge zu lieben. Es kam ein starkes, dürstendes Verlangen in mir ihrer stillen Schönheit entgegen. (80)

> (And so, I began to love these things. Within me there was a strong, thirsting desire for their quiet beauty.)

---

[249] Rauch-Rapaport, "The Melancholic Structure," 85.
[250] Ibid.

And:

> Indem ich nun anfing, die Natur persönlich zu lieben, ihr zu lauschen wie
> einem Kameraden und Reisegefährten, der eine fremde Sprache redet, ward
> meine Schwermut zwar nicht geheilt, aber veredelt und gereinigt. (82)

> (As I began to love nature, to listen to it like a friend and a traveling com-
> panion who speaks a foreign language, my melancholy was not entirely healed
> but ennobled and purified.)

Here Peter compares nature to a "friend and a traveling companion" which
brings to mind Richard and their journey to Italy. In addition, the fact that
Peter underscores that nature "ennobles" his melancholy accentuates a
connection with Plato's *Symposium* and its homoerotically charged *noble*
friendships between men. This quote strengthens the novel's intertwinement
of queerness and nature.

Throughout the story, both nature and Richard are portrayed as loveable,
honest, and true, whereas heterosexuality has overwhelmingly negative
connotations. Although these connotations do not cease completely after
Elisabeth's introduction, she herself is not primarily linked to heterosexuality
in the way that Erminia and Rösi were. Rather, she is linked with hetero-
sociality which is slightly less imposing.

Let us dwell for a moment on how the homosociality/heterosociality
dualism is manifested in *Peter Camenzind*. If one compares the two contexts
and asks which contains the most eroticism, it will rapidly become obvious
that male homosociality is far more erotic than Peter and Elisabeth's heterosociality. At the same time, viewing homosociality/heterosociality as equivalent with homosexuality/heterosexuality does not yield identical implications.
As an effect of heteronormativity, heterosociality oftentimes includes an
expectation of heterosexual desire, even if such desire never materializes (as
in Peter and Elisabeth's friendship).

Even though Elisabeth's presence raises some expectations of heterosexual
relationality for the novel's protagonist, she is fundamentally different from
the previous female love interests, chiefly because she is not truly a love
interest in the romantic meaning. Rather, we shall see, she becomes a loving
friend to Peter: "Sie begrüßte mich gütig, sogar herzlich und mit einer
vertrauten Freundschaftlichkeit, die mich glücklich machte." (85) (She
greeted me kindly, even warmly and with a familiar friendliness that made
me happy.) Elisabeth's actions pave the way for Peter's friendship with her,

and the two of them form a respectful bond that comes to challenge previous iterations of different-sex relations in the text, which therefore makes it a queer friendship. Peter and Elisabeth's friendship provides a queer speck of light in the bottomless pit of alienation and grief in which Peter has dwelled since Richard's death.

The protagonist, however, is still longing for something more: "meine Umgebung [gab] mir [nicht] die Menschen … die ich suchte" (100) (my surroundings did not provide me with the people I needed), he narrates, adding: "Mit Sehnsucht dachte ich an Italien." (100) (With desire I thought of Italy.) The longing back to Italy shows that Richard is still on Peter's mind, and it also reactivates Florence's connection with homosexuality. Heather Love states that while there is a danger in naturalizing the link between homosexuality and melancholia, "critiquing such a link ought to be distinguished from denying its existence."[251] Whether we like it or not, Love explains, "[s]ame-sex desire is marked by a long history of association with failure, impossibility, and loss."[252] This relationship, she argues, "has given queers special insight into love's failures and impossibilities (as well as, of course, wild hopes for its future)."[253] By not being able to get over the loss of Richard and their mutual hopes for a queer utopia, Peter exemplifies all of these arguments.

The reference to Italy shows that Peter's queerness is still active at this point in the story, despite his newly formed heterosocial bond with Elisabeth, which indicates that their friendship originates in something other than heterosexual desire. Curiously, even while Peter considers proposing marriage to Elisabeth, he acknowledges his own hesitation toward it:

> Bisher war ich von meiner völligen Unfähigkeit zur Ehe so überzeugt gewesen, daß ich mich darein mit bissiger Ironie ergeben hatte. Ich war Dichter, Wanderer, Trinker, Einspänner! (85)

> (Up until now, I had been utterly convinced of my incompatibility with marriage and with a biting irony I had accepted that fact. I was a writer, wanderer, drinker, loner!)

Apart from describing himself as a masculine countertype ("wanderer, drinker, loner"), heterosexual marriage is not upheld as romantic but

---

[251] Love, *Feeling Backward*, 20.
[252] Ibid., 21.
[253] Ibid., 23.

depicted as having a *practical* rather than an emotional purpose: "Jetzt glaubte ich mein Schicksal zu erkennen, das mir in der Möglichkeit einer Liebesehe die Brücke zur Menschenwelt schlagen wollte." (85) (Now I believed I could see my fate and that marriage could be a bridge between myself and humanity.) Being married to Elisabeth could, in Peter's words, be "a bridge between himself and humanity." Heterosexuality is endorsed as a form of salvation for Peter, the queer outsider. Hesse's text thereby imposes the idea that no matter how queer a person is, heteronormativity offers another, less troublesome way of life towards which one ought to strive.

When Peter finds out that Elisabeth is already engaged to another man his reaction is one of relief. Instead of mourning the lost opportunity for marriage, Peter is content with being her friend: "Die neue Liebe war doch stärker als ihre älteren Schwestern. Sie war auch stiller, bescheidener und dankbarer." (106) (This new love was stronger than her "older sisters." It was also softer, humbler, and more grateful.) Just as with Rösi, a sister metaphor is used to describe a different-sex relation, which confirms Peter and Elisabeth's relationship as nonsexual.

The use of the word *dankbar* (grateful) is especially telling. It is as if Peter's gratefulness arises because a marriage is impossible. As is evident at this point, female characters in *Peter Camenzind* are introduced simply to be rejected as love interests. Elisabeth's engagement paves the way for her loving queer friendship with Peter to flourish. Contrary to Erminia and Rösi, Elisabeth is never portrayed with misogynistic language, which is likely an effect of heterosexuality not being enforced by her. Furthermore, Peter's melancholia and status as an outsider are lessened after having become Elisabeth's friend. We see this indicated by a surprisingly harmonious reference to Peter and a boat: "Um mir die gute Stimmung zu bewahren, nahm ich ein Boot und ruderte behaglich langsam in den warmen, lichten See." (106) (To maintain my good mood, I took a boat and rowed slowly and comfortably on the warm, clear lake.)

As previously argued, boats in *Peter Camenzind* express heterosexuality, and this quote indicates that expectations of heterosexuality in Peter have evened out. At this point in the story, he is evidently able to master his boat without turning into a heterosexual man, conforming to heteromasculine norms. The waters on which Peter now rows are neither dark nor stormy, and it is apparent he has come closer to finding equilibrium. Heterosexuality no longer creates ambivalence or anxiety in Peter because heterosexuality is no longer something he is forced to perform.

Peter's emotional state is now characterized by satisfaction with the heterosocial bond that Elisabeth provides. At this point in this Bildungsroman, when the end is drawing closer, Peter's Bildung is about to be completed and Elisabeth turns out to be of great importance in Peter's learning process. Her friendliness helps facilitate his growth into a compassionate human being, which, as we shall see in the next chapter, has positive effects on the novel's second major male relationship.

"A Friendly and Neighborly Manner"

The fourth and final woman with whom Peter is socially involved is Signora Annunziata Nardini, a thirty-four-year-old Italian widow who he befriends when he wanders in Italy after Richard's death. In contrast to the previous women, Signora Nardini falls head over heels in love with Peter. Although Peter does not desire her, he still considers marriage. One of the main reasons why he finally decides not to marry Signora Nardini is that he wants to return to Switzerland and begin writing his novel. Whatever the reason, what is noteworthy is that in the previous relationships the women have been (more or less) romantically indifferent to Peter, whereas Signora Nardini is not. Even so, Peter still rejects heterosexual relationality.

As this chapter has showed, heterosexual ambivalence can be seen as a manifestation of queerness in *Peter Camenzind*. By juxtaposing Peter's relationships with women with his relationship with Richard, the latter comes across as a significantly more loving bond (with, perhaps, the sole exception of Peter and Elisabeth's respectful queer friendship).

At the end of the novel, when Peter returns home to care for his elderly father, the thematic link between him and his Uncle Konrad becomes significant again. The two men, neither of whom is married or romantically involved with someone, reminisce about Peter's father's old boat, which is now spoken of with an affirmative nostalgia:

> "Mußt Segel nehmen, Onkel Konrad", munterte ich ihn auf, und über dem Segel kamen wir dann jedesmal auf unsern alten Nachen zu sprechen, welcher nimmer da war und den er wie einen lieben Toten beklagte. Da auch mir das alte Stück lieb gewesen war und nun fehlte, gedachten wir seiner und aller mit ihm passierten Geschichten bis ins kleinste. (130)

> ("You must raise the sail, Uncle Konrad," I used to say to cheer him up, and this always led us to speak about our old boat which did not exist anymore and whom he lamented like a deceased loved one. Since the old thing had

been dear to me as well and I missed it, we remembered it and spoke in detail of all the stories that were linked with it.)

What used to be a mocking phrase—"'Mußt Segel nehmen, Konrad!'" ("You must raise the sail, Konrad!")—has now grown into something that cheers Peter and Konrad up, indicating that both men have come to terms with their status as outsiders. Now they recall their experiences of embodying difference with a certain form of fondness, as if their social trials have helped shape and strengthen their characters. Peter narrates: "Meine paar Zickzackflüge im Reich des Geistes und der sogenannten Bildung lassen sich füglich der berühmten Segelfahrt des Oheims vergleichen." (132) (My excursions into the realm of the intellectual and the so-called Bildung are very much comparable to my uncle's famous sailing trip.)

Peter pointing out the similarities between himself and Konrad emphasize their kinship. Both, in a sense, have failed to achieve heteronormative completeness. However, as the overall ambience of contentment and joy around Peter and Konrad shows at the end, neither have allowed their failure to force them into sadness or despair. Peter (who among other things has been linked with alcoholism and asocial behavior) is portrayed as thriving by not conforming. He gains a reputation in the village for being an upstanding and reasonable individual who speaks in a "[freundnachbarlich]" (131) (friendly and neighborly) manner. This is a considerable progress from the bottomless pit of grief in which Peter dwelt after Richard's death, a time when he was hateful of others.

If we recall Franco Moretti's statement that protagonists in Bildungsromane are forced to conform to normality and if they fail to do so must leave social life, *Peter Camenzind* nuances a genre convention. While he finally is part of village sociality, he does not need to conform to all its norms. He remains an outsider but gains a reputation for being an upstanding person. In effect, *Peter Camenzind* underlines that being "reasonable"—that is, sensible, practical, realistic, or intelligent—has absolutely nothing to do with an individual's ability (or desire) to conform to a heterosexual lifestyle.

CHAPTER 3

Facing the Other

Disability and Otherness

The main expression of otherness in *Peter Camenzind* can be identified in and around the character Boppi, whom Peter befriends after his school years and Richard's death. The affectionate bond between Peter and Boppi mirrors Peter's relationship with Richard—and can also be seen as a same-sex romance—but this chapter has wider implications. Continuing to highlight the ways with which queerness is manifested in *Peter Camenzind*, this chapter will examine how Boppi's disability works as a catalyst for expressions of queer/crip kinship in the text.

Although Boppi is essential to the way with which the conceptual link between queerness and disability is expressed in *Peter Camenzind*, the text never grants him the same amount of agency as the novel's eponymous character. Therefore, David T. Mitchell and Sharon L. Snyder's concept "narrative prosthesis" is suitable to draw on. Mitchell and Snyder suggest that a narrative prosthesis is a disabled character that is used as a mere prop in service of the personal development of an able-bodied protagonist.[254] This concept will be explained in detail under the next heading.

A common goal of queer theories and crip theory is critique of various forms of normativity. As previously clarified, queer theories challenge hegemonies and any queer theory's signifying trait is critique of ideas of what is considered desirable or normal. While queer theorists often direct their critique toward heteronormativity (that is, the assumption that people are cisgender and heterosexual), crip-theorists tend to critique ableist ideals of functionality (that is, the assumption that people are able-bodied).

Robert McRuer calls able-bodiedness compulsory for human beings and argues that "the system of compulsory able-bodiedness, which in a sense produces disability, is thoroughly interwoven with the system of compulsory heterosexuality that produces queerness."[255] In pointing out these parallels, McRuer illustrates, on the one hand, the potential for kinship between queer

---

[254] See David T. Mitchell and Sharon L. Snyder, *Narrative Prosthesis: Disability and the Dependencies of Discourse* (Ann Arbor: University of Michigan Press, 2000).

[255] Robert McRuer, *Crip Theory: Cultural Signs of Queerness and Disability* (New York: New York University Press, 2006), 2.

and disabled individuals and, on the other hand, the conceptual entanglement of queer and crip theories.

Throughout history disabled people have, just like queer people, been pathologized and labeled deviant and unnatural. Disabled people, however, are still commonly thought of as in need of repair, viewed as socioeconomic liabilities, or deemed unproductive and weak. Mitchell and Snyder state that disabled individuals are oftentimes regarded as "stubbornly inhuman."[256] And, as they argue elsewhere, narrative literature has a long history of relying on disability to convey conceptions of otherness:

> Most basic to the identification of character through disability is the way in which physical and cognitive differences have been narrated as alien to the normal course of human affairs. To represent disability is to engage oneself in an encounter with that which is believed to be off the map of "recognizable" human experiences. Making comprehensible that which appears to be inherently unknowable situates narrative in the powerful position of mediator between two separate worlds.[257]

In addition to Mitchell and Snyder's thoughts on literature, disability, and otherness, Judith Butler's writing on the concept of "precariousness" highlights how the bodies of Others—like disabled Others—exist in a particular state of vulnerability.[258] As will be substantiated shortly, vulnerability is a theme that frequents the passages that Boppi takes part in.

---

[256] David T. Mitchell and Sharon L. Snyder, "Introduction: Disability Studies and the Double Bind of Representation," in *The Body and Physical Difference: Discourses of Disability*, ed. David T. Mitchell and Sharon L. Snyder (Ann Arbor: University of Michigan Press, 1997), 4.

[257] Mitchell and Snyder, *Narrative Prosthesis*, 5–6.

[258] However, one ought to bear in mind, as Ellen Samuels points out, that applying Judith Butler's theories in the field of disability studies might be problematic. "Despite the obvious applicability of many of Butler's insights to the central questions of disability studies," she writes, "her work was largely absent from the seminal published works of disability studies, even in the writings of scholars who explicitly drew upon and aligned themselves with feminist and gender theory." (Ellen Samuels, "Critical Divides: Judith Butler's Body Theory and the Question of Disability," in *Feminist Disability Studies*, ed. Kim Q. Hall [Bloomington: Indiana University Press, 2011], 50–51.) Furthermore, Samuels explains, one potential problem with putting Butler's conceptions into dialogue with disability scholarship is that oftentimes terms such as "gender" and "sexuality" are merely swapped for "disability," which has the inevitable result that the specificity of the disabled experience is disregarded. "In its most extreme forms," Samuels maintains, "this exchange can become an apparent substitution that suggests a direct correspondence or equation between two very different realms of social and bodily existence." (Ibid., 54.)

Butler writes:

> The body ... is where we encounter a range of perspectives that may or may not be our own. How I am encountered, and how I am sustained, depends fundamentally on the social and political networks in which this body lives, how I am regarded and treated, and how that regard and treatment facilitates this life or fails to make it livable. ... [N]ormative frameworks establish in advance what kind of life will be a life worth living, what life will be a life worth preserving, and what life will become worthy of being mourned.[259]

Although Butler does not specifically refer to disability, the corporeality of which she speaks is useful here since Boppi's physical body stands out as the primary signifier of his difference. In the following it will be revealed that attitudes toward Boppi's disabled body—how this character is treated by others and whether the narrative deems him "livable"—effects both his and Peter's narrative fates.

"Narrative Prosthesis"

In *Narrative Prosthesis: Disability and the Dependencies of Discourse* (2000), Mitchell and Snyder propose that "disability pervades literary narrative, first, as a stock feature of characterization and, second, as an opportunistic metaphorical device."[260] The authors give literature's dependency on disability the name "narrative prosthesis," a phrase that "is meant to indicate that disability has been used throughout history as a crutch upon which literary narratives lean for their representational power, disruptive potentiality, and analytical insight."[261] Essentially, disabled literary characters are employed as mere props to be used in service of the personal development of able-bodied protagonists.

While disability has the potential to be a disruptive force that resists ideas of normalcy in literary narratives, it is, however, often enmeshed in other associations. Mitchell and Snyder write: "The inherent vulnerability and variability of bodies serves literary narratives as a metonym for that which refuses to conform to the mind's desire for order and rationality."[262] That is, the vulnerability that is frequently attributed to disabled characters tends to divert attention from a structural issue, namely normative culture's inability

---

[259] Judith Butler, *Frames of War: When is Life Grievable?* (London: Verso, 2009), 53.
[260] Mitchell and Snyder, *Narrative Prosthesis*, 47.
[261] Ibid., 49.
[262] Ibid., 48.

to acknowledge bodily difference as anything other than something in need of "fixing," "treatment," "rescue," and the like. In narrative fiction, therefore, disabled characters tend to emerge as *problems to be solved*.

In Mitchell and Snyder's conception, this "problem-solving trope" has a schematic structure consisting of four narrative stages:

> [F]irst, a deviance or marked difference is exposed to a reader; second, a narrative consolidates the need for its own existence by calling for an explanation of the deviation's origins and formative consequences; third, the deviance is brought from the periphery of concerns to the center of the story to come; and fourth, the remainder of the story rehabilitates or fixes the deviance in some manner.[263]

As we shall see throughout this chapter, Boppi's function in *Peter Camenzind* follows this schema. As such, he embodies Mitchell and Snyder's notion that "[d]isability marks a character as 'unlike' the rest of a fiction's cast, and once singled out, the character becomes a case of special interest who retains originality to the detriment of all other characteristics."[264]

While Boppi is disabled (which will momentarily be exemplified with textual examples) and thereby functions as the main expression of otherness in Hesse's novel, one should bear in mind that, as a character, he is also an *individual* who the text overall denies any form of personal agency. Although the interpretation in this chapter will emphasize Boppi's vulnerability/precariousness, it will also attempt to treat disability as something other than a problem to be solved.

Queerness in Emmanuel Levinas's Ethics

Alongside Judith Butler's ideas of precariousness and Mitchell and Snyder's narrative prosthesis concept, this chapter will also make use of notions of otherness voiced by philosopher Emmanuel Levinas. It should be noted from the outset that including Levinas's work in a queer/crip-theoretical analysis is not an obvious choice. In most of Levinas's writings he entertains a rather rigid and dualistic idea of gender (masculinity and femininity are perceived as opposites with inherent and gender-specific traits) and his writings project a heteronormative view on sexuality.

---

[263] Mitchell and Snyder, *Narrative Prosthesis*, 53.
[264] Ibid., 55–56.

For these reasons, Levinas's usefulness to queer theory has hitherto been quite underutilized.[265] But there are aspects of Levinasian ethics that can be employed within queer frameworks, primarily that he always emphasizes the importance of acknowledging the Other's otherness. Levinas writes that "the other is what I myself am not. … [N]ot because of the Other's character, or physiognomy, or psychology, but because of the Other's very alterity."[266] Essentially, to Levinas, the Other is to be considered entirely other and unique in their own right.

Levinas's contemplations entail a respect for difference that is promising to queer scholarship since his reverence for the Other's "very alterity" (what makes someone unique) can be seen as an expression of the belief that those who are deemed different by normative frameworks should not have their character traits, sense of self, or agency ascribed to them, or forcefully imprinted on them by those with privilege and power. In this study, Levinas's non-limiting view on difference is understood as an encouragement of diversity. This idea has previously been voiced by Robin Podolsky who highlights the queer core in Levinasian ethics: "[Levinas's] work champions multiplicity and pluralism, insisting on the uniqueness of the individual."[267] This description would suit almost any project with a foundation in identity politics and Levinas himself has suggested that identity and experience constitute one's understanding of the world. He writes: "language refers to the positions of the listener and the speaker, that is, to the contingency of their story."[268] In so doing, Levinas suggests that an individual's status in the world determines how they perceive the world. This idea can be seen as a conceptual predecessor to situated knowledge, a concept we previously explained as feminist objectivity based on embodiment and experience.

A final important aspect of Levinasian ethics that is significant in this reading of *Peter Camenzind* is his thoughts on *responsibility*. Levinas writes:

---

[265] Marc Demont underscores an undeveloped queer potential in Levinas's work and suggests that the philosopher's notion of the "face-to-face" (an encounter in which one realizes the Other's vulnerability as well as one's own) "is probably one of the most polemical and useful aspects to develop a queer ethics." (Marc Demont, "Caressing Radical Alterity: For a Queer Ethic of Embodiment in Contemporary Films and Literature" (PhD diss., University of South Carolina, 2017), 30, doi: https://scholarcommons. sc.edu/etd/4046 (accessed January 14, 2022). Although Demont's insightful analysis is rewarding, its emphases do not align with the aims of this study and is thus not referenced in the following. For further reading on queer potential in Levinas's thinking, see pages 27–43 in Demont's above-quoted work.

[266] Emmanuel Levinas, *Time and the Other [and other essays]*, trans. Richard A. Cohen (Pittsburgh: Duquesne University Press, 1987), 83.

[267] Robin Podolsky, "L'Aimé qui est l'aimée. Can Levinas' Beloved Be Queer?" *European Judaism* 48, no. 2 (2016): 50.

[268] Emmanuel Levinas, *Humanism of the Other*, trans. Nidra Poller (Urbana: University of Illinois Press, 2006), 11.

"The Other is, for example, the weak, the poor, 'the widow and the orphan,' … whereas I am the rich or the powerful."[269] He declares that when one encounters the Other "face-to-face" (which can be understood as truly *seeing* the Other and acknowledging their presence), one is bound by responsibility: "The expression the face introduces into the world does not defy the feebleness of my powers, but my ability for power."[270] Responsibility for the Other should be an instant response, Levinas claims, not least for those wielding power, and herein lies our humanity. Judith Butler also notes this, draws on Levinasian ethics, and writes: "To respond to the face, to understand its meaning, means to be awake to what is precarious in another life or, rather, the precariousness of life itself."[271]

We will, in a moment, move on to the interpretation of Peter and Boppi's relationship. Before doing so, however, let us note that this chapter makes use of two frameworks of otherness: otherness in the shape of disability and otherness in the Levinasian sense. Both definitions influence each other but they are not to be seen as a single theoretical perspective. Levinas's emphasis on responsibility for vulnerable Others is herein understood as a call for solidarity, equality, and justice that is advantageous to queer/crip-oriented political ends. His thoughts on the Other are thus understood in a conceptual sense, existing primarily on an intellectual level, whereas otherness in the shape of disability has a corporeal implication and is grounded in situated experience.

Regarding this difference, Sara Ahmed has voiced noteworthy criticism of Levinas. Ahmed writes that Levinas "erases the question of how a particular other may become a force in the ethical relation, rather than a term *through which otherness mediates its force*. In this sense, the figuring of the other as the dispossessed does not deal with the material embodiment of those who are dispossessed from moral discourse."[272] Ahmed emphasizes that Levinas's theoretical thinking about otherness does little (if anything) to support marginalized individuals in vulnerable positions. Consequently, an effort to put Levinasian ethics into dialogue with crip theory is a prospect with much potential. While these two distinct perspectives on otherness are not inter-

---

[269] Levinas, *Time and the Other*, 83.

[270] Emmanuel Levinas, *Totality and Infinity. An Essay on Exteriority*, trans. Alphonso Lingis (Pittsburgh: Duquesne University Press, 2016), 198.

[271] Judith Butler, *Precarious Life: The Powers of Mourning and Violence* (London: Verso, 2004), 134.

[272] Sara Ahmed, *Differences that Matter: Feminist Theory and Postmodernism* (Cambridge: Cambridge University Press, 1998), 61.

changeable in and of themselves, they clearly intersect in the portrayal of Boppi, as we shall see.

Boppi's Introduction

In the penultimate chapter of *Peter Camenzind* (after Richard's death and the time spent in Paris, but before Peter returns to his home village), Peter visits the home of a carpenter where Boppi is introduced. Boppi's presence immediately evokes reluctance in the protagonist: "ein armer, halbgelähmter Verwachsener, für welchen nach dem kürzlich erfolgten Tod seiner alten Mutter nirgends sich ein Plätzchen gefunden hatte." (108) (a poor, half-paralyzed monstrosity without a place to stay after the recent death of his old mother.) In addition:

> Widerstrebend hatte ihn der Schreiner einstweilen zu sich genommen, und die beständige Gegenwart des kranken Krüppels lag wie ein Schrecken auf dem gestörten Hauswesen. (108)

> (Unwillingly, the carpenter had taken him in for the time being, but the presence of the sickly cripple hung horribly over the household.[273])

Boppi, who is the brother of the carpenter's wife, is portrayed as a tremendous burden to the family, which mirrors assertions made in Walter Fandrey's *Krüppel, Idioten, Irre: Zur Sozialgeschichte behinderter Menschen in Deutschland* (1990) about living conditions for—and attitudes toward—disabled people in Germany from the Middle Ages and onward. Fandrey's study shows that at the end of the nineteenth century, the common social convic-

---

[273] While the term "cripple" is oftentimes used as a derogatory label within able-bodied culture, the term has (similarly to "queer") been reclaimed within the field of disability studies and crip theory. As Eli Clare writes: "*Queer* and *cripple* are cousins: words to shock, words to infuse with pride and self-love, words to resist internalized hatred, words to help forge a politics. They have been gladly chosen—*queer* by many gay, lesbian, bi, and trans peoples, *cripple*, or *crip*, by many disabled people." (Eli Clare, *Exile & Pride: Disability, Queerness, and Liberation* [Durham: Duke University Press, 2015], 84.) Mitchell and Snyder describe the act referred to by Clare as "transgressive reappropriation." They write: "Perversely championing the terms of their own stigmatization, marginal peoples alarm the dominant culture with a canniness about their own subjugation. The embrace of denigrating terminology forces the dominant culture to face its own violence head-on because the authority of devaluation has been claimed openly and ironically. Thus, the minority culture deflects the stigmatizing definition back on to the offenders by openly advertising them in public discourse. The effect shames the dominant culture into a recognition of its own dehumanizing precepts. What was most devalued is now righted by a self-naming that detracts from the original power of the condescending terms." (Mitchell and Snyder, *Narrative Prosthesis*, 35–36.) It bears underscoring that transgressive reappropriation is a current strategy to criticize dominant culture's subjugation of minorities. As a literary character, Boppi has not chosen the term cripple for himself—Hermann Hesse has done this for him.

tion was that physical and cognitive deviances were not only degenerate traits in individual family members but something that shamed the entire family.[274] Beliefs that alcoholism, poverty, and lower-class status were underlying reasons for disability resulted in stigma for entire households. Therefore, the demeaning attitude toward Boppi among the members of his own family are most likely a means of creating distance between themselves and him, that is, an attempt to forego their own social stigma and humiliation.

As we can see by Boppi's introduction, his otherness is accentuated straightaway. The protagonist and the reader are confronted with a character who is portrayed as a spectacle, which reminds us of the purpose of freak shows in the nineteenth and early twentieth centuries. In the words of Eli Clare: "the freak show probably was one big melting pot of difference and otherness."[275] And as a form of "entertainment," Clare explains, the freak show helped establish "an exaggerated divide between 'normal' and Other."[276] The process of differentiation between normal and grotesque that was perpetuated by the freak show abetted the marginalization of disabled people. Essentially, Clare concludes, disabled individuals "became freaks," not by means of natural selection but *because of the freak show*.[277]

Boppi's introduction mirrors the procedure described by Clare. Overall, he is depicted as a horrific freak and a burden:

> Man hatte sich noch nicht an ihn gewöhnt; den Kindern graute vor ihm, die Mutter was mitleidig, verlegen und gedrückt, der Vater offenbar verstimmt. (108)

> (They had not yet grown accustomed to him; the children dreaded him, the mother pitied him—she was embarrassed and miserable—and the father was clearly distraught.)

The feelings on display here—dread, pity, embarrassment, and misery— abound in literary representations of disability, as demonstrated by Rosemarie Garland-Thomson. She states that disabled characters tend to be objectified: "The plot or the work's rhetorical potential," she explains, "usu-

---

[274] See Walter Fandrey, *Krüppel, Idioten, Irre: Zur Sozialgeschichte behinderter Menschen in Deutschland* (Stuttgart: Silberburg, 1990), 99–104.

[275] Clare, *Exile & Pride*, 87.

[276] Ibid.

[277] Rosemarie Garland-Thomson, for example, writes about the historic entanglement of disability and freak shows (specifically in a North American context). Her work is highly recommended for further reading on this topic. See Rosemarie Garland-Thomson, *Extraordinary Bodies: Figuring Physical Disability in American Culture and Literature* (New York: Columbia University Press, 2017), 55–80.

ally benefits from the disabled figure remaining other to the reader—identifiably human but resolutely different."[278] Furthermore:

> Disabled literary characters usually remain on the margins of fiction as uncomplicated figures or exotic aliens whose bodily configurations operate as spectacles, eliciting responses from other characters or producing rhetorical effects that depend on disability's cultural resonance. ... From folktales and classical myths to modern and postmodern "grotesques," the disabled body is almost always a freakish spectacle presented by the mediating narrative voice. Most disabled characters are enveloped by the otherness that their disability signals in the text.[279]

Apart from being denied subjectivity and agency, disabled people in literature often conjure fear, repulsion, pity, and fascination in the able-bodied characters, as is the case in *Peter Camenzind*. Fear, repulsion, and pity are evident in Boppi's introduction, visible in both Boppi's family's and the narrator's blatantly ableist attitudes. The way Boppi is introduced also mimics Mitchell and Snyder's schematic problem-solving structure. The first and second stages have been touched upon so far, that is, Boppi's "deviance or marked difference" has been acknowledged and the reasons why he is in the care of the carpenter's family (the death of his old mother) has been explained.

Peter's repulsion upon seeing Boppi for the first time leads him to quickly leave the carpenter's home, not to return for a week. He confesses:

> [V]or der Begegnung mit dem Kranken hatte ich ein kindisches Grauen. Es war mir widerlich, ihn immer zu sehen, ihm die Hand geben zu müssen. (109)

> (Meeting the sick one instilled in me a childish fear. It was disgusting to see him and to be forced to shake his hand.)

Boppi being associated with expressions such as *widerstrebend* (unwillingly), *Schrecken* (horror), *widerlich* (disgusting), and *Grauen* (fear) show that he is regarded as barely human. He is described as: "eine groteske, schiefe Menschengestalt in einem Stuhl, der wie ein Kindersessel mit einer Brustwehr versehen war." (108) (a grotesque, crooked human figure in a chair with a parapet, like the chair of a child.)

---

[278] Garland-Thomson, *Extraordinary Bodies*, 11.
[279] Ibid., 9–10.

Boppi's comparison with a child mirrors how Richard is described as having a childlike nature, although their respective comparisons with childhood have vastly different implications. As we saw in chapter one, in Richard's case, his childlike nature suggests that he is not yet fully formed and accentuates the notion that boys, before growing into normative heterosexuality, go through a homosexual phase. In Boppi's case, being equated with a child primarily emphasizes stereotypical conceptions about disability, such as helplessness, being in need of care, and not being fully developed, what Clare calls "the perpetual childhood many disabled people are forced into."[280]

Being presented as frightening, deviant, and infantile, the text reduces Boppi to a representative of a disabled body that is characterized simply by otherness. As such, he embodies Mitchell and Snyder's conception that disabled literary characters are reduced to a common denominator (disability/otherness) to the detriment of other characteristics. As we can see, Boppi is equated with being disabled and comes to personify the conception of disability as an unnatural and/or inhuman affliction.

Mitchell and Snyder write: "The humanities component of disability studies offers scholars and students the ability to return to a history of representations to reassess our understanding of disability and thus of ourselves."[281] Moreover, they point out, "even the most 'derisive' portrait harbors within it an antithesis, its own disruptive potential."[282] With a basis in this argument, we will, throughout this chapter, underscore that the ableism in Hesse's novel is not *all* that Boppi can be associated with. Addressing *Peter Camenzind*'s ableism head-on may, in fact, open it up for reformulation and offer possibilities for associating Boppi with something other than otherness. One possible explanation for Peter's ableist emotions is that it is the *sameness* we recognize in Others—not their otherness—that makes people prone to phobic attitudes.

---

[280] Clare, *Exile & Pride*, 125. Moreover, equating Boppi with a child sheds light on the practice of *forced sterilization*—a legal practice well into modern times—which definitively denied disabled people the ability to move from childhood into adulthood and personal autonomy. Immediately after the Nazis came to power in 1933, the Sterilization Law was passed in Germany, which eventually resulted in the Nazi "euthanasia" program. During the twelve years of the Third Reich, disabled people were not only seen as inferior and threatening to the superiority of the Aryan race, but they were also systematically murdered in the concentration camps. "The eugenics movement was international," Carol Poore explains, "but it was only in Nazi Germany that it led to the mass killing of disabled people." (Carol Poore, *Disability in Twentieth-Century German Culture* [Ann Arbor: University of Michigan Press, 2007], 86.) For further reading, see pages 75–89 in Poore's book.

[281] Mitchell and Snyder, *Narrative Prosthesis*, 9.

[282] Ibid., 40.

If we agree to view the entanglement of queerness and disability as a means of challenging heteronormativity in *Peter Camenzind*, drawing on this idea would make Peter's initial aversion toward Boppi a possible iteration of internalized homophobia. Additionally, since Boppi's introduction emphasizes disability in derogatory terms, this character's otherness comes to function as a sort of diversion from Peter's own queerness. As chapters one and two have shown, at this point in the story, Peter has accumulated a fair number of queer connotations (from the homoerotic relationship with Richard to his heterosexual ambivalence). The "freakish otherness" that characterizes Boppi's introduction therefore comes to represent a form of difference that stands out as *even more Other* than Peter's queerness.

Responsibility for the Other

When one examines Boppi's introduction, it not only appears ableist, but what also stands out is that none of the other characters act responsibly toward him. The significance of responsibility as a theme in the text—which Boppi activates—makes Levinasian ethics a useful means to emphasize the character's function as a narrative prosthesis. When Boppi is introduced, Peter indicates that someone ought to assume responsibility for him, although he clearly considers that this person should be anyone but himself or someone from the carpenter's family: "Es mußte sich irgendeine Möglichkeit finden, ihn mit geringen Kosten in einem Spital oder Pfründhaus unterzubringen." (109) (There had to be some possibility, with minimum costs, of placing him in a hospital or another support facility.)

Boppi is clearly regarded a problem. His family members do not want him physically in their home and he is portrayed as an obstacle to Peter, whose social engagement with the carpenter is disturbed by the "elenden Existenz" (109) (miserable existence) of the disabled man. In time, however, Boppi comes to affect the novel's protagonist a great deal. Interestingly, from a Levinasian face-to-face perspective, Boppi shaking Peter to his core involves three examples emphasizing Boppi's "face"—essentially, instances when Peter sees him as a *person* rather than a problem:

> Boppi hatte auf einem häßlichen Doppelhöcker ohne Hals einen großen, starkzügigen Kopf mit breiter Stirn, starker Nase und schönem, leidendem Munde sitzen, die Augen waren klar, aber still und etwas verängstigt. (109)

(On an ugly double chin without a neck lay Boppi's large, strong-featured head. His forehead was broad, the nose was large. His mouth was beautiful but tormented, and his eyes were clear and still, but worried somehow.)

On the one hand, this first mention involving Boppi's actual face clarifies that Peter does not care for the man. On the other hand, the remark about Boppi's "beautiful but tormented mouth" signify a spark of introspection that activates Peter's ability to respond. As Wilbur B. Franklin states, Hesse often-times elevates suffering to a virtue, "for it is in suffering that man participates in a universal human experience. How he deals with the phenomenon," Franklin continues, "will reveal the substance of a person."[283] The spark of introspection in Peter indicates that by responding to Boppi's suffering—basically, taking it upon himself to *do good*—Peter himself might be able to grow as an individual. We will return to this interpretation and delve further into it under the next heading.

The second reference to Boppi's face—this time in the broader Levinasian sense (not limited to the *physical* face)—occurs when Peter has joined the carpenter's family on a Sunday excursion, and they have left Boppi alone in their home. The carpenter expresses relief in not being disturbed by the presence of the disabled man: "'Na, hier draußen kann man wenigstens noch eine Stunde vergnügt sein, ohne daß er einen stört!'" (110) ("Well, out here at least, one can enjoy one's time without being bothered by him!") Peter is affected by the harsh words, and he pictures Boppi:

> [Ich sah] plötzlich den armen Lahmen vor mir, flehend und leidend, ihn, den wir nicht liebten, den wir loszuwerden trachteten und der jetzt von uns verlassen und eingeschlossen einsam und traurig in der dämmernden Stube saß. (110)

> (I envisioned the ill-fated lame man, pleading and tormented; the one we did not love, who we sought to get rid of, who was now sitting abandoned and trapped, lonely and sad, in the dim-lit home.)

Peter seeing Boppi, truly acknowledging him as "pleading and tormented," signals that his attitude toward the disabled man is changing rapidly. Apparently, it is becoming rather upsetting to the protagonist that the carpenter so blatantly disregards Boppi's comforts.

---

[283] Franklin, "The Concept of the 'Human'," 94.

The growing responsibility in Peter reaches its culmination in the third Levinasian face-to-face example of Boppi, when Peter and Boppi meet in person later that same Sunday. At this point in the story, Peter confesses that he is ashamed of having left Boppi alone in the carpenter's home while he and the others went out. Straightforwardly, he asks Boppi if he is allowed to become his friend. When Boppi accepts the offer Peter looks at him: "sein Blick war so hell und kindlich schön, daß mir vor Beschämung das Blut ins Gesicht stieg." (113) (his gaze was so bright and youthfully beautiful that my face turned red with shame.)

Peter's shame reveals that his behavior vis-à-vis this individual has had a profound effect on his sense of self. Evidently, he is shaken by his own lack of responsibility:

> Die Hand eines mächtigen Unsichtbaren legte sich auf mein Herz, drückte es nieder und füllte es mit so viel Scham und Schmerz, daß ich zitterte und unterlag. … Mir war genau so zumute, als würde ich vor einen reinen, untrüglichen Spiegel gestellt, und ich erblickte mich darin als einen Lügner, als einen Maulhelden, als einen Feigling und Wortbrüchigen. (111)

> (A mighty invisible hand took hold of my heart, squeezed it, and filled it with so much shame and pain that I trembled and collapsed. It made me feel like I was placed in front of a clear truth-telling mirror, and I could see myself within it as the liar, faker, and selfish coward that I was.)

Facing one's image in a mirror is a common practice in Hesse's fiction, which aims at helping characters come to terms with who they truly are. As Andreas Kiryakakis writes: "Reflection via the mirror is one of Hesse's methods for allowing his hero to be confronted by himself after a long period of egotistical activity."[284] Salvatore Campisi voices a similar argument: "by reflecting and, occasionally, distorting their contours, the 'mirror' allows Hesse's characters to discover or acknowledge possibilities and hidden facets of their inner self. This introspective moment, implicit in the reflection process, often paves the way to a moment of revelation."[285] The passage quoted above is oozing with affect, as Peter's mirror image bluntly reflects his egotistical shortcomings.

So, Peter is confronted with his selfishness which makes him realize something that will influence the remainder of the story. Because of Boppi's disability and status as Other, Peter here comes to terms with his own lack of empathy. Boppi's introduction in Peter's life thereby shapes the conditions

---

[284] Kiryakakis, *The Ideal of Heimat*, 113.
[285] Campisi, "Dialectics of Time," 183.

for his own self-development. Essentially, Boppi's presence creates an opening for Peter to grow into a responsible individual. The text's emphasis on Peter's personal growth stresses Boppi's function as a narrative prosthesis.

As we have seen so far, Levinas's thoughts on the importance of the face when assuming responsibility for the Other can be identified in Peter's reactions to Boppi. Peter does not assume responsibility for Boppi as an instant response, rather, it develops via three references to Boppi's face (in the broader Levinasian sense) which, taken together, underscore the significance of responsibility in the text. The three-phased exposition may be the author's narrative strategy for strengthening Peter's obligation. As a reader it is difficult not to notice the three-step development, as well as its emphasis on responsibility. *Peter Camenzind* thus says something about our collective obligations toward people with disabilities and makes a statement about the value of ethics.

"Benevolent Paternalism"

After having realized that the carpenter's family neglects their responsibilities toward Boppi, Peter becomes his friend, and the two men move in together. As Boppi's roommate, Peter assumes the role of caretaker which, in the following, will be examined. While Hesse's novel makes a statement about the value of ethics, Peter does convey a form of paternalism in his newly formed bond with Boppi. Even though Peter's care is grounded in good intentions, one cannot ignore that he uses Boppi to learn something and to fuel his own personal growth. Also, by characterizing Boppi as a person who lives in a perpetual childhood, Peter's paternalism is enhanced.

The way that Boppi is treated from this point on in the novel can be compared with what Rosemarie Garland-Thomson calls "benevolent maternalism." In her work she interprets novels that make use of disabled characters as "essential rhetorical elements in their arguments for humanitarian social reform."[286] The texts Garland-Thomson reads foregrounds non-disabled characters who "prevail" or "triumph" whereas the disabled characters "stay on the narrative margins, degraded by oppressive institutions and ultimately sacrificed to the social problems the novels assail."[287] Garland-Thomson labels these disabled individuals "icons of vulnerability" whose function in the texts is to arouse sympathy and "propel readers from

---

[286] Garland-Thomson, *Extraordinary Bodies*, 81–82.
[287] Ibid., 82.

complacency to conviction."[288] While disabled characters possess the potential to instill sympathy in readers, a side-effect can be that they become mere signifiers (or symbols) rather than fleshed-out characters who readers can actually identify with.

Peter Camenzind conveys Garland-Thompson's concept—in this case as "benevolent *paternalism*"—which can be summarized as an elevation of grand humanitarian ideas (such as ethics, solidarity, or queer/crip kinship) by means of idealization and/or appropriation of disabled people's suffering.[289] When looked at in the light of this concept, the potential ethical ambitions in Hesse's novel are rendered ambiguous.

On the one hand, Peter's actions have paternalistic overtones. On the other hand, despite being an ableist novel, the emphasis on self-realization in *Peter Camenzind* can been seen as intertwined with an exploration of ethics. In Rudolf Koester's assessment, Hesse's views on individual development go as follows: "In childhood one is not yet responsible, one is ethically immature; whereas adolescence is a time of awakening to the ethical realities of the world. It involves an acquisition of the knowledge of good and evil and the realization that complete virtue cannot be attained."[290] This form of ethical awakening is clearly identifiable in Peter's attitude toward Boppi.

While Wilbur B. Franklin suggests that Hesse's early work primarily focuses on characters who are passive and "plagued with chronic indecision,"[291] in essence, individuals who *run from responsibility*, Peter is an exception. Peter exemplifies, in Franklin's words, that "[b]ecoming mature involves accepting responsibility for other people."[292] *Peter Camenzind* thus expresses a contradiction. Although Hesse's text underlines that ethics and responsibility are key features in cultivating one's humanity, the novel depicts a relationship in which the most tangible benefit (personal development) is attributed to the character who helps rather than the one who is helped. One

---

[288] Garland-Thomson, *Extraordinary Bodies*, 82.

[289] It is worth mentioning that Hermann Hesse seems to idealize Boppi's disability in a manner equal to the treatment of "grotesques" in Nietzsche's *Also sprach Zarathustra*. Hesse was deeply influenced by Nietzsche and so this idealization is likely not a coincidence. Mitchell and Snyder write: "Nietzsche's writing establishes an inverted hierarchy of physical forms wherein the physically grotesque are ironically 'protected' from the rampaging disease of Western nihilism. Shielded from some of the more debasing influences of human community, the cripples and grotesques of Nietzsche's work become primary weapons in his radical critiques of Christianity and philosophy proper." (Mitchell and Snyder, *Narrative Prosthesis*, 68.)

[290] Rudolf Koester, "Self-realization: Hesse's Reflections on Youth," *Monatshefte* 57, no. 4 (1965): 183.

[291] Franklin, "The Concept of the 'Human'," 134.

[292] Ibid., 139.

can also note that Boppi himself has not expressed a need for goodwill, neither from Peter nor anyone else.[293]

Seeing as Boppi has not asked for Peter's help, why do these men build a life together? After having settled in their shared apartment and procured a poodle, the men's relationship evolves into an intimate companionship:

> Es begann eine gute, erfreuliche Zeit für mich, an der ich zeitlebens reichlich zu zehren haben werde. Es ward mir gegönnt, klar und tief in eine prachtvolle Menschenseele zu schauen, über welche Krankheit, Einsamkeit, Armut und Mißhandlung nur wie leichte lose Wolken hinweggeflogen waren. (113)

> (Now began a happy and pleasant time for me, which will benefit me for the rest of my life. I was granted the privilege of looking clearly and deeply into a wonderful human soul, who had just been passed by illness, loneliness, poverty, and mistreatment like free, weightless clouds.)

The clouds in this quote are especially noteworthy since their association with nature and naturalness not only reminds us of the relationship with Richard, but also signals that this new queer friendship develops effortlessly. The free, weightless clouds that pass by Boppi also indicate that his disability should not be seen as an obstacle to the men's evolving relationship, and they also contrast the conception that disability is unnatural.

Henceforth, the narrative enters the third stage in Mitchell and Snyder's schematic problem-solving structure, in which the disabled character's deviance is brought from the narrative's margins to the center of the story. The effortlessness of Peter and Boppi's bond is now enhanced by a second reference to Richard:

---

[293] One likely reason for Peter's goodwill toward Boppi is that he is inspired by St. Francis of Assisi, a patron saint of Italy who propagated love for nature, animals, and all other living things. (Hesse himself was also inspired by St. Francis and wrote a short biography of him before *Peter Camenzind* was published.) Peter's reverence for St. Francis's teachings underlines a Christian foundation in his approach to Boppi. While this religious/spiritual basis for Peter's ethical awakening will not be examined here, it bears mentioning that religious beliefs have a history of influencing social attitudes toward disability. Walter Fandrey's study, for instance, shows that in nineteenth-century Germany, disabled people were believed to provide the nondisabled with a means of coming closer to God. Although taking care of the less fortunate meant that one performed "God's work," the care in question mainly involved keeping the disabled comfortable but isolated from the rest of society. (Fandrey, *Krüppel, Idioten, Irre*, 100.) Further references to St. Francis of Assisi as Peter's inspiration when caring for Boppi can be found in Tusken, *Understanding Hermann Hesse*, 47; and Franklin, "The Concept of the 'Human'," 78–79.

> Die besten Zeiten mit Richard waren nicht schöner gewesen als diese stillen, heiteren Tage, wenn draußen die Flocken tanzten und am Ofen wir zwei samt dem Pudel es uns wohl sein ließen. (121)

> (The best times with Richard were not lovelier than these peaceful days when the snow fell outside and the two of us and the poodle enjoyed ourselves in front of the fireplace.)

During this time, Peter confesses: "nun erlebte ich es, daß ich … der erstaunte und dankbare Schüler eines elenden Krummen werden sollte." (113) (now I learned that I was supposed to become an amazed and grateful disciple of an ill-fated hunchback.) The emphasis on becoming a *disciple* is important, not only because it relates to the Bildungsroman's overall theme of education, personal development, and social integration, but also because it is Peter who is educated by Boppi, not the other way around. When this is viewed in conjunction with Levinasian ethics, Boppi (who among other things is characterized by otherness and vulnerability) teaching Peter what it means to be a responsible individual becomes even more significant: according to Levinas, the Other's "alterity is manifested in a mastery that does not conquer, but *teaches*."[294]

"Queer/Crip Kinship"

In Levinas's definition, vulnerability is the aptitude for being uncovered and an openness to being harmed: "The one is exposed to the other as a skin is exposed to what wounds it,"[295] he writes, elsewhere stating: "To suffer by the other is to take care of him, bear him, be in his place, consume oneself by him."[296] Although Levinas's definition of vulnerability might come across as masochistic or submissive (exposing one's skin to the risk of being wounded), it can also be viewed as earnest. It indicates that we are all vulnerable beings (in various forms and levels of course) and that vulnerability is a shared condition of the human experience. It might, potentially, be Peter's acknowledgment of his own vulnerability as a queer outsider that makes him attached to Boppi. In that case, his own queerness parallels Boppi's disability and thereby accentuates the importance of queer/crip kinship in Hesse's text.

---

[294] Levinas, *Totality and Infinity*, 171. Emphasis added.

[295] Emmanuel Levinas, *Otherwise than Being, or Beyond Essence*, trans. Alphonso Lingis (Pittsburg: Duquesne University Press, 2016), 49.

[296] Levinas, *Humanism of the Other*, 64.

Peter shares Boppi's struggles and within the boundaries of the men's relationship, Levinasian ethics and crip theory intersect. This brings us to a crip-theoretical concept formulated by Merri Lisa Johnson and Robert McRuer. Aiming to critique science's historic disregard of situated disabled perspectives within the production of knowledge, Johnson and McRuer introduce "cripistemology" which is a term that plays on *epistemology* (the theory of knowledge). Cripistemology, the explain, "lurks" everywhere in theory and means "thinking from the critical, social, and personal position of disability."[297] Johnson and McRuer do not envision this concept as assuming epistemic privilege exclusively for disabled individuals, nor as restricting epistemic privilege for those with first-hand knowledge of disabled experience, stating that "the production of knowledge about disability comes not only from being disabled but from *being with and near* disability, thinking through disabled sensations and situations, whether yours or your friend's."[298] Peter caring for Boppi and sharing his struggles can be said to exemplify "being with and near disability." The men's cozy evenings in front of the fireplace, joined by their poodle while the snow falls outside, are also, when compared with Boppi's previous conditions, categorizable as queer specks of light.

Levinas's idea of vulnerability as the capacity to open oneself up to potential suffering is intrinsically linked to trust, dependence, responsibility, compassion, and love—themes that are all prevalent in *Peter Camenzind*. Levinas writes: "Love aims at the Other ; it aims at him in his frailty ... To love is to fear for another, to come to the assistance of his frailty."[299]

Throughout Peter and Boppi's relationship, love keeps on developing as a key motif, and Peter starts to talk about Boppi as "meinen Buckligen, dem ich meine ganze Liebe geschenkt und mit dem ich mein ganzes Leben geteilt hatte." (122) (my hunchback, whom I gave all my love and with whom I shared my entire life.) When viewed against the backdrop of the men's everyday life and mutual living quarters, the sentence's reference to life-long love becomes romantic love. As such, it mirrors the bond "for life" that was articulated by Peter and Richard in Florence.

As we could see earlier, in Boppi's introduction, he is surrounded by negative imagery in the shape of stereotypical conceptions of disability. Mitchell and Snyder underscore that in the field of disability studies, what

---

[297] Merri Lisa Johnson and Robert McRuer, "Cripistemologies: Introduction," *Journal of Literary & Cultural Disability Studies* 8, no. 2 (2014): 134.

[298] Ibid., 141.

[299] Levinas, *Totality and Infinity*, 256.

tends to stand out in analyses focusing on negative imagery "is the importance of plots that emphasize individual isolation as the overriding component of a disabled life. ... By depicting disability as an isolated and
individual affair, storytellers artificially [extract] the experience of disability
from its necessary social contexts."[300] In Boppi's portrayal we see iterations of
both isolation and inclusion since he is alienated at first but comes to be
included in a social context with Peter. Peter, however, is not the only one
with whom Boppi forms a bond. One beautiful day Elisabeth accompanies
the pair to the zoo, an event that greatly contrasts Boppi's previous situation
as isolated and lonely.

It is the relationship with Peter, however, that becomes Boppi's primary
social context, and the depth of the men's intimacy is most clearly hinted at
toward the end of Boppi's life, when he falls ill and is hospitalized. Peter then
narrates: "Ich war noch ein Anfänger in der ars amandi und sollte gleich mit
einem ersten Kapitel der ars moriendi beginnen." (122–123). (I was only a
novice in the ars amandi and was about to begin a first chapter of the ars
moriendi.) Two aspects of this quote merit closer examination, the first being
the expression "ars moriendi," which is a reference to a couple of Latin texts
from the late Middle Ages dealing with "the art of dying." This expression is
most likely referencing Boppi's illness and impending death.

The second important aspect is Hesse's curious use of the expression "ars
amandi"—Latin for "the art of love," specifically sexual love.[301] While Joseph
Mileck argues that Hesse's pre-*Demian* protagonists (Peter Camenzind
among them) "are outsiders consumed by their own loneliness, misfits to
whom the ars vivendi [the art of living] and the ars amandi are foreign,"[302]
Hesse's quote recognizes that sexual love is *not* a foreign concept to Peter. He
may describe himself as a novice, but it appears that he has some experience.
Peter using the conspicuous term "ars amandi" to label his bond with Boppi

---

[300] Mitchell and Snyder, *Narrative Prosthesis*, 19.

[301] The expression "ars amandi" is usually associated with ancient Roman poet Ovid's work *Ars amatoria* (circa 2 AD), a book of educational, erotic short stories. For further reading, see, e.g., Publius Ovidius Naso, *Ovid: in Six Volumes. 2, The Art of Love, and Other Poems*, trans. J. H. Mozley (Cambridge, MA: Harvard University Press, 1947). Another work of interest is the surviving fragments of an ancient sex manual written by Philaenis, which Ovid's *Ars amatoria* is said to have been modelled on. Philaenis's writings have a significantly queerer and more radical content than Ovid's writing, such as open and detailed descriptions of lesbian sexuality. In effect, the "ars amandi" passage in *Peter Camenzind* is shown to have originated from a context in which same-sex practices were a common occurrence. For references to Philaenis's lesbianism, see, e.g., Marguerite Johnson and Terry Ryan, *Sexuality in Greek and Roman Society and Literature: A Sourcebook* (London: Routledge, 2005), 142, 163, 205.

[302] Mileck, "The Prose of Hermann Hesse," 172. Emphasis in original.

indicates that their relationship—apart from being dog-sharing room-mates—is not only homoerotic, but also involves actual sexual activities.

Although it was suggested in chapter one that Peter and Richard's relationship can be interpreted as involving homosexual desire, the passage quoted above is the first clear-cut mention of sexual activity in *Peter Camenzind*. Not only does this passage give the relationship between Peter and Boppi a special significance, but also, by bringing the sexual facet of their bond to the forefront, it challenges stereotypical conceptions of disabled people's sexualities.

One common conception about the sexuality of disabled people is that it is either tragic in its deficiency or freakishly excessive. As pointed out by Anna Mollow and Robert McRuer: "Pity or fear … are the sensations most often associated with disabilities."[303] A stereotypical conception emphasized by Tobin Siebers is "the myth that [disabled people] do not experience sexual feelings or that they do not have or want to have sex."[304] Siebers argues against such claims: "the sexual activities of disabled people do not necessarily follow normative assumptions about what a sex life is."[305] Instead, he explains: "disabled sexuality has an ebb and flow that spreads it out among other activities, and its physiognomy does not necessarily mimic conventional responses of arousal, penetration, or orgasm."[306] Moreover, as shown by Mollow, everyday notions of disabled people's sexualities are profoundly contradictory. Mollow underlines that since disabled people are sometimes believed to be sexual predators and other times seen as asexual, "it seems nearly impossible for any expression of disabled sexuality to escape stigma."[307]

The fact that Hesse portrays an intimate relationship between Peter and Boppi and underscores its sexual dimension with the expression "ars amandi" makes it possible for the reader to experience disability representation beyond tragedy, pity, and paternalism. Also, by challenging hetero-normativity and compulsory able-bodiedness, both Peter and Boppi can be said to exist in precariousness, which emphasizes queer/crip kinship in the novel. As Courtney Andree has shown, in the early twentieth century, homo-

---

[303] Anna Mollow and Robert McRuer, "Introduction," in *Sex and Disability*, ed. Anna Mollow and Robert McRuer (Durham: Duke University Press, 2012), 1.

[304] Tobin Siebers, "A Sexual Culture for Disabled People," in *Sex and Disability*, ed. Anna Mollow and Robert McRuer (Durham: Duke University Press, 2012), 39.

[305] Ibid.

[306] Ibid., 49.

[307] Anna Mollow, "Is Sex Disability? Queer Theory and the Disability Drive," in *Sex and Disability*, ed. Anna Mollow and Robert McRuer (Durham: Duke University Press, 2012), 286.

sexuality was frequently lumped together with a range of other "degene-rative" disorders, such as communicable diseases, alcoholism, and dis-ability.[308] And, in the words of Eli Clare, "[t]he ways in which queer people and disabled people experience oppression follow, to a certain extent, parallel paths."[309] Paralleling each other does not mean that queer people and disabled people experience identical forms of oppression, but both groups having been labeled "freaks of nature" heightens their kinship potential. Essentially, the shared pathologizing histories of homosexuality and disability can be seen as strengthening Peter and Boppi's bond on the page. Their joint experience of outsiderness and otherness unites them.

The Implications of Boppi's Death

Boppi's death in *Peter Camenzind* remains to be addressed. When Boppi's health declines he is hospitalized. Throughout his illness Peter is by his bedside, and when Boppi dies he dies in Peter's arms: "Er … erkaltete mir in der Hand." (125) (He turned cold in my hand.) Hesse treats this incident gracefully and it expresses a sort of poetic peacefulness. However, Boppi's death reminds us of the historic tradition in literature (and all other media) to treat queer and disabled characters as expendable and having them achieve their narrative values by being punished for their deviances (and dying).

Boppi's death also mirrors Richard's death. It is apparent that both these characters die because they embody difference (disability and/or queerness) and because the genre—the Bildungsroman—rarely allows supporting characters to have narrative arcs that go full circle. Rather, supporting charac-ters are included to assist the protagonist in reaching his full potential. In this regard both Boppi and Richard can be seen as narrative prostheses.

When viewed in conjunction with Judith Butler's thoughts on which Others' lives are deemed livable within normative frameworks, Boppi's demise becomes interpretable as a form of punishment. Butler writes: "specific lives cannot be apprehended as injured or lost if they are not first apprehended as living. If certain lives do not qualify as lives or are, from the start, not conceivable as lives within certain epistemological frames, then these lives are never lived nor lost in the full sense."[310]

Since disabled individuals in able-bodied and heteronormative contexts are frequently regarded as unnatural and/or inhuman, they are, subsequently,

---

[308] Andree, "*Bildung* Sideways," 25.
[309] Clare, *Exile & Pride*, 112.
[310] Butler, *Frames of War*, 1.

not treated as really being alive in the first place and neither missed nor mourned when they die. Furthermore, as argued by Valerie Rohy, the "primitive" connotation of otherness tends to make majority culture afraid that Others will halt society's development: "it is not just that time stops *for the other*," Rohy writes, "but that the other—the 'primitive,' savage, or homosexual—wields the power to stop time for all the world."[311] In the case of *Peter Camenzind*, wherein the main expression of otherness materializes in Boppi, disability becomes a threat of societal arrested development. Being an Other in a narrative characterized by conceptions of progress (such as the Bildungsroman) means that one must die to make way for said progress. In essence, the Other's death is a final lesson for the protagonist to complete his learning process.

By means of Boppi's death we enter the fourth stage of Mitchell and Snyder's schematic problem-solving structure, namely the rehabilitation of the disabled character's deviance and it portrays how disability is "fixed" in some way. Boppi's death surely fixes the "problem" of disability in *Peter Camenzind*. Morbidly, as it definitively eases Boppi's life-long suffering, the text conveys his demise as the optimal solution for him and the others involved.

Boppi's un-livability being invoked at the end of *Peter Camenzind* shows that he must die for Peter to complete his transition into adulthood. In this Bildungsroman, Peter's experiences are constantly linked to concepts of learning and when he returns to his childhood village after Boppi's death, he claims to have learned all he needs to know: "Mir schien, ich habe nun ein hinreichendes Stück Leben und Tod gesehen." (126) (It seemed to me I had now seen a sufficient piece of life and death.) One must remember that while Peter's Bildung may be complete, this is achieved at the expense of Boppi's existence. If we recall Jill Ehnenn's argument that the Bildungsroman tends to "enforce normalcy" by adding deviant supporting characters to train readers in recognizing difference, what becomes visible is that Boppi's disability diverts attention from and normalizes many of the text's queer implications (that is, the queer connotations around the protagonist). Disability, in this way, becomes queerer than queerness itself.

As the primary purpose of a deviant supporting character in a Bildungsroman is to contrast the protagonist's assimilation into normalcy—at any cost (including premature death)—Hesse's novel breaks with a narrative

---

[311] Valerie Rohy, *Anachronism and Its Others: Sexuality, Race, Temporality* (Albany: State University of New York Press, 2009), x.

convention. The protagonist in Hesse's text is never fully assimilated into normalcy. Peter does not choose a heteronormative lifestyle after Boppi's death, he chooses to live the rest of his life alone. This choice, in fact, turns out to have implications for Boppi's representation and importance in the story. When the men's relationship is interpreted within the framework of a queer friendship—that is, a friendship that challenges heteronormative conceptions of relationality, sexuality, and desire—it gains a deeper meaning. Boppi's part to play becomes more than a contrast to the protagonist's path to normalcy. In lieu of being a narrative prosthesis, Boppi's role can be seen as a catalyst that conveys the importance of queer/crip kinship. Although Hesse's text does not allow him to be a fully-fleshed-out character in his own right, within the context of a queer friendship—or a same-sex romance—he comes into focus with a less ableist set of connotations.

Moreover, from a Levinasian angle, the depth of one's love manifests itself via the ways with which one is affected by the Other's death. Levinas writes: "the death of the other affects me more than my own."[312] Hence, in a Levinasian sense, Boppi's death is the event that defines the scope of Peter's affection. It is likely that if Boppi had not had such an impact on Peter's emotional life, Peter would be able to find another companion or romantic partner after his passing. Peter's view of Boppi as the person to whom he has given "all his love" and with whom he "shares his entire life" signifies that however long Peter lives himself, Boppi will forever be missed.

Worthy of Being Mourned

As discussed in chapter one, many scholars have argued that the Bildungsroman is inherently heteronormative, since its common conclusion is marriage. In this regard, *Peter Camenzind* breaks with convention. Marriage figures in the novel but only as a theme. After Peter's proposal to Elisabeth is turned down, he abandons the idea of marriage with ease. More notably, when he and Boppi live together, Peter describes the situation like this:

> Bald darauf bezog ich mit meinem armen Bucklinen eine neugemietete Wohnung. Ich kam mir vor, als hätte ich geheiratet, da ich nun statt der gewohnten Junggesellenbude einen ordentlichen kleinen Haushalt zu zweien beginnen sollte. Aber es ging, wenn ich auch im Anfang manche unglücklichen Wirtschaftsexperimente anstellte. Zum Ordnungmachen und Waschen kam ein Laufmädchen, das Essen ließen wir uns ins Haus tragen,

---

[312] Emmanuel Levinas, *God, Death, and Time*, trans. Bettina Bergo (Stanford: Stanford University Press, 2000), 105.

> und bald war uns beiden ganz warm und wohl bei diesem Zusammenleben. (118)

> (Soon afterwards, I moved in with my poor hunchback in a newly rented apartment. It seemed to me that I was now married, for now I had changed my bachelor quarters for a small, orderly household for two. And it went well, even though I initially was involved in some unfortunate housekeeping experiments. We had a daily help that saw to the cleaning and washing, our food was brought to the house, and soon we both found ourselves completely happy and at ease in our life together.)

On the surface of this quote, male companionship is clearly equated with marriage, the epitome of the heterosexual union. Let us recall the statement by Walter Naumann that was quoted in the overview chapter, that throughout Hesse's work, friendships between men resemble *marriages*, an observation also made by Franklin: "Friendship in Hesse's world resembles the role of marriage in that there is a commitment to one another, and a responsibility for one another."[313] In Peter's narration, moving in with Boppi "seems like being married." Accordingly, the homoerotic ambiguity inherent in literary marriages between men (which George Haggerty refers to in his study on queer friendships) indicates that these characters are to be understood as more than roommates. Ralph Freedman (who stated that Richard is "the novel's central love") also alludes to this and writes that Boppi's death represents "yet another great loss, another great love gone from the hero's life."[314]

The passage closes with Peter confessing to being "ganz warm und wohl" (completely happy) with Boppi, which merits further investigation. Within the framework of this queer reading (with homoeroticism as a main focus point), the word *warm* is significant because the German term *Warmer Bruder* (warm brother), which originated in eighteenth-century Berlin, specifically refers to "a homosexual man."[315] Clayton J. Whisnant explains that "'warm' is probably an allusion either to affected and emotional behavior or to sexual heat."[316] Because of this, Peter and Boppi being "ganz warm und wohl bei diesem Zusammenleben" (very *warm* and content while living

---

[313] Franklin, "The Concept of the 'Human'," 80.

[314] Freedman, *Pilgrim of Crisis*, 116.

[315] Jody Skinner, *Warme Brüder, Kesse Väter: Lexikon mit Ausdrücken für Lesben, Schwule und Homosexualität* (Essen: Blaue Euele, 1997), 172–173. For a longer discussion about the term "warm brother," see chapter two in Tobin, *Warm Brothers*, 24–43.

[316] Whisnant, *Queer Identities*, 128.

together) gains a queer meaning. As we can see, in *Peter Camenzind*, living like a married couple accentuates links with male homosexuality.

On the one hand, the marriage analogy supersedes the marginalizing effects of challenging heteronormativity in the ways that Peter and Boppi do, and also provides a queer speck of light in the narrative. On the other hand, in relation to the novel's queerness, death is still an unavoidable aspect. But possibly, drawing on the work of Jack Halberstam, we could reformulate the negative implications of this trope. The "queer art of failure," Halberstam explains, implies finding alternatives to standardized conceptions of what it means to be an accomplished individual in heteronormative, capitalist society: "To live is to fail," Halberstam writes, "to bungle, to disappoint, and ultimately to die; rather than searching for ways around death and disappointment, the queer art of failure involves the acceptance of the finite."[317] Halberstam's queer art of failure concept can be said to echo throughout Hesse's novel. In completing his Bildung and becoming an upstanding, responsible, and educated adult, Peter, on the one hand, succeeds. But on the other hand, he is never completely assimilated into heteronormativity—he never marries—and is thereby perceivable as failing. As we can see in *Peter Camenzind*, within the Bildungsroman's context of optimism, development, and achievement, failure can be equally manifested in the shape of queerness and disability.

Also, as Rudolf Koester underscores, Hesse "warns against common standards of achievement. Since each individual's destiny is unique, its fulfillment cannot be gauged by objective standards; they should instead be subjective, indicating only the extent to which individual potential has been realized."[318] From a queer standpoint, Koester's assessment casts light on a norm-challenging foundation in Hesse's thinking. As *Peter Camenzind* demonstrates, failure ought not to be perceived as the antithesis to success but rather as *an alternative path* to the standardized, heteronormative trajectory. As queers, Sara Ahmed suggests, we "can explore the strange and perverse mixtures of hope and despair, of optimism and pessimism, within forms of politics that take as a starting point a critique of the world as it is and a belief that the world could be different."[319] Ahmed calls for a refusal of fixed definitions of what it means to be hopeful, desperate, optimistic, pessimistic, or to succeed or to fail. For example, as queers and crips we can

---

[317] Jack Halberstam, *The Queer Art of Failure* (Durham: Duke University Press, 2011), 186–187.
[318] Koester, "Self-realization," 185.
[319] Sara Ahmed, "Happy Futures, Perhaps," in *Queer Times, Queer Becomings*, ed. E. L. McCallum and Mikko Tuhkanen (Albany: State University of New York Press, 2011), 161.

interpret failure as we choose ourselves and appropriate the term to suit our needs.

Since the queer characteristics of Peter and Boppi's bond—visible for example in the marriage analogy—are interlinked with Boppi's otherness, he comes to activate queer/crip kinship in *Peter Camenzind*, which adds to the overall queerness of the novel. This link, however, is not the only way that Boppi's presence affects the story. Peter does not choose a heteronormative lifestyle after Boppi's death but lives the rest of his life as a single man, and his actions therefore confirm that Boppi is clearly worthy of being mourned.

PART 2
The Runner: Steppenwolf

CHAPTER 4

Tracing the Wolf

An Outsider and Other

We will now turn our attention from *Peter Camenzind* to one of Hesse's most famous novels, *Der Steppenwolf* (published in 1927), and show that one of the novel's key expressions of otherness intersects with queerness. The otherness in focus is the animality of the middle-aged, intellectual protagonist Harry Haller: "*Er ging auf zwei Beinen, trug Kleider und war ein Mensch, aber eigentlich war er doch eben ein Steppenwolf.*"[320] (*He walked on two legs, wore clothes and was a human, but actually he was a wolf of the steppes.* [The italics here indicate a quote from the part of the original work that was printed in a separate pamphlet.[321]])

This chapter will diverge somewhat from the other chapters in this book in that it will not revolve around an iteration of a friendship (Harry's queer friendships with the characters Hermine and Pablo will be examined in subsequent chapters). In the following, it will be emphasized that the relationship between the human part and wolf part of Harry Haller constitutes the antithesis of friendship—that is, this bond is instead built on animosity.

Harry's conflicting nature as a wolf-man makes him different from other people. He embodies in-betweenness and since he is repeatedly associated with the word *Fremdheit* (strangeness), his status as an Other is accentuated. He is, however, also an outsider. In Colin Wilson's words (at this point almost habitually quoted within scholarship on Hesse), *Der Steppenwolf* "is one of the most penetrating and exhaustive studies of the Outsider ever written."[322] Harry's status as an outsider and Other are apparent in the following phrase:

---

[320] Hermann Hesse, *Der Steppenwolf*, in *Sämtliche Werke. Band 4: Die Romane. Der Steppenwolf, Narziß und Goldmund, Die Morgenlandfahrt*, ed. Volker Michaels (Berlin: Suhrkamp, 2001), 45. Further references will be given by page number in parentheses.

[321] Several italicized quotes will follow. In the first edition of *Der Steppenwolf* Hermann Hesse insisted that "the Treatise" (one of the novel's three parts) was to be included as a separate pamphlet, printed on low-quality paper with its own cover and own page numbers, inserted between the novel's pages. (Volker Michels, *Materialien zu Hermann Hesses* Der Steppenwolf [Frankfurt: Suhrkamp, 1972], 119.) In the standard edition of Hesse's works from 2001 (edited by Michels), which is used throughout this study, the text in the Treatise is italicized, with the intention to create a similar effect as with the first edition's separate pamphlet.

[322] Wilson, *The Outsider*, 60.

"um den ganzen Mann herum [war] eine fremde und … ungute oder feind-liche Atmosphäre." (8) (the man was enveloped in a strange and uncom-fortable or hostile atmosphere.) The protagonist's dual nature accentuates outsiderness and otherness in equal measure. Moreover, being part wolf, an animal believed to be "the ultimate symbol of wilderness"[323] signals that Harry is an untamed creature of the *wild*.

"Wild Thing"

Ever since Classical antiquity, humans have had a complicated relationship with the wolf. The animal's stereotypical and negative features appear in literature, for example, in Ovid's *Metamorphoses* (8 AD). Therein the myth of Lycaon of Arcadia is recounted, which describes how Lycaon is trans-formed into a wolf as a punishment for serving Zeus the roasted flesh of his own son.[324] Luigi Boitani points out other negative depictions, including the bestiaries of the Middle Ages (illustrated books that describe real animals and mythological creatures such as fauns, dragons, and unicorns), which con-tained "many tales of the wolf being portrayed as a deceitful and lascivious beast."[325] Another well-known and significant example is Little Red Riding Hood, of which Boitani writes: "This fable is a perfect example of a culture detaching itself from the biological reality of an animal in order to construct an image for its own use. This fable represents the ultimate 'other' wolf—that of the imagination as compared to the biological animal."[326]

Harry Haller being an outsider can be seen as a choice made by a mis-anthropic intellectual, and as exclusion from normative society because of his wild wolf-man nature: "ich lebe so etwas abseits, etwas am Rande" (18) (my life is sort of unusual, I exist somewhere in the margin), he explains. In contrast to the bourgeois humans around him, Harry's animality makes him a norm-challenger and this is enhanced by queer characteristics.

---

[323] Steven H. Fritts, Robert O. Stephenson, Robert D. Hayes, and Luigi Boitani, "Wolves and Humans," in *Wolves: Behavior, Ecology, and Conservation*, ed. L. David Mech and Luigi Boitani (Chicago: University of Chicago, 2003), 290.

[324] See Publius Ovidius Naso, *Ovid: in Six Volumes. 3, Metamorphoses, in Two Volumes, 1: Books IX–XV*, trans. Frank Justus Miller (Cambridge, MA: Harvard University Press, 1977); and Publius Ovidius Naso, *Ovid: in Six Volumes. 4, Metamorphoses, in Two Volumes, 2: Books I–VIII*, trans. Frank Justus Miller (Cambridge, MA: Harvard University Press, 1984).

[325] Luigi Boitani, "Ecological and Cultural Diversities in the Evolution of Wolf-Human Relationships," in *Ecology and Conservation of Wolves in a Changing World*, ed. Ludwig N. Carbyn, Steven H. Fritts, and Dale R. Seip (Edmonton: Canadian Circumpolar Institute, 1995), 8.

[326] Ibid.

When queer is understood as a signifier of that which disrupts normative conceptions of gender and sexuality, the wolf part of Harry accentuates a connection between animality and queerness. As George Chauncey points out (albeit in a North American context), the term "wolf" was frequently used in the early twentieth century within the context of male same-sex acts. Wolves, Chauncey explains, were men who "abided by the conventions of masculinity and yet exhibited a decided preference for male sexual partners."[327] The correlation between wolves and homosexuality is also alluded to by Sigmund Freud in his 1918 study of the "Wolfman," a man who exhibited latent homosexual desire.[328] The correlation also manifests itself in the figure of the werewolf, of which Phillip A. Bernhardt-House writes: "The werewolf is generally seen as a 'hybrid' figure of sorts — part human and part wolf — and its hybridity and transgression of species boundaries in a unified figure is, at very least, unusual, thus the figure of the werewolf might be seen as a natural signifier for queerness in its myriad forms."[329] Apart from signifying queerness and constituting a research field too large to be accounted for in full here, the figure of the werewolf was an often-invoked icon among the Nazis.[330] This connection will be examined in detail later, under the heading "Elitism and Nazi Wolf Symbolism."

The combination of this study's queer-theoretical framework and the wildness that has historically been attributed to wolves make Jack Halberstam's *Wild Things: The Disorder of Desire* (2020) a fruitful theoretical addition. In this work, Halberstam theorizes that the concept of "the wild" not only exists beyond the domestic sphere in the natural world but can be identified in all things that refuse and resist order. "Wildness," Halberstam

---

[327] George Chauncey, *Gay New York: Gender, Urban Culture, and the Making of the Gay Male World, 1890-1940* (New York: Basic Books, 1994), 87.

[328] See Sigmund Freud, *The 'Wolfman' [From the* History of an Infantile Neurosis *]*, trans. Louise Adey Huish (London: Penguin Books, 2010). For an examination of queerness in the relationship between men and wolves, see Michael Lundblad, *The Birth of a Jungle: Animality in Progressive-Era U.S. Literature and Culture* (Oxford: Oxford University Press, 2013), 49–74, in which wolf/man-centered writings by Jack London are analyzed.

[329] Phillip A. Bernhardt-House, "The Werewolf as Queer, the Queer as Werewolf, and Queer Werewolves," in *Queering the Non/Human*, ed. Noreen Giffney and Myra J. Hird (Aldershot, Hampshire: Ashgate, 2008), 159.

[330] The research field on the mythology of werewolves is too vast and varied to be accounted for in full here. For further reading, see, e.g., Montague Summers's groundbreaking study from 1933 (Montague Summers, *The Werewolf in Lore and Legend* [Mineola, NY: Dover, 2003]), in which historical documents and folklore from throughout Europe are examined. Further reading on werewolves in literature can be found in Brian J. Frost, *The Essential Guide to Werewolf Literature* (Madison: University of Wisconsin Press, 2003), in which the werewolf myth is traced from its origins in superstitious beliefs to its iterations in contemporary horror and fantasy fiction.

writes, "names simultaneously a chaotic force of nature, the outside of categorization, unrestrained forms of embodiment, the refusal to submit to social regulation, loss of control, the unpredictable."[331] As such, wildness is innately entangled with sexuality: "The wild plays a part in most theories of sexuality, and sexuality plays its role in most theories of wildness,"[332] Halberstam states.

Harry's wildness is key to his characterization. He continuously oscillates between wildness and bourgeois conventions, which suggests that he might also oscillate between opposing expressions of sexuality, a hypothesis that will be discussed at length in chapters five and six. But first, we will take a closer look at *Der Steppenwolf*'s human/animal motif, which not only affects how otherness and queerness are manifested, but also connotes elitist ideals and associations with the wolf symbolism perpetuated by the Nazis— connotations that make Hesse's novel a multifaceted and complex document of its time.

"May Each Person Make of It What Suits and Serves Him"

While the research field on Hesse's life and work is substantial, few scholars have given attention to *Der Steppenwolf*'s animal aspects.[333] An exception is Alexander Mathäs's research, which has an animal studies angle and therefore is a significant contribution here. Mathäs writes that Hesse's novel "seeks to reveal the human dependence on an instinctual, subconscious nature beyond rational control, thus exposing the myth that individuals are superior to other living beings by virtue of their ability to rationally know themselves."[334] Mathäs argues that *Der Steppenwolf* draws attention to the entanglement of human and non-human lives and that the ability of humans to *think* does not make them a superior species.

This chapter will "trace the wolf" in *Der Steppenwolf*, which means observing how the figure of the wolf appears in the text, as well as how the animality/otherness it brings to the narrative functions as a counterpoint to—and critique of—the anthropocentric (human-centered) paradigm, which presupposes humans as superior to non-human animals.

---

[331] Jack Halberstam, *Wild Things: The Disorder of Desire* (Durham: Duke University Press, 2020), 3.

[332] Ibid., 6.

[333] For research focusing on *Der Steppenwolf*'s animal aspects, see David Gallagher, *Metamorphosis: Transformations of the Body and the Influence of Ovid's* Metamorphoses *on Germanic Literature of the Nineteenth and Twentieth Centuries* (Amsterdam: Rodopi, 2009), 326–338.

[334] Alexander Mathäs, *Beyond Posthumanism: The German Humanist Tradition and the Future of the Humanities* (New York: Berghahn Books, 2020), 242.

But first: *Der Steppenwolf* has a complicated narrative that mirrors the fragmented nature of its protagonist. The story's events can be seen as occurring on different levels (reality, dream, hallucination) and the construction of the text is equally complex. The novel consists of three parts with different narrators: The first part is the "Foreword," narrated by a young bourgeois man who publishes the second part, "Harry Haller's Manuscript," which is narrated by the protagonist. The third part is the "Treatise of the Steppenwolf," whose narrator remains unknown throughout the novel. All three parts will be extensively quoted in this and the following chapters. Suffice it to say, for now, that summarizing the novel's events is a daunting task of which Martin Swales has pondered: "Are the events portrayed as genuinely occurring in a recognizable outer world? Or are they part of an elaborate dream sequence?"[335]

Many scholars have, with a basis in the theories of Carl Jung, interpreted the novel as the latter. Swales mentions that while writing *Der Steppenwolf*, Hesse was "in a state of profound psychological turmoil," which likely affected the novel's complex structure and its layers of psychological meaning.[336] Also, the fact that the author sought therapy from J. B. Lang, a student of Jung's—and that he had conversations with Jung himself—has prompted a plethora of scholarly work that highlights the influence of Jungian thought in Hesse's literary oeuvre. David G. Richards is therefore right in pointing out that "some knowledge of Jung's theories is an unavoidable prerequisite for interpreting texts which owe as much to Jung's psychology as *Demian* and *Steppenwolf* do."[337]

Those of Jung's concepts that strengthen this study's queer interpretations will be referenced in the following (especially in the next chapter, "The Function of Hermine").[338] It bears underscoring, however, that if one relies

---

[335] Martin Swales, "*Der Steppenwolf*," in *A Companion to the Works of Hermann Hesse*, ed. Ingo Cornils (Rochester, NY: Camden House, 2009), 172.

[336] Ibid., 178.

[337] Richards, *Exploring the Divided Self*, 111.

[338] This study will not rely as predominantly on Jungian ideas as some previous scholarship has. A principal reason for this tactic is that implementing Jung's thinking in a queer reading of *Der Steppenwolf* might incidentally pathologize the novel's queer implications. In the anthology *Homosexuality & Psychoanalysis* (2001), editors Tim Dean and Christopher Lane underscore that homosexuality and psychoanalysis have a long history of being at odds with one another. Even in the twenty-first century, negative attitudes in conservative campaigns persist, campaigns that perpetuate the myth that homosexuality is "curable" by means of reparative therapies (such as gay conversion camps). Because of the antagonistic history of homosexuality and psychoanalysis it is not desirable to rely too heavily on Jung's theories within this study, however refined Jung's thinking may be. "Neither psychoanalysts nor lesbian, gay, and queer people," Dean and Lane explains, "have forgotten that the mental health estab-

too heavily on Jung's psychoanalytical theories while simultaneously classifying Harry Haller as queer, one might, inadvertently, rouse speculations regarding Hermann Hesse's sexual orientation, for *Der Steppenwolf* and its protagonist are regarded as bearing striking resemblances to Hesse himself and his life.

Theodore Ziolkowski argues that *Der Steppenwolf* "is more overtly autobiographical than any of Hesse's other fiction. Almost every detail in the characterization of Harry Haller—from his sciatica and eyeglasses and general physical appearance to his reading habits and political views—is drawn from Hesse's own life and person."[339] Hence it is worth repeating that while this study takes some biographical aspects of the author's life into account, the primary point of interest is expressions of queerness in Hesse's *texts*, not in his private life.

In previous scholarship, Jung's theories have been proven useful for showing how *Der Steppenwolf* portrays its protagonist's journey toward *wholeness*. As we shall see later, however, it is enormously challenging for Harry to achieve a complete unification of all parts of his personality (in Jungian terminology: "individuation"), specifically because he resists and runs from the parts of him that have queer connotations.

Although Hesse claimed that *Der Steppenwolf* was his most misunderstood work—pointing out that the tendency to understand it as a narrative about misery and crisis overshadowed his intention to tell a story about faith and redemption—his ensuing statement clarifies that the text can be understood in a variety of ways. In a postscript to the 1941 edition of *Der Steppenwolf*, Hesse suggests: "Möge jeder aus [*Der Steppenwolf*] machen, was ihm entspricht und dienlich ist."[340] (May each person make of *Der Steppenwolf* what suits and serves him.) The novel has, accordingly, been given a range of diverse labels. Swales argues that *Der Steppenwolf* belongs to a group of novels that "represent the canonical contribution of the German novel to High Modernism,"[341] whereas drug guru Timothy Leary suggests: "Before

---

lishment routinely used to consider same-sex desire as a form of illness." (Tim Dean and Christopher Lane, "Homosexuality and Psychoanalysis: An Introduction," in *Homosexuality & Psychoanalysis*, ed. Tim Dean and Christopher Lane [Chicago: University of Chicago Press, 2001], 3.)

[339] Ziolkowski, *The Novels of Hermann Hesse*, 179. For another thorough comparison between the author's own life and Harry Haller's living conditions, see Jackson, "Ambivalent Modernist," 142–151.

[340] Hermann Hesse, "Nachwort (1941)," in *Sämtliche Werke. Band 4: Die Romane. Der Steppenwolf, Narziß und Goldmund, Die Morgenlandfahrt*, ed. Volker Michaels (Berlin: Suhrkamp, 2001), 208.

[341] Swales, "*Der Steppenwolf*," 171.

your LSD session, read *Siddhartha* and *Steppenwolf*. The last part of the *Steppenwolf* is a priceless manual."[342]

Summary of Key Events in *Der Steppenwolf*

At the beginning of the narrative, Harry becomes a lodger in a bourgeois home in the city. His fragmented human/animal nature—that he has "*zwei Naturen, eine menschliche und eine wölfische*" (45) (*a dual nature, one human and one wolfish*)—makes it impossible for him to identify with conformist society, leading him to contemplate suicide. One evening, after having aimlessly wandered the streets, he finds a doorway in an alley leading to a "Magic Theater." But Harry does not enter. Instead, he meets a man who gives him the "Treatise of the Steppenwolf."

The Treatise, surprisingly, is an inquiry into Harry's own existence. It explains that he is "*ein unzufriedener Mensch.*" (45) (*an unsatisfied person.*) The word *Mensch* (person) can be translated to "human being" as well. Either way, if Harry learns to perceive himself as more than just wolf and man—that is, if he can transcend the binary that they constitute—he will reach the peaceful realm of the Immortals.

The Immortals, we are told, are legendary artists like Johann Wolfgang von Goethe (1749–1832) and Wolfgang Amadeus Mozart (1756–1791) who have overcome the mediocrity of life through humor and laughter. "These immortals," Ralph Freedman explains, "are the great voices of art, and of humanistic culture, under whose aegis a personal struggle to accept oneself in all one's agonies and inner divisions could rise to an ascent toward an ideal."[343] In Harry's perception, Goethe and Mozart are supreme representations of a humanity that is more refined than that of the bourgeois masses.[344] The correlation between Johann *Wolf*gang von Goethe, *Wolf*gang Amadeus Mozart, and the Steppen*wolf* are most likely not coincidental.[345]

---

[342] Timothy Leary and Ralph Metzner, "Hermann Hesse: Poet of the Interior Journey," *The Psychedelic Review* 1 (1963): 181.

[343] Freedman, *Pilgrim of Crisis*, 286.

[344] The reverence for Goethe that is expressed in *Der Steppenwolf* is not only the protagonist's but the author's as well. Throughout his life Hesse greatly admired Goethe and saw him as a role model. For further reading, see, e.g., "Gratitude to Goethe," in Hermann Hesse, *My Belief: Essays on Life and Art*, ed. Theodore Ziolkowski, trans. Denver Lindley, with two essays trans. Ralph Manheim (St. Albans: Triad/Panther Books, 1978), 181–188; and Gunter E. Grimm, "Hermann Hesses Goethe-Lektüren. Stationen einer 'geistigen Beunruhigung'," in *Der Grenzgänger Hermann Hesse: Neue Perspektiven der Forschung*, ed. Henriette Herwig and Florian Trabert (Freiburg i. Br.: Rombach, 2013), 141–154.

[345] The correlation between Johann *Wolf*gang von Goethe, *Wolf*gang Amadeus Mozart, and the Steppen*wolf* has been pointed out previously. See, for example, Richards, *Exploring the Divided Self*, 31.

The connection between these figures underlines the ideal toward which Harry is striving.

After having read the mysterious Treatise, Harry meets the alluring young Hermine.[346] She teaches him how to dance and experience sexual pleasure, indulgences with which he is unfamiliar. Like Harry's human/animal nature, Hermine has two sides to her. She is a gender-nonconforming character with fluid gender expressions:

> In die stille glatte Stirn hing eine kurze Locke herab, von dort aus, von dieser Stirnecke mit der Locke her, strömte von Zeit zu Zeit wie lebendiger Atem jene Welle von Knabenähnlichkeit, von hermaphroditischer Magie. (107–108)

> (A short curl of hair hung over her calm, smooth forehead, and from time to time, like a living breath, a wave of boyishness—of hermaphroditic enchantment—radiated from her.)

Hermine's fluid gender expressions—that she appears as both female and male, and thus can be understood as a person whose gender expression is trans/non-binary (or "gender neutral")—makes Hesse's choice of pronoun ("she") part of her enigmatic qualities.[347] (Hermine's gender nonconformity and other queer characteristics will be discussed at length in the next chapter.) To avoid confusion when quoting Hesse's text, when referring to her in this study, the pronoun "she" will be used.

Through Hermine, Harry is acquainted with the prostitute Maria and the jazz musician Pablo. The novel culminates at a masked ball where Harry takes drugs supplied by Pablo, who invites him into the Magic Theater. Hidden

[346] The author/authors of the Treatise remain unknown throughout the novel. Readings that deal with who might have written it exist in appreciative numbers. Lynn Dhority identifies three primary positions interpreters have taken. The first: "the author remains unidentifiable." The second: "the author is one of the 'Immortals'." And the third: "the Treatise is a product of Haller's own imagination." (Lynn Dhority, "Who Wrote the *Tractat vom Steppenwolf*?" *German Life and Letters* 27, no. 1 [1973]: 60.) Colin Wilson belongs to the third category, claiming that the Treatise "is obviously Haller's own work" and "an important piece of self-analysis" that emphasizes his status as an outsider. (Wilson, *The Outsider*, 62.) Ziolkowski belongs to the second category and argues that the Treatise "must be understood as the work of the Immortals themselves," as it is written in a superior tone and projects an "all-encompassing view of the world." (Ziolkowski, *The Novels of Hermann Hesse*, 189.) For the present study, the first position (that the author remains unidentifiable) is the most useful, because speculation regarding the real author/authors of the Treatise is not as interesting as how the protagonist is affected by the content of the pamphlet, that is, how he chooses to respond to it.

[347] Hermine bears great resemblance to the character Mignon in Goethe's *Wilhelm Meisters Lehrjahre*. Mignon's gender expressions also oscillate between male and female, thereby activating homoerotic desires in Goethe's novel (as argued, for example, in Lindén, "It Takes a Real Man," 70).

parts of Harry's personality are revealed inside the theater and in an intricate, dream-like episode he discovers Hermine and Pablo in each other's arms, naked. Harry assumes that they have had sex and murders Hermine, an act that she, throughout the narrative, has commanded of him (textual examples will be provided later). For this crime and for having taken life too seriously, Harry is condemned by the Immortals. The novel ends with them all laughing at him and having now merged with Mozart, Pablo is shown to be one of the Immortals, waiting for Harry to join him.

Tierähnlichkeit and Animality

Concerning how one "traces animals in literature," Philip Armstrong (drawing on the work of John Simons) has written: "in seeking to go beyond the use of animals as mere mirrors for human meaning, our best hope is to locate the 'tracks' left by animals in texts, the ways cultural formations are affected by the materiality of animals and their relationships with humans."[348] Reading literary animals by paying attention to their tracks is, according to Armstrong, a notion with the purpose of challenging human/animal hierarchies and essentialist conceptions of species, as well as allowing animal agency—a stance shared by many in the critical animal studies field.

Susan McHugh, for instance, writes: "Although animals abound in literature across all ages and cultures, only in rarified ways have they been the focal point of systematic literary study."[349] McHugh suggests that "literary animal agency" derives from acknowledging literary animals as more than proxies for human subjectivity. Also, as Ann-Sofie Lönngren argues, even though we, as human beings, are incapable of completely escaping an anthropocentric worldview, "it is certainly possible to question the centrality of 'the human' in the humanities, to point out the consequences of this bias, and to employ theoretical concepts and methods according to which more-than-anthropocentric knowledge can be produced."[350]

Attempting to read the wolf in Hesse's novel exclusively as a "real" animal poses somewhat of a challenge, however. *Der Steppenwolf* does not involve any clear-cut representations of an actual wolf. Rather, as Richards suggests, the wolf is a symbol that signifies demons or the devil. "Hesse consistently

---

[348] Philip Armstrong, *What Animals Mean in the Fiction of Modernity* (London: Routledge, 2008), 3.

[349] Susan McHugh, *Animal Stories: Narrating Across Species Lines* (Minneapolis: University of Minnesota Press, 2011), 6.

[350] Ann-Sofie Lönngren, *Following the Animal: Power, Agency, and Human-Animal Transformations in Modern, Northern-European Literature* (Newcastle upon Tyne: Cambridge Scholars Publishing, 2015), 22.

develops lupine imagery to describe the bestial side of Harry,"[351] he writes. Although Hesse's novel does not involve a real wolf, this study aims at acknowledging the wolf as more than mere "imagery" and thereby emphasizes literary animal agency.

As the first quote presented in this chapter shows, *Der Steppenwolf* gives us an amalgamation of a human and an animal, a creature in which even the human part is imbued with wolf-like traits. The author's construction of Harry's animality is thus comparable with Theodor Adorno's concept *Tierähnlichkeit*, that is, "humans' resemblance to animals." In Adorno's "Notes on Kafka" he perceives a conflict between the ultimate bourgeois concept of human dignity and the likeness between man and animal.[352] Recognizing our Tierähnlichkeit as humans—how we resemble animals—is, to Adorno, a means of addressing human beings' subjugation of the other animals, as well as an appeal to find balance in this unequal relationship.

In Camilla Flodin's assessment, Adorno does not regard non-human animals to be slaves to their primal instincts. Flodin explains that Adorno sees Tierähnlichkeit "as having both critical and utopian potential: when we humans deny our likeness to animals, defining ourselves as radically distinct from other animals, we become increasingly like the false (but socially real) conception of animals subtending this denial—*instinctual creatures trapped in existing conditions.*"[353] That is, when we humans ignore our likeness to animals, we exemplify the primitive behavior that we otherwise ascribe to the non-human animals we subjugate.

Christina Gerhardt points out: "Animals remind us that nature for Adorno is the condition of possibility not only for reading the self, humans, and culture but also for an unreadable other, alterity."[354] In so doing, she follows Adorno and Max Horkheimer's contention in *Dialectic of Enlightenment* (1947) about animal otherness: "The idea of man in European history," they write, "is expressed in the way in which he is distinguished from the animal. Animal irrationality is adduced as proof of human dignity."[355]

---

[351] Richards, *Exploring the Divided Self*, 120. In this quote, Richards draws on David Artiss, "Key Symbols in Hesse's *Steppenwolf*," *Seminar* 7, no. 2 (1971): 87–88.

[352] Theodor W. Adorno, "Notes on Kafka," in *Prisms*, trans. Samuel and Shierry Weber (Cambridge, MA: The MIT Press, 1981), 270.

[353] Camilla Flodin, "Adorno's Utopian Animals," in *Critical Theory: Past, Present, Future*, ed. Anders Bartonek and Sven-Olov Wallenstein (Huddinge: Södertörns högskola, 2021), 112.

[354] Christina Gerhardt, "The Ethics of Animals in Adorno and Kafka," *New German Critique* 33, no. 1 (2006): 160.

[355] Max Horkheimer and Theodor W. Adorno, *Dialectic of Enlightenment*, trans. John Cumming (New York: Continuum, 1989), 245.

Although the animal in *Der Steppenwolf* is portrayed as an Other, it is not irrational but has intelligence and subjectivity, and a shared corporeality with a human. These factors make it possible to understand Hesse's novel as critical of the perception that humans alone are the superior species.

Interestingly, alongside being conveyed thematically in *Der Steppenwolf*, Tierähnlichkeit can also be identified on a material level. Although Harry's physical body is that of a human being (he walks, for instance, on two legs), his animal characteristics are expressed with a couple of bodily wolf-like attributes. First, "[Harry] hatte seinen scharfen kurzhaarigen Kopf witternd in die Höhe gereckt, schnupperte mit der nervösen Nase um sich her." (8) (Harry reached out his sharp-looking, short-haired head and sniffed around with his nose nervously.) Harry's sharp-looking head reminds us of the pointy shape of a wolf's face. Second, he is described as having "ganz [kurzes] Kopfhaar, das hier und dort ein wenig grau flimmerte." (8) (short hair that flickered in shades of gray.) This description mirrors the fact that while wolves' furs can be either black or white, most wolves are mottled gray.[356] And third, Harry often *sniffs*; an activity with animal-like connotations. At one point, while sniffing, he contemplates entering a jazz club full of people:

> Ich stand einen Augenblick schnuppernd, roch an der blutigen grellen Musik, witterte böse und lüstern die Atmosphäre dieser Säle. (38)

> (I stood there sniffing for a moment, smelled the bloody, bright music, viciously and lustfully sensing the atmosphere of these halls.)

This example highlights the previously mentioned devilish connotations of the wolf. As Harry is sniffing—likely for prey—he is depicted as being a threat to humans, as an antagonist. As such, his otherness is emphasized.

While Mauro Ponzi argues that Hesse's prose is characterized by "relationships with otherness" that are never depicted as threatening,[357] *Der Steppenwolf* is an exception to this rule, since the novel's wolf-man represents the ways with which wolves have historically been viewed: "In Western cultures," Garry Marvin states, "wolves, more than any other animal, have been emblematic of the wild and particularly of the dangerous and threatening qualities of the wild."[358] And Peter Arnds writes: "Though admired as a

---

[356] L. David Mech and Luigi Boitani, "Introduction," in *Wolves: Behavior, Ecology, and Conservation*, ed. L. David Mech and Luigi Boitani (Chicago: University of Chicago, 2003), xv.
[357] Mauro Ponzi, "Hermann Hesses Umgang mit dem Fremden," in *Hermann-Hesse-Jahrbuch. Band 1*, ed. Mauro Ponzi (Tübingen: Max Niemeyer, 2004), 1.
[358] Garry Marvin, *Wolf* (London: Reaktion, 2012), 7.

skillful predator by hunting and war-mongering societies, [the wolf] has also been feared as an animal that is able to kill and devour humans."[359]

Harry Haller/the wolf as the antagonist of humans is enhanced by having his outsiderness and otherness continually emphasized. He is a shy but wild animal: "ein verirrtes Tier, das seine Umwelt nicht begriff." (36) (a stray animal that did not understand his environment.) Other characters' reactions convey that Harry exudes something animalistic, even though he passes for a human. But as David Gallagher points out, the reader must neither see the wolf in a literal sense, nor witness Harry's transformation between wolf and human to understand the significance of his animal nature.[360] The importance of wolfishness in Harry's characterization suggests that animality is key to understanding Hesse's text.[361]

Because of two species merging in Harry—that is, the wolf and the human, one might say, co-constructed—Michael Lundblad's conception of animality is relevant. Lundblad argues that rather than seeking to improve relationships between humans and nonhumans, the emphasis in the field of animality studies "remains more on discursive constructions of animalities in relation to human cultural politics."[362] Instead of focusing on real animals, Lundblad suggests that "animalities" are "a set of dynamics that move beyond the human, to be defined as texts (broadly conceived, not just literary), discourses, and material relationships that construct animals, on the one hand, or humans in relation to animals, on the other hand, or both."[363]

Not tracing an actual animal but instead highlighting the discursive co-construction of the human and wolf within Harry Haller is not to be seen as surrendering to anthropocentrism. As will be disclosed in this reading,

---

[359] Peter Arnds, *Lycanthropy in German Literature* (Basingstoke: Palgrave Macmillan, 2015), 1.

[360] Gallagher, *Metamorphosis*, 336.

[361] Hesse's fascination with wolves encompasses more than the novel in focus here. In 1907, he authored a short story about a wolf who is hunted and killed, and *Der Steppenwolf* was preceded by a collection of "Steppenwolf poems" that were originally published in the literary magazine *Die Neue Rundschau* in 1926 with the title "Steppenwolf: A Piece of Diary in Verse." While they share many similarities with *Der Steppenwolf* (summarized in Freedman, *Pilgrim of Crisis*, 281–283) and have often been regarded as predecessors to the novel, they are, as argued by Eugene L. Stelzig, more than "raw material for the fictional frame of *Steppenwolf*." (Eugene L. Stelzig, "The Aesthetics of Confession: Hermann Hesse's 'Crisis' Poems in the Context of the 'Steppenwolf' Period," *Criticism* 21, no. 1 [1979]: 50.) Although a comparison of the Steppenwolf poems and *Der Steppenwolf* from a queer-theoretical perspective is an interesting prospect, such an examination is beyond the scope of this study. After the publication of *Der Steppenwolf*, the poems were made into a book of their own named *Krisis* (*Crisis*, 1928).

[362] Michael Lundblad, "Introduction: The End of the Animal — Literary and Cultural Animalities," in *Animalities: Literary and Cultural Studies Beyond the Human*, ed. Michael Lundblad (Edinburgh: Edinburgh University Press, 2017), 11.

[363] Ibid., 1–2.

Harry's wolfish nature is never inferior to his human nature. Harry, we shall see, is dependent on the qualities of his inner wolf. In addition, the animal side of him—that which makes him Other—is consistently elevated as an ideal.

The Human/Animal Dualism

In this study's overview chapter, it was mentioned that, in the scholarship on Hesse, it has been common to emphasize dualisms that the author attempts to synthesize. One of the many dualisms that figure in *Der Steppenwolf* (examples that will be examined throughout the remainder of this study) can be observed by Harry taking "an uncanny pleasure in the juxtaposition of chaos and order,"[364] as suggested by Theodore Saul Jackson. This chaos/order dualism relates to the previously mentioned conception of wildness as chaotic, unrestrained, and unpredictable: "wildness is the absence of order," Halberstam writes, "the entropic force of a chaos that constantly spins away from biopolitical attempts to manage life and bodies and desires."[365]

The significance of wildness within the chaos/order dualism makes another important pair of opposites at the center of Hesse's novel evident, that is, the dualism between human and animal. This dichotomy is articulated through the juxtaposition of bourgeois culture and Harry's status as an outsider and Other. One could argue, of course, that the categories of human and animal are not really dual because humans are also animals. As far as we know, though, non-human animals are not concerned with the concept of bourgeois ideology, and it is thus safe to assume that the bourgeoisie in *Der Steppenwolf* stands for humanistic qualities whereas Harry (while also being human) represents that which is animalistic as well.

The bourgeoisie in *Der Steppenwolf* manifests itself as the norm against which the wolf's untamed otherness is measured, something to which Theodore Ziolkowski also alludes. With the wolf of the steppes, he claims, "Hesse was attempting to delineate his own specific situation: that of a man who felt himself to be so cut off from the world of normal people that he was like a wolf among the lambs of bourgeois society because his very existence threatened their ideals, beliefs, and way of life."[366] An iteration of this is visible in the novel, when the protagonist moves into the neat, bourgeois home.

[364] Jackson, "Ambivalent Modernist," 142.
[365] Halberstam, *Wild Things*, 7.
[366] Ziolkowski, *The Novels of Hermann Hesse*, 179.

When the landlady and her nephew (who is the man who publishes Harry's manuscript and the narrator of the "Foreword") talk about Harry, she says:

> Es riecht hier bei uns nach Sauberkeit und Ordnung und nach einem freundlichen und anständigen Leben … Er sieht aus, wie wenn er daran nicht mehr gewöhnt wäre und es entbehrt hätte. (10)

> (Here it smells of cleanliness and order, and a welcoming, civilized life. He looks like he is no longer used to that and has missed it.)

But Harry does not miss such a life. He is proud to be *"gänzlich außerhalb der bürgerlichen Welt"* (53) (*completely cut off from the bourgeois world*) and although he grew up in a middle-class home, he has revolted against it. Harry believes himself to be someone who rises above *"die kleinen Normen des Durchschnittlebens"* (53) (*the petty norms of average life*) but at the same time he finds himself strangely drawn to bourgeois settings (likely because of his human side). Choosing to lodge in a clean apartment in an urban environment, rather than remaining in nature, indicates that Harry is ambivalent about where he belongs. As Ralph Freedman points out: "*Steppenwolf* was the first and actually the only work by Hesse in which the entire action takes place in a contemporary metropolis."[367] Usually, Hesse's texts include depictions of grand natural settings. Hence, the fact that Hesse chose an urban environment to tell a story about a wolf-man indicates that animality is a motif that should be acknowledged.

Harry's ambivalence about where he belongs takes the shape of an (oftentimes forcefully) uttered disdain for the bourgeoisie, which at the same time makes visible a cluster wherein masculine, antimodernist, animalistic, and warrior-praising sentiments become central to his self-perception as a wolf-man. Let us recall Robert Deam Tobin's statement from the overview chapter that the German Männerbunde (groups of men in which masculinity bordering on homoeroticism was celebrated) entertained antiliberal, antibourgeois, and antimodernist ideas. While Harry is a devoted pacifist, his wolf-like qualities actually connote war and aggressiveness. "In German culture," Peter Arnds writes, "wolves are a part of an extensive terrain of folklore and myths in the proximity of the hunt and war."[368] Also, as Luigi Boitani points out, the link between wolves, warriors, and masculinity has a long history: "When hunters settled down and became farmers, bands of

---

[367] Freedman, *Pilgrim of Crisis*, 277.
[368] Arnds, *Lycanthropy in German Literature*, 6.

people protected small villages from wild animals and from potential human invaders. These people were the first 'military bodies,' the Indo-German 'Mannerbunde' [*sic*] that behaved much like a group of wolves."[369]

As this pacifist/warrior dichotomy illustrates, ambivalence is a central component in Harry's character. Craig Bernard Palmer argues the same: "Harry Haller does not fit comfortably into the social expectations of a middle-class, masculine identity. Because he conceives of himsetf [*sic*] as both man and wolf, he cannot feel synonymous with either image, cannot possess a single identity, masculine or otherwise."[370] While the wolf part of Harry connotes strength, his human side is portrayed as weak. "Seine Gesundheit schien nicht gut zu sein" (16) (His health appeared to be bad), the landlady's nephew narrates. The pain in Harry's leg makes him limp up the stairs, and he has trouble with digestion and lack of sleep. The nephew ascribes Harry's ailments to his frequent alcohol consumption: "Ich schreib es vor allem seinem Trinken zu." (16) (I attributed it all to his drinking habits.)

These observations stress a correlation between the protagonists in *Der Steppenwolf* and *Peter Camenzind*. Peter's alcoholism accentuates unmanliness, as we saw in chapter two. While Harry is far better at controlling his drinking than Peter, the observation above clearly shows that alcohol affects his health. If we interpret Harry's alcohol habits as we did Peter Camenzind's, that is, that lacking impulse control can make male characters associated with George Mosse's concept of the masculine countertype, Harry's contradictory qualities are highlighted. As a wolf-man Harry is *animal* and *human*, *strong* and *weak*, *manly* and *unmanly*, *warrior* and *pacifist*—essentially, he appears to be innately ambivalent.

"A Creature from Another World"

The bourgeois culture surrounding Harry illuminates the conditions of his status as *Sonderling* (outsider), *Einsiedler* (hermit), or better yet, lone wolf. The novel's protagonist, we learn, belongs among "*[d]ie friedlosen Steppenwölfe.*" (57) (*the lawless Steppenwolves.*[371]) Being *friedlos* implies not being

---

[369] Boitani, "Ecological and Cultural Diversities," 6.

[370] Palmer, "The Significance of Homosexual Desire," 1.

[371] As I have argued elsewhere, Harry's qualities as a lone wolf resonates with Giorgio Agamben's thoughts on the *homo sacer* ("the sacred or accursed man" in ancient Roman law). In Agamben's definition, the homo sacer comes into being in "a zone of indistinction between the human and the animal;" he is "a man who is transformed into a wolf and a wolf who is transformed into a man." (Giorgio

obedient to the law, as well as to be "without peace." Although Hesse's novel is set between the two World Wars, Harry is in a perpetual war with himself. The human and the wolf within him are far from friends; instead, they are in "*ständiger Todfeindschaft gegeneinander.*" (46) (*endless bitter animosity with each other.*)

Harry's friedlos-qualities are visible to others, such as the landlady's nephew. He observes Harry avoiding the police, which he perceives as suspicious and threatening:

> Gerade zu dem Unvertrauten und Fremden, das der Mann an sich hatte, schien mir diese Scheu vor der Polizei allzu gut zu passen, um nicht als verdächtig aufzufallen. (9)

> (The man's wariness of seeming suspicious to the police matched his strange and otherworldly appearance.)

Harry's "otherworldly appearance" can be attributed to the fact that he is not a forest wolf, which according to Peter Arnds is the more usual version of the wolf in German literature: "Being a wolf of the steppes and not of the forest (*Waldwolf*) may be a significant detail in connection with [Haller's] lack of patriotism, with Haller's un-German, if not foreign nature."[372] In the German context the word "steppe" may appear foreign. It refers to ecoregions in Eurasia characterized by desolate grassland plains without trees. The word also connotes perceptibility, since on a steppe there are no trees to hide behind. We are thus encouraged to truly observe the part of Harry's nature that the Steppenwolf dominates, to identify with this Other who rejects bourgeois conformism.

Arnds suggests that, in German literature, the wolf is used as a metaphor to reflect "bourgeois anxieties about crime, vagrancy, invasion, and idleness."[373] In Hesse's novel there are examples of all these fears: The landlady's nephew notices Harry's apprehensive behavior toward the police (*crime*); Harry is homeless and has a nomadic lifestyle (*vagrancy*); the fact that Harry passes for a normal bourgeois human makes him an infiltrating threat to that society (*invasion*); and since his purpose in the world of the bourgeoisie is

Agamben, *Homo Sacer: Sovereign Power and Bare Life*, trans. Daniel Heller-Roazen [Stanford: Stanford University Press, 1998], 106.) For further reading on the parallels between Agamben's homo sacer figure and Harry Haller, see Oscar von Seth, "Tracing the Wolf in Hermann Hesse's *Der Steppenwolf*," in *Squirrelling: Human–Animal Studies in the Northern-European Region*, ed. Amelie Björck, Claudia Lindén, and Ann-Sofie Lönngren (Huddinge: Södertörns högskola, 2022), 119–140.

[372] Arnds, *Lycanthropy in German Literature*, 103.

[373] Ibid., 8.

unclear—that he, an intellectual, prefers to contemplate in solitude rather than partake in bourgeois sociality—may in fact be regarded as a threat to modernist conceptions of progress (*idleness*).

Harry is, accordingly, labeled "ungesellig" (7) (asocial), and:

> [E]r war wirklich, wie er sich zuweilen nannte, ein Steppenwolf, ein fremdes, wildes und auch scheues, sogar sehr scheues Wesen aus einer anderen Welt. (7)

> (Truly he was, as he occasionally called himself, a wolf of the steppes, a strange, wild, and shy—even very shy—creature from another world.)

As we have seen, Harry has little reverence for the norms of the bourgeoisie. He manages to tolerate the middle-class because he is not a part of it:

> [I]ch habe auch den Kontrast gern, in dem mein Leben, mein einsames, liebloses und gehetztes, durch und durch unordentliches Leben, zu diesem Familien- und Bürgermilieu steht. (29)

> (I also appreciate the contrast between my life—my lonely, loveless, and haunted, thoroughly messy life—and this family-like, bourgeois environment.)

Although throughout history, the wolf has often been regarded a threat to humans, Arnds states that it has also been a bearer of superior characteristics such as valiancy and nobility.[374] This vacillation between antagonistic and idealized Other turns out to be integral to the character Harry Haller. Accentuating the wolf part of him thus echoes the aesthetic movement primitivism, in which primitive aspects of human life (in essence, that which preceded civilization) was idealized. Ben Etherington explains:

> Primitivism was an aesthetic project formed in reaction to the zenith of imperialist expansion at the start of the twentieth century. As those spaces in which "primitive" modes of existence were imagined to be possible either were directly colonized or otherwise forcibly integrated into a geographically totalized capitalist system, so dissenting spirits responded by trying to rekindle the primitive by means of their art. As such, primitivism was a pro-

---

[374] Arnds, *Lycanthropy in German Literature*, 1.

ject specific to this world-historical situation: an undertaking to become primitive in a world where, it seemed, such a possibility had been voided.[375]

What sets Harry apart from human culture are his primitive instincts as part wolf and that he desires "Wonne, Erlebnis, Ekstase und Erhebung." (32) (enjoyment, experience, ecstasy, and elevation.) In particular, the final expression, elevation, suggests that Hesse employs the animal part of his protagonist as a means of illuminating transcendence from the one-sidedness and mediocrity of civilized, bourgeois, and human life.

References to Nietzsche's Thinking

While Friedrich Nietzsche's animal philosophy does not constitute a primary theoretical source in this study, the fact that Hesse was an admirer of his thinking, and that *Der Steppenwolf* mirrors some of Nietzsche's conceptions of animality, makes his thoughts interesting when tracing the novel's wolf.[376]

For instance, in *Also sprach Zarathustra*, Nietzsche refers to the wolf as an outsider of sorts: "But the free spirit," he writes, "the enemy of fetters, the non-adorer who dwells in the woods, is as hateful to the people as a wolf to dogs. To hound him out of his lair—that is what the people have ever called 'a sense of decency'; and against him the people still set their fiercest dogs."[377] The wolf, to Nietzsche, represents something wild, something deviant that lurks in the forest and is despised by humans. As such, Nietzsche's wolf can be said to connote queerness (queerness in the sense that it is marginalized,

---

[375] Ben Etherington, *Literary Primitivism* (Stanford: Stanford University Press, 2018), xi. Etherington differentiates between two forms of primitivism, namely "philo-primitivism" (*identification* with the primitive) and "emphatic primitivism" (a desire *to become* primitive). The latter is the one he is interested in. "Primitivism," Etherington writes, "has been regarded as a unidirectional ideological projection from the colonizer onto the colonized: a racial and imperialistic 'discourse' according to which Western artists and thinkers idealize those non-Western peoples whom they suppose to be 'primitive.'" (Ibid., xii.) The purpose of Etherington's study is to not revisit such conceptions of primitivism but rather to "change the object." He does not view literary primitivism as an imperialist exercise of power, but as a practice in which colonized peoples themselves took part, thus challenging Western oppression. With readings of Aimé Césaire, D. H. Lawrence, Claude McKay, and Franz Fanon, Etherington argues that the most subversive primitivist literary works were produced by colonized subjects under imperialist rule.

[376] Research on animal imagery in Nietzsche's philosophy includes Margot Norris's groundbreaking study *Beasts of the Modern Imagination: Darwin, Nietzsche, Kafka, Ernst, and Lawrence* (Baltimore: Johns Hopkins University Press, 1985); the comprehensive anthology *A Nietzschean Bestiary: Becoming Animal Beyond Docile and Brutal*, ed. Christa Davis Acampora and Ralph R. Acampora (Lanham, MD: Rowman & Littlefield, 2004); and Vanessa Lemm, *Nietzsche's Animal Philosophy: Culture, Politics, and the Animality of the Human Being* (New York: Fordham University Press, 2009).

[377] Friedrich Nietzsche, *Thus Spoke Zarathustra: A Book for All and None*, trans. Walter Kaufmann (Harmondsworth: Penguin Books, 1978), 102–103.

outside of majority culture), much like the wolf in Hesse's novel. Additionally, the wolf in *Der Steppenwolf* is perceivable as a depiction of Nietzsche's *Übermensch* ("superhuman," or "overman").[378]

For Nietzsche, Ralph R. Acampora writes, "the European herd-history of common civilization has produced animals spiritually sickened by becoming all-too-humanly *tame*; their illness can, however, be overcome by trans-human (*übermenschlich*) individuals who have the courage and control to instinctually and artistically reappropriate—redeem and transvalue—ancestral animality from the prehistoric wild."[379] What Acampora labels "European herd-history" can be compared with the bourgeois culture against which Hesse charges in *Der Steppenwolf*. In choosing a wolf—an animal we have established is far from tame—as a contrast to the bourgeoisie, and infusing that wolf with idealized qualities, Hesse's protagonist becomes interpretable as an iteration of Nietzsche's Übermensch.

Interestingly, being an iteration of this figure also accentuates queer connotations around Harry. Robert Deam Tobin remarks that "Nietzsche's notion of the Übermensch appealed tremendously to [Adolf Brand and other masculinist] writers, who were smitten by the phantasy of the superman as blond beast. The concept of [self-ownership]," Tobin underscores, "overlapped extensively with Nietzsche's Übermensch."[380] Tobin also mentions that Brand published a poem entitled "Der Übermensch" in the magazine.[381] As we can see here, an interconnectedness between the Übermensch, homoeroticism, and animality exists, three concepts with which Hesse's novel is linked.

As Acampora's writing suggests, cultivating one's animality (an aspect of the human that has been lost throughout civilization) is necessary in order to become an Übermensch. Vanessa Lemm makes a similar point, writing that "becoming overhuman is dependent upon one's openness to the animality of the human being."[382] *Der Steppenwolf* is an apt example of these scholars'

---

[378] It is probably not a coincidence that Harry Haller's greatest idol, Johann Wolfgang von Goethe, was perceived by Nietzsche as an example of humanity's "great redemptive men," that is, an iteration of the Übermensch. (See Friedrich Nietzsche, *Schopenhauer as Educator* [1874], in Friedrich Nietzsche, *Untimely Meditations*, ed. Daniel Breazeale, trans. R. J. Hollingdale [Cambridge: Cambridge University Press, 1997].) For further reading, see Nicholas Martin, "Nietzsche's Goethe: In Sickness and in Health," *Publications of the English Goethe Society* 77, no. 2 (2008): 113–124.

[379] Ralph R. Acampora, "Nietzsche's Feral Philosophy: Thinking Through an Animal Imaginary," in *A Nietzschean Bestiary: Becoming Animal Beyond Docile and Brutal*, ed. Christa Davis Acampora and Ralph R. Acampora (Lanham, MD: Rowman & Littlefield, 2004), 2.

[380] Tobin, *Peripheral Desires*, 57. Emphasis in original.

[381] Ibid., 57–59.

[382] Lemm, *Nietzsche's Animal Philosophy*, 5.

interpretations of Nietzsche's conception, as Harry Haller idealizes the wolf part within himself. Harry can be said to embody Acampora's and Lemm's interpretations because he elevates his wolfishness and cultivates animality.

In Wilbur B. Franklin's research on Hesse, however, it is argued that since Hesse's writing "dwells on the inner, subjective experience of his heroes" and focuses less on interpersonal relationships, it is primarily useful in defining what is *human*.[383] Franklin adopts the position that being human means to be able to think, which is a common characteristic of Hesse's heroes. *Der Steppenwolf* is an exception to this rule, however, since it attempts to demarcate what it might mean to be an animal (at least in part). In the novel, Hesse not only posits an animal as a thinker but also suggests that this animal is more "real" than human beings. We see this in a conversation with Hermine about Harry's dual wolf-man nature, when she expresses criticism of terms such as *Bestie* (beast) and *Raubtier* (predator) when one speaks about animals:

> Man sollte nicht so von den Tieren reden. Sie sind ja oft schrecklich, aber sie sind doch viel richtiger als die Menschen. ... Sie wollen dir nicht schmeicheln, sie wollen dir nicht imponieren. Kein Theater. Sie sind, wie sie sind. (111)

> (One should not speak of animals in such a way. While they are often horrifying, they are much more real than people. They do not seek to flatter you; they do not wish to impress you. No fuss. They are what they are.)

In Hermine's words we hear an echo of Nietzsche's notion that animals are unhistorical: "the animal lives *unhistorically*: for it is contained in the present," Nietzsche writes, "it does not know how to dissimulate, it conceals nothing and at every instant appears wholly as what it is."[384]

Although Hermine reiterates Nietzsche's idea, her words also express ambivalence; that is, her argument both contradicts and correlates with his. While animals are "more real than people" most of them resemble humans that are sad, Hermine claims. Then she says:

---

[383] Franklin, "The Concept of 'the Human'," 77.
[384] Friedrich Nietzsche, *On the Uses and Disadvantages of History for Life* [1874], in Friedrich Nietzsche, *Untimely Meditations*, ed. Daniel Breazeale, trans. R. J. Hollingdale (Cambridge: Cambridge University Press, 1997), 61.

[W]enn ein Mensch sehr traurig ist … dann sieht er immer ein wenig einem Tier ähnlich – er sieht dann traurig aus, aber richtiger und schöner als sonst. (111–112)

(When a person is very sad, then he always resembles an animal – he looks sad but truer and more beautiful than usual.)

The sadness of animals that Hermine refers to contradicts Nietzsche's ideas because he proposes that animals—living unhistorically—are *happy* because of their forgetfulness.

Although Hermine regards Harry's sadness as true and beautiful, his dual nature—being neither wolf nor human completely, and his inability to synthesize this duality—makes him sad and suicidal: "ein unzufriedener Mensch" (an unsatisfied human being). As we can see, it is Harry's human side that makes him discontented, while the animal part of him is elevated. The proposed synthesis of both sides, however, is the desirable alternative. Here we might recall Colin Wilson's conceptualization of the Outsider as someone who, while at odds with society, yearns to *cease being an outsider*; but ceasing to be an outsider does not mean that one conforms to the ideals of majority culture. We see an iteration of Wilson's Outsider in Harry, since he desires transcendence from the dualisms of his being. Harry wants to become something higher, an Immortal, but his inability to accept all parts of himself makes him a raging cynic.

Harry's pessimistic view of his time, as well as his scorn of its bourgeois values, can be seen as another reflection of Nietzsche's thinking. Nietzsche writes: "If happiness, if reaching out for new happiness, is in any sense what fetters living creatures to life and makes them go on living, then perhaps no philosopher is more justified than the Cynic: for the happiness of the animal, as the perfect Cynic, is the living proof of the rightness of Cynicism."[385] This Nietzschean concept pervades Harry's worldview; to really live one must learn forgetfulness which the human part of him, unfortunately, makes impossible.

Elitism and Nazi Wolf Symbolism

While Harry is both suicidal and pessimistic, his intellectual and philosophical aptitudes supersede the bourgeois majority, which is an aspect of the

---

[385] Nietzsche, *On the Uses*, 61.

text that makes his elitism visible. We see this from the perspective of the landlady's nephew when he observes Harry in a lecture hall:

> [D]er Blick des Steppenwolfes durchdrang unsre ganze Zeit … der Blick … ging noch viel weiter als bloß auf Mängel und Hoffnungslosigkeiten unsrer Zeit, unsrer Geistigkeit, unsrer Kultur. Er ging bis ins Herz alles Menschentums, er sprach beredt in einer einzigen Sekunde den ganzen Zweifel eines Denkers, eines vielleicht Wissenden aus an der Würde, am Sinn des Menschenlebens überhaupt. Dieser Blick sagte: "Schau, solche Affen sind wir! Schau, so ist der Mensch!" (12–13)

> (The gaze of the Steppenwolf pierced our whole time. The gaze went further than the mere defects and futility of our time, our spirituality, our culture. The gaze of the Steppenwolf pierced the heart of humanity, it eloquently voiced in a single second the doubt of a thinker regarding the dignity, even the entire meaning of human life. That gaze said: "Look, such monkeys! That is what humans are!")

Hesse using another animal, a monkey, as a symbol for the futility of human culture is yet another noticeable reference to Nietzsche's thinking. In *Also sprach Zarathustra*, Nietzsche writes: "What is the ape to man? A laughingstock or a painful embarrassment. And man shall be just that for the overman: a laughingstock or a painful embarrassment. You have made your way from worm to man, and much in you is still worm. Once you were apes, and even now, too, man is more ape than any ape."[386]

Nietzsche suggests that the human is to the Übermensch what the ape is to the human, namely lesser, something to be ridiculed and ashamed by.[387] In making this claim, Nietzsche degrades the ape, a species he associates with something primitive and intellectually deficient.[388] Even though primates are

---

[386] Nietzsche, *Thus Spoke Zarathustra*, 12.

[387] For a conclusive and exciting analysis of the figure of the Ape in Nietzsche's writing, see Peter S. Groff, "Who Is Zarathustra's Ape?" in *A Nietzschean Bestiary: Becoming Animal Beyond Docile and Brutal*, ed. Christa Davis Acampora and Ralph R. Acampora (Lanham, MD: Rowman & Littlefield, 2004), 17–31.

[388] While the discursive link between Nietzsche's thinking and Nazi ideology that this study notes can be seen as unfair (that is, that Nietzsche's ideas, at large, have been misinterpreted), much has been written about the appropriation of Nietzschean thought within racist and fascist movements. Nietzsche's views on "racial purity" and "regulated reproduction," for instance, were in fact propagated by the Nazis. For further reading, see the epilogue in Rüdiger Safranski, *Nietzsche: A Philosophical Biography*, trans. Shelley Frisch (London: Granta Books, 2002), 317–350; Gregory Moore, *Nietzsche: Biology and Metaphor* (Cambridge: Cambridge University Press, 2002); and Robert Bernasconi, "Nietzsche as a Philosopher of Racialized Breeding," in *The Oxford Handbook of Philosophy and Race*, ed. Naomi Zack (New York: Oxford University Press, 2017), 54–64.

generally regarded as intelligent, humans described as monkeys can be seen in two ways. On the one hand, such a description functions as a signifier of the animal side of man, that man is an animal too. On the other hand, the monkey metaphor in *Der Steppenwolf* primarily represents unevolved humans. While both humans and primates can be intelligent, problem-solving, have high levels of cognition, and possess language, Harry's wolf-man nature represents a more evolved being. Therefore, the novel establishes a hierarchy among animals in which primates are designated as a lesser species.

The quote above ("Look, such monkeys! That is what humans are!") mirrors Nietzsche's notion but, in Hesse's novel, the low hierarchical status of monkeys has an increased meaning since monkeys are equated with black people. *Der Steppenwolf* repeatedly uses the N-word,[389] sometimes in conjunction with depictions of black people as monkey-like and uncultivated. The racism that is conveyed in *Der Steppenwolf* will be addressed in detail in the last chapter, under the heading "Intersections of Jazz, Racism, and Sex." Suffice it to say, for now, that although one could interpret Harry's elitist disdain for others as a reaction to being on the margins himself (that he, as an outsider and Other, challenges the norms of majority culture in a queer way), the fact that the novel equates black people with monkeys while at the same time idealizing a *white* wolf-man makes its racist facet impossible to ignore.

As we can see, the novel's human/animal motif not only connotes otherness and queerness, but also racism. Additionally, giving the wolf within Harry the label "ideal" has other discursive associations. Although the Nazi reign in Germany began a few years after the publication of *Der Steppenwolf*, there are similarities between Hesse's application of the wolf and the Nazis' wolf symbolism. Wolves became greatly revered in Nazi Germany and from the beginning of the Second World War, lycanthropic folklore was revitalized by fascists who upheld the mythical figure of the werewolf as a representation

---

[389] Since language is a powerful tool, both to reproduce and to critique inequalities, this study will not make use of the racist terminology that *Der Steppenwolf* employs for black people, neither in quotes from the original text, nor in quotes from secondary sources. Racist terminology in *Der Steppenwolf* occurs, for example, on pages 38, 39, 60, 63, 98, and 154. For readers unable to grasp why one would choose to refrain from reproducing racist terminology in a study such as this one, further reading on systemic racism, colonialism/postcolonialism/decolonialism as well as white privilege in academia and society is recommended. See, e.g., Reni Eddo-Lodge, *Why I'm No Longer Talking to White People About Race* (London: Bloomsbury, 2017); Robin DiAngelo, *White Fragility: Why It's So Hard for White People to Talk About Racism* (Boston: Beacon Press, 2018); Sara Ahmed, *Living a Feminist Life* (Durham: Duke University Press, 2017); and Alana Lentin, *Why Race Still Matters* (Cambridge: Polity Press, 2020).

of German purity and strength.[390] For example, Nazi U-boats were referred to as "wolf packs" and Hitler gave three of his headquarters wolfish names, among them *Wolfsschanze* (Wolf's Lair) in East Prussia.[391] The name "Adolf" itself is derived from *Athalwolf,* an Old High German name meaning "noble wolf" which may account for why Hitler referred to himself as a wolf—his "Lieblingspseudonym"[392] (favorite pseudonym)—on several occasions during the war.

Additional connections between *Der Steppenwolf* and Nazi ideology are pointed out by Andrew Hollis who suggests that Hesse's writings are characterized by political ambiguity. The author himself was a pacifist and anti-nationalist whose work was nevertheless read by many of his adversaries, that is, people whose political and ideological convictions bordered on National Socialism.[393] *Der Steppenwolf*'s wolf theme makes Hesse's political ambiguity visible. Harry Haller may be openly critical of nationalism but in the early twentieth century when the novel takes place, other German wolf-man narratives, such as Hermann Löns's *Der Wehrwolf* (1910) and Ernst Wiechert's *Der Totenwolf* (1924), tended to give voice to national conservative ideas.[394] Axel Goodbody explains that these "wolf and wolf-man narratives" perpetuated nationalist fantasies of independence and strength, and were "written in the context of 'völkisch' thinking (racist-nationalist conservatism)."[395] For instance, *"Der Wehrwolf,"* he writes, "was a source of inspiration for the right-wing paramilitary groups which proliferated in the years after Germany's defeat in the First World War and sought to undermine Weimar democracy."[396]

---

[390] Eric Kurlander, *Hitler's Monsters: A Supernatural History of the Third Reich* (New Haven, CT: Yale University Press, 2018), 278–281.

[391] Marvin, *Wolf,* 75–78.

[392] Marcel Atze, *"Unser Hitler": Der Hitler-Mythos im Spiegel der deutschsprachigen Literatur nach 1945* (Göttingen: Wallstein, 2003), 385.

[393] Andrew Hollis, "Political Ambivalence in Hesse's 'Steppenwolf," *The Modern Language Review* 73, no. 1 (1978): 110.

[394] Axel Goodbody, "Wolves and Wolf Men as Literary Tropes and Figures of Thought: Eco- and Zoopoetic Perspectives on Jiang Rong's *Wolf Totem* and Other Wolf Narratives," in *Texts, Animals, Environments: Zoopoetics and Ecopoetics,* ed. Frederike Middelhoff, Sebastian Schönbeck, Roland Borgards, and Catrin Gersdorf (Freiburg i. Br.: Rombach, 2019), 318–320. Goodbody, however, exempts *Der Steppenwolf* from the context of racist-nationalist German wolf-man narratives. In a footnote he writes: "The link between wolfishness and aggressive nationalism is, however, notably absent in the German wolf-man story of the time which found an international readership, Hermann Hesse's novel, *Steppenwolf.*" (Ibid., 319.)

[395] Ibid., 318.

[396] Ibid., 319.

Although Hesse's intention was likely not to promote aggressive nationalism, there are indications in *Der Steppenwolf* that the protagonist considers the *Bürger* (common man) expendable: "*es kommt auf ein paar Millionen mehr oder weniger nicht an, sie sind Material, sonst nichts.*" (66) (*a few million more or less do not matter, they are substance, nothing else.*) Harry's view of the middle-class is juxtaposed with his own elevated wolf-man nature and in the wake of the Nazi reign, Harry's attitude regarding the dispensability of the masses—as well as the text's ominous reference to "*ein drittes Reich*" (57) (*a third Reich*) for those who can outgrow bourgeois mediocrity—adds to the complexities of the novel.[397]

A Myriad of Contradictions

As an iteration of otherness, the wolf in Hesse's novel vacillates between antagonistic and idealized. These multifaceted and contradictory implications of *Der Steppenwolf*'s protagonist are also stressed by Alexander Mathäs who argues that "the Steppenwolf, as a symbol with manifold meanings, stands for 'the Animal' in general, and as such for the human other, in that it both distinguishes itself from the human but also embodies it. The Steppenwolf, on the one hand, marks the uncivilized abject, and on the other a purportedly more genuine, uncorrupted human nature worthy of preservation."[398] If we recall the previously quoted passage by Adorno and Horkheimer about how human beings in European history have "distinguished themselves from animals," Hesse's novel reverses this assessment—in *Der Steppenwolf* it is an animal Other that distinguishes itself *from humans.*

In elevating the wolf (a non-human animal), *Der Steppenwolf* criticizes the anthropocentric paradigm; moreover, it can be said to offer an expanded

---

[397] Today's readers should bear in mind that Hesse's interest in wolves began long before he authored *Der Steppenwolf* as well as before Hitler began to publicly idealize the animal, and there is thus no immediately obvious causality. Any conceptual correlation between the two should not warrant guilt by association or reflect negatively on Hesse, a position also held by David G. Richards, who underscores: "To compare Hesse with Hitler or Hesse's thought with the ideology of the Third Reich is certainly unjust." (Richards, *Exploring the Divided Self*, 78.) Furthermore, Richards emphasizes, Hesse "was one of the first German writers to publicly attack Hitler and National Socialism. In July 1922, a year after Hitler became the head of the National Socialist Party, Hesse wrote in an essay entitled 'Verrat am Deutschtum' (Betrayal of the German Ideal) that it was now time 'to say something about one of the most despicable and most ridiculous forms of young-German nationalism, about the idiotic, pathological hatred of Jews (Judenfresserei) on the part of these swastikabards and their numerous, especially student supporters.'" (Ibid., 81. The quote within the quote is from Volker Michels, "Zwischen Duldung und Sabotage. Hermann Hesse und der Nationalsozialismus," in *Hermann Hesse und die Politik*, 7th International Hermann-Hesse Colloquium in Calw, ed. Martin Pfeifer [Bad Liebenzell: Verlag Bernhard Gegenbach, 1992], 87.)
[398] Mathäs, *Beyond Posthumanism*, 244–245.

concept of diversity and inclusivity that moves far beyond the human/wolf binary. As the following quote suggests, Hesse, in fact, advocates peaceful co-existence and kinship between human beings and *all* non-human animals:

> *Die Zweiteilung in Wolf und Mensch, in Trieb und Geist, durch welche Harry sich sein Schicksal verständlicher zu machen sucht ist eine sehr große Vereinfachung … Harry besteht nicht aus zwei Wesen, sondern aus hundert, aus tausenden. (59–60)*

> *(The division of wolf and man, instinct, and spirit, through which Harry seeks to understand his fate is a great simplification. Harry does not consist of two beings but of hundreds, of thousands.)*

But by elevating his inner wolf while simultaneously comparing the narrative's peripheral black people with a low, monkey-like animality, Harry appears racist. In reproducing racist stereotypes and promoting racial inequality to foster wolf agency in *Der Steppenwolf*, its anthropocentric critique becomes arbitrary. Overall, it is apparent that a great deal of ambivalence surrounds the wolf as a figure. *Der Steppenwolf* produces an array of associations: its protagonist is interpretable as queer, he is an outsider and Other, an antagonist, an Übermensch, and the elevated wolf qualities in Hesse's late-1920s text are equal to those that were shortly afterwards appropriated by the Nazis.

Before concluding this chapter, a final word on the internal animosity between the human part and the wolf part of Harry, which, as we know, leads him to consider taking his own life. Harry's suicidal drive derives from an inability to synthesize the polarities within himself, which in Andreas Kiryakakis interpretation limits Harry's options significantly. Harry's "way of salvation is either suicide," Kiryakakis writes, "or an integration into the bourgeois society."[399] The second option is a fate worse than death in Harry's mind, which intensifies his suicidal contemplations. Kiryakakis underlines the following: "Pessimism is the chief determinant in Haller's life, and there is only one response to it: self-annihilation."[400]

At the end of the novel, when Pablo and Mozart appear as the same person, we see an iteration of what Harry aspires to be. If he can finally learn to perceive himself as more than just part wolf and part man—that is, to synthesize into "not two beings but hundreds, thousands"—he will be

---

[399] Kiryakakis, *The Ideal of Heimat*, 105.
[400] Ibid., 104–105.

allowed to enter the peaceful realm of the Immortals. To Harry, achieving peace is thus more than synthesizing the human/animal dualism. Rather, the synthesis that he craves is between a myriad of contradictions.

CHAPTER 5

The Function of Hermine

"The Other Other"

The preceding chapter showed, among other things, that Harry Haller's animality is linked with queerness. Aside from being part wolf (an animal as well as an early-twentieth-century euphemism for masculine homosexual men), Harry's friendship with the gender-nonconforming Hermine shows that queerness, in fact, is tightly entangled with otherness in *Der Steppenwolf*; the wolf in Hesse's text is not the only figure that is characterized by otherness, as we will discover momentarily. Hermine's fluid gender expressions mirror the protagonist's wolf-man nature and makes her the novel's "other Other."

Hermine will be the character of interest in this chapter, and her queer characteristics and function in the novel will be explored. When she first appears in the narrative it quickly becomes clear that gender is key to her characterization. While she is referred to as a "girl," she has a boyish haircut and "ein Knabengesicht" (105) (a boy's face), and she reminds Harry of someone from his adolescence: "aus ihrem Gesicht [sprach] etwas, was mich an frühe Jugendzeiten erinnerte." (88) (her face expressed something that reminded me of my youth.) Then we find out that the person Harry is reminded of is his childhood friend Hermann, which is supposed to be understood as the male equivalent of the name Hermine: "'Wenn du ein Knabe wärst', sagte ich staunend, 'müßtest du Hermann heißen.'" (105) ("If you were a boy," I said full of surprise, "your name had to be Hermann.")

Hermine's answer reflects gender performativity: "'Wer weiß, vielleicht bin ich einer und bin bloß verkleidet', sagte sie spielerisch." (105) ("Who knows, maybe I am a boy but simply in disguise," she said teasingly.) When she finds out what Harry is called, she exclaims: "Harry? Ein Bubenname!" (89) (Harry? A boy's name!) The astonishment of both characters shows that fluid conceptions of gender are supposed to be noticed when reading this novel.

As Craig Bernard Palmer writes, however: "many interpreters have not known whether to view Hermine as an incredibly insightful callgirl or a symbolic projection of Harry's imagination."[401] Since the ideas of Carl Jung influenced Hesse when he was writing *Der Steppenwolf*, a common move among scholars has been to interpret Hermine not as a person but as emblematic of the protagonist's "anima."[402] In Jung's conception of the collective unconscious, the anima, in short, is the unconscious feminine side of a man. While feminine aspects of Harry's persona would be interesting to investigate, reading Hermine mainly as a representation of the protagonist's femininity is a disservice to her as a character. Also, when reading the surface of *Der Steppenwolf*, it would be strange to regard Hermine as a symbol. Viewing her function as allegorical—that is, as signifying something hidden, latent, or unexplored within the male protagonist—would also diminish her own potential and agency.

Hermine's Androgynous Traits

Since Hermine not only has feminine traits but expresses a variety of genders—female, male, and trans/non-binary (gender neutral)—she is more complex and nuanced than some previous readings have allowed her to be. Instead of choosing one or the other—callgirl or symbolic projection— Palmer suggests that "viewing Hermine as both produces greater possibilities for understanding the text."[403] Moreover, as Kamakshi P. Murti argues, to view the concept of androgyny as a symbolic representation of a female/male synthesis in Hesse's work makes it possible to ignore the possibility of homoeroticism completely, as most previous scholarship has done.[404]

In some respects, Hermine's multidimensionality makes her readable as a reversed embodiment of Karl Ulrichs's conception of Urnings. Rather than having the body of a man and the soul of a woman, she can be seen as having a female body and a male soul. While Ulrichs's sexual science included classifications such as *Uranodioningins* (female bisexuals) and "hermaphro-

---

[401] Palmer, "The Significance of Homosexual Desire," 19.

[402] Eugene Webb, for instance, writes that from a Jungian perspective the road to self-knowledge includes the anima as a symbol for one's unconscious. In her role both as a guide and temptation to Harry Haller, Hermine is perceivable as this figure, Webb argues. "The anima," he writes, "will usually take the form of an appealing feminine figure representing the attractiveness of self-knowledge to a person who has begun to outgrow his initial fear of learning the truth about those aspects of himself of which he has previously suppressed all awareness." (Eugene Webb, "Hermine and the Problem of Harry's Failure in Hesse's *Steppenwolf*," *Modern Fiction Studies* 17, no. 1 [1971]: 118.) Overall, however, Webb heterosexualizes the relationship between Harry and Hermine by arguing that since Harry "falls in love" with his anima, he fails to master her and assimilate that which she represents into his own personality.

[403] Palmer, "The Significance of Homosexual Desire," 19.

[404] Murti, "'Ob die Weiber Menschen seyn?'," 270.

dites," these sexual varieties are not fully satisfactory when studying Hermine.[405] Although she can be labeled bisexual (more on this shortly), she is not only female. While her name, Hermine, brings the term hermaphrodite to mind, viewing her as such is less rewarding than seeing her fluid gender expressions as queer. While reading Hermine as a reversed embodiment of an Urning makes her interesting, the duality she brings to the text—which mirrors Harry's human/animal nature—differs from his in a significant way: Harry is at perpetual war with himself over his wolf/man duality, whereas Hermine is portrayed as a complete being. "Her androgyny," David G. Richards writes, "symbolizes the wholeness [Harry] lacks and which is his goal, and she is his guide to that goal."[406]

As Catriona MacLeod has shown (drawing on Aristophanes's speech in Plato's *Symposium*): "The myth of the primal being as a cosmic androgyne whose original unity disintegrates into a world of conflicting parts has persisted throughout Western philosophy, theology, psychology, and literature."[407] MacLeod suggests that "the androgynous myth seems to hold particular fasciation for those historical moments when cultures are actively engaged in rethinking the most basic assumptions about gender and sexuality."[408] Writing against the backdrop of the field of sexology in the first half of the twentieth century, Hesse constructing Hermine as someone whose gender expressions are (at the very least) different is therefore most likely not a coincidence.

Although the figure of the androgyne is interesting (and Hermine can certainly be regarded as such a figure, as she has been in most studies), to grapple with "transgender realness," as Jack Halberstam suggests, "we have to leave the androgyne behind."[409] One viable reason why is that the figure of the androgyne, to certain extent, fortifies heteronormative conceptions of gender as binary. Moreover, to view the concept of androgyny as a symbol of a female/male synthesis in *Der Steppenwolf* not only makes it possible to ignore the possibility of homoeroticism (as Murti argues), but it also diminishes the potential to read Hermine as a person with a trans/non-binary

---

[405] Ulrichs wrote very little about "female uranism" as a sexual variety. For further reading on the concept, Ralph M. Leck refers to chapter five in Ulrichs's *Ara Spei* (1865). However, Leck writes: "Ulrichs says very little about lesbian love, because it was not proscribed by German law." (Leck, *Vita Sexualis*, 241.)

[406] Richards, *Exploring the Divided Self*, 56.

[407] Catriona MacLeod, *Embodying Ambiguity: Androgyny and Aesthetics from Winckelmann to Keller* (Detroit: Wayne State University Press, 1998), 13.

[408] Ibid.

[409] Jack Halberstam, *Female Masculinity* (Durham: Duke University Press, 1998), 215.

gender identity. What is attempted in this chapter is to read Hermine as a character that certainly possesses androgynous traits, but who is not, however, a clear-cut representation of the classic figure of the androgyne.

While Hermine's symbolic function in *Der Steppenwolf* is an interesting starting point—for example, the way she activates certain parts of the protagonist's personality by "mirroring" him—she will, in the following, predominantly be approached as a person in her own right, that is, as someone whose characteristics and actions have meaning in and of themselves.

Female Characters and Lesbianism in *Der Steppenwolf*

In the words of Kurt J. Fickert: "Hermine leads Harry into a hedonistic world. However, her ultimate function is to take Harry to the Magic Theater."[410] Bringing Harry to the Magic Theater at the end of the novel is certainly an important aspect of Hermine's function in the text. But Hermine spending most of her time with Harry by introducing him to a world of hedonism is equally (if not more) meaningful.

When attempting to understand Hermine's function in *Der Steppenwolf*, we must take a closer look at the ways with which female characters and femininity occur in the text, and what sort of desires they are associated with. *Der Steppenwolf* is, on the one hand, a fitting example of Murti's claim that female figures in Hesse's fiction are utilized as mere props for the male protagonists' self-development. Androgynous figures such as Frau Eva and Beatrice in *Demian*, Kamala in *Siddhartha*, and Hermine tend "to reflect and enable the consummation of the protagonist's homoerotic desires," Murti argues, "resulting in the annihilation of the woman as subject."[411]

On the other hand, although Hermine is murdered by Harry (which is a clear depiction of being annihilated), her fluid gender expressions and choices of sexual partners allow her more agency than other female characters in Hesse's fiction. This agency turns out to be especially evident when one measures which characters express their sexuality more freely in *Der Steppenwolf*. The text's female characters (Hermine and Maria) appear, we shall see, to be freer than the men in matters of lovemaking.

Since Hermine and Maria challenge certain norms they can be seen as transgressive characters. As we know, Hermine's gender fluidity differs from other characters in *Der Steppenwolf*. Although her gender expressions are

---

[410] Kurt J. Fickert, "The Development of the Outsider Concept in Hesse's Novels," *Monatshefte* 52, no. 4 (1960): 177.
[411] Murti, "'Ob die Weiber Menschen seyn?'," 270.

met with neither suspicion nor hostility, she is still an embodiment of otherness and defies standardized binary conceptions of gender. Harry is curious about, and attracted to, the multidimensionality she embodies, and when this quality is juxtaposed with his own inability to fit in anywhere, some critics might argue that Hermine's transgressive traits are not equally challenging. From such a viewpoint the lack of resistance Hermine experiences on account of her queerness would indicate that she, in fact, is not much of a rebel. Norms that are not imposed forcefully, however, are not to be seen as any less governing, particularly if an individual is alone in challenging them.

Both Hermine and Maria are prostitutes, and their mutual openness about sexual expression challenge moralist conceptions of what female sexuality ought to be. The female characters in *Der Steppenwolf* thus contrast the women in *Peter Camenzind*. Neither Hermine nor Maria are portrayed as unattainable or saint-like (like Rösi and Elisabeth are) and while they are desired by men, they are not placed on pedestals to be worshipped from afar. Instead, they have a grit to them, something authentic and unapologetic that Harry finds seductive. There is, of course, a Madonna/whore complex at work here. But it bears underscoring that the female characters in *Der Steppenwolf* still appear to have more agency than the women in *Peter Camenzind* do. The purpose here is not to suggest that women must be prostitutes to exercise sexuality freely, but rather to emphasize that while one might not agree with Hermine and Maria's lifestyle choices (prostitution and partying), neither one expresses hesitation toward their reality, and at least within the narrative, their choices appear to be their own.

In addition, the scrupulousness with which they both engage in same-sex sexual practices accentuates their transgressive qualities. In an unfazed manner, Hermine discloses to Harry that she and Maria sometimes have sex: "Ich habe oft genug bei ihr geschlafen und mit ihr gespielt." (140) (I have slept and played with her often enough.) Hermine treats her and Maria's sexual engagement as a self-evident aspect of their relationship precisely because they are friends: "wir sind doch Freunde." (140) (but we are friends.) Since Hermine does not use the feminine German version of "friends," that is, *Freundinnen* (female friends), the gender-transgressive qualities in each of them are emphasized. Moreover, stating "wir sind doch Freunde" could also be interpreted as meaning "but we are *boyfriends*," a statement in which the intertwinement of male friendship and same-sex desire in the era echoes.

Because Hermine sometimes presents herself as male, her fluid gender expressions could make sex with Maria interpretable as heterosexual. But Maria is openly prone to lesbian lovemaking: "Maria [war] auch in der Liebe mit beiden Geschlechtern erfahren." (132) (Maria also had experience loving both sexes.) Additionally, during the masked ball, while presenting as female, Hermine seduces a woman: "sie habe diese Frau nicht als Mann erobert, sondern als Frau, mit dem Zauber von Lesbos." (159) (she had not conquered this woman as a man but as a woman, with allure from Lesbos.)

It is the lesbian implications of Hermine and Maria's bond that activate Harry's own interest in same-sex practices, as he narrates when in bed with Maria:

> Als ich wieder mit Maria zusammenkam, war es mir wunderlich und geheimnisvoll, zu wissen, daß sie Hermine ebenso an ihrem Herzen gehabt hatte wie mich, daß sie deren Glieder, Haar und Haut genauso befühlt, geküßt, gekostet und geprüft habe, wie die meinen. Neue, indirekte, komplizierte Beziehungen und Verbindungen tauchten vor mir auf, neue Liebes- und Lebensmöglichkeiten. (140)

> (When I got back together with Maria, it was strange and mysterious to know that she had had Hermine as close to her heart as me, that she had touched, kissed, tasted, and examined her limbs, her hair and skin, just as she had mine. New, unforeseen, and complicated relationships and liaisons appeared to me, new prospects for love and life.)

At this point in the story, a curiosity is awoken in Harry regarding sexual practices that are not strictly heterosexual. The last phrase of the quote makes this visible. Harry's experiences in bed with Maria open him up to facing something "new, unforeseen, and complicated," which is henceforth understood as references to something queerer than straight sex. While male same-sex desire is not yet indicated (Pablo will activate this later), the text renders lesbianism a gateway for Harry to discover his own sexual potential. Being an embodiment of complexity, however, Harry's marvel at the sexual relationship between Hermine and Maria is rivalled by contrasting emotions. While their lesbianism tickles his imagination, its suggestion that he himself might have potential for same-sex desire results in ambivalence.

After meeting Hermine, Harry has an elaborate dream wherein he meets Goethe and encounters a scorpion: "Außerdem beunruhigte mich ein Skorpion, der soeben noch sichtbar gewesen war und an meinem Bein hochzuklettern versucht hatte." (93) (I was also worried about a scorpion that had appeared and attempted to climb my leg.) Harry expresses ambivalence toward this tiny but deadly creature. In a similar manner to the contradictory way with which Peter Camenzind speaks of women (they are, at first, labeled beautiful only to be perceived as unattractive a mere moment later), the scorpion is depicted as dangerous at first, but then shortly thereafter (within the same sentence in fact), not so much so:

> Der Skorpion aber, wenn auch gefährlich und vielleicht in meiner nächsten Nähe versteckt, war doch vielleicht nicht so schlimm; er konnte, so schien mir, vielleicht auch Freundliches bedeuten. (93–94)

> (The scorpion, while dangerous and perhaps hidden in my immediate surroundings, was perhaps not that bad; it seemed to me it might also mean something friendly.)

Several scholars have pointed out that the scorpion in Harry's dream is associated with women, sensuality, and danger. Reso Karalaschwili, for instance, sees it as representing sexual passion while also signifying illness and the threat of death.[412] Theodore Ziolkowski interprets Harry's ambivalence toward the scorpion as representing his conflicting feelings regarding the sensuality and danger that Hermine has activated by entering his life.[413] And Richards corroborates that view, writing that "[t]he scorpion of the Goethe dream may indicate both desire for and fear of sex, but it also contains a warning that the anima can be dangerous."[414]

Harry wonders whether the name of the scorpion might be "Vulpius" (the name of Goethe's wife), and in the following quote, the feminine and treacherous (even sinful) connotations of the creature are intertwined:

> [E]s schien mir sehr möglich, daß er irgend etwas mit Molly zu tun habe, eine Art Bote von ihr sei oder ihr Wappentier, ein schönes, gefährliches Wappentier der Weiblichkeit und der Sünde. (94)

> (It seemed very possible that it might have something to do with Molly, that it was her messenger or emblem, a beautiful, dangerous emblem of femininity and sin.[415])

---

[412] Reso Karalaschwili, "Harry Hallers Goethe-Traum: Vorläufiges zu einer Szene aus dem *Steppenwolf* von Hermann Hesse," *Goethe-Jahrbuch* 97 (1980): 228.

[413] Ziolkowski, *The Novels of Hermann Hesse*, 209.

[414] Richards, *Exploring the Divided Self*, 130.

[415] Theodore Ziolkowski regards "Molly" in the quote as a reference to the muse in the ballads of pre-Romantic German poet Gottfried August Bürger (1747–1794). (Ziolkowski, *The Novels of Hermann Hesse*, 209.) For the purpose of this reading, however, Molly accentuates a noteworthy link to the British

At the end of the dream, when Goethe presents Harry with a velvet covered box containing a miniature female leg, Harry's indecision is unmistakable:

> Ich streckte die Hand aus und wollte das kleine Bein an mich nehmen, das mich ganz verliebt machte, aber sowie ich mit zwei Fingern zugreifen wollte, schien das Spielzeug sich mit einem winzigen Zuck zu bewegen, und es kam mir plötzlich der Verdacht, dies könne der Skorpion sein. Goethe ... hielt mir das reizende Skorpiönchen ganz nahe vors Gesicht, sah mich danach verlangen, sah mich davor zurückschaudern. (97)

> (Enamored with the little leg I reached out wanting to take it, but as soon as I tried to grab it with two fingers, the figurine seemed to move with a tiny twitch, and I suddenly suspected this might be the scorpion. Goethe held the charming little scorpion close to my face, saw my desire for it, saw me shudder from it.)

Harry being enamored while also shuddering illustrates that he experiences both desire and hesitation. However, the scorpion in his dream is not only associated with women, female attributes, and sensuality, but it also has a curious queer connotation worth highlighting. The title of the most well-known and loved trilogy of lesbian novels from the interwar period is *Der Skorpion* (*The Scorpion*, 1919–1932) by Anna Elisabeth Weirauch.[416] While it is unknown whether Hesse was familiar with Weirauch's work, the causality between the scorpion in Hesse's text and the title of Weirauch's trilogy (wherein "scorpion" is a code word for lesbian women with masculine features) emphasizes that female characters in Hesse's novel and lesbianism are interrelated.

Harry's fear of the scorpion is not only interpretable as ambivalence toward women and sensuality, but specifically as *fear of lesbianism*. As we have seen, female–female desire awakens unease of queer potential in Harry. Like Peter Camenzind, he is inherently ambivalent but for somewhat different reasons. As we saw in chapter two, one factor that emphasizes queerness in Peter is that he is heterosexually ambivalent. Harry's relationship with Maria conveys that he is not ambivalent about heterosexuality. Still, as his

---

"Molly houses" in the eighteenth and nineteenth centuries, social establishments where homosexual men could meet sexual partners.

[416] Claudia Schoppmann explains that what makes *Der Skorpion* different from other lesbian novels from the 1920s is that it does not treat its protagonist's sexuality as a sickness but rather authentically portrays the discrimination and stigmatism she faces. (Claudia Schoppmann, "Ein Lesbenroman aus der Weimarer Zeit: 'Der Skorpion'," in *Eldorado: Homosexuelle Frauen und Männer in Berlin 1850–1950; Geschichte, Alltag und Kultur* ed. Michael Bollé (Berlin: Frölich & Kaufmann, 1984), 197.)

attitude toward lesbianism illustrates, he does swing between fascination for and fear of homosexuality.

When measuring which characters express their sexuality more freely in *Der Steppenwolf*, the female characters exercise more freedom than the men. While the lesbian implications of Hermine and Maria's relationship activate Harry's homosexual ambivalence, they are, as characters, never met with hostility or resentment. Pablo's bisexuality, on the other hand, is often met with homophobia by Harry. While Harry's homophobia does not make Pablo any less of a bisexual, the text provides different conditions for women and men when conveying what makes them queer.

"Queersociality" and Bisexuality

Despite the presence of Pablo, who becomes a friend of Harry's, male homosociality is notably absent in *Der Steppenwolf* (it occurs primarily as a *theme*), which differs from most other novels by Hesse. As is a commonplace in Hesse's writing, when the theme of male friendship figures, it is linked to youth. Harry indicates this when he is alone in a bar:

> Oh, wenn ich jetzt einen Freund gehabt hätte, einen Freund in irgendeiner Dachkammer, der bei einer Kerze grübelt und die Violine danebenliegen hat! Wie hätte ich ihn in seiner Nachtstille beschlichen, wäre lautlos durchs winklige Treppenhaus emporgeklettert und hätte ihn überrascht, und wir hätten mit Gespräch und Musik ein paar überirdische Nachtstunden gefeiert! Oft hatte ich dies Glück gekostet, einst, in vergangenen Jahren, aber auch dies hatte sich mit der Zeit von mir entfernt und losgelöst, verwelkte Jahre lagen zwischen hier und dort. (37)

> (Oh, if I had only had a friend now, in an attic room, ruminating with a lit candle and a violin next to him! In the stillness of the night, I would have crept into his space, silently climbed up the winding stairs and surprised him; with conversation and music we would have spent a few celebratory and unearthly hours together! In past years I had often tasted such happiness, but with the passing of time this too had slipped away from me, withered years now lay between here and there.)

The passage reminds us of the sort of male friendships that are central in *Peter Camenzind*: male same-sex bonds that provide space for young men to escape the pressures of heterosexuality, like, for example, adulthood's impending marriage. At the same time, the passage clarifies that such homosocial relationships are no longer part of Harry's life.

While *Der Steppenwolf* can be categorized as a Bildungsroman, its protagonist is not a version of the genre's typical hero, Martin Swales argues. Harry "is old," he writes, "whereas the protagonists of the Bildungsroman are typically adolescents."[417] As mentioned in the earlier chapters of this study, the end of the Bildungsroman usually entails the end of homosocial bonds and in its common conclusion, same-sex friendships are replaced with heterosexual marriage.

On the one hand, Harry having left male homosocial relationships behind corresponds to the Bildungsroman's usual conclusion. On the other hand, being an unmarried middle-aged man in the middle of this Bildungsroman's storyline contradicts the genre's conventions. Egon Schwarz writes:

> After all, the most important feature of a Bildungsroman is the gradual awakening of a dormant *youth* who, at the beginning, is a toy of circumstances but becomes a mature, seasoned individual … But as soon as one formulates the idea of a novel of development or apprenticeship in this way, it becomes clear that *Steppenwolf*, although not completing this prescribed scheme in a straightforward fashion, nonetheless has a strong relationship to it. It is possible to state without reservation that *Steppenwolf* is obviously a Bildungsroman but one that has been stood on its head.[418]

Moreover, Schwarz suggests that in cultivating a carefree existence and experimenting sexually, Harry undergoes "an education backwards, a development in the opposite direction."[419] Viewed in this way, the conclusion of Harry's educational journey would be male friendship instead of heterosexual marriage. Because of his age, however, Harry is supposed to have evolved past youth infatuations and instead adhere to heterosexuality. But he is neither married nor free from longing for the homosocial friend-ships of his youth (as the longer quote above showed), which generates friction within him. His fervent statement "Einsamkeit ist Unabhängigkeit" (38) (Loneliness is independence) therefore comes across as a motto he has persuaded himself to believe in, to be able to cope with life.

In fact, it is recurringly underscored that Harry does not celebrate his freedom and independence: "*der Steppenwolf [ging] an seiner Unabhängigkeit zugrunde.*" (49–50) (*the Steppenwolf perished from his independence.*) And:

---

[417] Swales, "*Der Steppenwolf*," 183.

[418] Egon Schwarz, "Hermann Hesse: *Steppenwolf* (1927)," in *Reflection and Action: Essays on the Bildungsroman*, ed. James Hardin (Columbia: University of South Carolina Press, 1991), 403. Emphasis added.

[419] Ibid., 404.

"*seine Freiheit [war] ein Tod.*" (50) (*his freedom was a sort of death.*) While being a lone wolf, Harry still craves friendship. Choosing to be a loner therefore implies that he has yet to find someone who truly understands him—someone who understands what makes him an outsider and Other—which Hermine's presence in his life will remedy.

As we shall see in the following, friendship in *Der Steppenwolf* is depicted in a manner that differs from Hesse's early novels (such as *Peter Camenzind, Unterm Rad, Demian* and *Knulp*) in which friendship commonly occurs in the shape of sexually ambiguous bonds between men. The fact that lesbian practices are acknowledged in *Der Steppenwolf,* and that Pablo's bisexuality is openly addressed, affect how the novel's homosocial relationships can be interpreted. In the friendship that evolves between Harry and Pablo, Harry experiences not only homosexual ambivalence but also a sometimes-active homophobic hesitation toward him (more on this later). And in Harry's bond with Hermine, her transgressive gender expressions give way for a sort of "queersociality" to materialize, that is, their bond is neither strictly homo-social nor strictly heterosocial but rather an amalgamation of both, which, in turn, makes it an exemplary representation of a queer friendship.

On this topic, Craig Bernard Palmer states: "In addition to being both real and symbolic, Hermine is also simultaneously male and female and thus can bond with Harry on both the homosocial and heterosexual level."[420] Palmer argues that Hermine's gender fluidity allows for a form of male bonding that, in turn, allows Harry to express repressed homoerotic urges: "By fulfilling Harry's homosocial needs in her female persona," he writes, "she is able to bypass the shame associated with those needs by men."[421] Since Hermine also introduces Harry to Pablo she facilitates the sexual attraction hinted at in their interactions, which mirrors the way with which homoerotic desire is portrayed in Hesse's *Demian.*

Palmer underscores that the similarities between homoeroticism in *Der Steppenwolf* and *Demian* reside in their manly female characters (Hermine and Frau Eva) facilitating male same-sex desire by means of their fluid gender expressions. Frau Eva, for instance, sends the protagonist, Emil Sinclair, a kiss through her son Max Demian. About this act, Palmer writes: "While the kiss is symbolically heterosexual, it is homosexual in terms of the gendered bodies performing it."[422] Palmer goes on to argue that in *Der Steppenwolf* the impli-cations are even queerer because Hermine attracts Harry both when she

---

[420] Palmer, "The Significance of Homosexual Desire," 19.
[421] Ibid., 20.
[422] Ibid., 2.

presents herself as female *and* male, and because Pablo disregards Harry's attempt at conventional male homosocial bonding (that is, an intellectual or spiritual sort of bonding) and instead suggests a threesome with himself and Maria.

Although Harry declines Pablo's sexual advances, one of the hidden traits of his personality revealed in the Magic Theater is his latent potential to desire other men. During the surrealistic episode (which will be closely examined in the final chapter), Harry sees several representations of himself in a mirror; for one of them, Pablo is the main object of desire: "ein junger eleganter Kerl, sprang dem Pablo lachend an die Brust, umarmte ihn und lief mit ihm davon." (169) (a young, elegant fellow threw himself laughing at Pablo, embraced him and ran away with him.)

The episode in the Magic Theater, however, also reminds Harry of all the love he has ever felt for every woman he has known or desired. This juxtaposition of homosexual and heterosexual desires makes a homosexuality/heterosexuality dualism manifest. While Theodore Ziolkowski does not state it clearly, he hints that the homosexuality/heterosexuality dualism in this concluding episode opens for a range of sexual desires. He writes: "The complete resolution of any polarity in matters of physical love is clearly implied."[423]

Because of the examples above, Harry, too, can be interpreted as bisexual (something Ziolkowski's interpretation does not express clearly). And Jack Halberstam's arguments from the previous chapter help clarify that Harry's bisexuality can be seen as a natural consequence of being a "wild thing." Halberstam writes:

> Other histories of sexuality ... lie nestled in the category of the wild, sexualities that are ... "untimely" in the sense that they were not properly scooped up by new classifications of homosexuality in the late nineteenth and early twentieth centuries, but lingered in the unspoken forms of address, gesture, and relation that preceded the sexual order of things.[424]

Harry's wildness as part wolf mirrors his wildness as bisexual, a sexual variety that, while it was acknowledged by sexologists, was not given equal attention as (male) homosexuality in the late nineteenth and early twentieth cen-

---

[423] Ziolkowski, *The Novels of Hermann Hesse*, 219.
[424] Halberstam, *Wild Things*, 11.

turies.[425] When reviewing the study of sexuality at the time, the homosexuality/heterosexuality binary tends to overshadow sexual varieties that did not fit neatly into one pole or the other, as Halberstam's quote suggests. Harry is not either/or but both. He is wolf *and* man, homosexual *and* heterosexual, and transcends these binaries by embodying in-betweenness.

Alongside the sexual ambiguity that the presence of Pablo creates, Harry's own bisexuality—or *sexual fluidity*—is most perceptible when he meets Hermine at the masked ball. She then oscillates between presenting herself as a female and male, and Harry is equally attracted to her when she presents both genders. At first, he sees her as "ein hübscher Jüngling" (157) (a good-looking young man) dressed in a tuxedo. Harry asks: "'Ist dies das Kostüm, Hermine, in dem du mich in dich verliebt machen willst?'" (157) ("Is it in this costume you want to make me fall in love with you, Hermine?")

Harry feels that he cannot possibly dance with her when she is dressed as a man but confesses that he does fall in love with her: "ohne daß Hermine sich darum irgendwelche Mühe zu geben schien, wurde ich sehr bald in sie verliebt." (157–158) (without seeming to give it an effort, Hermine made me fall in love with her.) Even more so, however, we see that Harry's sexual desire has potential to exceed the woman/man binary completely:

> [Hermine] unterhielt sich mit mir über Hermann und über die Kindheit, über meine und ihre, über jene Jahre vor der Geschlechtsreife, in denen das jugendliche Liebesvermögen nicht nur beide Geschlechter, sondern alles und jedes umfaßt. (158)

> (Hermine and I conversed about Hermann and childhood, both mine and hers, the years before puberty in which the youthful capacity for love not only includes both sexes but everything and everyone.)

As the quote above shows, before becoming an adult, Harry's "capacity for love" included more than "both sexes," an idea that is henceforth understood as more than the female/male gender binary. The queersociality that

---

[425] One example of bisexuality as a category of interest in the sexology discourse can be found in *Memnon* (1868), wherein Ulrichs classified human sexual varieties into seven categories with *uranodionings* (male bisexuals) divided into two sub-categories: "conjunctive" and "disjunctive." Ralph M. Leck explains the difference between them by emphasizing that while the men in the latter category were able to have emotionally loving bonds with both sexes, they were only sexually inclined toward one sex, whereas the men in the first category were sexually attracted to both: "Conjunctive uranodionings … felt a unified love toward both sexes. However, in the sexual consciousness of disjunctive uranodionings, erotic and amatory feelings were disjoined. Bisexuals of this sort might feel sentimental or intellectual love for one sex and sensual love for another." (Leck, *Vita Sexualis*, 43.)

Hermine brings to Harry's life prompts him to recognize trans/non-binary persons as sex object choices (as can be seen in the word *everyone*). Hermine's function, evidently, is to encourage Harry to recall the sexual openness of his youth, assent to it, and continue to experiment with his sexuality as an adult.

Three Examples of an "Erotic Triangle"

After meeting Hermine, Harry's sexual experimentation is portrayed in three depictions of an erotic triangle.[426] The first triangle toward which we will direct our attention is perhaps the most traditional, since it most clearly correlates with Eve Kosofsky Sedgwick's concept. As previously explained, within the context of any erotic triangle, the homosocial bond between the two male rivals is more potent and erotic than either of their desire for the woman. Sedgwick also underlines that the woman is commonly devoid of agency, functioning rather as a commodity to be exchanged between the men.

The characters involved in the first of *Der Steppenwolf*'s triangles are Harry, Pablo, and Maria. The rivalry between the men is especially prominent here as Harry, who at this point in the story has begun sleeping with Maria on a regular basis, becomes jealous of Pablo when he shows interest in her. We see this in a couple of examples where Harry measures himself against Pablo: "Diesen Pablo, den schönen, schien auch Maria sehr zu lieben!" (134) (Maria also seemed to love this Pablo, the beautiful one!) Harry is both jealous of Pablo's beauty, which he has no trouble acknowledging, and surprised by Maria's interest in him, since his own perception of Pablo is that he is not much of a lover:

> Ich hätte diesen Pablo in der Liebe für etwas schläfrig, verwöhnt und passiv gehalten, aber Maria versicherte mir, daß er zwar nur langsam in Glut zu bringen, dann aber gespannter, härter, männlicher und fordernder sei als irgendein Boxer oder Herrenreiter. (137–138)

> (In terms of lovemaking I would have thought this Pablo to be a bit sluggish, blasé, and passive, but Maria assured me that although he was slow to get aroused, he became more excited, harder, more manly, and demanding than any boxer or rider.)

---

[426] Anjeana Kaur Hans's analysis briefly addresses the possibility of triangular desires in *Der Steppenwolf* (see Hans, "Defining Desires," 136–137). While Hans draws on parts of Eve Kosofsky Sedgwick's theories, she does not examine (nor mention) erotic triangles in Hesse's novel to the extent that they are investigated in this study.

First, Harry measuring his own merits as a lover with Pablo's signals that he regards them as adversaries. Drawing on Sedgwick's conception of erotic triangles, these men's rivalry turns their bond into an erotic one. And second, Harry imagining how Pablo behaves in bed has additional homoerotic implications.

The homoerotic tension between these men is perceptible by Harry clearly being able to picture Pablo as a sexual being (as the quote above shows) and Pablo clearly being interested in Harry sexually (which his offer of a three-some suggests). The straightforwardness of their homoerotic tension—that it is neither hidden nor hinted at, but in the open—makes another feature of Sedgwick's theory relevant. Since male homosocial desire depends on ambiguity between homoeroticism and homophobia, actual homoerotic deeds—especially homosexuality—must not be spoken aloud, Sedgwick explains. She exemplifies this with one of the most characteristic of tropes in Gothic literature, namely the "unspeakable." Historically the very "namelessness" of sexuality between men, its secrecy, has played a huge part in how homosexuality has been kept in check, she argues.[427] The fact that *Der Steppenwolf* openly flirts with homoeroticism is thus perceivable as radical and augments the novel's queerness. This queerness is also evident when one compares its actual depictions of heterosexual intercourse with the homoerotic tension between Harry and Pablo. For a modern reader the heterosexual sex scenes in *Der Steppenwolf* have, as Hans Mayer writes, "a somewhat puerile effect [and] are portrayed in a remarkably unsensual manner."[428] An effect of this lack of heterosexual passion is that the homoerotic tension that characterizes the novel stands out as more passionate and more exciting.

A final example about the first erotic triangle that parallels Sedgwick's theory concerns how the woman (in Sedgwick's view) is usually commodified and treated as an object to be exchanged between the male rivals. We see this commodification when Pablo needs to borrow money from Harry and offers Maria to him in exchange for the funds: "Er biete mir dafür an, diese Nacht statt seiner über Maria zu verfügen." (139) (In exchange he offered me to have Maria at my disposal tonight instead of him.) However, Pablo is not Maria's pimp, and she is not his to offer to anyone. The fact that the men talk about her in this manner, as if she were merchandise, says more about their relationship than their respective relationships with her.

---

[427] Sedgwick, *Between Men*, 94.

[428] Hans Mayer, *Steppenwolf and Everyman: Outsiders and Conformists in Contemporary Literature*, trans. Jack D. Zipes (New York: Crowell, 1971), 2.

A similar transactional occurrence is repeated in the second erotic triangle, once again for the purpose of cementing the bond between the men. The characters involved in the second triangle are Harry, Maria, and Hermine, the latter of whom in this example presents herself as male. Hermine facilitates the relationship between Harry and Maria, and Harry regards Maria as a gift: "Auch die [Maria] hast ja du mir geschenkt." (141) (Maria was also a gift from you.)

Male rivalry occurs in the second erotic triangle as well, albeit slightly less charged than between Harry and Pablo. When Hermine and Harry attend the masked ball, it is also made clear that Maria is not the only woman over whom they compete:

> Wir traten als Nebenbuhler auf, strichen beide eine Weile derselben Frau nach, tanzten abwechselnd beide mit ihr, suchten beide sie zu gewinnen. Und doch war dies alles nur Maskenspiel, war nur ein Spiel zwischen uns beiden, flocht uns beide enger zusammen, entzündete uns beide füreinander. (158)

> (We appeared as rivals, followed the same woman for a while, we took turns dancing with her and both of us tried to win her over. And yet this was all just a masque, a game between the two of us which wove us closer together and ignited our sparks for each other.)

In contrast to the rivalry between Harry and Pablo, the rivalry between Harry and Hermine is characterized by camaraderie and playfulness. As the quote above shows, their competitiveness is a friendly game meant to cement their bond rather than a consequence of any desire to conquer women.

A likely reason why the bond between Harry and Hermine is not as charged as Harry's liaison with Pablo is that while Hermine presents herself as male, Harry is always conscious of her duality—that she is *also female*. He is thus able to disregard the homoerotic implications of his desire. Harry's feelings for Hermine are characterized by respect and admiration, which differs from his homophobic hesitation toward Pablo. Because of Hermine's gender fluidity she is, within the framework of an erotic triangle, less threatening than Pablo.

Harry's negative perception of Pablo is in focus in the third and final of *Der Steppenwolf*'s erotic triangles as well. The characters involved here are Harry, Pablo, and Hermine, who in this example presents herself as both female and male. It is instantly palpable that Harry regards Pablo a rival for her attention:

> Zu meiner eigenen Verwunderung empfand ich gegen diesen harmlosen, hübschen Musikanten etwas wie Eifersucht, nicht Liebeseifersucht, denn von Liebe war ja zwischen mir und Hermine gar nicht die Rede, aber eine mehr geistige Freundschaftseifersucht, denn er schien mir des Interesses und der auffallenden Auszeichnung, ja Verehrung, die sie für ihn zeigte, nicht so recht würdig zu sein. (117–118)

> (To my own amazement I felt something resembling jealousy toward this harmless, handsome musician, although not the kind of jealousy one experiences in love—since between me and Hermine there was no such thing—but rather the kind of jealousy one experiences in friendship of the spiritual kind, since to me he did not seem worthy of the interest—or rather, ennobling—that she showed him.)

The ambiguity of Harry's desires is made manifest in this quote since he clearly states that Hermine is not a love interest. Between them there "is no such thing" as romantic love but rather a spiritual sort of love between friends that Harry cherishes. The romantic implications of the previously mentioned male bonds of Harry's youth are thus reactivated, as well as infused with importance. Rather than regarding Pablo as a rival for a woman's affection, Harry is jealous of him because he threatens the friendship between him and Hermine. This mirrors the behavior of Peter Camenzind, whose jealousy toward Richard's friends bestows their relationship with homoerotic meaning. An additional connection with *Peter Camenzind* is the protagonist's use of the word *Verehrung* (ennobling) when describing Hermine's attitude toward Pablo, which also reminds us of the homoerotic *noble* male bonds at the center of Plato's *Symposium*.

Comparing *Der Steppenwolf* with *Demian*, Palmer writes: "the androgynous Hermine … leads the protagonist ostensibly by heterosexual means, to the object of his homosocial desire, and thus unites them homosexually. Upon completing this task, [she] can and must disappear so that the protagonist can realize the unified desire that he could previously only imagine by dividing it and attributing it to two genders."[429] Hermine's death thus becomes the means for uniting Harry and Pablo and allowing the homoeroticism in their relationship to materialize. Herein we see the backwards education of which Egon Schwarz speaks. In this Bildungsroman, the conclusion of Harry's journey is not heterosexual marriage (or even heterosexual romance) but a bond between men. We will return to this bond

---

[429] Palmer, "The Significance of Homosexual Desire," 3.

later. Suffice it to say, for now, that in the third erotic triangle, when Hermine presents herself as female, the homoerotically charged rivalry between Harry and Pablo is accentuated. When she presents herself as male, however, she underlines the profound significance of friendship in *Der Steppenwolf*, which holds homoerotic connotations. Heterosexual desire is thus rendered close to completely insignificant (at least within this triangle), which accentuates the queer implications of *Der Steppenwolf*.

An Iteration of *Symposium*'s Diotima

What stands out as Hermine's most important function in *Der Steppenwolf* is that she is Harry's teacher, primarily in matters of pleasure and love. "Harry is an educated man, or so he believes," Seymour L. Flaxman writes, "but it is clear to Hermine that he has not been educated for life."[430] Along with providing Harry with a queer friendship that brings about a link to *Symposium*, the educational function of Hermine makes similarities between her and the portrayal of the ancient Greek philosopher Diotima in Plato's text visible.

When Socrates, in *Symposium*, gives his celebratory speech to Eros he accounts for what Diotima taught him in his youth about "the right method of boy-loving."[431] Diotima describes Eros as a development from earthly beauty in the shape of beautiful bodies (reserved for when one is young) to spiritual beauty in the shape of beautiful souls (when one has grown in maturity). If we recall the personal growth of Peter Camenzind for a moment, Diotima's teachings are identifiable therein. As we saw in chapter one, in Peter's youth, his homoerotic relationship with Richard (which through its intertwinement with nature can be seen as *earthly*) takes center stage. And as we saw in chapter three, when Peter grows older and forms a loving relationship with Boppi (which through its emphasis on responsibility can be seen as *spiritual*), he devotes himself to ethical ideals such as solidarity. This progression from earthly pleasures to spiritual principles can also be said to characterize Harry Haller's journey. Throughout *Der Steppenwolf* Harry experiences a sexual awakening, but when the story ends, he appears closer to reaching the peaceful realm of the Immortals and their undying philosophies.

While Socrates's account of Diotima's teachings refer to heterosexual and reproductive relationships to a greater extent than the other speakers in

---

[430] Seymour L. Flaxman, "*Der Steppenwolf*: Hesse's Portrait of the Intellectual," *Modern Language Quarterly* 15, no. 4 (1954): 356.
[431] Plato, *The Symposium of Plato*, 211b.

Symposium, Diotima acknowledges male same-sex relationships with the metaphor of *pregnancy*. She distinguishes between men who acquire immortality by means of relationships with women (relationships that result in children) and men who devote their lives to more honorable pursuits (such as philosophy or public affairs). Men in the latter category exemplifies what Diotima calls "pregnancy of soul"[432] and "men in this condition," she explains, "enjoy a far fuller community with each other than that which comes with children."[433] Both Peter Camenzind and Harry Haller fit this description. Neither of their stories end in heterosexual marriage or child rearing; rather, they adhere to philosophical or spiritual ideals. Peter lives as a single man in honor of Richard and Boppi who have died, and Harry is allowed entry into the realm of the Immortals.

Like Diotima, Hermine educates Harry about both heterosexuality and homosexuality. Her fluid gender expressions and sexual ambiguity make her adept in a variety of contexts. She can engage in heterosexual practices, both when presenting female and male, as well as in lesbian sex (when presenting female) and gay sex (when presenting male). Teaching Harry how to affirm his own sexual fluidity (to desire both women and men) can be seen as an iteration of what David M. Halperin investigates in *How to be Gay* (2012), namely that to develop one's gay subjectivity one must learn gayness from others who are gay. "Unlike the members of minority groups defined by race or ethnicity or religion," Halperin writes, "gay men cannot rely on their birth families to teach them about their history or their culture."[434] Learning one's history and culture from a chosen family thus takes the shape of an initiatory process of sorts.

"As a cultural practice," Halperin continues, "male homosexuality involves a characteristic way of receiving, reinterpreting, and reusing mainstream culture, of decoding and recoding the heterosexual or heteronormative meanings already encoded in that culture, so that they come to function as vehicles of gay or queer meaning."[435] Halperin lists various cultural forms such as art, opera, musicals, and style as essential when learning one's gay sensibilities from elders, and he emphasizes the importance of cultural practices. Gayness, he proposes, is "a mode of perception, an attitude, an ethos: in short, it is a practice."[436] Although Hermine is neither exclusively

---

[432] Plato, *The Symposium of Plato*, 209a.
[433] Ibid., 209c.
[434] Halperin, *How to be Gay*, 7.
[435] Ibid., 12.
[436] Ibid., 13.

male nor exclusively gay (in the modern definition of the word), the fact that she herself challenges heteronormativity and gender norms makes her receptive to, and knowledgeable of, gayness's specific characteristics. Halperin's idea of gayness as an attitude and practice can thus be identified in the ways with which Hermine educates Harry about living.

The most practical example of Hermine as a teacher happens when she gives Harry dance lessons in preparation for the masked ball. Dancing has historically been seen as a seductive and sinful practice, primarily associated with young people challenging authority and other norms, which makes it a fitting activity for a queer character like Hermine to be teaching. Another view is given by Theodore Saul Jackson, who sees dancing in *Der Steppenwolf* as a heterosexual mating ritual that aids in the process of reproduction: "Dance, of all the access points Hesse could have chosen for Haller's entrance to the realm of socialization, is more tolerable for Haller precisely because the activity itself acknowledges its own natural aspects, i.e. continuation of the species."[437] Ziolkowski also emphasizes heterosexual implications of dancing, labeling Hermine and Harry's dance at the masked ball "a symbolic wedding dance" which symbolizes the "marriage of the two poles of existence in [Harry's] soul: the intellectual or spiritual with the sensual or natural."[438]

However, when these characters' "wedding dance" is seen as representing a psychological process within the protagonist, Hermine becomes a mere symbol for a part of Harry's identity. As previously mentioned, scholars have usually interpreted Hermine as Harry's anima or as a symbolic projection that represents hidden facets of his identity. Some view her as a product of the protagonist's imagination. Eike Middel, for example, substantiates this claim by underscoring that the "Foreword" (which is narrated from the perspective of the landlady's nephew) does not acknowledge Hermine's visits to Harry's room—or the dance lessons she gives him there—at all.[439]

If one views Hermine as a product of Harry's imagination, their "wedding dance" receives a curious implication, however. On a realistic level, if Hermine does not exist, Harry is dancing alone in the scene. If so, any heterosexual implications of the activity of dancing must be regarded irrelevant. Interestingly, Ziolkowski also seems to want to dismiss the heterosexual implications, stating that the merging of Hermine with Harry's

---

[437] Jackson, "Ambivalent Modernist," 170.

[438] Ziolkowski, *The Novels of Hermann Hesse*, 214.

[439] Eike Middell, *Hermann Hesse: Die Bilderwelt seines Lebens* (Leipzig: Reclam, 1975), 188, referenced in Richards, *Exploring the Divided Self*, 92.

boyhood friend Hermann results in "distinct implications of homo-sexuality."[440]

In this study, the dancing part of Harry and Hermine's relationship is seen as having a mainly educational function and the scenes in which the dance lessons occur are categorizable as queer specks of light, contrasting with Harry's often bleak existence. This does not mean than dancing is not *also* portrayed as a heterosexual mating ritual, but the heterosexual implications of the practice are primarily identifiable in Harry's relationship with Maria. Although Harry fears that he is too old for Maria, Hermine encourages him to invite her to dance, saying that being laughed at is a risk he must take.

By pairing Harry and Maria, Hermine schools Harry in heterosexuality. Evidently, she does not only teach Harry how to be gay but provides an education in how to be straight as well. It is Hermine that makes sure Maria finds her way to Harry's bed one night, which, characteristically, is met with ambivalent emotions: "Erstaunen, Befremden, Schreck und Entzücken." (129) (amazement, surprise, horror, and delight.)

Despite Harry's initial ambivalence, he and Maria become lovers. As a wolf, Harry's sexual engagement with her is unusual since among wolves the common social formation is a male and a female with the intent to breed—a reproductive unit.[441] But neither Harry nor Maria express desire to mate long-term or have children; their sex is recreational, for fun. The wolf part in Harry thus rejects his species-specific heterosexual breeding convention, which is mirrored by the human part of him: "*er [kannte] weder Familien-leben noch sozialen Ehrgeiz.*" (53) (*he knew neither family life nor social ambition.*) Harry calls his previous family life "zusammengebrochen" (69) (collapsed) and his vague hints of a distant girlfriend do not indicate an ambition to procreate and live a "normal life" ("wir lebten seit langem in sehr loser Verbindung." [74] [we had been living in an uncommitted relationship for a long time.])

It appears that *Der Steppenwolf* is a coming-out tale in which Harry undergoes a heterosexual liberation. While engaging in heterosexual love-making can be seen as a way of keeping Harry's homoerotic desire at bay, challenging bourgeois, normative, and reproductive sexuality by having sex with Maria for fun makes heterosexuality part of what makes the novel queer.

The reason that Hermine is key to Harry's sexual liberation is that she teaches him how to let loose. Ziolkowski suggests: "In order [for Harry] to

---

[440] Ziolkowski, *The Novels of Hermann Hesse*, 214.

[441] L. David Mech and Luigi Boitani, "Wolf Social Ecology," in *Wolves: Behavior, Ecology, and Conservation*, ed. L. David Mech and Luigi Boitani (Chicago: University of Chicago, 2003), 1–2.

overcome his bourgeois inhibitions he must expand his soul to the point of embracing every aspect of life."[442] With the assistance of Pablo and Maria, Hermine guides him into a hedonistic world of sexual experimentation, dancing, and jazz, which "is symbolic for his repudiation of the entire narrow world of the Bürger and his new dimensions as an aspirant to the kingdom of the Immortals."[443]

As we saw in the preceding chapter, when Harry's existence is contrasted with the bourgeois majority, his animality makes him a norm-challenger which, in turn, is enhanced by his queer characteristics. The surrounding bourgeois culture also illuminates his status as an outsider and Other. Both contexts referred to by Ziolkowski above (the friendship circle of Harry/Hermine/Pablo/Maria and the realm of the Immortals) provide possibilities for Harry, the lone wolf, to finally *belong* to something. Hermine's dance lessons, Pablo's jazz music, and Harry's sexual escapades in bed with Maria become what Colin Wilson calls "an education of the senses."[444] Wilson's phrase emphasizes that Maria, like Hermine, has an educational role in Harry's life:

> Maria lehrte mich – in jener wunderlichen ersten Nacht und in den folgenden Tagen – vieles, nicht nur holde neue Spiele und Beglückungen der Sinne, sondern auch neues Verständnis, neue Einsichten, neue Liebe. (133)

> (During that wonderful first night and in the following days, Maria taught me a lot, not only lovely new games and delights of the senses, but also new understanding, new insights, new love.)

In addition to teaching Harry how to dance, Hermine's function as a teacher is expressed through a sort of tough love in which firm instructions are combined with references to motherhood. During their first meeting Hermine buys Harry a sandwich and, he says, "befahl mir, es zu essen." (87) (ordered me to eat it.) Hermine instantly identifies Harry's need to be commanded: "Wollen wir wetten, daß es lange her ist, seit du zum letztenmal jemandem hast gehorchen müssen" (87) (I bet it has been a long time since you last had to obey someone), she says, and Harry admits that her behavior makes him satisfied:

---

[442] Ziolkowski, *The Novels of Hermann Hesse*, 210.
[443] Ibid. Emphasis in original.
[444] Wilson, *The Outsider*, 66.

> Es tat ungeheuer wohl, jemand zu gehorchen, neben jemand zu sitzen, der einen ausfragte, einem befahl, einen ausschalt. (89)

> (It was tremendously gratifying to obey someone, to sit next to someone who interrogated me, gave me orders, berated me.)

Hermine's associations with motherhood can be seen in her conduct toward Harry, whom she labels a "Kindskopf" (91) (big kid), "ein kleiner Bub" (91) (a little boy), and "Kleiner." (92) (little one.) She is called both "Gouvernante" (91) (governess) and mother: "Sie war in der Tat wie eine Mama mit mir." (91) (She was indeed like a mother to me.) It is clear, based on these labels, that her function is to nurture.

Let us for a moment recall Lewis W. Tusken's argument that, in Hesse's fiction, themes of masculinity and femininity are primarily manifested in representations of the "father-world" and "mother-world," as he labels them. "In the early prose," Tusken writes, "the domains are relatively simple; that of the mother is loving and gentle, that of the father authoritative and demanding."[445] In Hesse's later prose these themes become more complex, Tusken explains, which *Der Steppenwolf* and the portrayal of Hermine exemplifies. The novel does not include any notable references to fathers or father figures, but its most flagrant iteration of a mother, Hermine, embodies all the qualities listed above. She is loving, gentle, authoritative, and demanding.

Hesse's primary characters usually have troubled relationships with their mothers, Angelika Rauch-Rapaport suggests, which is true also in *Der Steppenwolf.* As children, she explains, "they were not securely attached to their caregiver, and hence are always in search of what they never properly had. They do not quite know what they have lost and roam through the world, suffering from a tremendous loss and attempting to find themselves."[446] Roaming the world in search of himself is an apt description of Harry, and although he finds a mother in Hermine, their relationship is far from perfect, as proven by her murder.

As we have seen so far, Hermine's function as Harry's teacher mainly involves encouraging him to experiment sexually and tutoring him about how to interact with others. In this regard, her gender fluidity and bisexuality make her an ideal teacher: "ich [bin] deine Lehrerin und werde dir eine bessere Lehrerin sein, als deine ideale Geliebte es war." (123) (I am your teacher, and I will be a better teacher than your ideal lover has been.) As

---

[445] Tusken, "A Mixing of Metaphors," 626.
[446] Rauch-Rapaport, "The Melancholic Structure," 84.

Harry's teacher, Hermine facilitates his homoerotic bond with Pablo and when teaching him how to seduce Maria, she actually leads by example (having also had sex with her): "ich mußte sie doch für dich verführen!" (140) (I had to seduce her for you!)

The teacher motif that Hermine activates mirrors how otherness is portrayed in *Peter Camenzind*, in which the character Boppi is also labeled a teacher. There are, however, further similarities between these Others. For one, the murder of Hermine has similar implications as Boppi's death. As we saw in chapter three, for a protagonist in a Bildungsroman to complete his Bildung, the death of an Other is a final lesson of sorts. Since Hermine is also utilized in this way she can be labeled, like Boppi, a narrative prosthesis.

Overall, we can say that Hermine socializes Harry. As an iteration of *Symposium*'s Diotima, she teaches him how to be gay and straight which challenges the heteronormative conception that heterosexuality is natural whereas other sexualities are not. Hesse's novel shows that both gayness and straightness must be learned and, most importantly, the fact that a character like Hermine (who transcends heteronormative conceptions of sexuality and gender) is the protagonist's educator in these matters enhances *Der Steppenwolf*'s queerness.

Harry's Self-Hatred and Internalized Phobias

Before concluding this chapter, we will turn our attention toward Harry's self-hatred and internalized phobias, which can be seen as effects of Hermine's function in the text. It is clearly conveyed that the point of Hermine's entry into Harry's life is to make him *fall in love*. She says: "Ich will dich in mich verliebt machen." (108) (I will make you fall in love with me.) While it would be possible to interpret this as an offer for a love affair, Hermine's statement is more complex than that. Primarily, we see the complexity of her statement manifest itself in her function as Harry's "mirror."

Ralph Freedman, among many other Hesse scholars, argues that "the characters [in *Der Steppenwolf*] are intricate mirrors for one another,"[447] and Hermine says outright: "ich [bin] wie eine Art Spiegel für dich." (106) (I am a sort of mirror for you.) Hermine's declaration underlines her profound connection with Harry as well as accentuates that her role involves making him see himself more clearly. Salvatore Campisi writes that "the mirror motif … resonates with Hesse's use of self-irony, which is that particular type of 'self-

---

[447] Freedman, *Pilgrim of Crisis*, 287.

reflection' which leads his characters to be confronted with the cleavage between their real and ideal – or idealized – self and to laugh at this discrepancy."[448] As argued in the previous chapter, the wolf part of Harry's identity (which is active, masculine, and wild) is idealized. If the mirror metaphor in *Der Steppenwolf* signifies the link between Harry's real and ideal selves, as Campisi's quote suggests, Hermine—with her gender and sexual fluidity—turns out to be a more real reflection of Harry than the ideal figure of the wolf.

Theodore Saul Jackson, who also recognizes the importance of mirrors in *Der Steppenwolf*, asserts "that the mirror symbols are themselves a symbol of Haller's internal reflection, the self-examination that he undergoes. Mirrors, though," he continues, "are capable of reversing, bending, and distorting the image they reflect."[449] Drawing on this claim, mirrors can be regarded as unreliable conveyers of one's identity. If Harry wants to disavow certain parts of his character, mirrors, as such, could work to his advantage. Hermine reflecting characteristics of Harry that he himself does not want to acknowledge (his own sexual fluidity for example) leads to conflicting emotions within him. But the fact that mirrors are also able to reverse, bend, and distort their reflections makes it possible for Harry to suppress what makes him and Hermine similar.[450]

As we can see, romantic love is a too simple description of Harry and Hermine's bond. Besides, she is more often than not treated as his friend than a potential lover, for instance: "sie war mein Kamerad" (121) (she was my friend), and although Harry admits that he would sacrifice anything for her, he would do so "ohne doch im mindesten in sie verliebt zu sein." (103) (without being the slightest in love with her.)

Harry's feelings for Hermine are, evidently, not conventionally romantic. The bond between them is more reminiscent of the kind of kinship that can be found between siblings, individuals who share experiences and attributes. Harry and Hermine are frequently compared to brother and sister. Harry mentions that Hermine has shown him "daß ich Geschwister habe." (100) (that I have siblings.) She calls him "Brüderchen" (107) (my little brother), and he calls her "Schwester." (121, 144) (sister.) As such, their bond is based

---

[448] Campisi, "Dialectics of Time," 185.

[449] Jackson, "Ambivalent Modernist," 160.

[450] Furthermore, the link between mirrors and the myth of Narcissus (who drowns when enamored by his own reflection) has historically been interpreted as representing homoeroticism, as argued by several scholars. For further reading, see, e.g., Steven Bruhm's previously mentioned study, *Reflecting Narcissus*, especially the introductory chapter. While not predominantly focused on homoeroticism, another interesting take on the Narcissus theme can be found in Niclas Johansson, *The Narcissus Theme from Fin de Siècle to Psychoanalysis: Crisis of the Modern Self* (Frankfurt am Main: Peter Lang, 2017).

on respect and understanding which Hermine's words confirm: "Ich verstehe dich. Darin sind wir Geschwister." (142) (I understand you. In that regard we are siblings.)

Even in situations when physical intimacy occurs between the two, which could be read as indications of romance, the association of siblingship is present:

> Ich nahm Herminens Kopf in meine Hände, kußte sie auf die Stirn und lehnte ihn Wange an Wange zu mir, geschwisterlich, so blieben wir einen Augenblick. (146)

> (I took Hermine's head in my hands, kissed her on the forehead and leaned my cheek to hers like brother and sister, and for a moment we remained like that.)

It is interesting to note that while the quote above includes physical touch, it comes across as less sexualized than, for instance, Peter Camenzind's nose rubbing with Richard, making the implications of siblingship in Harry and Hermine's relationship even stronger. Additionally, if Hermine were to be read only as female, she would, because of her "sister label," be as asexualized as the female love interests in *Peter Camenzind* (like Rösi and Elisabeth).

In effect, Hermine does not enter Harry's life to offer him a romance with her—she introduces Maria to take care of that—but rather to teach him how to love himself: "[Harrys] ganzes Leben [war] ein Beispiel dafür, daß ohne Liebe zu sich selbst auch die Nächstenliebe unmöglich ist." (14) (Harry's life exemplified that if one cannot love oneself, love for one's neighbor is impossible.) While it is unknown to this author whether legendary drag queen RuPaul Charles has ever read *Der Steppenwolf,* Hesse's suggestion in the previous quote reverberates in contemporary queer culture, as RuPaul's reality competition television series *RuPaul's Drag Race* (2009–present) ends all episodes with the motto: "If you can't love yourself, how in the hell are you gonna love somebody else?"

So, Harry needs to learn how to love himself in all his complexity, but he is, unfortunately, unable to do so. This has grave consequences. His potential for queerness provokes anxiety within him which manifests itself through internalized phobias. Contrary to the heterosexual ambivalence that is prevalent in *Peter Camenzind, Der Steppenwolf* includes homosexual ambivalence (as we established earlier when discussing lesbianism). Lesbianism activates both curiosity and fear in Harry of his own sexual fluidity, in essence, internalized homophobia. When he murders Hermine, who is a gender nonconformist, her murder is, in reality as well as on the surface of the text, a crime of passion with transphobic overtones.

Ziolkowski, however, sees the murder differently. He argues that on a realistic level the murder of Hermine "amounts to no more than an exclamation of jealousy and disgust when [Harry] realizes that the woman [who] he had elevated to symbolic stature, rather than being the ethereal personification of an ideal, is indeed very much of the flesh."[451] That jealousy is a motive behind Harry's action is not disputed here. Viewing Hermine only as female, however, is.

When Harry finds Hermine and Pablo in the Magic Theater, naked and in each other's arms, something snaps in him. There are two likely reasons as to why he becomes jealous enough to kill Hermine. First, if we recall the erotic triangle between Harry, Pablo, and Hermine, her death makes homoeroticism between the men possible. In this interpretation Harry is jealous because Hermine has had sex with the man that he secretly desires. Second, if we rely on the mirror motif for a moment—in which Hermine activates Harry's self-perception—his masculine identity (which the wolf part in him accentuates) is threatened by her fluid sexuality and gender expressions. Reflecting Harry makes her death an iteration of Harry's fear of his own fragmented nature, as well as his fear of his own sexual and gender fluidity. Hermine's command: "Du wirst meinen Befehl erfüllen und *wirst mich töten*" (108) (You will follow my command and *kill me*), also brings Harry's suicidal contemplations to mind. As Hermine is perceivable as Harry's mirror, her death can, in Andreas Kiryakakis words, be seen as "the substitute for Haller's own suicide."[452]

Hermine's presence brings everything that Harry lacks to light and the text implies that he sees her bisexuality and capacity to transcend the female/male binary as enviable: "Du bist ja mein Gegenteil; du hast alles, was mir fehlt" (106) (You are my opposite; you possess everything I lack), Harry says to her. As opposed to Harry, who suffers from his dual nature as a wolf-man, Hermine accepts herself as multifaceted and she is therefore complete. Harry fears such transgressive completeness within himself, and Hermine's murder, therefore, comes to represent his self-hatred and internalized trans- and homophobia.

---

[451] Ziolkowski, *The Novels of Hermann Hesse*, 219–220.
[452] Kiryakakis, *The Ideal of Heimat*, 138.

In conclusion, although Harry's wolf-man nature is a symbol of complexity, it is the queerness of Hermine—that she is female, male, and trans/non-binary, as well as straight, lesbian, gay, and bisexual—that makes *Der Steppenwolf* a truly radical text.

CHAPTER 6

Queer Sounds, Times, and Places

"Actually Animal Eyes"

With Harry's friend Pablo as the primary person of interest, this chapter will examine queer connotations in and around *Der Steppenwolf*'s portrayals of sounds, times, and places, all aspects that are linked with Pablo. We will begin by examining the novel's most noticeable depiction of sound, that is, how music—mainly jazz—figures in *Der Steppenwolf*.[453]

In Hesse's fiction musicians abound. Theodore Ziolkowski underscores that "[t]here is scarcely a novel whose hero is not in some way musical: *Gertrude* (1909) is the story of a composer, H. H. in *The Journey to the East* is a violinist, and Joseph Knecht in *The Glass Bead Game* is an accomplished pianist and music theorist."[454] To this list we can add supporting characters like Richard and Elisabeth in *Peter Camenzind,* who are both pianists, and the saxophone-playing Pablo, who is crucial to the ways with which jazz is presented in *Der Steppenwolf.*

As we will see in the following, jazz music has somewhat contradictory connotations in the novel. Jazz connotes both queerness and racism in Hesse's text, which, in addition, heightens the music genre's association with otherness. Since Pablo is inextricably linked with the text's depictions of jazz, he connotes otherness as well. Furthermore, Pablo is depicted as a "Latin

---

[453] Throughout Hermann Hesse's work (both within his poetry and prose), he cultivated musical structures and analogies. Therefore, the relationship between Hesse and music "is as many-faceted as the man and poet himself," C. Immo Schneider writes, "and cannot be reduced to a common denominator." (Schneider, "Hermann Hesse and Music," 373.) "Aside from tempo and flow," Schneider continues, "contemporary poetry generally no longer observes specific metric or rhyming schemes. Some poets, however, like Hesse, continued to cultivate such forms, following traditions reaching from the Middle Ages and Renaissance to the mid-twentieth cetury [sic]." (Ibid., 375.) Moreover, Colin Wilson states that Hesse's musical structures induce a mood of sorts in the writing: "As the clear, limpid prose carries you along, it is possible to feel how closely Hesse's literary art is allied to music." (Wilson, *Hermann Hesse*, 23. In the quote, Wilson refers specifically to *Knulp*.) Among the novels by Hesse that incorporate musical analogies or structures, *Der Steppenwolf* stands out as a key example. Hesse himself suggested as much in a letter in 1930 when defending his novel against a charge of "formlessness." *Der Steppenwolf*, Hesse replied, is "so streng und straff gebaut wie eine Sonate." (Hesse, *Briefe*, 36–37.) (as strictly and tightly built as a sonata.) This specific idea was drawn on later by Theodore Ziolkowski in his interpretation of the novel as a sonata in prose (see Ziolkowski, *The Novels of Hermann Hesse*, 178–228).

[454] Ibid., 190–191.

lover," but his otherness is equally manifested in a conspicuous reference to animality that mirrors the otherness of the novel's wolf-man. When Harry and Hermine meet up with Pablo at the masked ball he is described as having glowingly happy eyes, "welche eigentlich Tieraugen waren." (163) (which were actually animal eyes.)

Although jazz in *Der Steppenwolf* often signifies otherness founded in racist stereotypes (which will become evident under the next heading), it can also be viewed in a contrasting light. At the time of the novel's publication, jazz culture in Weimar Germany also signified the antithesis to traditionalism. As stated by Jonathan O. Wipplinger, jazz "contributed to, rather than merely reflected, the period's vaunted modernism and modernity."[455] Moreover, Wipplinger calls the Weimar Republic "Germany's own 'jazz age' … an age syncopated by experiences of revolution and betrayal, defeat and 'victory' gone awry, hope and despair, progress and reaction."[456] For those who wanted to rebel against convention, jazz stood for something modern, exciting, and liberating. Hesse's novel, however, makes it clear that its protagonist does not regard jazz in such a positive manner, at least not to begin with.

Intersections of Jazz, Racism, and Sex

It has been argued that jazz, which originated in African American culture in North America, is North America's answer to classical music. "Though jazz has utilized and restructured materials from many other musical traditions," William "Billy" Taylor writes, "its basic elements were derived from traditions and aesthetics which were non-European in origin and concept. It is an indigenous *American* music whose roots and value systems are *African*."[457]

As we established in chapter four, a predominant dualism in *Der Steppenwolf* is Harry's split human/animal identity. Alongside this human/animal dualism (and other hitherto discussed dualisms), the novel contains a dualism between classical music and jazz. In the first half of the novel, Harry expresses no reverence whatsoever for jazz. In his elitist manner he considers it a lesser, distasteful form of music, unworthy of serious attention: "Natürlich war sie, mit Bach und Mozart und wirklicher Musik verglichen, eine

---

[455] Jonathan O. Wipplinger, *The Jazz Republic: Music, Race, and American Culture in Weimar Germany* (Ann Arbor: University of Michigan Press, 2017), 3.
[456] Ibid.
[457] William "Billy" Taylor, "Jazz: America's Classical Music," *The Black Perspective in Music* 14, no. 1 (1986): 22.

Schweinerei." (38) (In comparison with Bach and Mozart and "real music," jazz was, of course, filth.)

Travis A. Jackson underscores that as a musical genre, jazz has seldom been described on its own terms as much as in the ways it differs from European concert music.[458] In *Der Steppenwolf* in particular, "jazz is the negation of 'serious' music," Mark Christian Thompson writes, "it is anti-music that structures one's positive experience of the classical tradition."[459] It is the opinion of Harry, as explained by Andreas Kiryakakis, "that there are no new artists after the manner of 'immortals' such as Mozart, and consequently Haller's view of art and the world is oriented to the past: only the venerable artists and geniuses of well-established tradition rank in his view."[460] Harry's musical hero, Mozart, is upheld as antithetical to jazz and he is the definitive symbol for classical music in Hesse's text. Within the context of *Der Steppenwolf*, however, jazz is frequently characterized as much more dynamic and vibrant than classical music, which is a contrast that will be emphasized in what follows.

The juxtaposition of classical music and jazz in *Der Steppenwolf* brings yet another significant dualism to light—that is, a dualism between racial whiteness and racial blackness, where the former is deemed sophisticated and the latter crude:

> Aus einem Tanzlokal, an dem ich vorüberkam, scholl mir, heiß und roh wie der Dampf von rohem Fleisch, eine heftige Jazzmusik entgegen. Ich blieb einen Augenblick stehen; immer hatte diese Art von Musik, sosehr ich sie

---

[458] Travis A. Jackson, "Jazz as Musical Practice," in *The Cambridge Companion to Jazz*, ed. David Horn and Mervyn Cooke (Cambridge: Cambridge University Press, 2002), 83.

[459] Thompson, *Anti-Music*, 59. Thompson's reading (which will be frequently quoted in this chapter) contrasts with Theodore Ziolkowski's interpretation of *Der Steppenwolf* as a sonata in prose. *Der Steppenwolf* can, according to Thompson, also be seen as a textual imitation of jazz. The novel's "narrative structure," he writes, "suggests a combination of the sonata *and* jazz musical composition." (Ibid.) And regarding structural implications of jazz in the novel, Thompson underlines the following: "In terms of form and content, jazz plays a significant role in the text; it acts as dialectical partner and foil to the problematized presence of classical music." (Ibid., 61.) Alongside Thompson's work, music-theory analyses of *Der Steppenwolf*, with an emphasis on jazz, include Gustav Landgren, "'Untergangsmusik war es, im Rom der letzten Kaiser mußte es ähnliche Musik gegeben haben.' Hesses Verhältnis zur Musik in *Der Steppenwolf*," in *Der Grenzgänger Hermann Hesse: Neue Perspektiven der Forschung*, ed. Henriette Herwig and Florian Trabert (Freiburg i. Br.: Rombach, 2013), 111–122; and Alexander Honold, "Der Geist, der in die Beine fährt. Hermann Hesses *Der Steppenwolf* – ein Jazz-Roman?" in *Der Grenzgänger Hermann Hesse: Neue Perspektiven der Forschung*, ed. Henriette Herwig and Florian Trabert (Freiburg i. Br.: Rombach, 2013), 73–92. In Landgren's chapter, Harry Haller's conflicting attitude toward jazz and radio music is the starting point for an examination of Hesse's media aesthetics. Honold labels *Der Steppenwolf* a jazz novel because of the Americanization in Europe in the 1920s.

[460] Kiryakakis, *The Ideal of Heimat*, 106.

> verabscheute, einen heimlichen Reiz für mich. Jazz … traf mit ihrer frohen rohen Wildheit auch bei mir tief in die Triebwelt und atmete eine naive redliche Sinnlichkeit. (38)

> (I passed a dance hall from which intense jazz music was heard, hot and raw like the steam of raw flesh. I stopped for a moment; this kind of music, however much I hated it, was still secretly enticing for me. With its raw and savage wildness, jazz struck me deeply into an underworld of instinct and breathed a simple, honest sensuality.)

Although one could interpret this quote within the frame of the previously mentioned connotations of jazz culture in Weimar Germany (that is, as exciting, liberating, and the antithesis of traditionalism), several stereotypical features of black people can be seen in the way it depicts jazz. For instance, using a phrase like "hot and raw like the steam of raw flesh" to describe the way it sounds, as well as "wildness," "instinct," and "sensuality," connote racist stereotypes such as cannibalism, animality, and uncontrolled primal sexuality.

In Thompson's interpretation of Hesse's quote, he writes: "Haller is here not describing an intellectual music, a form of art to be savored by the mind. He presents instead a music that is viscerally of the body, or viscerally embodied."[461] Harry's attitude toward jazz mirrors his ambivalence regarding his sexual awakening. As Harry's sexual instincts and desire for jazz are of the body, that is, that they overcome him physically, it is difficult for him to suppress them.

Thompson suggests that jazz is equated with racial blackness in *Der Steppenwolf* and that the novel treats jazz as the "symptomatic focal point of European *racial* degeneration."[462] His claim is convincing, since Harry's considers jazz to be "Untergangsmusik" (38) (doomsday music) that threatens German culture.[463] "Jazz is primal music," Thompson explains, "befitting the

---

[461] Thompson, *Anti-Music*, 67.

[462] Ibid., 58.

[463] Gustav Landgren also points out that Hesse portrays jazz as "doomsday music" in *Der Steppenwolf* but suggests that the Dionysian implications of jazz have a positive influence on the protagonist. He also argues that Hesse's notion of *Untergang* (doom) has more than only negative connotations. Landgren substantiates this claim with a reference to a review that Hesse wrote in 1922 about "exotic art," wherein the author states that doom makes rebirth a possibility (see Landgren, "Untergangsmusik war es," 121–122.). This attitude regarding doom and rebirth is not very prevalent in *Der Steppenwolf*, however. The possible rebirth in focus mainly concerns the protagonist *as an individual*, not German culture in general.

degeneration and barbarism of the age."[464] However, he adds, blackness is not only a threat from the outside but an element of Harry's own multifaceted identity: "To represent race and near-vestigial blackness in Haller, Hesse simply figures his 'inner crisis' as that between man (European, German) and animal (black, jazz, recalling that both blackness and jazz were considered bestial [in the Western world] before, during, and well beyond the 1920s)."[465]

Drawing on Thompson's conception, Harry fears what is black within himself, characteristics that are exemplified with his animality and ambivalent feelings for jazz. If we recall the earlier example of him sniffing outside the dance hall, contemplating whether to enter, he senses its inner atmosphere in a lustful manner, which indicates ambivalence. It appears that Harry persistently resists the allure of jazz culture, perhaps because he secretly longs to be part of it? In any case, sensing the atmosphere of the dance hall makes Harry acknowledge his own otherness and he does not enter because his otherness frightens him.

As previously argued, Harry's primitiveness as a white wolf-man is idealized in *Der Steppenwolf* whereas the primitive implications of monkeys and racial blackness is demonized. The demonization of racial blackness is abetted with racist terminology and associations, which highlights a fundamental paradox in Hesse's text. Although Harry expresses fear of his own blackness and uses racist expressions, he also betrays curiosity for jazz as both music and culture. This tension brings about a complex entanglement of desire and disdain that can be traced back to primitivism.

In Jack Halberstam's words, "movements like primitivism … direct desire and fear onto a precivilized past represented using the language of racial otherness."[466] The term "racial otherness" refers to difference that is determined by race or origin and is often surrounded by stereotypical conceptions. Additionally, Halberstam writes, "as these movements show, wildness has been associated with racialized forms of precivilized disorder, as a mode of being that, even though it represents something that white Europeans felt they had lost, must nonetheless be tamed and governed."[467] Such a wildness—one that since the dawn of colonialism has been attributed to black people—is identifiable in *Der Steppenwolf* and represents yet another contradiction. As we saw in chapter four, Harry/the wolf is himself an iteration of wildness, but he also expresses fear of the wildness that the text, through jazz, ascribes

---

[464] Thompson, *Anti-Music*, 68.
[465] Ibid., 62.
[466] Halberstam, *Wild Things*, 9.
[467] Ibid.

to racial blackness. Essentially, otherness in the shape of racial blackness is portrayed as *more Other* than Harry's own otherness as a wolf-man and thus works to normalize the primitiveness of the protagonist.

Harry's ambivalent desire for jazz and disdain of his own blackness thereby mirror his internalized trans- and homophobia. He is clearly also suffering from internalized racism, an iteration of the white man's irrational fear of having his land invaded by black people. As Thompson puts it, "jazz does not so much introduce a foreign element into European culture as awaken and release a long-dormant, indigenous inner white savagery."[468] The wildness that Harry dreads in jazz already exists within himself.

For the purpose of this study, the link between jazz and sex is patricularly interesting. The word jazz has always been a bearer of many meanings, and in the 1920s, Krin Gabbard explains, "the term was appearing in literary works as a synonym for sexual intercourse."[469] Uta G. Poiger adds: "Since musicians first introduced Germans to jazz during the Weimar years, its critics linked the music to feminized men and lascivious women, to racial degeneration and to commercialism. In the 1920s, conservatives, for example, described jazz as music created by [the N-word], marketed by Jews and expressing a 'primitive sexuality.'"[470] Not surprisingly, the Nazis tried to ban jazz and persecuted many jazz fans.

All the above-mentioned associations brought about by jazz can be identified in *Der Steppenwolf*. The association between jazz and feminized men occurs in Harry's homophobia toward Pablo. The link between jazz and lascivious women emerges by means of Hermine and Maria's affinity for dancing to jazz, as well as in their openness about sexual expression. With a basis in Thompson's work, jazz as a symbol for racial degeneration has been underlined above. Jazz as a symbol for commercialism can be seen in Harry's elitism and preference for classical music. And finally, the primitive sexuality that jazz signifies and activates is identifiable not only in *Der Steppenwolf* but in all of Germany between the World Wars. Thompson writes: "The German attitude toward [black people] themselves in the Weimar period was … ambivalent at best. By the start of the '30s, it was openly hostile."[471] To this description, Laurie Marhoefer's work adds that hostile attitudes toward black

---

[468] Thompson, *Anti-Music*, 73.

[469] Krin Gabbard, "The Word Jazz," in *The Cambridge Companion to Jazz*, ed. David Horn and Mervyn Cooke (Cambridge: Cambridge University Press, 2002), 2.

[470] Uta G. Poiger, "American Jazz in the German Cold War," in *Music and German National Identity*, ed. Celia Applegate and Pamela Potter (Chicago: The University of Chicago Press, 2002), 218.

[471] Thompson, *Anti-Music*, xviii.

people were founded in "a national hysteria about the supposed violent hypersexuality of black men that gripped white Germans in the early 1920s."[472] A consequence of Harry's internalized racism (that he dreads that which is black within himself) is that his feelings come to signify fear for an uncontrollable sexuality deep within himself that struggles, essentially, to come out.

Because sexually transgressive characters like Hermine and Pablo are connected with jazz in *Der Steppenwolf*, this link between jazz and sex can be labeled queer. While not specifically mentioning queerness, David G. Richards gives a similar argument: "As [Harry] comes to accept jazz and popular dance music with their social and cultural implications, he undergoes a transformation of social consciousness which is reflected ... in his changed attitude toward Pablo and the sense of community he feels with others at the masked ball."[473] Building on this argument, jazz becomes a means by which Harry opens himself up to queer aspects of life.

It bears mentioning, however, that Harry does not partake in jazz culture on its own terms. He is a white man who appropriates jazz to let go of his own inhibitions. Pablo, being a jazz musician, plays a crucial role in this formative process, as will be demonstrated below.

The Function of Pablo

In the words of Wilbur B. Franklin: "Music, perhaps more than any other of the art forms, is elevated by Hesse to the highest of the disciplines that produce reconciliation of the opposites within man."[474] Drawing on this statement, certain expectations on the function of Pablo are raised.

Pablo, as we know, is a jazz musician and at the end of *Der Steppenwolf* he merges with Harry's musical hero, Mozart. This type of synthesis is seldom realized in Hesse's work. In the Pablo/Mozart figure, the novel's jazz/classical dualism is amalgamated, which in Salvatore Campisi's view "has the fundamental and reassuring consequence for the reader that there is no gap between 'high and low art' and that they have always been interdependent."[475] Thompson arrives at a similar conclusion, noting that "Haller thinks of culture as a phenomenon that is always understood through the historical

---

[472] Marhoefer, *Sex and the Weimar Republic*, 16.
[473] Richards, *Exploring the Divided Self*, 107. In this quote, Richards draws on Marc A. Weiner, *Undertones of Insurrection: Music, Politics, and the Social Sphere in the Modern German Narrative* (Lincoln, NE: University of Nebraska Press, 1993).
[474] Franklin, "The Concept of 'the Human'," 117.
[475] Campisi, "Dialectics of Time," 96.

mediation of its contemporary products."[476] Harry needs Pablo, the modern-day jazz musician, to contrast the greatness of Mozart so that the music of the latter perseveres. (This idea is connected with the ways that the radio is spoken of in *Der Steppenwolf* and how Harry regards the device, which will be addressed momentarily.)

Scholars like Reso Karalaschwili have argued that Hesse's characters are symbols with metaphorical meanings and that Hesse's secondary characters often function as projections of the protagonists' unconsciousnesses.[477] In chapter five, we addressed such ideas regarding Hermine. It was argued that from a queer surface reading perspective, she benefits from not being viewed in a strict symbolic sense, as certain aspects of her character then risk being downplayed or overlooked. The same ought to be true about Pablo. While the Pablo/Mozart synthesis at the end of *Der Steppenwolf* is fantastical (they blend with one another in a surrealistic manner), there is certainly more to Pablo than being a symbol. While most scholars acknowledge that Pablo is important, his bisexuality is often treated as secondary to other aspects, such as his similarities with Jungian archetypes like the "wise old man," "animus," or "shadow."

The wise old man, in Jung's definition, is "the superior master and teacher, the archetype of the spirit, who symbolizes the pre-existent meaning hidden in the chaos of life."[478] The animus archetype is the opposite of the anima, in short, one's unconscious masculine side. The shadow, in Jung's words, is "the dark half of the personality,"[479] which in Heidi M. Rockwood's view is an archetype associated with "negative and frightening, even criminal, impulses."[480] Since all these descriptions correlate with Pablo's personality, they are tempting explanations when examining his function in the text. In "The Function of Pablo in Hesse's *Steppenwolf*" (1994), Rockwood assesses the links between Pablo and Jung's archetypal figures, emphasizing, however, the many contradictions in scholarly attempts to fit the character neatly into one category or the other.

Instead, Rockwood suggests, Hesse's novel portrays an "alchemical development." Alchemy, she explains, "is in its philosophical manifestation a

---

[476] Thompson, *Anti-Music*, 81.

[477] Reso Karalaschwili, *Hermann Hesses Romanwelt* [Literatur und Leben, n.s., vol. 29] (Cologne: Böhlau, 1986), 175.

[478] C.G. Jung, *The Collected Works of C.G. Jung. Vol. 9. P. 1: The Archetypes and the Collective Unconscious*, trans. R. F. C. Hull (London: Routledge & Paul, 1968), 74.

[479] Ibid., 442.

[480] Heidi M. Rockwood, "The Function of Pablo in Hesse's *Steppenwolf*," *South Atlantic Review* 59, no. 4 (1994): 48.

discipline that presents a path toward individuation and psychological wholeness."[481] When the events in *Der Steppenwolf* are seen as progressing in an alchemical manner (and when one refrains from forcing Pablo into a standard Jungian archetypal pattern), Pablo "has a completely natural and organic function," Rockwood writes, "as the catalyst for the events that take place in the novel."[482] As such, Pablo's duality is emphasized, a conclusion that makes it curious that Rockwood's article only mentions his bisexuality once. Undoubtedly, Pablo's potential to desire two (or more) sexes provides a possibility for underlining the depth of his duality, an interpretation that Rockwood leaves out of her analysis.

Rockwood is, however, far from the only scholar to overlook the significance of Pablo's bisexuality. Although some interpreters acknowledge the ways with which Pablo brings Dionysian aspects into Harry's life (with the aid of Hermine and Maria), his norm-challenging traits are frequently downplayed. Emphasizing Pablo's Dionysian elements, Seymour L. Flaxman labels him "a *Naturmensch* [an earthbound, natural human being]" who "is completely uninterested in Harry's long-winded academic opinions. What counts is not musical theories," Flaxman underscores, "or even value judgments, but *making* music."[483] To Harry's aggravation, Pablo is not interested in bonding with him intellectually and speaking of music. Harry says:

> Ich habe mehrmals den Versuch gemacht, mit Ihnen über Musik zu sprechen … aber Sie haben es verschmäht, mir auch nur die geringste Antwort zu geben. (127)

> (I have tried several times to converse with you about music, but you have avoided giving me even the slightest answer.)

Pablo explains that "es hat nach meiner Meinung gar keinen Wert, über Musik zu sprechen." (127) (in my opinion, speaking of music is of no value whatsoever.) Harry's failed attempt at conventional male bonding (that is, to engage in intellectual conversation) is contrasted with Pablo's actual music-making. Let us remember that music, in Hesse's description, is "the most feminine and sweetest of the arts" (as it is described in *Peter Camenzind*). Pablo's preference to make music rather than to talk about it mirrors the way the relationship between Peter and Richard commences, since Richard

---

[481] Rockwood, "The Function of Pablo," 53.
[482] Ibid., 59.
[483] Flaxman, "Hesse's Portrait of the Intellectual," 354. Emphasis added.

introduces himself to Peter with the question: "'Ich wollte fragen, ob Sie nicht Lust hätten, ein wenig mit mir zu musizieren'." (38) ("I wanted to ask if you would like to make some music with me.") Pablo, like Richard, is a man of action rather than words. Both characters' invitations to make music (with Peter and Harry respectively) suggest that their function in the novels is to introduce and encourage a more-than-heteromasculine practice of male bonding.

Apart from Rockwood, other scholars whose interpretations minimize the importance of Pablo's norm-challenging traits include David Artiss and Edward F. Abood, who labels Pablo a "guru" for Harry.[484] And following Pablo's (and Mozart's) association with humor, Campisi calls him a "joker" and a fool in the Shakespearean tradition, that is, a character "who, protected by his role, can afford to voice discomforting truths couched in their (sometimes irreverent) jokes."[485]

If we recall that Peter Camenzind's Uncle Konrad is also a fool and that his foolishness amplifies his queerness, Pablo's association with the fool figure becomes curious. The queer implications of the fool figure that are underlined by Konrad and Pablo's transgressive qualities make it noteworthy that Harry associates *himself* with that category as well: "wir Narren" (39) (us fools), he says, which can be interpreted as an indication that deep down he knows he is himself a challenger of sexual norms.

In certain instances when Pablo's bisexuality is acknowledged in scholarship, it is seen as exercising a negative influence on the novel's protagonist. Franklin, for instance, calls Pablo "amoral" and describes him as a person who desires nothing other than to play music, take drugs, and engage in various forms of sexual activates (straight, gay, and group sex), which suggests, he writes, "that nothing is expected of man."[486] What Franklin's quote implies is that Pablo's amorality accentuates his earth-boundness and diminishes his impact as a supreme immortal being. In contrast, it is suggested here that Pablo belongs to *both* realms (the earthly world of pleasure and the spiritual realm of the Immortals) and that his function, therefore, is to show Harry that it is possible to move freely between the two.

Being at the center of the concluding synthesis in the Magic Theater, while at the same time being openly bisexual, makes Pablo essential to the ways with which queerness occurs in *Der Steppenwolf*. The fact that Pablo is "an

---

[484] See Artiss, "Key Symbols in Hesse's *Steppenwolf*," 91; and Edward F. Abood, *Underground Man* (San Francisco: Chandler & Sharp, 1973), 71.

[485] Campisi, "Dialectics of Time," 188.

[486] Franklin, "The Concept of the 'Human'," 155.

authority figure"[487] (as Richards labels him) is important when clarifying his role in the novel. Let us for a moment recall Heather Love's argument that most characters that are openly acknowledged as queer end up dead. Even if they survive the narrative's trials and tribulations, their lives are usually miserable enough to make death appear a better option. While Hermine, due to her transgressive gender expressions, ends up dead, Pablo's survival challenges Love's statement. It is, of course, significant that Pablo is male whereas Hermine (oftentimes) is perceivable as female. The fact that Pablo survives despite his sexual transgressiveness underlines the overall male homosocial tendencies in Hesse's authorship, wherein female characters are seldom allowed cohesive agency.

Pablo being in a position of authority implies that he has power, which is an uncommon trait for queer literary characters (regardless of gender). His importance in the conclusion of *Der Steppenwolf* thus elevates the novel's queerness. "Like Hermine," Richards writes, "Pablo represents what Harry needs in order to become whole."[488] Hermine's gender fluidity makes her complete and Pablo is also whole, not simply because he is crucial to synthesizing the jazz/classical dualism, but also by means of his bisexuality. Unlike Harry, both Pablo and Hermine are themselves to the fullest, which is why he is attracted to them.

That Harry needs Pablo to become whole himself strongly suggests that he idealizes him, perhaps because of Pablo's confident qualities and strong sense of self, that is, the Eigensinn (self-will) that he projects. In fact, both Pablo and Hermine—who are characterized as Others—project Eigensinn, which demonstrates that Eigensinn is not an exclusive outsider-trait in Hesse's writing. A difference, however, is that in order to march to the beat of their own drums—essentially, to *be themselves*, as Hesse would put it—outsiders like Peter Camenzind and Harry Haller appear to depend on their Eigensinn in a more calculated way that the Others. The characters in the latter category (Boppi, Hermine, and Pablo, as well as Richard and Elisabeth) do not need any deliberate Eigensinn to express the "Be yourself" ideal because all of them are themselves already.

Andreas Kiryakakis interprets Pablo as "the alter ego of Haller, or his other side. [Pablo] is that which Haller could have been."[489] As Pablo is bisexual, Kiryakakis's quote accentuates a possibility that Harry could be bisexual as well. Similarly, in Richards's words, Pablo "represents the part of life Haller

---

[487] Richards, *Exploring the Divided Self*, 137.
[488] Ibid., 138.
[489] Kiryakakis, *The Ideal of Heimat*, 133.

has suppressed or failed to develop."[490] But let us pose these questions: What is Pablo if not someone who shows Harry that living as a bisexual man is truly possible? And has Harry really "failed to develop" bisexual desires himself?

Pablo's bisexuality is not meant to be understood as contagious, that is, as something that would influence Harry to adopt sexual fluidity against his natural inclinations: "Ich kann Ihnen nichts geben, was nicht in Ihnen selbst schon existiert" (165) (I cannot give you anything that you do not already have within you), Pablo explains. Drawing on this statement, Harry already possesses queerness. Not because he is acquainted with queer characters like Hermine and Pablo, but because queerness is within him to begin with.

Now, a word on the merging of Pablo and Mozart and its implications when reading the surface of *Der Steppenwolf*. While the amalgamation of these characters is a fantastical element that is tempting to interpret symbolically, one is not obliged to understand the Pablo/Mozart figure as a mere metaphor. Throughout the events of the novel Pablo is undoubtedly a real person. As mentioned in chapter five, the characters in *Der Steppenwolf* have, in previous scholarship, frequently been described as mirrors for each other, which in conjunction with Jungian approaches to the novel tends to result in interpretations that emphasize symbolism. It is thus noteworthy that when Harry sees himself in a real mirror it is held in front of him by Pablo. In this scene, Pablo is not a symbolic projection of a mirror that conveys a facet of the protagonist's identity, but an actual person who holds up a reflecting object, in which Harry sees his human face merged with the face of the wolf:

> Er hielt mir das Spiegelein vor die Augen … und ich sah, etwas zerflossen und wolkig, ein unheimliches, in sich selbst bewegtes, in sich selbst heftig arbeitendes und gärendes Bild: mich selber, Harry Haller, und innen in diesem Harry den Steppenwolf. (165)

> (He held the small mirror in front of me and I saw, somewhat misty and cloudy, a creepy, fluid, vividly moving, and seething reflection of myself, Harry Haller, and inside this Harry, the Steppenwolf.)

In Eugene Webb's interpretation, the wolf part of Harry is a symbol for the Jungian archetype the shadow, "a figure representing those aspects of the self which have been repressed by the conscious personality and which have consequently begun to live a life of their own in the unconscious."[491] However,

---

regardless of whether the shadow represents the wolf within Harry (or his repressed bisexuality), Pablo holding a physical mirror indicates that he is not a symbol.

Mozart, however, does not exist in Harry's earthbound world and is thus more of a symbol than Pablo. The link between him and Goethe (both are Immortals), and especially the fact that Harry visits Goethe in a dream, makes it likely that Mozart also occurs on a dream level. The merging of Pablo and Mozart takes place when Harry is on drugs, and it is therefore possible to view as a hallucination, which is comparable to a dream-like event. On a realistic level, Pablo is physically present during Harry's drug-induced state, whereas Mozart's symbolic function seems to be to help Harry accept his sexual desire for Pablo. We see this in Harry's description of Mozart as: "dem Gott meiner Jugend, dem lebenslangen Ziel meiner Liebe und Verehrung." (192) (the God of my youth, the lifelong recipient of my love and ennobling.)

In this quote, Mozart is upheld as the prime signifier of homoerotic friendships between men, the type of friendship from Harry's adolescence (as we saw in the earlier quote about longing for a friend in an attic room). Mozart being an admired "God" of Harry's youth as well as the endpoint of Harry's journey also mirror Egon Schwarz's conception of *Der Steppenwolf* as a Bildungsroman that has been "stood on its head," a backwards education. Instead of ending in heterosexual marriage, Harry's education concludes in male companionship with the Pablo/Mozart figure. The very last phrases of the novel confirm its homosocial foundation: "Pablo wartete auf mich. Mozart wartete auf mich." (203) (Pablo waited for me. Mozart waited for me.) As we can see, Harry does not only need Pablo to acknowledge the greatness of Mozart, but he also needs Mozart to rationalize his suppressed homoerotic desire for Pablo.

Moreover, throughout the novel there are several examples of Pablo's looks being commented upon by the protagonist, which clarifies that Harry considers Pablo to be a beautiful man. In one example, Harry refers to the attractiveness of Pablo no less than five times over the course of two pages: "der hübsche junge Herr Pablo" (119) (the beautiful, young Mr. Pablo); "Schön war er, das war nicht zu leugnen, schön von Wuchs und schön von Gesicht" (119) (He was handsome, that could not be denied, handsome in stature and with a handsome face); "dieser hübsche Caballero" (120) (this beautiful gentleman); "er [war] sichtlich zu nichts andrem in der Welt, als um schön zu sein" (120) (he was, evidently, not meant for anything else in this world than to be good-looking); and finally, Harry ruminates:

> Seine dunklen, schönen Kreolenaugen, seine schwarzen Locken verbargen
> keine Romantik, keine Probleme, keine Gedanken – aus der Nähe besehen
> war der schöne exotische Halbgott ein vergnügter und etwas verwöhnter
> Junge mit angenehmen Manieren, nichts weiter. (120)

> (His beautiful dark creole eyes and black curls did not conceal romance,
> problems, or thoughts—when seen up close, this beautiful exotic demigod
> was a jovial and somewhat spoiled youngster with pleasant manners, nothing
> more.)

It is remarkable really that Harry, in one and the same breath, manages to
exotify Pablo in a homoerotic way and trivialize that he finds him attractive
by labeling him shallow. The conflict between homoerotic desire and homophobia within Harry makes his sexual ambivalence tremendously palpable.
Pablo's connection with jazz in the text (a type of music that Harry is drawn
to) and particularly that Pablo is a saxophone player, also stresses ambivalence in Harry since the saxophone, Thompson writes, was the "most hated
of jazz's instruments."[492]

Not surprisingly, when Harry is given various drugs by Pablo (cocaine,
opium), he has a more consenting attitude toward male same-sex activity.
Although he refuses to engage in a sexual threesome with Pablo and Maria,
he allows another homoerotic approach. Intoxicated by Pablo's drugs, Harry
lays down on a bed to get some rest:

> [A]ls ich für einige Minuten die Augen schloß, spürte ich auf jedem Augenlid
> einen ganz flüchtigen, gehauchten Kuß. Ich nahm ihn hin, als sei ich der
> Meinung, er komme von Maria. Aber ich wußte wohl, daß er von ihm war.
> (139)

> (When I closed my eyes for a few minutes I felt a fleeting kiss on each eyelid,
> light as a breath. I accepted it and told myself that it came from Maria. But I
> knew very well that the kiss was from him.)

The events described above correlate with Hesse's novel *Demian,* in which
the sequence of events framing the kiss between the characters Emil and Max
is almost identical. Emil's eyes are also closed when the kiss takes place and
he falls asleep afterwards.[493] First, the fact that both protagonists have their

---

[492] Thompson, *Anti-Music,* xviii.
[493] Hermann Hesse, *Demian,* in *Sämtliche Werke. Band 3: Die Romane. Roßhalde, Knulp, Demian, Siddhartha,* ed. Volker Michaels (Berlin: Suhrkamp, 2001), 365.

eyes closed when the same-sex kiss occurs signifies ambivalence and ambiguity. Second, that they both fall asleep afterwards makes it possible to confuse the event with a dream. In the case of Harry and Pablo, however, the homoerotic implications of the kiss are not easily obscured.

In Kiryakakis's analysis, Pablo's kiss differs from other examples of men kissing men in Hesse's writing (further instances include Govinda kissing Siddhartha, and a kiss between Hermann Heilner and Hans Giebenrath in *Unterm Rad*). Pablo's kiss is more "dangerous," Kiryakakis suggests, since it has no other function than acknowledging homoeroticism.[494] Since Pablo is openly bisexual, kissing Harry cannot be understood metaphorically and Harry's awareness that the kiss is "from him" accentuates its homoerotic meaning. The function of Pablo, as we can see, is to activate homoeroticism in *Der Steppenwolf* and (like Hermine) to guide its protagonist toward sexual fluidity.

Desiring Timelessness

In addition to activating homoeroticism, Pablo works as a catalyst for the ways in which the novel's musical and temporal facets are aligned. His role in the concluding synthesis in *Der Steppenwolf* has been discussed above. Under this heading, we will see that the jazz/classical dualism—and Pablo's function within it—also draw attention to temporal motifs in Hesse's novel.

Hesse considered music and time to be related: "das Wesen der Musik [ist] Zeit,"[495] (the essence of music is time), he wrote in a letter in 1940. As previously suggested, jazz is a means by which Harry opens himself up to queer aspects of life, a formative process in which Pablo has a crucial function. In what follows, we will use the phrase in Hesse's letter ("the essence of music is time") as a bridge between *Der Steppenwolf*'s musical theme and its portrayals of time, and suggest that time, like jazz music, has queer connotations in the novel.

To begin with, the emphatic critique of modernity in *Der Steppenwolf* casts light on time as a major theme therein. Later on we will explore the possibility that Harry's aversion toward modernity is interpretable as queer, but first we will take a look at some of the cases in which his critique of modernity is palpable. For one, Harry does not understand why the land-lady's nephew chooses to spend his evenings in his room listening to a radio: "hingerissen von der Idee der Drahtlosigkeit, anbetend auf frommen Knien

---

[494] Kiryakakis, *The Ideal of Heimat*, 130–131.
[495] Hesse, *Briefe*, 193.

vor dem Gott der Technik." (102) (entranced by the idea of the wireless, on his knees worshiping before the God of technology.)

As we know, Harry needs Pablo, a modern-day jazz musician, to contrast the greatness of Mozart, thereby allowing the music of the latter to persevere. The radio is key in this process, but "jazz," Thompson writes, "is the true voice of the radio."[496] Additionally, he suggests, "with the radio it can no longer be said that an essential connection exists between the event of the concert and the musical score. Technology diffuses musical 'essence'."[497] In Harry's mind, the radio is a threat to the sublimity of classical music, which should be experienced in palaces or salons, and therefore he scorns the music he links with the device. Jazz and radio are emblematic of what Thompson labels modernity's "disease and poison"[498] in *Der Steppenwolf*.

As we can see, the theme of time appears in conjunction with the jazz/classical dualism (which is embodied by Pablo). Mirroring this pair of opposites is another dualism, namely a dualism between past and present. There is a potent conflict between the old (classical music, Mozart) and the new (jazz and other radio genres) which underscores a pervading temporal tension. Harry considers Pablo's music to be "billige Eintagsmusik" (128) (cheap popular music), and with great indignation he exclaims: "es [geht] nicht an, Mozart und den neuesten Foxtrott auf eine Stufe zu stellen." (128) (one simply cannot place Mozart and the latest Foxtrot on the same level.) One example that can be seen as making modernity and jazz associated with queerness is that although Pablo could have been offended by Harry's ignorant remark, he instead gives him a friendly smile and (as narrated by Harry): "strich mir kosend über den Arm." (128) (caressed my arm.) Pablo's intimate carress enhances the homoerotic implications of the men's relationship, thus accentuating queerness in the text.

Furthermore, Harry's distaste for the cinema, whose audiences pay entrance fees for what he considers "Schweinerei" (153) (filth), is another example of the novel's critique of modernity. Cinema, Harry believes, is "ein hübsches kleines Einzelbild aus dem riesigen Ramsch und Kulturausverkauf dieser Zeit." (153) (a pretty little image of the profound junk and culture sell-out of our time.) In addition to the entertainment movies and jazz music in themselves, it is the *increased accessibility* of culture that radio and cinema offer the bourgeoisie that is offensive to Harry. In these perceptions his elitism is forcefully activated. When it comes to experiencing culture, Harry

---

[496] Thompson, *Anti-Music*, 85.
[497] Ibid., 78.
[498] Ibid.

wants exclusivity, which explains why he is drawn to the mysterious Magic Theater, a place that is not open to everyone: "*Eintritt nicht für jedermann*" (33) (*Entry not for everyone*).

When Harry first finds the doorway leading to the Theater, what stands out is his contempt for the luminous sign above the entrance: "Nun haben sie, dachte ich, richtig auch diese alte gute Mauer zu einer Lichtreklame mißbraucht!" (33) (Now, I thought, they have really made a misuse of this good old wall as an illuminated advertisement!) Harry does not enter but is noticeably entranced by the enigmatic venue into which this doorway leads, and he is unable to take his mind off it: "Viel war mir da versprochen worden, gewaltig hatten die Stimmen jener fremden Welt meine Neugierde ange-stachelt." (73) (Much had been promised to me there, mighty voices of a strange world had aroused my curiosity.) His assumption that the Theater may offer what he so desperately desires can be seen in the following reference to music: "Dort vielleicht war das, was ich begehrte, dort vielleicht würde meine Musik gespielt?" (39) (Maybe what I desired could be found in there, maybe my music was played inside?)

The novel does not clarify which genre Harry considers "his" music. It is, however, questionable that the modern entrance (with its illuminated sign) should lead to a venue where classical music is played. It is equally unlikely that it should lead to a place where jazz is played, as this scene occurs shortly after Harry has been standing outside a jazz club sniffing and choosing not to enter. "My music" thus points to something else, perhaps a mix of modern and classical melodies—a synthesis—which underscores Pablo/Mozart's importance yet again.

Alongside the fact that Harry's critique of modernity accentuates time as a theme in *Der Steppenwolf*, his antagonistic feelings toward modernity can be said to have queer implications. First, the classic/old-fashioned type of male friendship that Harry romanticizes belongs to a time in which male homosociality was not as intertwined with homoeroticism as it is in his present. As has been discussed, after the emergence of the modern category of homosexuality around the turn of the twentieth century, male friendship started to become associated with same-sex desire. Because Harry is ambivalent about his own sexual fluidity, he idealizes the past, a time when male–male relations did not automatically connote homoeroticism. As such, he comes to express the type of backwardness that Heather Love proposes in *Feeling Backward*, essentially, a melancholic queer structure of feeling directed toward the past. Second, Harry is hesitant about modern life because it makes transgressive sexualities and gender expressions actual possibilities (as in the cases of Pablo and Hermine). These possibilities frighten Harry because they pressure him to recognize his own queerness.

Harry is caught in-between the past and the present, and he consequently cannot live life to the fullest. When speaking about Harry's manuscript, the landlady's nephew says the following on this topic: "Diese Aufzeichnungen … sind ein Versuch, die große Zeitkrankheit … zu überwinden." (23) (These records are an attempt to overcome the great illness of time.) Thereafter, he clarifies: "Haller gehört zu denen, die zwischen zwei Zeiten hineingeraten." (24) (Haller belongs to those who have fallen in-between two times.)

Let us ponder for a moment what it means to exist in such a temporal space. In Harry's case, the in-betweenness is described as a "great illness" that is brought on by the conflict between the old and the new. Unambiguously, Harry explains: "ich war kein moderner Mensch noch auch ein altmodischer, ich war aus der Zeit herausgefallen und trieb dahin." (151) (I was neither a modern individual, nor an old-fashioned one, I had fallen out of time and was drifting.) In essence, Harry exists in what appears to be a broken temporal continuum.

In Theodore Saul Jackson's words: "The lesson of Haller's journey is that transitory beings such as himself must approach eternity [where Mozart, Goethe, and the other Immortals reside] by first accepting their own temporality: by first achieving a unity and understanding of the Zeitgeist."[499] Harry, however, is unable to accept his current conditions—including himself and his time—and his hunger for eternity is thus proven impossible to satiate. Here it is worth underscoring that the concept of eternity as it appears in *Der Steppenwolf* bears great resemblance to José Esteban Muñoz's thoughts on utopia as a queer domain, out of reach but toward which one can strive: "Queerness is utopian," Muñoz writes, "and there is something queer about the utopian. … Indeed, to live inside straight time and ask for, desire, and imagine another time and place is to represent and perform a desire that is both utopian and queer."[500]

As we established at the end of chapter one, straight time refers to a temporal framework that elevates heterosexual/reproductive relationships as the only natural option; and straight time progresses linearly, that is, uninterrupted. Consequently (in Muñoz's words): "Queerness's time is a stepping out of the linearity of straight time."[501]

---

[499] Jackson, "Ambivalent Modernist," 180.
[500] Muñoz, *Cruising Utopia*, 26.
[501] Ibid., 25.

Eternity, in *Der Steppenwolf*, is equivalent with timelessness, which Goethe explains to Harry when he encounters the author in the dream involving the scorpion:

> Wir Unsterblichen lieben das Ernstnehmen nicht, wir lieben den Spaß. Der Ernst, mein Junge, ist eine Angelegenheit der Zeit; er entsteht, soviel will ich dir verraten, aus einer Überschätzung der Zeit. ... In der Ewigkeit aber, siehst du, gibt es keine Zeit; die Ewigkeit ist bloß ein Augenblick, gerade lange genug für einen Spaß. (96–97)

> (We Immortals prefer not to be taken seriously; we love to have fun. Seriousness, my boy, is a matter for time itself; I will tell you this much, it arises from an overestimation of time. In eternity, however, you see, there is no time at all; eternity is a mere moment that only lasts long enough for a joke.)

Harry learns an important lesson here. Before one can become timeless/eternal/immortal one must learn how to laugh about life. This realization, we shall see, affects Harry's experience in the Magic Theater, wherein Pablo guides him toward a unification of all parts of his personality through humor (we will return to the themes of humor and laughter at the end of this chapter).

Hermine also plays a crucial role in activating Harry's desire to enter a state of timelessness:

> Das heilige Jenseits, das Zeitlose, die Welt des ewigen Wertes, der göttlichen Substanz war mir heute von meiner Freundin und Tanzlehrerin wiedergeschenkt worden. (147)

> (The sacred hereafter, the timeless, the world of eternal values and divine substance was given back to me today by my friend and dance teacher.)

In the straight time that is Harry's actual reality (both straight as a temporal context that is heteronormative and bourgeois, and straight as time that progresses linearly), his longing for eternity/timelessness can be seen as an iteration of Muñoz's ideas on queer utopia. Muñoz writes: "The here and now is a prison house. We must strive, in the face of the here and now's totalizing rendering of reality, to think and feel a *then and there*."[502] These phrases are well-suited descriptions of Harry's condition in *Der Steppenwolf*. With a basis

---

[502] Muñoz, *Cruising Utopia*, 1.

in Muñoz's theories, Harry's longing for eternity/timelessness becomes a queer form of longing. It also suggests that queerness and portrayals of time are entangled in *Der Steppenwolf*.

Another noticeable connection between queerness and time in Hesse's novel is that the timelessness that the Immortals exist in does not adhere to linear conceptions of time. Rather, the timelessness in which the Immortals reside exists "beyond time and space,"[503] Kiryakakis writes. Theirs is a metaphysical realm that Kiryakakis identifies as Harry's Heimat. And David G. Richards explains that the "higher form of humor" that Harry must learn in order to overcome his split identity "involves a flight from reality to the transcendent realm of the Immortals, which is outside time and space and beyond life."[504]

If we refer back to Jack Halberstam's quote from the overview chapter, that queer time seldom revolves around family, inheritance, and children, then the realm of the Immortals, with its non-linear timelessness, can be said to signify such a temporal context. Neither family, inheritance, nor bringing up children characterize the timeless state of the Immortals. This collective of supreme beings consists exclusively of male individuals (*Der Steppenwolf* gives no indication that there should be female artists or geniuses among the Immortals), which makes aspects such as heteronormative family life unlikely among them. Because they are eternal, there is no need for them to partake in continuing their species.

Mozart and Goethe function as the primary signifiers of the timelessness Harry desires. As we have seen, it is not until Pablo merges with Mozart at the end that it is possible for him/them to invite Harry into the Immortals' timeless realm. Goethe, on the other hand, is throughout the novel portrayed as existing beyond common conceptions of time. For example, a copy of Goethe's collected works can be found among the books in Harry's room, which indicates that the author is not only Harry's hero, but despite having passed away long ago, he is (through his art) ever present in the protagonist's life and, as Campisi writes, "explicitly contrasts eternity with time."[505] Also, Goethe's connection with time as a theme makes Hesse's debt to Romanticism visible (the era with which Goethe himself is associated). While the Romantic period was long over when Hesse was writing, what makes him a modern writer, Ralph Freedman argues, "is found in his manner of

---

[503] Kiryakakis, *The Ideal of Heimat*, 132.
[504] Richards, *Exploring the Divided Self*, 94.
[505] Campisi, "Dialectics of Time," 6.

formulating romantic thought and techniques."[506] For instance, in this study's chapters on *Peter Camenzind*, we saw how nature is elevated and celebrated as an ideal. However, it is "[t]he resolution of conflict," Freedman writes, "ultimately in mystical vision or aesthetic imagination, [that] is Hesse's most consistent romantic theme, which extends into the culminating novels of his old age."[507]

Because of the Pablo/Mozart synthesis, *Der Steppenwolf* is a good example of what Freedman calls resolution of conflict. Additionally, the presence of Goethe activates the novel's temporal implications of Romantic thought. In Freedman's words, "many romantic definitions of the function of the novel relate progression in time to aesthetic reconciliation beyond time [and] Hesse borrows a good deal from romantic sources ... to portray the relation between the time-bound experiences which his protagonists encounter and their reflections in timeless art."[508]

Harry's desire to enter a state of timelessness is awoken by Goethe. When he finally achieves this goal, it is facilitated by the synthesized Pablo/Mozart figure who says:

> Sie sehnen sich danach, diese Zeit, diese Welt, diese Wirklichkeit zu verlassen und in eine andre, Ihnen gemäßere Wirklichkeit einzugehen, in eine Welt ohne Zeit. (165)

> (You long to leave this time, this world, this reality, and enter another reality that is more suitable to you: a world without time.)

With a basis in Muñoz's concept of queer utopia as something beyond one's grasp but which one can strive toward, as well as Halberstam's account of queer time as a temporality in which heteronormative notions of relationality are challenged, Goethe and Mozart become symbols of a timelessness that can be seen as queer in *Der Steppenwolf*. Furthermore, the implication that the realm of the Immortals is a homosocial space reserved for men enhances its queer overtones.

---

[506] Ralph Freedman, "Romantic Imagination: Hermann Hesse as a Modern Novelist," *PMLA* 73, no. 3 (1958): 275.
[507] Ibid., 276.
[508] Ibid., 282.

In Queer Times and Places

Under the headings above, examples have been given of the ways that sound (jazz music) and time (modernity, eternity) are perceivable as queer in *Der Steppenwolf*. In the following, links between queerness and places in Hesse's novel will be addressed.

In addition to defining queer time as a temporality that challenges heteronormative conceptions of relationality, Halberstam also conceptualizes it as "a different mode of temporality that might arise out of an immersion in club cultures or queer sex cultures."[509] Places such as bars and clubs have always had an important function in the lives of queer people. In James D. Steakley's work on the homosexual emancipation movement in Germany, it is underlined that having queer venues where people could socialize were, by many, actually regarded as more important than legal rights:

> [I]t appears that the almost legendary flowering of the homosexual subculture during the heyday of the "Golden Twenties" worked to the detriment of the emancipation movement: a contradiction between personal and collective liberation emerged, for it was far easier to luxuriate in the concrete utopia of the urban subculture than to struggle for an emancipation which was apparently only formal and legalistic.[510]

Queer subcultures (of which bars and dancefloors are part) offer release to queer people from the restrictions of heteronormative life and (as described by Halberstam) "produce alternative temporalities by allowing their participants to believe that their futures can be imagined according to logics that lie outside of those paradigmatic markers of life experience—namely, birth, marriage, reproduction, and death."[511] As we have seen so far in this study, Harry Haller does not conform to the heteronormative conceptions of life that Halberstam lists (he is neither married, nor a parent) and therefore he fits in within the kind of queer subculture that both Steakley and Halberstam refer to.

The suggestion that was made earlier, that the timelessness Harry desires is characterized by queerness, is enhanced during the masked ball, which, we shall see, is perceivable as both a queer time and place. Immersed in the bacchanalian activates on the dancefloor, Harry says: "Das Zeitgefühl war mir verlorengegangen, ich weiß nicht, wie viel Stunden oder Augenblicke

---

[509] Halberstam, *In a Queer Time and Place*, 174.
[510] Steakley, *Homosexual Emancipation Movement*, 78–81.
[511] Halberstam, *In a Queer Time and Place*, 2.

dies Rauschglück dauerte." (161) (I had lost all sense of time and did not know how many hours or moments this intoxicated happiness had lasted.) But is the masked ball categorizable as a queer subculture? Well, we know that queer forms of desire occur in this place as it includes an erotic triangle between Harry and Hermine (as rivals) and various women, one of whom Hermine seduces "with allure from Lesbos." Moreover, during the ball Harry's sense of belonging grows which suggests that he is coming to terms with who he is.

That the venue where the ball is held is interpretable as a queer place can be seen in several examples in which bodies and desires are entangled in an orgy-like fashion on the dancefloor. Hesse calls this dance-orgy context "Rausch der Gemeinschaft" (159) (shared intoxication), and in this euphoric state, he explains, "Musik, Rhythmus, Wein und Geschlechtslust" (160) (music, rhythm, wine, and sexual desire) are essential components.

Although Harry is initially skeptical as to whether he truly belongs in this vibrant crowd, he soon becomes passionately entangled with the other bodies:

> Aufgelöst schwamm ich im trunkenen Tanzgewühl, von Düften, Tönen, Seufzern, Worten berührt, von fremden Augen begrüßt, befeuert, von fremden Gesichtern, Lippen, Wangen, Armen, Brüsten, Knien umgeben, von der Musik wie eine Welle im Takt hin und wieder geworfen. (161)

> (Excitedly I swam through the drunken crowd on the dancefloor, touched by scents, sounds, moans, and words; I was greeted and fired up by strangers' eyes, surrounded by faces, lips, cheeks, arms, breasts, and knees—and thrown back and forth by the music like a synchronized wave.)

Although the above quotation does not make any overt references to male bodies, Harry narrates that before having these experiences on the dancefloor, he has witnessed all sorts of men to whom a "shared intoxication" has brought pleasure, hundreds of times in his life, in fact. For instance, among "besoffenen Rekruten und Matrosen" (159) (drunken recruits and sailors), "Künstlern" (159) (artists), "Soldaten" (159) (soldiers), and most recently in Pablo. Besides, the orgy-like state on the dancefloor *does* include men, as this quote about the passionate entanglements during the masked ball demonstrates:

> [A]lle hatten wir einander teil. Und auch die Männer gehörten dazu, auch in ihnen war ich, auch sie waren mir nicht fremd, ihr Lächeln das meine, ihr Werben das meine, meines das ihre. (160)

> (We were all part of each other. Even the men were part of it; I was inside of them too, they were no strangers to me either; their smiles were mine; their lust was mine, and mine was theirs.)

Harry realizes that he belongs in this subculture which activates one of the text's queerly connoted temporal motifs. His sexual liberation occurs at a late stage in life, which differs from common conceptions of subcultures as reserved for the young. On this topic, Halberstam writes:

> [Q]ueer subcultures offer us an opportunity to redefine the binary of adolescence and adulthood that structures so many inquiries into subcultures. Precisely because many queers refuse and resist the heteronormative imperative of home and family, they also prolong the periods of their life devoted to subcultural participation. This challenge to the notion of the subculture as a youth formation could, on the one hand, expand the definition of subculture beyond its most banal significations of youth in crisis and, on the other hand, challenge our notion of adulthood as reproductive maturity.[512]

With a basis in this conception, Harry's sexual liberation taking place at a late stage in life suggests that it is queer. Let us therefore once more recall Egon Schwarz's idea that Harry's personal development progresses in reverse, essentially, that Harry's Bildung leads toward a free-spirited and youthful way of living (rather than resulting in heterosexual marriage and family life).

While not making any references to subcultures, Schwarz's idea correlates with Halberstam's and shows that the middle-aged protagonist in *Der Steppenwolf* has prolonged the part of his life wherein subcultural activity is an option. However, Harry does not find his queer subcultural space on the dancefloor before he is a middle-aged man, and this may account for his initial skepticism. It can, after all, be hard for old dogs to learn new tricks.

Let us now move on from the queer implications of the masked ball to another important place that Harry visits during the drug-induced final scenes in *Der Steppenwolf*. When examining whether the Magic Theater is also perceivable as a queer place, we will look at the phrase that initiates the "Treatise of the Steppenwolf." The opening phrase of the Treatise, "*Nur für*

---

[512] Halberstam, *In a Queer Time and Place*, 161–162.

verrückte" (44) (For madmen only) can be said to signify both madness in the conventional sense and being *displaced*.[513] This ambiguity or dual meaning is emphasized by Kamakshi P. Murti who writes: "The German word 'verrückt' — to be mad or crazy — is much closer to what Haller experiences if one separates the prefix 'ver-' from 'rücken,' that is, dis-place, or re-move from reality, for example move into an alternate reality."[514] While the most common translation of the German adjective *verrückt* is "mad" or "crazy" it can also, as Murti's idea suggests, be understood as *von etwas gerückt*, that is, "torn *from* something." This double meaning of the term affects the queerness of the events occurring in the Magic Theater.

In the following quote, Harry contemplates a call he hears from the voices in the mysterious pages of the Treatise, which illustrates the duplicity of "verrückt":

> Verrückt also mußte ich sein und weit abgerückt von "jedermann", wenn jene Stimmen mich erreichen, jene Welten zu mir sprechen sollten. Mein Gott, war ich denn nicht längst weit genug entfernt vom Leben jedermanns, vom Dasein und Denken der Normalen, war ich nicht längst reichlich abgesondert und verrückt? Und dennoch verstand ich im Innersten den Zuruf recht wohl, die Aufforderung zum Verrücktsein, zum Wegwerfen der Vernunft, der Hemmung, der Bürgerlichkeit, zur Hingabe an die flutende gesetzlose Welt der Seele, der Phantasie. (73)

> (So, if those voices reached me, if those worlds spoke to me, mad is what I had to be, as well as removed from the lives of "everyone else." Good God, had I not long ago been torn from the life, existence, and thinking of normal people; was I not already isolated and out of my mind? And yet in my heart I understood it all quite well, the summons to madness, the call to throw away reason, inhibition, the bourgeois ideals; to surrender to the flood of the lawless world of the soul and imagination.)

Scrutinizing the passage above, what Hesse labels madness is synonymous with challenging the conventions of normal people—that is, in the sense that madness challenges norms of sanity, being mad is queer in *Der Steppenwolf.* Hesse's quote underlines that madness/queerness means being removed or torn from the lives of the ordinary masses. "Verrückt," in this regard, includes both being *crazy* and *displaced.*

---

[513] Apart from being the opening phrase of the Treatise, "Nur für verrückte" is also the opening phrase of "Harry Haller's Manuscript" (27) and thus echoes throughout the entire story.
[514] Murti, "'Ob die Weiber Menschen seyn?'," 286.

So, instead of understanding "Nur für verrückte" solely as "For madmen only," one could interpret it as an invitation more along the lines of: "Only for those who are displaced." As being displaced is equivalent with living in the margins or being an outsider, the queer implications of the phrase are elevated. Additionally, when we emphasize the previously mentioned expression "Entry not for everyone," the Magic Theater is bestowed a distinct queerness. This exclusive venue is clearly a place where only some individuals belong, people who are on the outskirts of mainstream culture's normalcy. The purpose here is not to suggest that being displaced is always equivalent with being queer. Harry's particular situation, however—that he is a lost soul, torn between poles, in-between times, at war with himself, and that he does not find a true sense of belonging until he fully engages with others at the masked ball—indicates that being displaced, in this particular novel, is an expression of queerness.

Contrary to the corporeal, sweaty, and sensual entanglements on the dancefloor, the Magic Theater is a different type of venue. When the ball has reached its end and the guests have left, only Hermine, Pablo, and Harry remain. They enter the Magic Theater where Harry, behind various doors, can dissect parts of his personality in an organized manner. The signs on the doors read, for example, "*Alle Mädchen sind dein!*" (169) (*All girls are yours!*) or offer experiences like suicide in the form of laughing oneself to death, or practices from the *Kama Sutra* (an ancient Indian text which among other things include references to love-making and sexual positions). These rooms make Harry's experience in the Magic Theater more methodical and cerebral than the corporeal, sweaty, and euphoric bacchanal on the dancefloor.

It was mentioned in chapter four that one of the hidden traits of Harry's personality that is revealed in the Magic Theater is his latent attraction to Pablo (Harry sees an image of himself in a mirror, throwing himself in Pablo's arms). As we will see, however, in this queer place, Pablo is not the only person that Harry associates with same-sex desire. Behind one door, "unspeakable" sexual experiences return to Harry's consciousness:

> Auch jene Verführung kehrte wieder, die mir Pablo einst angeboten hatte, und andere, frühere, die ich zu ihrer Zeit nicht einmal ganz begriffen hatte, phantastische Spiele zu dreien und vieren, lächelnd nahmen sie mich in ihren Reigen mit. Viele Dinge geschahen, viele Spiele wurden gespielt, nicht mit Worten zu sagen. (190)

> (Even the seduction I was once offered by Pablo returned, as well as others, earlier ones that I had not even fully understood when they occurred, amazing

games involving three or four, smiling they drew me into their circle. Many things happened, many games were played, not to be spoken of.)

As this confession shows, Pablo's suggestion for a threesome with himself and Maria is not the only *ménage à trois* that Harry is linked with. Sexual games involving more than two people that are "not to be spoken of" are clearly part of Harry's sexual history, albeit suppressed or forgotten until he enters the Magic Theater. Therein, all corners of his personality are illuminated. Recalling Eve Kosofsky Sedgwick's argument that the very namelessness of male–male sexuality—*its secrecy*—throughout history has aided in keeping homosexuality in check, echoes in Harry's narration.

The Magic Theater brings all the homoerotic implications of Harry's sexuality to light. Alongside the example above, and Pablo's continuous presence, Harry's childhood friend Gustav makes an appearance behind a door with the promise of a "hunt for automobiles." Behind this door, Harry encounters a full-scale war between men and machines, which apart from reactivating the novel's critique of modernity, includes phrases with similar descriptions of male friendship that appeared in *Peter Camenzind*. Gustav's appearance is described as "Das Schönste von allem" (170) (The most beautiful of all), Harry is "glücklich" (171) (happy) to meet his friend after many years apart, and: "Mir lachte das Herz, als ich seine hellblauen Augen mir wieder zuzwinkern sah." (171) (As I saw his pale blue eyes wink at me again my heart rejoiced.)

Further similarities between Harry and Gustav's friendship and Peter and Richard's bond can be seen in the following example: At one point Harry and Gustav travel to the mountains where they climb a tree and shoot at cars passing by. Visiting this mountain mirrors Peter and Richard's mountain-climb. Instead of gazing at a queer horizon, however, Harry and Gustav attempt to stop time completely. When asked why they shoot at the passing cars they clarify that although the vehicles were moving at normal car speeds, that speed was still too fast:

> "Was gestern normal war, ist es heute nicht mehr … Wir sind heute der Meinung, es sei jegliche Geschwindigkeit, mit welcher ein Auto fahren möge, zu groß. Wir machen die Autos jetzt kaputt, alle, und die andern Maschinen auch." (173–174)

> ("What was considered normal yesterday is no longer normal today. We are of the opinion that any speed at which a car may travel is too great. We are wrecking cars now, all of them, and all other machines as well.")

Here, cars are a symbol for modernity, and modernity, it is stated, is moving too fast. Harry and Gustav's effort to interrupt this development emphasizes a connection between the critique of modernity in *Der Steppenwolf* and the neo-Romantic idealizing of nature in *Peter Camenzind*. Not insignificantly, both examples link temporal motifs with male friendship.

The quote above also signifies that which was suggested earlier about Harry's preference for a classic/old-fashioned type of male friendship. Harry romanticizes the past, a time when male–male relations did not automatically connote homoeroticism, since within such liaisons he is able to experience same-sex desire without having to come out as bi- or homosexual.

Evidently, the Magic Theater is an arena wherein all parts of Harry's identity are intentionally ambiguous, as if the protagonist is testing the limits of how multidimensional he is able to become. Behind the door "*Wunder der Steppenwolfdressur*" (182) (*The wonder of Steppenwolf training*) we see, for instance, the text's human/animal dualism being physically negotiated. In this room, Harry witnesses an animal trainer who resembles himself. He is holding a large but scrawny wolf on a leash. The trainer has tamed this wolf. It is made to perform tricks for an audience, such as playing dead and eating chocolate from a human's hand. It is appalling to Harry that the animal has been made to disguise its true nature, but soon the roles of the performers are reversed, and when the trainer is forced to perform the wolf's tricks the act takes a turn for the macabre. Bound with the leash, crawling on all fours, the human trainer devours a lamb and a rabbit which makes Harry flee the room. He explains: "Angstvoll lief ich auf und ab, spürte den Geschmack von Blut und den Geschmack von Schokolade im Munde." (184) (In fear I ran back and forth with the taste of blood and chocolate in my mouth.)

Harry tasting blood (the human part of him having eaten the animals) and chocolate (the wolf within him having eaten from the trainer's hand) stresses his inherent duality. The phrase underlines that his human and animal parts are equally prevalent, which suggests that he has taken a large step toward embodying a similar synthesis as the one of Pablo and Mozart.

Accepting his own complexity comes across as Harry's primary purpose in the Magic Theater. Wilbur B. Franklin also argues for this interpretation, writing that it is in this place that Harry "learns to stop viewing life as a dichotomy and to accept all aspects of his personality as being natural."[515] If one accepts Franklin's argument, all aspects of Harry's personality include his queer traits, which are a natural part of him. Subsequently, moving on

---

[515] Franklin, "The Concept of 'the Human'," 122.

from the Magic Theater into the realm of the Immortals would make all worldly dichotomies irrelevant. "The Immortals," Theodore Ziolkowski writes, "accept chaos as the natural state of existence, for they inhabit a realm where all polarity has ceased and where every manifestation of life is approved as necessary and good. … [T]heir cosmos is expansive enough to encompass all of the apparent polar extremes in the Bürger's limited sphere."[516] As this portrayal of the Immortals' realm shows ("where every manifestation of life is approved as necessary and good"), there is no place more suited for a norm-challenging and queerly connoted character like Harry Haller to dwell.

Throughout the second part of this study, it has been shown that Harry has trouble fitting in in contexts that are characterized by normative bourgeois conventions. At the end of the novel, when Harry visits the masked ball and the Magic Theater, he enters arenas that heighten his chances to find out who he really is. In Hesse's oftentimes cynical text, which presents the reader with a chaotic and frequently dark outlook on its protagonist's existence, both the masked ball and the Magic Theater are examples of queer specks of light.

The bacchanalian queer place in which the masked ball occurs is perceivable as a sort of gateway to the Magic Theater, in which all facets of Harry's personality (including his queerness) are negotiated. With the Pablo/Mozart figure as inspiration, the Magic Theater offers a glimpse of a future synthesis of Harry's inner dualisms. This synthesis will be possible if Harry follows the bisexual Pablo into the timeless realm of the Immortals, which is the quintessential manifestation of a queer time and place in *Der Steppenwolf*.

The Liberating Sound of Laughter

Many scholars have emphasized that humor and laughter—which are Romantic themes—are frequently used in Hesse's writing.[517] In *Der Steppen-*

---

[516] Ziolkowski, *The Novels of Hermann Hesse*, 187. Emphasis in original.

[517] Günter Baumann, for instance, mentions Romantic irony and humor when suggesting a possible solution for Harry's inner division, albeit a compromise of sorts, wherein all parts of his personality can be reconciled and integrated. (Günter Baumann, *Hermann Hesses Erzählungen im Lichte der Psychologie C.G. Jungs* [Rhenfelden: Schäuble, 1989], 201–203, referenced in Richards, *Exploring the Divided Self*, 135.) Further references to the frequent use Romantic themes in Hesse's oeuvre can be found in, for example, Campisi, "Dialectics of Time," 163–196; Freedman, "Romantic Imagination," 275–284; Franklin, "The Concept of 'the Human'," 31–37; and Osman Durrani, "'Cosmic Laughter' or the Importance of Being Ironical. Reflections on the Narrator of Hermann Hesse's *Glasperlenspiel*," *German Life and Letters* 34, no. 4 (1981): 398–408.

wolf humor is associated with the Immortals (Goethe in particular) who encourage Harry to laugh at himself. When Harry first enters the Magic Theater and Pablo introduces himself as his guide, Pablo clarifies that to successfully leave his current reality and enter the realm of the Immortals, Harry must let go of his "sogenannten Persönlichkeit" (166) (so-called personality) and commit a "Scheinselbstmord." (167) (pretended suicide.) The only way to complete this task, Harry is told, is to learn how to laugh at himself:

> Sie sind hier in eine Schule des Humors, Sie sollen lachen lernen. Nun, aller höhere Humor fängt damit an, daß man die eigene Person nicht mehr ernst nimmt. (167)

> (Here you are in a school of humor, you should learn how to laugh. Now, all higher humor begins with one no longer taking oneself so seriously.)

Here, Pablo reiterates Goethe's suggestion from Harry's dream that one should never take life too seriously. To become complete, one must cultivate humor. Franklin writes that in Hesse's work, "humor serves as a mediator between the real and ideal"[518] which suggests that humor is a means by which one achieves wholeness. And wholeness in *Der Steppenwolf* includes the potential syntheses of dualisms such as human/animal, female/male, black/white, jazz/classical, past/present, and homosexuality/heterosexuality.

Drawing on the work of David Artiss, David G. Richards sees laughter as a bridge between opposites that can help balance conflicting elements in Harry.[519] Since laughter is essential to synthesizing polarities in *Der Steppenwolf*, the queer connotations of laughter augment the novel's overall queerness. But what is it that makes laughter a queer sound in Hesse's text? In general, as remarked by Anjeana Kaur Hans, laughter has "subversive potential" in *Der Steppenwolf* and signifies something beyond normative

---

[518] Franklin, "The Concept of 'the Human'," 119.

[519] David Artiss draws on Nietzsche's thoughts on laughter, which Richards cites: "Hesse shares Nietzsche's distinction between two kinds of laughter, the base laughter of the multitude or bourgeois and the *Gelächter der Höhe* (laughter of the heights) or *Gelächter des Jenseits* (laughter of the beyond). The goal of philosophy, according to Nietzsche, is to be able to laugh well and live well, which is precisely the standpoint of Pablo and Mozart. The initially humorless Harry Haller is given the opportunity in the Magic Theater to confront the chaos of his Self and to gain the insight and distance of humor and laughter, which would enable him to bridge the gap between polar opposites and to bring disparate elements of his personality into a healthy and creative balance, to take possession and control of his Self." (Richards, *Exploring the Divided Self*, 122.)

definition.[520] More specifically, while not underlining queerness per se, Campisi points out the following: "Richard's resounding laughter in *Peter Camenzind* … resonates with the immortal laughter of Mozart."[521] As we saw in chapter one, Richard's happy manner (that he has an intoxicating laughter) adds a certain flair to his character and accentuates his queer qualities. Additionally, as this chapter has shown, by means of Pablo's bisexuality, the synthesized and laughing Pablo/Mozart figure is bestowed a distinct queer significance.

At the end of *Der Steppenwolf*, the following is clear: If Harry could ultimately allow himself to embrace his sexual fluidity—that is, to open himself up to a complete unification of all aspects of his personality—he would embody a synthesis as well. As such, queerness stands out as the key to solving conflicts and synthesizing dualisms in Hesse's novel. Consequently, Harry's reaction to Pablo's command that he should learn how to laugh—"ich [ausbrach] in ein erlösendes Gelächter" (167) (I broke out in a liberating laughter)—suggests that at the end of Harry's journey, he might finally be ready to stop running from the norm-challenging characteristics of his identity and begin to cultivate his queerness.

[520] Hans, "Defining Desires," 130.
[521] Campisi, "Dialectics of Time," 170.

Conclusion

Imperfect Syntheses

Eighteen years after writing *The Outsider*, Colin Wilson revisited Hesse's body of work with a biographical essay covering Hesse's entire career. The essay's assessment is occasionally harsh: "In a sense," Wilson writes, "Hesse has never grown up; he keeps on writing the same novel over and over again."[522] Furthermore, Wilson argues that no apparent process of maturing has occurred in Hesse's authorship: "He has learned to *state* his problems more clearly; but the solution is as far away as ever."[523]

However, presenting solutions was likely never Hesse's goal as a writer. Peter Heller points out that "Hesse thrives on contradictions."[524] Without contradictions there would be less tension in Hesse's texts, and they would be less engaging. Moreover, if Hesse's work aims at showing its characters' potential to affirm multiple aspects of their personalities, a solution of the sort that Wilson seems to propose (essentially, that one should make a choice *between one or the other*) is neither likely nor desirable. Wilson is right to point out that Hesse's texts never provide clear-cut answers to the questions they pose. But could not an intended ambiguousness be understood as an answer? If so, Hesse's texts achieve what they set out to do. Although the syntheses that are sought throughout his writing most often end up as imperfect, the queer readings in this study have substantiated that their contradictions invite complex, multifaceted, and diverse interpretations.

Hesse's Queer Legacy

It is, for this study, interesting to note that in the instances when syntheses *are* reached in *Peter Camenzind* and *Der Steppenwolf*, they materialize within the novels' queer friendships. When the outsider-protagonists (Peter and Harry) are alone, they experience everything from loneliness to contempt for others, depression, bad health, alcoholism, and failure, whereas the bonds they form with other people (Richard, Elisabeth, Boppi, Hermine, and Pablo) provide queer specks of light in the dark—a sense of belonging and complete-

---

[522] Wilson, *Hermann Hesse*, 34–35.
[523] Ibid., 25.
[524] Peter Heller, "The Writer in Conflict with His Age. A Study in the Ideology of Hermann Hesse," *Monatshefte* 46, no. 3 (1954): 146.

ness. As we can now conclusively determine, in Hesse's fictional worlds, it is possible to categorize queer specks of light and queer friendships as more or less the same thing.

We are now approaching the end of this book but let us first, for a moment, recollect the "Hesse Boom" in the United States in the 1960s and 70s, that is, the era in which Hesse's popularity among countercultures was enormous. Regarding Hesse's appeal to readers at that time, Theodore Ziolkowski has pointed out that "anyone wishing to understand the [Hesse] phenomenon must be concerned not so much with what Hesse actually says in his works as with what his readers think or like to believe that he says."[525] While some may be content with regarding the conclusions in this study as "reading too much into things," Hesse himself actually encouraged readers to interpret his stories queerly, as the letter that was quoted in the overview chapter confirmed. Hence, reading Hesse's work queerly today has less to do with wanting to "believe" that he says something queer and more to do with recognizing unexplored depth in his work. In fact, *Peter Camenzind* and *Der Steppenwolf* provoke the question, why should one presuppose heterosexuality as a norm in Hesse's writing at all? The queer friendships in the stories that have been at the center of this study clearly challenge such an assumption.

In addition, the two novels in focus here can be said to express queerness in the following way: That which is idealized in the texts—for example, homoerotic bonds, or characters who embody various forms of otherness— is always juxtaposed with heteronormativity or other norms. For instance, when contrasted with what is considered normal (able-bodiedness, heterosexual relationships, bourgeois values), Boppi's status as a disabled Other, Hermine's gender nonconformity, and the idealized wolf part of Harry Haller underline the importance of queerness in the texts. *Peter Camenzind* and *Der Steppenwolf* also convey that queerness is essential to the ways with which the novels portray completeness, and to the characters' desires to become whole. As the last chapter suggested, the key to synthesizing dualisms in *Der Steppenwolf* is Harry embracing his queerness. And in the reading of *Peter Camenzind*, queerness in the shape of homoerotic bonds between men is presented as essential, since Peter's relationships with Richard and Boppi provide him with the leeway to truly become himself.

Contrary to the times in which Hesse's novels were written—when terms like queer, gay, and homosexual were not as prevalent as they are today—our

---

[525] Ziolkowski, "Saint Hesse among the Hippies," 20.

current era provides greater possibilities for interpreting characters in historical texts as queer: "If their trajectory to a queer future seems inevitable," Heather Love writes, "this appearance is perhaps best explained by the fact that *we are that future*. Our existence in the present depends on being able to imagine these figures reaching out to us."[526] An informal intention with this study has been to do exactly that: to imagine what characters like Peter Camenzind and Harry Haller are actually trying to tell us. And moreover, by emphasizing, embracing, and celebrating queer specks of light in Hesse's novels—that is, representations of queer companionship, affection, desire, and romance—this study has shown that Hermann Hesse can be seen as a campaigner for queer subjectivity, which from now on ought to make his place within the queer literary canon self-evident.

[526] Love, *Feeling Backward*, 40.

Bibliography

Abood, Edward F. *Underground Man*. San Francisco: Chandler & Sharp, 1973.

Acampora, Ralph R. "Nietzsche's Feral Philosophy: Thinking Through an Animal Imaginary." In *A Nietzschean Bestiary: Becoming Animal Beyond Docile and Brutal*, edited by Christa Davis Acampora and Ralph R. Acampora, 1–13. Lanham, MD: Rowman & Littlefield, 2004.

Adorno, Theodor W. "Notes on Kafka." In *Prisms*, translated by Samuel and Shierry Weber. Cambridge, MA: The MIT Press, 1981.

Agamben, Giorgio. *Homo Sacer: Sovereign Power and Bare Life*, translated by Daniel Heller-Roazen. Stanford: Stanford University Press, 1998.

Ahmed, Sara. *Differences that Matter: Feminist Theory and Postmodernism*. Cambridge: Cambridge University Press, 1998.

Ahmed, Sara. "Happy Futures, Perhaps." In *Queer Times, Queer Becomings*, edited by E. L. McCallum and Mikko Tuhkanen, 159–182. Albany: State University of New York Press, 2011.

Ahmed, Sara. *Living a Feminist Life*. Durham: Duke University Press, 2017.

Aldrich, Robert. *The Seduction of the Mediterranean: Writing, Art and Homosexual Fantasy*. London: Routledge, 1993.

Andree, Courtney J. "*Bildung* Sideways: Queer/Crip Development and E. M. Forster's 'Fortunate Failure'." *Journal of Literary & Cultural Disability Studies* 12, no. 1 (2018), 19–34.

Armstrong, Philip. *What Animals Mean in the Fiction of Modernity*. London: Routledge, 2008.

Arnds, Peter. *Lycanthropy in German Literature*. Basingstoke: Palgrave Macmillan, 2015.

Artiss, David. "Key Symbols in Hesse's *Steppenwolf*." *Seminar* 7, no. 2 (1971): 85–101.

Atze, Marcel. "*Unser Hitler*": *Der Hitler-Mythos im Spiegel der Deutschsprachigen Literatur nach 1945*. Göttingen: Wallstein, 2003.

Ball, Hugo. *Hermann Hesse: Sein Leben und sein Werk*. Berlin: S. Fischer, 1927.

Baumann, Günter. *Hermann Hesses Erzählungen im Lichte der Psychologie C.G. Jungs*. Rhenfelden: Schäuble, 1989.

Beachy, Robert. "To Police *and* Protect: The Surveillance of Homosexuality in Imperial Berlin." In *After* The History of Sexuality: *German Genealogies With and Beyond Foucault*, edited by Scott Spector, Helmut Puff, and Dagmar Herzog, 109–123. New York: Berghahn Books, 2012.

Beauvoir, Simone de. *The Second Sex*. Translated by H. M. Parshley. London: Jonathan Cape, 1953.

Benjamin, Walter. "The Task of the Translator." Translated by Harry Zohn. In *The Translation Studies Reader*, edited by Lawrence Venuti, 15–25. London: Routledge, 2000.

Berggren, Kalle. "Reading Rap: Feminist Interventions in Men and Masculinity Research." PhD diss., Uppsala University, 2014.

Bernasconi, Robert. "Nietzsche as a Philosopher of Racialized Breeding." In *The Oxford Handbook of Philosophy and Race*, edited by Naomi Zack, 54–64. New York: Oxford University Press, 2017.

Bernhardt-House, Phillip A. "The Werewolf as Queer, the Queer as Werewolf, and Queer Werewolves." In *Queering the Non/Human*, edited by Noreen Giffney and Myra J. Hird, 159–183. Aldershot, Hampshire: Ashgate, 2008.

Best, Stephen and Sharon Marcus. "Surface Reading: An Introduction." *Representations* 108, no. 1 (2009): 1–21.

Björklund, Jenny and Ann-Sofie Lönngren. "Now You See It, Now You Don't: Queer Reading Strategies, Swedish Literature, and Historical (In)visibility." *Scandinavian Studies* 92, no. 2 (2020): 196–228.

Björklund, Jenny. "Queer Readings/Reading the Queer." *Lambda Nordica* 23, no. 1–2 (2018): 7–15.

Boes, Tobias. "Modernist Studies and the Bildungsroman: A Historical Survey of Critical Trends." *Literature Compass* 3, no. 2 (2006), 230–243.

Boitani, Luigi. "Ecological and Cultural Diversities in the Evolution of Wolf-Human Relationships." In *Ecology and Conservation of Wolves in a Changing World*, edited by Ludwig N. Carbyn, Steven H. Fritts, and Dale R. Seip, 3–11. Edmonton: Canadian Circumpolar Institute, 1995.

Bruhm, Steven. *Reflecting Narcissus: A Queer Aesthetic*. Minneapolis: University of Minnesota Press, 2000.

Brunotte, Ulrike. *Zwischen Eros und Krieg: Männerbund und Ritual in der Moderne*. Berlin: Wagenbach, 2004.

Bruns, Claudia. *Politik des Eros. Der Männerbund in Wissenschaft, Politik und Jugendkultur (1880–1934)*. Köln: Böhlau, 2008.

Butler, Judith. *Frames of War: When is Life Grievable?* London: Verso, 2009.

Butler, Judith. *Gender Trouble: Feminism and the Subversion of Identity*. New York: Routledge, 1990.

Butler, Judith. *Precarious Life: The Powers of Mourning and Violence*. London: Verso, 2004.

Butler, Judith. *Undoing Gender*. New York: Routledge, 2004.

Campisi, Salvatore. "Hermann Hesse and the Dialectics of Time." PhD diss., University of Salford, 2010. Doi: https://www.yumpu.com/en/document/view/7240583/hermann-hesse-and-the-dialectics-of-time-salvatore-c-p- (accessed January 14, 2022).

Carlsson, Anni, ed. *Der Briefwechsel Hermann Hesse–Thomas Mann*. Frankfurt am Main: Suhrkamp, 1968.

Carroll, Rachel. "Introduction: feminism, queer theory and heterosexuality." In *Rereading Heterosexuality: Feminism, Queer Theory and Contemporary Fiction*, edited by Rachel Carroll, 1–21. Edinburgh: Edinburgh University Press, 2012.

Carstensen, Thorsten and Marcel Schmid. "Die Literatur der Lebensreform: Kontexte, Orte und Autoren." In *Die Literatur der Lebensreform: Kulturkritik und Aufbruchstimmung um 1900*, edited by Thorsten Carstensen and Marcel Schmid, 9–26. Bielefeld: transcript, 2016.

Chauncey, George. *Gay New York: Gender, Urban Culture, and the Making of the Gay Male World, 1890-1940*. New York: Basic Books, 1994.

Clare, Eli. *Exile & Pride: Disability, Queerness, and Liberation*. Durham: Duke University Press, 2015.

Colby, Thomas E. "The Impenitent Prodigal: Hermann Hesse's Hero." *The German Quarterly* 40, no. 1 (1967): 14–23.

Cornils, Ingo. "Introduction: From Outsider to Global Player — Hermann Hesse in the Twenty-First Century." In *A Companion to the Works of Hermann Hesse*, edited by Ingo Cornils, 1–16. Rochester, NY: Camden House, 2009.

Crompton, Louis. *Homosexuality and Civilization*. Cambridge, MA: The Belknap Press of Harvard University Press, 2003.

Crouthamel, Jason. "'Comradeship' and 'Friendship': Masculinity and Militarisation in Germany's Homosexual Emancipation Movement after the First World War." *Gender & History* 23, no. 1 (2011): 111–129.

Crouthamel, Jason. "Love in the Trenches: German Soldiers' Conceptions of Sexual Deviance and Hegemonic Masculinity in the First World War." In *Gender and the First World War*, edited by Christa Hämmerle, Osvald Überegger, and Birgitta Bader Zaar, 52–71. London: Palgrave Macmillan, 2014.

Davis Acampora, Christa and Ralph R. Acampora, ed. *A Nietzschean Bestiary: Becoming Animal Beyond Docile and Brutal*. Lanham, MD: Rowman & Littlefield, 2004.

Dean, Tim and Christopher Lane. "Homosexuality and Psychoanalysis: An Introduction." In *Homosexuality & Psychoanalysis*, ed. Tim Dean and Christopher Lane, 3–42. Chicago: University of Chicago Press, 2001.

Decker, Gunnar. *The Wanderer and His Shadow*. Translated by Peter Lewis. Cambridge, MA: Harvard University Press, 2018.

Demont, Marc. "Caressing Radical Alterity: For a Queer Ethic of Embodiment in Contemporary Films and Literature." PhD diss., University of South Carolina, 2017. Doi: https://scholarcommons.sc.edu/etd/4046 (accessed January 14, 2022).

Dhority, Lynn. "Who Wrote the *Tractat vom Steppenwolf?*" *German Life and Letters* 27, no. 1 (1973): 59–66.

DiAngelo, Robin. *White Fragility: Why It's So Hard for White People to Talk About Racism*. Boston: Beacon Press, 2018.

Doty, Alexander. *Making Things Perfectly Queer: Interpreting Mass Culture*. Minneapolis: University of Minnesota Press, 1993.

Dover, Kenneth James. *Greek Homosexuality*. London: Duckworth, 1978.

Durrani, Osman. "'Cosmic Laughter' or the Importance of Being Ironical. Reflections on the Narrator of Hermann Hesse's *Glasperlenspiel*." *German Life and Letters* 34, no. 4 (1981): 398–408.

Eddo-Lodge, Reni. *Why I'm No Longer Talking to White People About Race*. London: Bloomsbury, 2017.

Edelman, Lee. *No Future: Queer Theory and the Death Drive*. Durham: Duke University Press, 2004.

Ehnenn, Jill. "Reorienting the *Bildungsroman*: Progress Narratives, Queerness, and Disability in *The History of Sir Richard Calmady* and *Jude the Obscure*." *Journal of Literary & Cultural Disability Studies* 11, no. 2 (2017), 151–168.

Etherington, Ben. *Literary Primitivism*. Stanford: Stanford University Press, 2018.

Faderman, Lillian. *Odd Girls and Twilight Lovers: A History of Lesbian Life in Twentieth-Century America*. London: Penguin, 1992.

Faderman, Lillian. *Surpassing the Love of Men: Romantic Friendship and Love Between Women from the Renaissance to the Present*. London: Women's Press, 1985.

Fandrey, Walter. *Krüppel, Idioten, Irre: Zur Sozialgeschichte behinderter Menschen in Deutschland*. Stuttgart: Silberburg, 1990.

Fassnacht, Max. "On the Ground of Nature: Sexuality and Respectability in *Die Freundschaft*'s *Wandervogel* Stories." *Journal of Homosexuality* 68, no. 3 (2021): 434–460.

Felski, Rita. *Hooked: Art and Attachment*. Chicago: The University of Chicago Press, 2020.

Felski, Rita. *The Limits of Critique*. Chicago: The University of Chicago Press, 2015.

Fickert, Kurt J. "The Development of the Outsider Concept in Hesse's Novels." *Monatshefte* 52, no. 4 (1960): 171–178.

Flaxman, Seymour L. "*Der Steppenwolf*: Hesse's Portrait of the Intellectual." *Modern Language Quarterly* 15, no. 4 (1954): 349–358.

Flodin, Camilla. "Adorno's Utopian Animals." In *Critical Theory. Past, Present, Future*, edited by Anders Bartonek and Sven-Olov Wallenstein, 103–117. Huddinge: Södertörns högskola, 2021.

Franklin, Wilbur B. "The Concept of 'the Human' in the Work of Hermann Hesse and Paul Tillich." PhD diss., University of St Andrews, 1977. Doi: https://core.ac.uk/download/pdf/96709396.pdf (accessed January 14, 2022).

Freccero, Carla. *Queer/Early/Modern*. Durham: Duke University Press, 2006.

Freedman, Ralph. *Hermann Hesse: Pilgrim of Crisis. A Biography*. New York: Pantheon, 1978.

Freedman, Ralph. "Romantic Imagination: Hermann Hesse as a Modern Novelist." *PMLA* 73, no. 3 (1958): 275–284.

Freud, Sigmund. *The 'Wolfman' [From the* History of an Infantile Neurosis*].* Translated by Louise Adey Huish. London: Penguin Books, 2010.

Fritts, Steven H., Robert O. Stephenson, Robert D. Hayes, and Luigi Boitani. "Wolves and Humans." In *Wolves: Behavior, Ecology, and Conservation*, edited by L. David Mech and Luigi Boitani, 289–316. Chicago: University of Chicago, 2003.

Frost, Brian J. *The Essential Guide to Werewolf Literature.* Madison: University of Wisconsin Press, 2003.

Fumagalli, Maddalena. "Pablo contra Mozart? Das 'magische Teater' der Musik." In *Hermann-Hesse-Jahrbuch. Band 1*, edited by Mauro Ponzi, 111–120. Tübingen: Max Niemeyer, 2004.

Gabbard, Krin. "The Word Jazz." In *The Cambridge Companion to Jazz*, edited by David Horn and Mervyn Cooke, 1–6. Cambridge: Cambridge University Press, 2002.

Gallagher, David. *Metamorphosis: Transformations of the Body and the Influence of Ovid's* Metamorphoses *on Germanic Literature of the Nineteenth and Twentieth Centuries.* Amsterdam: Rodopi, 2009.

Garland-Thomson, Rosemarie. *Extraordinary Bodies: Figuring Physical Disability in American Culture and Literature.* New York: Columbia University Press, 2017.

Geist, Kathrin. "Der Nacktkletterer vom Monte Verità: Hermann Hesses *In den Felsen* als kritische Auseinandersetzung mit der Lebensreform." In *Die Literatur der Lebensreform: Kulturkritik und Aufbruchstimmung um 1900*, edited by Thorsten Carstensen and Marcel Schmid, 193–207. Bielefeld: transcript, 2016.

Gerhardt, Christina. "The Ethics of Animals in Adorno and Kafka." *New German Critique* 33, no. 1 (2006): 159–178.

Giffney, Noreen. "Introduction: The 'q' Word." In *The Ashgate Research Companion to Queer Theory*, edited by Noreen Giffney and Michael O'Rourke, 1–13. Farnham: Ashgate, 2009.

Gontrum, Peter Baer. "Natur- und Dingsymbolik als Ausdruck der inneren Welt Hermann Hesses." PhD diss., Munich, 1958.

Goodbody, Axel. "Wolves and Wolf Men as Literary Tropes and Figures of Thought: Eco- and Zoopoetic Perspectives on Jiang Rong's *Wolf Totem* and Other Wolf Narratives." In *Texts, Animals, Environments: Zoopoetics and Ecopoetics*, edited by Frederike Middelhoff, Sebastian Schönbeck, Roland Borgards, and Catrin Gersdorf, 307–324. Freiburg i. Br.: Rombach, 2019.

Grimm, Gunter E. "Hermann Hesses Goethe-Lektüren. Stationen einer 'geistigen Beunruhigung'." In *Der Grenzgänger Hermann Hesse: Neue Perspektiven der Forschung*, edited by Henriette Herwig and Florian Trabert, 141–154. Freiburg i. Br.: Rombach, 2013.

Groff, Peter S. "Who Is Zarathustra's Ape?" In *A Nietzschean Bestiary: Becoming Animal Beyond Docile and Brutal*, edited by Christa Davis Acampora and Ralph R. Acampora, 17–31. Lanham, MD: Rowman & Littlefield, 2004.

Haggerty, George E. *Queer Friendship: Male Intimacy in the English Literary Tradition.* Cambridge: Cambridge University Press, 2018.

Halberstam, Jack. *Female Masculinity*. Durham: Duke University Press, 1998.

Halberstam, Jack. *In a Queer Time and Place: Transgender Bodies, Subcultural Lives*. New York: New York University Press, 2005.

Halberstam, Jack. *The Queer Art of Failure*. Durham: Duke University Press, 2011.

Halberstam, Jack. *Wild Things: The Disorder of Desire*. Durham: Duke University Press, 2020.

Hall, Donald E. *Queer Theories*. Basingstoke: Palgrave Macmillan, 2003.

Halperin, David M. *How to be Gay*. Cambridge, MA: The Belknap Press of Harvard University Press, 2012.

Hans, Anjeana Kaur. "Defining Desires: Homosexual Identity and German Discourse 1900–1933." PhD diss., Harvard University, 2005.

Haraway, Donna. *Simians, Cyborgs, and Women: The Reinvention of Nature*. New York: Routledge, 1991.

Heilbut, Anthony. *Thomas Mann: Eros and Literature*. New York: Knopf, 1996.

Heller, Peter. "The Writer in Conflict with His Age. A Study in the Ideology of Hermann Hesse." *Monatshefte* 46, no. 3 (1954): 137–147.

Herwig, Henriette and Sikander Singh, ed. *"Magischer Einklang": Dialog der Künste im Werk Hermann Hesses*. Göttingen: Wallstein, 2011.

Hesse, Hermann. *Briefe*. Frankfurt am Main: Suhrkamp, 1964.

Hesse, Hermann. *Demian*. In *Sämtliche Werke. Band 3: Die Romane. Roßhalde, Knulp, Demian, Siddhartha*. Edited by Volker Michaels. Berlin: Suhrkamp, 2001.

Hesse, Hermann. *Der Steppenwolf*. In *Sämtliche Werke. Band 4: Die Romane. Der Steppenwolf, Narziß und Goldmund, Die Morgenlandfahrt*. Edited by Volker Michaels. Berlin: Suhrkamp, 2001.

Hesse, Hermann. *Die Antwort bist du selbst: Briefe an junge Menschen*. Edited by Volker Michels. Frankfurt am Main: Insel, 2000.

Hesse, Hermann. "Eigensinn." In *Eigensinn macht Spaß: Individuation und Anpassung*, edited by Volker Michels, 84–92. Frankfurt am Main: Insel, 2002.

Hesse, Hermann. "Eigensinn macht Spaß." In *Eigensinn macht Spaß: Individuation und Anpassung*, edited by Volker Michels, 8–11. Frankfurt am Main: Insel, 2002.

Hesse, Hermann. "Gratitude to Goethe." In *My Belief: Essays on Life and Art*, edited by Theodore Ziolkowski, translated by Denver Lindley, with two essays translated by Ralph Manheim, 181–188. St. Albans: Triad/Panther Books, 1978.

Hesse, Hermann. *Krieg und Frieden: Betrachtungen zu Krieg und Politik seit dem Jahr 1914*. Zürich: Fretz & Wasmuth, 1946.

Hesse, Hermann. *Kursgefaßter Lebenslauf*. In *Sämtliche Werke. Band 12: Autobiographische Schriften II. Selbstzeugnisse. Erinnerungen. Gedenkblätter und Rundbriefe*. Edited by Volker Michaels. Frankfurt am Main: Suhrkamp, 2003.

Hesse, Hermann. "Nachwort (1941)." In *Sämtliche Werke. Band 4: Die Romane. Der Steppenwolf, Narziß und Goldmund, Die Morgenlandfahrt*, edited by Volker Michaels, 207–208. Berlin: Suhrkamp, 2001.

Hesse, Hermann. *Peter Camenzind*. In *Sämtliche Werke. Band 2: Die Romane. Peter Camenzind, Unterm Rad, Gertrud*. Edited by Volker Michaels. Berlin: Suhrkamp, 2001.

Hesse, Hermann. *Steppenwolf*, translated by Basil Creighton, updated translation by Joseph Mileck and Horst Frenz. New York: Bantam Books, 1963.

Hesse, Hermann. "Vom Bücherlesen." In *Die Welt der Bücher: Betrachtungen und Aufsätze zur Literatur*, edited by Volker Michels, 188–193. Frankfurt am Main: Suhrkamp, 1977.

Hesse, Hermann. *Wanderung. Aufzeichnungen* [1920]. In *Sämtliche Werke. Band 11: Autobiographische Schriften 1. Wanderung, Kurgast, Die Nürnberger Reise, Tagebücher*. Edited by Volker Michaels. Berlin: Suhrkamp, 2003.

Hesse, Hermann. *Zarathustras Wiederkehr: Ein Wort an die deutsche Jugend*. Bern: Stämpfli & Cie, 1919.

Hollis, Andrew. "Political Ambivalence in Hesse's 'Steppenwolf'." *The Modern Language Review* 73, no. 1 (1978): 110–118.

Honold, Alexander. "Der Geist, der in die Beine fährt. Hermann Hesses *Der Steppenwolf* – ein Jazz-Roman?" In *Der Grenzgänger Hermann Hesse: Neue Perspektiven der Forschung*, edited by Henriette Herwig and Florian Trabert, 73–92. Freiburg i. Br.: Rombach, 2013.

Horkheimer, Max and Theodor W. Adorno. *Dialectic of Enlightenment*, translated by John Cumming. New York: Continuum, 1989.

Hsia, Adrian. "Siddhartha." In *A Companion to the Works of Hermann Hesse*, edited by Ingo Cornils, 149–170. Rochester, NY: Camden House, 2009.

Hubbard, Thomas K., ed. *Homosexuality in Greece and Rome: A Sourcebook of Basic Documents*. Berkeley: University of California Press, 2003.

Jackson, Theodore Saul. "Hermann Hesse as Ambivalent Modernist." PhD diss., Washington University, 2010. Doi: https://doi.org/10.7936/K71R6NKW (accessed January 14, 2022).

Jackson, Travis A. "Jazz as Musical Practice." In *The Cambridge Companion to Jazz*, edited by David Horn and Mervyn Cooke, 83–95. Cambridge: Cambridge University Press, 2002.

Jameson, Fredric. *The Political Unconscious: Narrative as a Socially Symbolic Act*. London: Methuen, 1981.

Johansson, Niclas. *The Narcissus Theme from Fin de Siècle to Psychoanalysis: Crisis of the Modern Self*. Frankfurt am Main: Peter Lang, 2017.

Johnson, Marguerite and Terry Ryan. *Sexuality in Greek and Roman Society and Literature: A Sourcebook*. London: Routledge, 2005.

Johnson, Merri Lisa and Robert McRuer. "Cripistemologies: Introduction." *Journal of Literary & Cultural Disability Studies* 8, no. 2 (2014): 127–147.

Jung, C.G. *The Collected Works of C.G. Jung. Vol. 9. P. 1: The Archetypes and the Collective Unconscious.* Translated by R. F. C. Hull. London: Routledge & Paul, 1968.

Karalaschwili, Reso. "Harry Hallers Goethe-Traum: Vorläufiges zu einer Szene aus dem *Steppenwolf* von Hermann Hesse." *Goethe-Jahrbuch* 97 (1980): 224–234.

Karalaschwili, Reso. *Hermann Hesses Romanwelt* [Literatur und Leben, n.s., vol. 29]. Cologne: Böhlau, 1986.

Karstedt, Claudia. *Die Entwicklung des Frauenbildes bei Hermann Hesse.* Frankfurt am Main: Peter Lang, 1983.

Keilson-Lauritz, Marita. "Tanten, Kerle und Skandale: Die Geburt des 'modernen Homosexuellen' aus den Flügelkämpfen der Emanzipation." In *Homosexualität und Staatsräson: Männlichkeit, Homophobie und Politik in Deutschland 1900–1945*, edited by Susanne zur Nieden, 81–99. Frankfurt: Campus, 2005.

Kiryakakis, Andreas. *The Ideal of Heimat in the Works of Hermann Hesse.* New York: Peter Lang, 1988.

Kivilaakso, Katri, Ann-Sofie Lönngren, and Rita Paqvalén. "Förord." In *Queera läsningar*, edited by Katri Kivilaakso, Ann-Sofie Lönngren, and Rita Paqvalén, 8–16. Hägersten: Rosenlarv, 2012.

Koester, Rudolf. "Self-realization: Hesse's Reflections on Youth." *Monatshefte* 57, no. 4 (1965): 181–186.

Konstan, David. *Friendship in the Classical World.* Cambridge: Cambridge University Press, 1997.

Kontje, Todd. "The German Tradition of the Bildungsroman." In *A History of the Bildungsroman*, edited by Sarah Graham, 10–32. Cambridge: Cambridge University Press, 2019.

Krafft-Ebing, Richard von. *Psychopathia Sexualis: With Especial Reference to the Antipathetic Sexual Instinct.* Translated by Franklin S. Klaf. London: Mayflower-Dell, 1965.

Kramer, Max. "From Georg Simmel to Stefan George: Sexology, Male Bonding, and Homosexuality." *German Studies Review* 41, no. 2 (2018): 275–295.

Kurlander, Eric. *Hitler's Monsters: A Supernatural History of the Third Reich.* New Haven, CT: Yale University Press, 2018.

Köhn, Lothar. *Entwicklungs- und Bildungsroman: Ein Forschungsbericht.* Stuttgart: Metzler, 1969.

Lachman, Gary. *Turn Off Your Mind: The Mystic Sixties and the Dark Side of the Age of Aquarius.* New York: Disinformation, 2001.

Landgren, Gustav. "'Untergangsmusik war es, im Rom der letzten Kaiser mußte es ähnliche Musik gegeben haben': Hesses Verhältnis zur Musik in *Der Steppenwolf*." In *Der Grenzgänger Hermann Hesse: Neue Perspektiven der Forschung*, edited by Henriette Herwig and Florian Trabert, 111–122. Freiburg i. Br.: Rombach, 2013.

Leary, Timothy and Ralph Metzner. "Hermann Hesse: Poet of the Interior Journey." *The Psychedelic Review* 1 (1963): 167–182.

Leck, Ralph M. *Vita Sexualis: Karl Ulrichs and the Origins of Sexual Science.* Urbana: University of Illinois Press, 2016.

Lemm, Vanessa. *Nietzsche's Animal Philosophy: Culture, Politics, and the Animality of the Human Being.* New York: Fordham University Press, 2009.

Lentin, Alana. *Why Race Still Matters.* Cambridge: Polity Press, 2020.

Levinas, Emmanuel. *God, Death, and Time.* Translated by Bettina Bergo. Stanford: Stanford University Press, 2000.

Levinas, Emmanuel. *Humanism of the Other.* Translated by Nidra Poller. Urbana: University of Illinois Press, 2006.

Levinas, Emmanuel. *Otherwise than Being, or Beyond Essence.* Translated by Alphonso Lingis. Pittsburg: Duquesne University Press, 2016.

Levinas, Emmanuel. *Time and the Other [and other essays].* Translated by Richard A. Cohen. Pittsburgh: Duquesne University Press, 1987.

Levinas, Emmanuel. *Totality and Infinity. An Essay on Exteriority.* Translated by Alphonso Lingis. Pittsburgh: Duquesne University Press, 2016.

Levitas, Ruth. *The Concept of Utopia.* Syracuse, NY: Syracuse University Press, 1990.

Lindén, Claudia. "It Takes a Real Man to Show True Femininity. Gender-transgression in Goethe's and Humboldt's concept of Bildung." In *The Humboldtian Tradition: Origins and Legacies,* edited by Peter Josephson, Thomas Karlsohn, and Johan Östling, 58–78. Leiden: Brill Publisher, 2014.

Love, Heather. *Feeling Backward: Loss and the Politics of Queer History.* Cambridge, MA: Harvard University Press, 2007.

Lundblad, Michael. "Introduction: The End of the Animal – Literary and Cultural Animalities." In *Animalities: Literary and Cultural Studies Beyond the Human,* edited by Michael Lundblad, 1–21. Edinburgh: Edinburgh University Press, 2017.

Lundblad, Michael. *The Birth of a Jungle: Animality in Progressive-Era U.S. Literature and Culture.* Oxford: Oxford University Press, 2013.

Lönngren, Ann-Sofie. *Following the Animal: Power, Agency, and Human-Animal Transformations in Modern, Northern-European Literature.* Newcastle upon Tyne: Cambridge Scholars Publishing, 2015.

MacFarlane, Scott. *The Hippie Narrative: A Literary Perspective on the Counterculture.* Jefferson, NC: McFarland & Co, 2007.

MacLeod, Catriona. *Embodying Ambiguity: Androgyny and Aesthetics from Winckelmann to Keller.* Detroit: Wayne State University Press, 1998.

Maier, Emmanuel. "The Psychology of C.G. Jung in the Works of Hermann Hesse [An Abridgment]." PhD diss., New York University, 1953. Doi: http://hesse.projects. gss.ucsb.edu/papers/maier.pdf (accessed January 14, 2022).

Marcus, Sharon. *Between Women: Friendship, Desire, and Marriage in Victorian England.* Princeton: Princeton University Press, 2007.

Marhoefer, Laurie. *Sex and the Weimar Republic: German Homosexual Emancipation and the Rise of the Nazis.* Toronto: University of Toronto Press, 2015.

Martin, Nicholas. "Nietzsche's Goethe: In Sickness and in Health." *Publications of the English Goethe Society* 77, no. 2 (2008): 113–124.

Marvin, Garry. *Wolf.* London: Reaktion, 2012.

Mathäs, Alexander. *Beyond Posthumanism: The German Humanist Tradition and the Future of the Humanities.* New York: Berghahn Books, 2020.

Mayer, Hans. *Steppenwolf and Everyman: Outsiders and Conformists in Contemporary Literature*, translated by Jack D. Zipes. New York: Crowell, 1971.

McHugh, Susan. *Animal Stories: Narrating Across Species Lines.* Minneapolis: University of Minnesota Press, 2011.

McRuer, Robert. *Crip Theory: Cultural Signs of Queerness and Disability.* New York: New York University Press, 2006.

Mech, L. David and Luigi Boitani. "Introduction." In *Wolves: Behavior, Ecology, and Conservation*, edited by L. David Mech and Luigi Boitani, xv–xvii. Chicago: University of Chicago, 2003.

Mech, L. David and Luigi Boitani. "Wolf Social Ecology." In *Wolves: Behavior, Ecology, and Conservation*, edited by L. David Mech and Luigi Boitani, 1–34. Chicago: University of Chicago, 2003.

Mecocci, Micaela. "Die Bedeutung der weiblichen Gestalten in Hermann Hesses Prosa." In *Hermann-Hesse-Jahrbuch. Band 1*, edited by Mauro Ponzi, 73–79. Tübingen: Max Niemeyer, 2004.

Michels, Volker. *Materialien zu Hermann Hesses* Der Steppenwolf. Frankfurt: Suhrkamp, 1972.

Michels, Volker. "Zwischen Duldung und Sabotage. Hermann Hesse und der Nationalsozialismus." In *Hermann Hesse und die Politik*, 7th International Hermann-Hesse Colloquium in Calw, edited by Martin Pfeifer, 87–105. Bad Liebenzell: Verlag Bernhard Gegenbach, 1992.

Middell, Eike. *Hermann Hesse: Die Bilderwelt seines Lebens.* Leipzig: Reclam, 1975.

Mileck, Joseph. *Hermann Hesse: Life and Art.* Berkeley: University of California Press, 1978.

Mileck, Joseph. "The Prose of Hermann Hesse: Life, Substance and Form." *The German Quarterly* 27, no. 3 (1954): 163–174.

Mileck, Joseph. "Trends in Literary Reception: The Hesse Boom." *The German Quarterly* 51, no. 3 (1978): 346–354.

Miller, Meredith. "Lesbian, Gay and Trans Bildungsromane." In *A History of the Bildungsroman*, edited by Sarah Graham, 239–266. Cambridge: Cambridge University Press, 2019.

Mitchell, David T. and Sharon L. Snyder. "Introduction: Disability Studies and the Double Bind of Representation." In *The Body and Physical Difference: Discourses of Disability*, edited by David T. Mitchell and Sharon L. Snyder, 1–31. Ann Arbor: University of Michigan Press, 1997.

Mitchell, David T. and Sharon L. Snyder. *Narrative Prosthesis: Disability and the Dependencies of Discourse*. Ann Arbor: University of Michigan Press, 2000.

Mix, York-Gothart. "'Ja, ich bin ein Anderer' – Hermann Hesses Konzept des Eigensinns Genese und kulturkritischer Impetus." In *Der Grenzgänger Hermann Hesse: Neue Perspektiven der Forschung*, edited by Henriette Herwig and Florian Trabert, 359–369. Freiburg i. Br.: Rombach, 2013.

Moi, Toril. *Revolution of the Ordinary: Literary Studies after Wittgenstein, Austin, and Cavell*. Chicago: The University of Chicago Press, 2017.

Mollow, Anna and Robert McRuer. "Introduction." In *Sex and Disability*, edited by Anna Mollow and Robert McRuer, 1–34. Durham: Duke University Press, 2012.

Mollow, Anna. "Is Sex Disability? Queer Theory and the Disability Drive." In *Sex and Disability*, edited by Anna Mollow and Robert McRuer, 285–312. Durham: Duke University Press, 2012.

Moore, Gregory. *Nietzsche: Biology and Metaphor*. Cambridge: Cambridge University Press, 2002.

Moretti, Franco. *The Way of the World: The Bildungsroman in European Culture*. London: Verso, 1987.

Moriz, Julia. "Die musikalische Dimension der Sprachkunst: Hermann Hesse, neu gelesen." PhD diss., Hamburg University, 2007. Doi: https://ediss.sub.uni-hamburg. de/bitstream/ediss/1206/1/Dissertation.pdf (accessed January 14, 2022).

Mosse, George L. *The Crisis of German Ideology: Intellectual Origins of the Third Reich*. New York: Grosset & Dunlap, 1964.

Mosse, George L. *The Image of Man: The Creation of Modern Masculinity*. New York: Oxford University Press, 1996.

Muñoz, José Esteban. *Cruising Utopia: The Then and There of Queer Futurity*. New York: New York University Press, 2009.

Murti, Kamakshi P. "'Ob die Weiber Menschen seyn?' Hesse, Women, and Homo-eroticism." In *A Companion to the Works of Hermann Hesse*, edited by Ingo Cornils, 263–299. Rochester, NY: Camden House, 2009.

Musil, Robert. "Über echte deutsche Dichter [Um 1910]." In *Gesammelte Werke. 2, Prosa und Stücke. Kleine Prosa, Aphorismen. Autobiographisches. Essays und Reden. Kritik*, edited by Adolf Frisé, 1303–1304. Reinbek bei Hamburg: Rowohlt, 1978.

Naumann, Walter. "The Individual and Society in the Work of Hermann Hesse." *Monatshefte* 41, no. 1 (1949): 33–42.

Nealon, Christopher S. *Foundlings: Lesbian and Gay Historical Emotion Before Stonewall*. Durham: Duke University Press, 2001.

Nieden, Susanne zur. "Einleitung." In *Homosexualität und Staatsräson: Männlichkeit, Homophobie und Politik in Deutschland 1900–1945*, edited by Susanne zur Nieden, 7–14. Frankfurt: Campus, 2005.

Nietzsche, Friedrich. *On the Uses and Disadvantages of History for Life* [1874]. In Friedrich Nietzsche, *Untimely Meditations*. Edited by Daniel Breazeale. Translated by R. J. Hollingdale. Cambridge: Cambridge University Press, 1997.

Nietzsche, Friedrich. *Schopenhauer as Educator* [1874]. In Friedrich Nietzsche, *Untimely Meditations*. Edited by Daniel Breazeale. Translated by R. J. Hollingdale. Cambridge: Cambridge University Press, 1997.

Nietzsche, Friedrich. *Thus Spoke Zarathustra: A Book for All and None*, translated by Walter Kaufmann. Harmondsworth: Penguin Books, 1978.

Norris, Margot. *Beasts of the Modern Imagination: Darwin, Nietzsche, Kafka, Ernst, and Lawrence*. Baltimore: Johns Hopkins University Press, 1985.

Oosterhuis, Harry. "Homosexual Emancipation in Germany Before 1933: Two Traditions." In *Homosexuality and Male Bonding in Pre-Nazi Germany: The Youth Movement, the Gay Movement and Male Bonding before Hitler's Rise: Original Transcripts from Der Eigene, the First Gay Journal in the World*, edited by Harry Oosterhuis and Hubert Kennedy, 1–27. New York: Haworth Press, 1991.

Ovidius Naso, Publius. *Ovid: in Six Volumes. 2, The Art of Love, and Other Poems*. Translated by J. H. Mozley. Cambridge, MA: Harvard University Press, 1947.

Ovidius Naso, Publius. *Ovid: in Six Volumes. 3, Metamorphoses, in Two Volumes, 1: Books IX–XV*. Translated by Frank Justus Miller. Cambridge, MA: Harvard University Press, 1977.

Ovidius Naso, Publius. *Ovid: in Six Volumes. 4, Metamorphoses, in Two Volumes, 2: Books I–VIII*. Translated by Frank Justus Miller. Cambridge, MA: Harvard University Press, 1984.

Palmer, Craig Bernard. "The Significance of Homosexual Desire in Modern German Literature." PhD diss., Washington University, 1997. Doi: http://hesse.projects.gss.ucsb.edu/papers/palmer-chap5.pdf (accessed January 14, 2022).

Plant, Richard. *The Pink Triangle: The Nazi War Against Homosexuals*. New York: H. Holt, 1986.

Plato. *The Symposium of Plato*. Translated by R. G. Bury. Cambridge: Heffner and sons, 1909.

Podolsky, Robin. "L'Aimé qui est l'aimée. Can Levinas' Beloved Be Queer?" *European Judaism* 48, no. 2 (2016): 50–70.

Poiger, Uta G. "American Jazz in the German Cold War." In *Music and German National Identity*, edited by Celia Applegate and Pamela Potter, 218–233. Chicago: The University of Chicago Press, 2002.

Ponzi, Mauro. "Hermann Hesses Umgang mit dem Fremden." In *Hermann-Hesse-Jahrbuch. Band 1*, edited by Mauro Ponzi, 1–18. Tübingen: Max Niemeyer, 2004.

Poore, Carol. *Disability in Twentieth-Century German Culture*. Ann Arbor: University of Michigan Press, 2007.

Radermacher, Martin. "Hermann Hesse – Monte Verità: Wahrheitssuche abseits des Mainstreams zu Beginn des 20. Jahrhunderts." *Zeitschrift für junge Religionswissenschaft* 6 (2011). Doi: https://doi.org/10.4000/zjr.710 (accessed January 14, 2022).

Rauch-Rapaport, Angelika. "The Melancholic Structure of the Mind: The Absence of Object Relations in the Work of Hermann Hesse." In *Hermann Hesse Today = Hermann Hesse Heute*, edited by Ingo Cornils and Osman Durrani, 83–93. Amsterdam: Rodopi, 2005.

Reichert, Herbert W. *The Impact of Nietzsche on Hermann Hesse*. Mt. Pleasant, MI: Enigma Press, 1972.

Richards, David G. *Exploring the Divided Self: Hermann Hesse's* Steppenwolf *and its Critics*. Columbia: Camden House, 1996.

Riordan, Colin. "Hermann Hesse and the Ecological Imagination." In *Hermann Hesse Today = Hermann Hesse Heute*, edited by Ingo Cornils and Osman Durrani, 95–105. Amsterdam: Rodopi, 2005.

Rocke, Michael. *Forbidden Friendships: Homosexuality and Male Culture in Renaissance Florence*. New York: Oxford University Press, 1996.

Rocke, Michael. "The Ambivalence of Policing Sexual Margins." In *At the Margins: Minority Groups in Premodern Italy*, edited by Stephen J. Milner, 53–70. Minneapolis: University of Minnesota Press, 2005.

Rockwood, Heidi M. "The Function of Pablo in Hesse's *Steppenwolf*." *South Atlantic Review* 59, no. 4 (1994): 47–61.

Rogers, Kathrine M. *The Troublesome Helpmate: A History of Misogyny in Literature*. Seattle: University of Washington Press, 1966.

Rohy, Valerie. *Anachronism and Its Others: Sexuality, Race, Temporality*. Albany: State University of New York Press, 2009.

Rose, Ernst. *Faith from the Abyss: Hermann Hesse's Way from Romanticism to Modernity*. New York: New York University Press, 1965.

Rousseau, Jean-Jacques. *The Social Contract* and *The First and Second Discourses* [1762, 1750, 1755]. Edited by Susan Dunn. New Haven: Yale University Press, 2002.

Safranski, Rüdiger. *Nietzsche: A Philosophical Biography*, translated by Shelley Frisch. London: Granta Books, 2002.

Said, Edward W. *Orientalism*. New York: Pantheon Books, 1978.

Samuels, Ellen. "Critical Divides: Judith Butler's Body Theory and the Question of Disability." In *Feminist Disability Studies*, edited by Kim Q. Hall, 48–66. Bloomington: Indiana University Press, 2011.

Schneider, C. Immo. "Hermann Hesse and Music." In *A Companion to the Works of Hermann Hesse*, edited by Ingo Cornils, 373–394. Rochester, NY: Camden House, 2009.

Schoppmann, Claudia. "Ein Lesbenroman aus der Weimarer Zeit: 'Der Skorpion'." In *Eldorado: Homosexuelle Frauen und Männer in Berlin 1850–1950; Geschichte, Alltag und Kultur*, edited by Michael Bollé, 197–199. Berlin: Frölich & Kaufmann, 1984.

Schwarz, Egon. "Hermann Hesse: *Steppenwolf* (1927)." In *Reflection and Action: Essays on the Bildungsroman*, edited by James Hardin, 382–414. Columbia: University of South Carolina Press, 1991.

Sedgwick, Eve Kosofsky. *Between Men: English Literature and Male Homosocial Desire*. New York: Columbia University Press, 1985.

Sedgwick, Eve Kosofsky. "Paranoid Reading and Reparative Reading; or, You're So Paranoid, You Probably Think This Introduction Is About You." In *Novel Gazing: Queer Readings in Fiction*, edited by Eve Kosofsky Sedgwick, 1–37. Durham: Duke University Press, 1997.

Seidlin, Oskar. "Hermann Hesse: The Exorcism of the Demon." In *Hermann Hesse: A Collection of Criticism*, edited by Judith Liebmann, 7–28. New York: McGraw-Hill, 1977.

Seth, Oscar von. "Tracing the Wolf in Hermann Hesse's *Der Steppenwolf*." In *Squirrelling: Human–Animal Studies in the Northern-European Region*, edited by Amelie Björck, Claudia Lindén, and Ann-Sofie Lönngren, 119–140. Huddinge: Södertörns högskola, 2022.

Serrano, Miguel. *C.G Jung and Hermann Hesse: A Record of Two Friendships*. Translated by Frank MacShane. London: Routledge and Kegan Paul, 1971.

Siebers, Tobin. "A Sexual Culture for Disabled People." In *Sex and Disability*, edited by Anna Mollow and Robert McRuer, 37–53. Durham: Duke University Press, 2012.

Skinner, Jody. *Warme Brüder, Kesse Väter: Lexikon mit Ausdrücken für Lesben, Schwule und Homosexualität*. Essen: Blaue Euele, 1997.

Sorell, Walter. *Hermann Hesse: The Man Who Sought and Found Himself*. London: Oswald Wolff, 1974.

Stark, Suzanne J. *Female Tars: Women Abord Ship in the Age of Sail*. London: Constable, 1996.

Steakley, James D. "Iconography of a Scandal: Political Cartoons and the Eulenburg affair." In *Hidden from History: Reclaiming the Gay and Lesbian past*, edited by Martin Duberman, Martha Vicinus, and George Chauncey, Jr., 233–263. New York: NAL, 1989.

Steakley, James D. *The Homosexual Emancipation Movement in Germany*. Salem, NH: Ayer, 1982.

Stein, Jess, ed. *The Random House Dictionary of the English Language* [The Unabridged Ed.]. New York: Random House, 1969.

Stelzig, Eugene. *Hermann Hesse's Fictions of the Self: Autobiography and the Confessional Imagination*. Princeton: Princeton University Press, 1988.

Stelzig, Eugene L. "The Aesthetics of Confession: Hermann Hesse's 'Crisis' Poems in the Context of the 'Steppenwolf' Period." *Criticism* 21, no. 1 (1979): 49–70.

Stuckrad, Kocku von. "Utopian Landscapes and Ecstatic Journeys: Friedrich Nietzsche, Hermann Hesse, and Mircea Eliade on the Terror of Modernity." *Numen* 57, no. 1 (2010): 78–102.

Summers, Montague. *The Werewolf in Lore and Legend.* Mineola, NY: Dover, 2003.

Swales, Martin. "*Der Steppenwolf.*" In *A Companion to the Works of Hermann Hesse,* edited by Ingo Cornils, 171–186. Rochester, NY: Camden House, 2009.

Swales, Martin. *The German Bildungsroman from Wieland to Hesse.* Princeton: Princeton University Press, 1978.

Szondi, Peter. *Introduction to Literary Hermeneutics.* Cambridge: Cambridge University Press, 1995.

Takács, Judith. "The Double Life of Kertbeny." In *Past and Present of Radical Sexual Politics: Working Papers: Fifth Meeting of the Seminar "Socialism and sexuality", Amsterdam, October 3–4, 2003,* edited by Gert Hekma, 51–62. Amsterdam: Mosse Foundation, 2004.

Tamagne, Florence. *A History of Homosexuality in Europe: Volume 1 & 2: Berlin, London, Paris 1919–1939.* New York: Algora, 2006.

Taylor, Charles Senn. "The Platonism of Hesse's 'Das Glasperlenspiel'." *Monatshefte* 74, no. 2 (1982): 156–166.

Taylor, Harley Ustus. "Homoerotic Elements in the Novels of Hermann Hesse." *West Virginia University Philological Papers* 16, (1967): 63–71.

Taylor, William "Billy." "Jazz: America's Classical Music." *The Black Perspective in Music* 14, no. 1 (1986): 21–25.

Theis, Wolfgang and Andreas Sternweiler. "Alltag im Kaiserreich und in der Weimarer Republik." In *Eldorado: Homosexuelle Frauen und Männer in Berlin 1850–1950; Geschichte, Alltag und Kultur,* edited by Michael Bollé, 48–73. Berlin: Frölich & Kaufmann, 1984.

Theweleit, Klaus. *Männerphantasien.* Frankfurt am Main: Roter Stern, 1977–1978.

Thompson, Mark Christian. *Anti-Music: Jazz and Racial Blackness in German Thought Between the Wars.* Albany: State University of New York Press, 2018.

Tobin, Robert Deam. *Peripheral Desires: The German Discovery of Sex.* Philadelphia: University of Pennsylvania Press, 2015.

Tobin, Robert Deam. *Warm Brothers: Queer Theory and the Age of Goethe.* Philadelphia: University of Pennsylvania Press, 2000.

Tusken, Lewis W. "A Mixing of Metaphors: Masculine-Feminine Interplay in the Novels of Hermann Hesse." In *The Modern Language Review* 87, no. 3 (1992): 626–635.

Tusken, Lewis W. *Understanding Hermann Hesse: The Man, His Myth, His Metaphor.* Columbia: University of South Carolina Press, 1998.

Ulrichs, Karl Heinrich. *Vindex: Social-juristische Studien über mannmännliche Geschlechtsliebe* [1864]. In *Forschungen über das Rätsel der mannmännlichen Liebe.* Leipzig: Max Spohr, 1898.

Waldecke, St. Ch. "Eros in the German Youth Movement." In *Homosexuality and Male Bonding in Pre-Nazi Germany: The Youth Movement, the Gay Movement and Male Bonding before Hitler's Rise: Original Transcripts from Der Eigene, the First Gay Journal in the World,* edited by Harry Oosterhuis and Hubert Kennedy, 199–206. New York: Haworth Press, 1991.

Webb, Eugene. "Hermine and the Problem of Harry's Failure in Hesse's *Steppenwolf.*" *Modern Fiction Studies* 17, no. 1 (1971): 115–124.

Weiner, Marc A. *Undertones of Insurrection: Music, Politics, and the Social Sphere in the Modern German Narrative.* Lincoln, NE: University of Nebraska Press, 1993.

Weininger, Otto. *Sex and Character: An Investigation of Fundamental Principles.* Edited by Daniel Steuer with Laura Marcus. Translated by Ladislaus Löb. Bloomington: Indiana University Press, 2005.

Whisnant, Clayton J. *Queer Identities and Politics in Germany: A History 1880–1945.* New York: Harrington Park Press, 2016.

White, Edmund. *A Boy's Own Story.* London: Picador, 2016.

Williams, John Alexander. "Ecstasies of the Young: Sexuality, the Youth Movement, and Moral Panic in Germany on the Eve of the First World War." *Central European History* 34, no. 2 (2001): 163–189.

Wilson, Colin. *Hermann Hesse.* London: Village Press, 1974.

Wilson, Colin. *The Outsider.* London: Pan, 1963.

Wipplinger, Jonathan O. *The Jazz Republic: Music, Race, and American Culture in Weimar Germany.* Ann Arbor: University of Michigan Press, 2017.

Ziolkowski, Theodore. "Saint Hesse Among the Hippies." *American-German Review* 35, no. 2 (1969): 19–23.

Ziolkowski, Theodore. *The Novels of Hermann Hesse: A Study in Theme and Structure.* Princeton: Princeton University Press, 1967.

Summary

This dissertation explores how characters who embody outsiderness and/or otherness intersect with and connote queerness—such as, for instance, homoeroticism and nonconformism—in the novels *Peter Camenzind* (1904) and *Der Steppenwolf* (1927) by German-language author Hermann Hesse (1877–1962).

In most of Hesse's novels, the narrative revolves around a male protagonist who is characterized as an outsider. This outsider comes to know himself through friendship with another man. The friend is desired by the outsider and tends to embody some form of otherness; he is almost always portrayed as different—rebellious, beautiful, enigmatic, and inspiring—and he comes to play a key role in the protagonist's personal development and journey through life. The hypothesis in this study is that the friendships formed by these characters are queer friendships, that is, that they challenge heteronormative conceptions of relationality, sexuality, and desire.

The study's main theoretical apparatus encompasses a selection of queer theories and concepts, including (among others) José Esteban Muñoz's conceptualization of the horizon as a signifier for "queer utopia," as well as Heather Love's thoughts on "backwardness." In addition, Eve Kosofsky Sedgwick's early queer-theoretical work on male homosocial desire and Jack Halberstam's recent theorizing about sexuality and wildness are drawn on. The method with which Hesse's novels are approached is a "queer surface reading," which means that attention is given to what appears on the texts' surfaces rather than plunging their depths for hidden meaning. Essentially, surface signs of queerness are emphasized and interpreted.

The study begins with an overview chapter on Hesse's authorship that provides historical context followed by two parts (one on *Peter Camenzind* and one on *Der Steppenwolf*) with three analytical chapters each. The overview chapter revolves around certain norm-challenging aspects of Hesse's time and reception. Hesse was active alongside the German homosexual emancipation movement and emerging field of sexology in the early 1900s, and his work was embraced by contemporary countercultures such as the German *Wandervogel* groups and later anti-conformist movements like beatniks and hippies. Despite these connections, however, Hesse's novels have rarely been interpreted with an ambition to emphasize queerness.

The common thread in the study's six analytical chapters is depictions of queer friendship. In each chapter, one character is in primary focus, and that character's portrayal as an outsider or Other (or both) is examined. In some instances, the protagonist is the key person of interest; at other times, the protagonist's friend is in focus.

In the first chapter, "Romantic Friendship in a *Bildungsroman*," the focus is on Peter, the outsider-protagonist in *Peter Camenzind*, and his homosocial bond with the character Richard. The chapter examines how defining traits of the *Bildungsroman* (novel of formation) and the concept of romantic friendship intersect in the novel. Apart from emphasizing the many expressions of homoeroticism in the novel, the chapter highlights how its portrayals of nature are entwined with male friendship, which, furthermore, is shown to elevate *Peter Camenzind*'s queer qualities. All in all, the chapter makes evident that Hesse's novel challenges conventions of the Bildungsroman, and that the bond between Peter and Richard transcends a romantic friendship, becoming, instead, interpretable as a same-sex romance.

In the second chapter, "Without Leaving Children Behind," heterosexual ambivalence, which Peter conveys in his interactions with women, is interpreted as a manifestation of queerness. While the chapter concerns a number of female characters, Peter's friend Elisabeth is the key character. In contrast to the other women in the book (who are oftentimes described with misogynistic language), Elisabeth does not enforce heterosexuality on Peter, and she is therefore never spoken of in such a manner. Additionally, drawing on George Mosse's concept of the masculine countertype, the chapter demonstrates that Peter personifies a dualism of manliness and unmanliness that makes him readable as inherently ambivalent.

In the third chapter, "Facing the Other," Peter's friend Boppi is the character in focus. The otherness ascribed to Boppi by means of his disability is examined, as well as the ways that disability works as a catalyst for expressions of "queer/crip kinship" in the text. Alongside its queer-theoretical core, the chapter relies on a selection of theories from disability studies, mainly the concept of "narrative prosthesis," which refers to a disabled character that is used as a mere prop in service of the personal development of an able-bodied protagonist. Moreover, Emmanuel Levinas's conceptualization of the Other is put into dialogue with crip-theoretical concepts, which ultimately underlines Boppi's importance in the story.

In the fourth chapter, "Tracing the Wolf," a key expression of otherness in *Der Steppenwolf* is examined, namely, the animality of its protagonist, the wolf-man (and outsider) Harry Haller. This chapter is different from the rest because it does not revolve around queer friendship per se. Rather, it emphasizes the antithesis of friendship, that is, a bond built on animosity, a major characteristic in the relationship between the human part and the wolf part of the protagonist. The chapter stresses that Hesse's wolf vacillates between antagonistic and idealized. The wolf invokes associations such as queerness, Nietzsche's *Übermensch* ("superhuman," or "overman"), and Nazi wolf symbolism, which demonstrates that the novel is a multifaceted and complex document of its era.

In the fifth chapter, "The Function of Hermine," the fluid gender expressions and queer characteristics of Harry's friend Hermine are explored. Hermine is a character whose otherness mirrors the protagonist's dual nature. Her role as Harry's teacher, mainly in matters of pleasure and love, is underscored. Hermine teaches Harry how to dance and introduces him to a world of transgressiveness that he finds alluring. The chapter concludes that although Harry's wolf-man nature is a symbol of complexity, it is the queerness of Hermine—that she can be seen as female, male, and trans/non-binary, as well as straight, lesbian, gay, and bisexual—that makes *Der Steppenwolf* a truly radical text.

The sixth and final chapter, "Queer Sounds, Times, and Places," puts the spotlight on the character Pablo, another of Harry's friends, and examines how the novel's portrayal of sounds (such as jazz music), times (the conflict between the old and the new), and places (like the dance floor) connote queerness in various ways. The chapter demonstrates that the function of Pablo, who is a jazz-musician, is to activate homoeroticism in the text—since he is himself openly bisexual—and to guide the protagonist toward sexual fluidity and completeness.

Ultimately, this study shows that Hermann Hesse's stories include queerness in two ways. First, queerness is identified in the shape of nonconformity in the characters, which is expressed through an elevation of outsiderness, *Eigensinn* (self-will), and Hesse's frequently invoked "Be yourself" ideal. Second, queerness is perceived in norm-challenging sexuality (such as Hermine and Pablo's bisexuality) and the prevalence of homoeroticism. Furthermore, *Peter Camenzind* and *Der Steppenwolf* convey that queerness is essential to both their protagonists' longings to become whole as well as the ways with which the novels portray completeness. Hesse's fervent use of queerness as an essential aspect in his stories makes him, in a sense, a campaigner for queer subjectivity, which, it is argued, should make his place within the queer literary canon self-evident.

Index

Acknowledgments

In 2018, at a conference in Comparative Literature, I took part in a doctoral student workshop attended by the two keynote speakers. I had not been a PhD student for very long and had barely grasped the competitive climate in academia, much less acclimatized to it, when one of these senior researchers belittled and invalidated my research project (which was, at the time, only a couple of months in the making). While the experience was demotivating, I learned an important lesson: When in doubt, make sure only to listen to the opinions of the bobble-head figures on your desk—in my case, Boba Fett from *Star Wars*, Michonne and Jesus from *The Walking Dead*, Special Agent Dana Scully, and Captain America. For me, to finish my PhD, these figures' heads, nodding in approval ("Just keep going! You're on the right path! You've got this, Oscar!"), have been more helpful than any opinions of that keynote speaker could ever be.

Apart from my approval-giving bobble-heads, completing this book would not have been possible without the support of several individuals. Among them, of course, are my supervisors Claudia Lindén and Mattias Pirholt. I am enormously grateful that you both, throughout this process, have allowed me the freedom to beat my own path—and the freedom to march on that path to the beat of my own drum. Claudia, having been introduced to the field of queer theory by you a decade ago makes me forever in your debt. And Mattias, thank you for consistently challenging me to think outside my (queer) comfort zone.

My gratitude encompasses my colleagues at Södertörn University, in particular those who have provided thoughtful comments, encouragement, and support during my writing process: Ann-Sofie Lönngren, Ulla Manns, Camilla Flodin, Karl Axelsson, Teresa Kulawik, Amelie Björck, Christina Svens, Maria Mårsell, Christine Farhan, Eva Jonsson, Bengt Lundgren, Charlotta Weigelt, Anna Bark Persson, Kajsa Gustavsson, and Stefano Fogelberg Rota. Special thanks to Ramona Rat for helping me untangle many of the complex thoughts in the writings of Emmanuel Levinas.

During the process of writing this book, I have enjoyed exchanging ideas and experiences with PhD students and post-doctoral researchers at Södertörn University's Centre for Baltic and East European Studies. Their contributions to an intellectual atmosphere of curiosity, inclusivity, and unpretentiousness make me hopeful for the future. Many thanks to Gilda Hoxha, Kristin Halverson, Philipp Seuferling, Paul Sherfey, Jenny Gustafsson, Matilda Tudor, Emil Edenborg, Maria Brock, and Camilla Larsson. Among the helpful administrative staff at Södertörn University, I am especially grateful to Ewa Rogström and Elina Nylander.

For providing the financial support that made my PhD studies, and this book, possible to begin with, my gratitude includes The Foundation for Baltic and East European Studies. Also, many thanks to Stiftelsen Roos af Hjelmsäter Testamentsfond for awarding me yearly scholarships while being a PhD student. Thank you as well to Jonseredsstiftelsen and Stiftelsen Fru Mary von Sydows, född Wijk, donationsfond for granting me a residency in Villa Martinson to complete my dissertation in February 2022.

In 2019, about halfway through my doctoral studies, a grant from Erasmus+ funded my stay at the Nordeuropa-Institut at Humboldt University in Berlin as a guest researcher. There I had the privilege of presenting parts of my work and received valuable feedback from the faculty and students. To Stefanie von Schnurbein especially, thank you for creating such an open-minded and exploratory environment that rekindled my academic ambitions.

In the fall of that same year, I took part in founding the Ratatoskr Research Group for Literary Animal Studies at Södertörn University. During our inaugural symposium, I got confirmation by one of my academic idols, Michael Lundblad, that my project was on the right path—thank you for that. Alongside all of the inspiring academics already mentioned, I am indebted to Niclas Johansson and Sam Holmqvist for providing insightful and thorough comments at my half-time seminar and final seminar respectively.

To my family, immediate and extended, thank you for being patient with me, always. My sisters Gabriella and Johanna, my nephew Carl, and my mother Fredrika, I love you and now that this endeavor is at an end, I promise to explain what I have actually been up to the past five years. Many thanks also to Robert's parents, sisters, and their families.

I am immensely thankful for the many stimulating conversations with friends and chosen family over the years, all of which have shaped me and my views on literature and life. The original "Sacred Wednesday" gang: Jenny, Johanna, and Lill-Oscar. My film studies crew: Anna-Carin, Emma, and Elliot. Sara Lewerth, who was there at the beginning of my literature studies in 2003, as well as Matias, Mateusz, and "Robert's girls." To Nina Hall, your input on my writing, be it academic or fiction, always makes it grow. My friends from Berlin: Sofia, Isabella, and last but not least, Carolin Friese, whose generous help with my translations from German to English in this book has been invaluable. *Vielen lieben Dank!*

Now. Finishing my PhD would neither have been possible, nor bearable, without my habibi, Robert Hannouch, whose unconditional love and support has transcended my wildest dreams. Bhebak ya albe, ktir, ktir, ktir. Thank you for reading my book at so many of its stages. "Because reading is what?"

"*Fundamental!*" And so are you.

With love and admiration, I am dedicating the third chapter—the one about Boppi—to my godmother Jenny Persson.

And as always, the memory of my late father has shaped my writing in this book. It would have been tremendously rewarding to discuss it, at length, with you.

Södertörn Doctoral Dissertations

1. Jolanta Aidukaite, *The Emergence of the Post-Socialist Welfare State: The case of the Baltic States: Estonia, Latvia and Lithuania*, 2004

2. Xavier Fraudet, *Politique étrangère française en mer Baltique (1871–1914): de l'exclusion à l'affirmation*, 2005

3. Piotr Wawrzeniuk, *Confessional Civilising in Ukraine: The Bishop Iosyf Shumliansky and the Introduction of Reforms in the Diocese of Lviv 1668–1708*, 2005

4. Andrej Kotljarchuk, *In the Shadows of Poland and Russia: The Grand Duchy of Lithuania and Sweden in the European Crisis of the mid-17th Century*, 2006

5. Håkan Blomqvist, *Nation, ras och civilisation i svensk arbetarrörelse före nazismen*, 2006

6. Karin S Lindelöf, *Om vi nu ska bli som Europa: Könsskapande och normalitet bland unga kvinnor i transitionens Polen*, 2006

7. Andrew Stickley. *On Interpersonal Violence in Russia in the Present and the Past: A Sociological Study*, 2006

8. Arne Ek, *Att konstruera en uppslutning kring den enda vägen: Om folkrörelsers modernisering i skuggan av det Östeuropeiska systemskiftet*, 2006

9. Agnes Ers, *I mänsklighetens namn: En etnologisk studie av ett svenskt biståndsprojekt i Rumänien*, 2006

10. Johnny Rodin, *Rethinking Russian Federalism: The Politics of Intergovernmental Relations and Federal Reforms at the Turn of the Millennium*, 2006

11. Kristian Petrov, *Tillbaka till framtiden: Modernitet, postmodernitet och generationsidentitet i Gorbačevs glasnost' och perestrojka*, 2006

12. Sophie Söderholm Werkö, *Patient patients? Achieving Patient Empowerment through Active Participation, Increased Knowledge and Organisation*, 2008

13. Peter Bötker, *Leviatan i arkipelagen: Staten, förvaltningen och samhället. Fallet Estland*, 2007

14. Matilda Dahl, *States under scrutiny: International organizations, transformation and the construction of progress*, 2007

15. Margrethe B. Søvik, *Support, resistance and pragmatism: An examination of motivation in language policy in Kharkiv, Ukraine*, 2007

16. Yulia Gradskova, *Soviet People with female Bodies: Performing beauty and maternity in Soviet Russia in the mid 1930–1960s*, 2007

17. Renata Ingbrant, *From Her Point of View: Woman's Anti-World in the Poetry of Anna Świrszczyńska*, 2007

18. Johan Eellend, *Cultivating the Rural Citizen: Modernity, Agrarianism and Citizenship in Late Tsarist Estonia*, 2007

19. Petra Garberding, *Musik och politik i skuggan av nazismen: Kurt Atterberg och de svensk-tyska musikrelationerna*, 2007

20. Aleksei Semenenko, *Hamlet the Sign: Russian Translations of Hamlet and Literary Canon Formation*, 2007

21. Vytautas Petronis, *Constructing Lithuania: Ethnic Mapping in the Tsarist Russia, ca. 1800–1914*, 2007

22. Akvile Motiejunaite, *Female employment, gender roles, and attitudes: the Baltic countries in a broader context*, 2008

23. Tove Lindén, *Explaining Civil Society Core Activism in Post-Soviet Latvia*, 2008

24. Pelle Åberg, *Translating Popular Education: Civil Society Cooperation between Sweden and Estonia*, 2008

25. Anders Nordström, *The Interactive Dynamics of Regulation: Exploring the Council of Europe's monitoring of Ukraine*, 2008

26. Fredrik Doeser, *In Search of Security After the Collapse of the Soviet Union: Foreign Policy Change in Denmark, Finland and Sweden, 1988–1993*, 2008

27. Zhanna Kravchenko. *Family (versus) Policy: Combining Work and Care in Russia and Sweden*, 2008

28. Rein Jüriado, *Learning within and between public-private partnerships*, 2008

29. Elin Boalt, *Ecology and evolution of tolerance in two cruciferous species*, 2008

30. Lars Forsberg, *Genetic Aspects of Sexual Selection and Mate Choice in Salmonids*, 2008

31. Eglė Rindzevičiūtė, *Constructing Soviet Cultural Policy: Cybernetics and Governance in Lithuania after World War II*, 2008

32. Joakim Philipson, *The Purpose of Evolution: 'struggle for existence' in the Russian-Jewish press 1860–1900*, 2008

33. Sofie Bedford, *Islamic activism in Azerbaijan: Repression and mobilization in a post-Soviet context*, 2009

34. Tommy Larsson Segerlind, *Team Entrepreneurship: A process analysis of the venture team and the venture team roles in relation to the innovation process*, 2009

35. Jenny Svensson, *The Regulation of Rule-Following: Imitation and Soft Regulation in the European Union*, 2009

36. Stefan Hallgren, *Brain Aromatase in the guppy, Poecilia reticulate: Distribution, control and role in behavior*, 2009

37. Karin Ellencrona, *Functional characterization of interactions between the flavivirus NS5 protein and PDZ proteins of the mammalian host*, 2009

38. Makiko Kanematsu, *Saga och verklighet: Barnboksproduktion i det postsovjetiska Lettland*, 2009

39. Daniel Lindvall, *The Limits of the European Vision in Bosnia and Herzegovina: An Analysis of the Police Reform Negotiations*, 2009

40. Charlotta Hillerdal, *People in Between – Ethnicity and Material Identity: A New Approach to Deconstructed Concepts*, 2009

41. Jonna Bornemark, *Kunskapens gräns – gränsens vetande*, 2009

42. Adolphine G. Kateka, *Co-Management Challenges in the Lake Victoria Fisheries: A Context Approach*, 2010

43. René León Rosales, *Vid framtidens hitersta gräns: Om pojkar och elevpositioner i en multietnisk skola*, 2010

44. Simon Larsson, *Intelligensaristokrater och arkivmartyrer: Normerna för vetenskaplig skicklighet i svensk historieforskning 1900–1945*, 2010

45. Håkan Lättman, *Studies on spatial and temporal distributions of epiphytic lichens*, 2010

46. Alia Jaensson, *Pheromonal mediated behaviour and endocrine response in salmonids: The impact of cypermethrin, copper, and glyphosate*, 2010

47. Michael Wigerius, *Roles of mammalian Scribble in polarity signaling, virus offense and cell-fate determination*, 2010

48. Anna Hedtjärn Wester, *Män i kostym: Prinsar, konstnärer och tegelbärare vid sekel-skiftet 1900*, 2010

49. Magnus Linnarsson, *Postgång på växlande villkor: Det svenska postväsendets organisation under stormaktstiden*, 2010

50. Barbara Kunz, *Kind words, cruise missiles and everything in between: A neoclassical realist study of the use of power resources in U.S. policies towards Poland, Ukraine and Belarus 1989–2008*, 2010

51. Anders Bartonek, *Philosophie im Konjunktiv: Nichtidentität als Ort der Möglichkeit des Utopischen in der negativen Dialektik Theodor W. Adornos*, 2010

52. Carl Cederberg, *Resaying the Human: Levinas Beyond Humanism and Antihuman-ism*, 2010

53. Johanna Ringarp, *Professionens problematik: Lärarkårens kommunalisering och väl-färdsstatens förvandling*, 2011

54. Sofi Gerber, *Öst är Väst men Väst är bäst: Östtysk identitetsformering i det förenade Tyskland*, 2011

55. Susanna Sjödin Lindenskoug, *Manlighetens bortre gräns: Tidelagsrättegångar i Liv-land åren 1685–1709*, 2011

56. Dominika Polanska, *The emergence of enclaves of wealth and poverty: A sociological study of residential differentiation in post-communist Poland*, 2011

57. Christina Douglas, *Kärlek per korrespondens: Två förlovade par under andra hälften av 1800-talet*, 2011

58. Fred Saunders, *The Politics of People – Not just Mangroves and Monkeys: A study of the theory and practice of community-based management of natural resources in Zan-zibar*, 2011

59. Anna Rosengren, *Åldrandet och språket: En språkhistorisk analys av hög ålder och åldrande i Sverige cirka 1875–1975*, 2011

60. Emelie Lilliefeldt, *European Party Politics and Gender: Configuring Gender-Balanced Parliamentary Presence*, 2011

61. Ola Svenonius, *Sensitising Urban Transport Security: Surveillance and Policing in Berlin, Stockholm, and Warsaw*, 2011

62. Andreas Johansson, *Dissenting Democrats: Nation and Democracy in the Republic of Moldova*, 2011

63. Wessam Melik, *Molecular characterization of the Tick-borne encephalitis virus: Environments and replication*, 2012

64. Steffen Werther, *SS-Vision und Grenzland-Realität: Vom Umgang dänischer und „volksdeutscher" Nationalsozialisten in Sønderjylland mit der „großgermanischen" Ideologie der SS*, 2012

65. Peter Jakobsson, *Öppenhetsindustrin*, 2012

66. Kristin Ilves, *Seaward Landward: Investigations on the archaeological source value of the landing site category in the Baltic Sea region*, 2012

67. Anne Kaun, *Civic Experiences and Public Connection: Media and Young People in Estonia*, 2012

68. Anna Tessmann, *On the Good Faith: A Fourfold Discursive Construction of Zoroastripanism in Contemporary Russia*, 2012

69. Jonas Lindström, *Drömmen om den nya staden: stadsförnyelse i det postsovjetisk Riga*, 2012

70. Maria Wolrath Söderberg, *Topos som meningsskapare: retorikens topiska perspektiv på tänkande och lärande genom argumentation*, 2012

71. Linus Andersson, *Alternativ television: former av kritik i konstnärlig TV-produktion*, 2012

72. Håkan Lättman, *Studies on spatial and temporal distributions of epiphytic lichens*, 2012

73. Fredrik Stiernstedt, Mediearbete i mediehuset: produktion i förändring på MTG-radio, 2013

74. Jessica Moberg, *Piety, Intimacy and Mobility: A Case Study of Charismatic Christianity in Present-day Stockholm*, 2013

75. Elisabeth Hemby, *Historiemåleri och bilder av vardag: Tatjana Nazarenkos konstnärskap i 1970-talets Sovjet*, 2013

76. Tanya Jukkala, *Suicide in Russia: A macro-sociological study*, 2013

77. Maria Nyman, *Resandets gränser: svenska resenärers skildringar av Ryssland under 1700-talet*, 2013

78. Beate Feldmann Eellend, *Visionära planer och vardagliga praktiker: postmilitära landskap i Östersjöområdet*, 2013

79. Emma Lind, *Genetic response to pollution in sticklebacks: natural selection in the wild*, 2013

80. Anne Ross Solberg, *The Mahdi wears Armani: An analysis of the Harun Yahya enterprise*, 2013

81. Nikolay Zakharov, *Attaining Whiteness: A Sociological Study of Race and Racialization in Russia*, 2013

82. Anna Kharkina, *From Kinship to Global Brand: the Discourse on Culture in Nordic Cooperation after World War II*, 2013

83. Florence Fröhlig, *A painful legacy of World War II: Nazi forced enlistment: Alsatian/Mosellan Prisoners of war and the Soviet Prison Camp of Tambov*, 2013

84. Oskar Henriksson, *Genetic connectivity of fish in the Western Indian Ocean*, 2013

85. Hans Geir Aasmundsen, *Pentecostalism, Globalisation and Society in Contemporary Argentina*, 2013

86. Anna McWilliams, *An Archaeology of the Iron Curtain: Material and Metaphor*, 2013

87. Anna Danielsson, *On the power of informal economies and the informal economies of power: rethinking informality, resilience and violence in Kosovo*, 2014

88. Carina Guyard, *Kommunikationsarbete på distans*, 2014

89. Sofia Norling, *Mot "väst": om vetenskap, politik och transformation i Polen 1989–2011*, 2014

90. Markus Huss, *Motståndets akustik: språk och (o)ljud hos Peter Weiss 1946–1960*, 2014

91. Ann-Christin Randahl, *Strategiska skribenter: skrivprocesser i fysik och svenska*, 2014

92. Péter Balogh, *Perpetual borders: German-Polish cross-border contacts in the Szczecin area*, 2014

93. Erika Lundell, *Förkroppsligad fiktion och fiktionaliserade kroppar: levande rollspel i Östersjöregionen*, 2014

94. Henriette Cederlöf, *Alien Places in Late Soviet Science Fiction: The "Unexpected Encounters" of Arkady and Boris Strugatsky as Novels and Films*, 2014

95. Niklas Eriksson, *Urbanism Under Sail: An archaeology of fluit ships in early modern everyday life*, 2014

96. Signe Opermann, *Generational Use of News Media in Estonia: Media Access, Spatial Orientations and Discursive Characteristics of the News Media*, 2014

97. Liudmila Voronova, *Gendering in political journalism: A comparative study of Russia and Sweden*, 2014

98. Ekaterina Kalinina, *Mediated Post-Soviet Nostalgia*, 2014

99. Anders E. B. Blomqvist, *Economic Natonalizing in the Ethnic Borderlands of Hungary and Romania: Inclusion, Exclusion and Annihilation in Szatmár/Satu-Mare, 1867–1944*, 2014

100. Ann-Judith Rabenschlag, *Völkerfreundschaft nach Bedarf: Ausländische Arbeitskräfte in der Wahrnehmung von Staat und Bevölkerung der DDR*, 2014

101. Yuliya Yurchuck, *Ukrainian Nationalists and the Ukrainian Insurgent Army in Post-Soviet Ukraine*, 2014

102. Hanna Sofia Rehnberg, *Organisationer berättar: narrativitet som resurs i strategisk kommunikation*, 2014

103. Jaakko Turunen, *Semiotics of Politics: Dialogicality of Parliamentary Talk*, 2015

104. Iveta Jurkane-Hobein, *I Imagine You Here Now: Relationship Maintenance Strategies in Long-Distance Intimate Relationships*, 2015

105. Katharina Wesolowski, *Maybe baby? Reproductive behaviour, fertility intentions, and family policies in post-communist countries, with a special focus on Ukraine*, 2015

106. Ann af Burén, *Living Simultaneity: On religion among semi-secular Swedes*, 2015

107. Larissa Mickwitz, *En reformerad lärare: konstruktionen av en professionell och betygssättande lärare i skolpolitik och skolpraktik*, 2015

108. Daniel Wojahn, *Språkaktivism: diskussioner om feministiska språkförändringar i Sverige från 1960-talet till 2015*, 2015

109. Hélène Edberg, *Kreativt skrivande för kritiskt tänkande: en fallstudie av studenters arbete med kritisk metareflektion*, 2015

110. Kristina Volkova, *Fishy Behavior: Persistent effects of early-life exposure to 17α-ethinylestradiol*, 2015

111. Björn Sjöstrand, *Att tänka det tekniska: en studie i Derridas teknikfilosofi*, 2015

112. Håkan Forsberg, *Kampen om eleverna: gymnasiefältet och skolmarknadens framväxt i Stockholm, 1987–2011*, 2015

113. Johan Stake, *Essays on quality evaluation and bidding behavior in public procurement auctions*, 2015

114. Martin Gunnarson, *Please Be Patient: A Cultural Phenomenological Study of Haemodialysis and Kidney Transplantation Care*, 2016

115. Nasim Reyhanian Caspillo, *Studies of alterations in behavior and fertility in ethinyl estradiol-exposed zebrafish and search for related biomarkers*, 2016

116. Pernilla Andersson, *The Responsible Business Person: Studies of Business Education for Sustainability*, 2016

117. Kim Silow Kallenberg, *Gränsland: svensk ungdomsvård mellan vård och straff*, 2016

118. Sari Vuorenpää, *Literacitet genom interaction*, 2016

119. Francesco Zavatti, *Writing History in a Propaganda Institute: Political Power and Network Dynamics in Communist Romania*, 2016

120. Cecilia Annell, *Begärets politiska potential: Feministiska motståndsstrategier i Elin Wägners 'Pennskaftet', Gabriele Reuters 'Aus guter Familie', Hilma Angered-Strandbergs 'Lydia Vik' och Grete Meisel-Hess 'Die Intellektuellen'*, 2016

121. Marco Nase, *Academics and Politics: Northern European Area Studies at Greifswald University, 1917–1992*, 2016

122. Jenni Rinne, *Searching for Authentic Living Through Native Faith – The Maausk movement in Estonia*, 2016

123. Petra Werner, *Ett medialt museum: lärandets estetik i svensk television 1956–1969*, 2016

124. Ramona Rat, *Un-common Sociality: Thinking sociality with Levinas*, 2016

125. Petter Thureborn, *Microbial ecosystem functions along the steep oxygen gradient of the Landsort Deep, Baltic Sea*, 2016

126. Kajsa-Stina Benulic, *A Beef with Meat Media and audience framings of environmentally unsustainable production and consumption*, 2016

127. Naveed Asghar, *Ticks and Tick-borne Encephalitis Virus – From nature to infection*, 2016

128. Linn Rabe, *Participation and legitimacy: Actor involvement for nature conservation*, 2017

129. Maryam Adjam, *Minnesspår: hågkomstens rum och rörelse i skuggan av en flykt*, 2017

130. Kim West, *The Exhibitionary Complex: Exhibition, Apparatus and Media from Kulturhuset to the Centre Pompidou, 1963–1977*, 2017

131. Ekaterina Tarasova, *Anti-nuclear Movements in Discursive and Political Contexts: Between expert voices and local protests*, 2017

132. Sanja Obrenović Johansson, *Från kombifeminism till rörelse: Kvinnlig serbisk organisering i förändring*, 2017

133. Michał Salamonik, *In Their Majesties' Service: The Career of Francesco De Gratta (1613–1676) as a Royal Servant and Trader in Gdańsk*, 2017

134. Jenny Ingridsdotter, *The Promises of the Free World: Postsocialist Experience in Argentina and the Making of Migrants, Race, and Coloniality*, 2017

135. Julia Malitska, *Negotiating Imperial Rule: Colonists and Marriage in the Nineteenth century Black Sea Steppe*, 2017

136. Natalya Yakusheva, *Parks, Policies and People: Nature Conservation Governance in Post-Socialist EU Countries*, 2017

137. Martin Kellner, *Selective Serotonin Re-uptake Inhibitors in the Environment: Effects of Citalopram on Fish Behaviour*, 2017

138. Krystof Kasprzak, *Vara – Framträdande – Värld: Fenomenets negativitet hos Martin Heidegger, Jan Patočka och Eugen Fink*, 2017

139. Alberto Frigo, *Life-stowing from a Digital Media Perspective: Past, Present and Future*, 2017

140. Maarja Saar, *The Answers You Seek Will Never Be Found At Home: Reflexivity, biographical narratives and lifestyle migration among highly-skilled Estonians*, 2017

141. Anh Mai, *Organizing for Efficiency: Essay on merger policies, independence of authorities, and technology diffusion*, 2017

142. Gustav Strandberg, *Politikens omskakning: Negativitet, samexistens och frihet i Jan Patočkas tänkande*, 2017

143. Lovisa Andén, *Litteratur och erfarenhet i Merleau-Pontys läsning av Proust, Valéry och Stendhal*, 2017

144. Fredrik Bertilsson, *Frihetstida policyskapande: uppfostringskommissionen och de akademiska konstitutionerna 1738–1766*, 2017

145. Börjeson, Natasja, *Toxic Textiles – towards responsibility in complex supply chains*, 2017

146. Julia Velkova, *Media Technologies in the Making – User-Driven Software and Infrastructures for computer Graphics Production*, 2017

147. Karin Jonsson, *Fångna i begreppen? Revolution, tid och politik i svensk socialistisk press 1917–1924*, 2017

148. Josefine Larsson, *Genetic Aspects of Environmental Disturbances in Marine Ecosystems – Studies of the Blue Mussel in the Baltic Sea*, 2017

149. Roman Horbyk, *Mediated Europes – Discourse and Power in Ukraine, Russia and Poland during Euromaidan*, 2017

150. Nadezda Petrusenko, *Creating the Revolutionary Heroines: The Case of Female Terrorists of the PSR (Russia, Beginning of the 20th Century)*, 2017

151. Rahel Kuflu, *Bröder emellan: Identitetsformering i det koloniserade Eritrea*, 2018

152. Karin Edberg, *Energilandskap i förändring: Inramningar av kontroversiella lokaliseringar på norra Gotland*, 2018

153. Rebecka Thor, *Beyond the Witness: Holocaust Representation and the Testimony of Images - Three films by Yael Hersonski, Harun Farocki, and Eyal Sivan*, 2018

154. Maria Lönn, *Bruten vithet: Om den ryska femininitetens sinnliga och temporala villkor*, 2018

155. Tove Porseryd, *Endocrine Disruption in Fish: Effects of 17α-ethinylestradiol exposure on non-reproductive behavior, fertility and brain and testis transcriptome*, 2018

156. Marcel Mangold, *Securing the working democracy: Inventive arrangements to guarantee circulation and the emergence of democracy policy*, 2018

157. Matilda Tudor, *Desire Lines: Towards a Queer Digital Media Phenomenology*, 2018

158. Martin Andersson, *Migration i 1600-talets Sverige: Älvsborgs lösen 1613–1618*, 2018

159. Johanna Pettersson, *What's in a Line? Making Sovereignty through Border Policy*, 2018

160. Irina Seits, *Architectures of Life-Building in the Twentieth Century: Russia, Germany, Sweden*, 2018

161. Alexander Stagnell, *The Ambassador's Letter: On the Less Than Nothing of Diplomacy*, 2019

162. Mari Zetterqvist Blokhuis, *Interaction Between Rider, Horse and Equestrian Trainer – A Challenging Puzzle*, 2019

163. Robin Samuelsson, *Play, Culture and Learning: Studies of Second-Language and Conceptual Development in Swedish Preschools*, 2019

164. Ralph Tafon, *Analyzing the "Dark Side" of Marine Spatial Planning – A study of domination, empowerment and freedom (or power in, of and on planning) through theories of discourse and power*, 2019

165. Ingela Visuri, *Varieties of Supernatural Experience: The case of high-functioning autism*, 2019

166. Mathilde Rehnlund, *Getting the transport right – for what? What transport policy can tell us about the construction of sustainability*, 2019

167. Oscar Törnqvist, *Röster från ingenmansland: En identitetsarkeologi i ett maritimt mellanrum*, 2019

168. Elise Remling, *Adaptation, now? Exploring the Politics of Climate Adaptation through Post-structuralist Discourse Theory*, 2019

169. Eva Karlberg, *Organizing the Voice of Women: A study of the Polish and Swedish women's movements' adaptation to international structures*, 2019

170. Maria Pröckl, *Tyngd, sväng och empatisk timing - förskollärares kroppsliga kunskaper*, 2020

171. Adrià Alcoverro, *The University and the Demand for Knowledge-based Growth The hegemonic struggle for the future of Higher Education Institutions in Finland and Estonia*, 2020

172. Ingrid Forsler, *Enabling Media: Infrastructures, imaginaries and cultural techniques in Swedish and Estonian visual arts education*, 2020

173. Johan Sehlberg, *Of Affliction: The Experience of Thought in Gilles Deleuze by way of Marcel Proust*, 2020

174. Renat Bekkin, *People of reliable loyalty…: Muftiates and the State in Modern Russia*, 2020

175. Olena Podolian, *The Challenge of 'Stateness' in Estonia and Ukraine: The international dimension a quarter of a century into independence*, 2020

176. Patrick Seniuk, *Encountering Depression In-Depth: An existential-phenomenological approach to selfhood, depression, and psychiatric practice*, 2020

177. Vasileios Petrogiannis, *European Mobility and Spatial Belongings: Greek and Latvian migrants in Sweden*, 2020

178. Lena Norbäck Ivarsson, *Tracing environmental change and human impact as recorded in sediments from coastal areas of the northwestern Baltic Proper*, 2020

179. Sara Persson, *Corporate Hegemony through Sustainability – A study of sustainability standards and CSR practices as tools to demobilise community resistance in the Albanian oil industry*, 2020

180. Juliana Porsani, *Livelihood Implications of Large-Scale Land Concessions in Mozambique: A case of family farmers' endurance*, 2020

181. Anders Backlund, *Isolating the Radical Right – Coalition Formation and Policy Adaptation in Sweden*, 2020

182. Nina Carlsson, *One Nation, One Language? National minority and Indigenous recognition in the politics of immigrant integration*, 2021

183. Erik Gråd, Nudges, *Prosocial Preferences & Behavior: Essays in Behavioral Economics*, 2021

184. Anna Enström, *Sinnesstämning, skratt och hypokondri: Om estetisk erfarenhet i Kants tredje Kritik*, 2021

185. Michelle Rydback, *Healthcare Service Marketing in Medical Tourism – An Emerging Market Study*, 2021

186. Fredrik Jahnke, *Toleransens altare och undvikandets hänsynsfullhet – Religion och meningsskapande bland svenska grundskoleelever*, 2021

187. Benny Berggren Newton, *Business Basics – A Grounded Theory for Managing Ethical Behavior in Sales Organizations*, 2021

188. Gabriel Itkes-Sznap, *Nollpunkten. Precisionens betydelse hos Witold Gombrowicz, Inger Christensen och Herta Müller*, 2021

189. Oscar Svanelid Medina, *Att forma tillvaron: konstruktivism som konstnärligt yrkesarbete hos Geraldo de Barros, Lygia Pape och Lygia Clark*, 2021

190. Anna-Karin Selberg, *Politics and Truth: Heidegger, Arendt and The Modern Political Lie*, 2021

191. Camilla Larsson, *Framträdanden: Performativitetsteoretiska tolkningar av Tadeusz Kantors konstnärskap*, 2021

192. Raili Uibo, *"And I don't know who we really are to each other": Queers doing close relationships in Estonia*, 2021

193. Ignė Stamolkaitė, *New Tides in Shipping: Studying incumbent firms in maritime energy transitions*, 2021

194. Mani Shutzberg, *Tricks of the Medical Trade: Cunning in the Age of Bureaucratic Austerity*, 2021

195. Patrik Höglund, *Skeppssamhället: Rang, roller och status på örlogsskepp under 1600-talet*, 2021

196. Philipp Seuferling, *Media and the refugee camp: the historical making of space, time, and politics in the modern refugee regime*, 2021

197. Johan Sandén, *Närbyråkrater och digitaliseringar: hur lärares arbete formas av tidsstrukturer*, 2021

198. Ulrika Nemeth, *Det kritiska uppdraget: diskurser och praktiker i gymnasieskolans svensk-undervisning*, 2021

199. Helena Löfgren, *Det legitima ägandet: Politiska konstruktioner av allmännyttans privatisering i Stockholms stad 1990–2015*, 2021

200. Vasileios Kitsos, *Urban policies for a contemporary periphery: Insights from eastern Russia*, 2021

201. Jenny Gustafsson, *Drömmen om en gränslös fred: Världsmedborgarrörelsens reaktopi, 1949-1968*, 2022

202. Oscar von Seth, *Outsiders and Others: Queer Friendships in Novels by Hermann Hesse*, 2022